Ancient Peoples of the Great Basin and the Colorado Plateau

Ancient Peoples of the Great Basin and the Colorado Plateau

Steven R. Simms

Original Artwork by
Eric Carlson and Noel Carmack

Routledge
Taylor & Francis Group

LONDON AND NEW YORK

First published 2008 by Left Coast Press, Inc.

Published 2016 by Routledge
2 Park Square, Milton Park, Abingdon, Oxon OX14 4RN
711 Third Avenue, New York, NY 10017, USA

Routledge is an imprint of the Taylor & Francis Group, an informa business

Library of Congress Cataloging-in-Publication Data:

Simms, Steven R.
Ancient peoples of the Great Basin and Colorado Plateau/Steven R.
Simms ; original artwork by Eric Carlson and Noel Carmack.
    p. cm.
Includes bibliographical references and index.
  ISBN 978-1-59874-295-4 (hardback : alk. paper)
  ISBN 978-1-59874-296-1 (pbk. : alk. paper)
1. Paleo-Indians—Great Basin. 2. Paleo-Indians—Colorado Plateau. 3. Indians of North America—Great Basin—Antiquities. 4. Indians of North America—Colorado Plateau—Antiquities. 5. Great Basin—Antiquities. 6. Colorado Plateau—Antiquities. 7. Great Basin—Environmental conditions—History. 8. Colorado Plateau—Environmental conditions—History. I. Title.
  E78.G67S54 2008   978.004'97—dc22   2008003539

Cover design by Hannah Jennings

ISBN 978-1-59874-295-4 hardcover
ISBN 978-1-59874-296-1 paperback

Contents

Illustrations

Plates   following p. 224

Preface

This book is about the ancient peoples of the Great Basin and the northern Colorado Plateau, a region occupying most of Nevada and Utah and portions of California, Oregon, Idaho, Wyoming, and Colorado.[1] It is an investigation of once real lives across an expanse of time too large to comprehend in terms of our short lives, through empathy, or by appeal to our imagined histories.

My aim is toward those who know something about the region and something about archaeology, and who want to understand why the ancient histories happened the way they did. This book is not a compendium of archaeological "digs," or a list of relics found, or a guide to identifying arrowhead collections. Neither is it an exhaustive textbook recitation of the scholarly studies pertaining to the region. It is an interpretation of the physical record of past cultures, ecosystems, and climates. As such, it includes examples of the evidence found at archaeological sites to back up my interpretations, although this treatise is certainly not encyclopedic. I intend it to be synthetic, but it is my own set of perceptions and interpretations.

Two premises anchor my story. The first is that a scientific approach must be the foundation for knowing the past. This is not because science is truth, but because all interpretations of the past,

FIGURE P-1

Western North America showing the Great Basin, a land of internal drainage and the Colorado Plateau, a land of high mesas dissected by deep canyons. They constitute the Basin-Plateau because of the cultural similarities of Native American groups and some degree of unity in the ancient history of the region. What occurred in the Basin-Plateau was shaped by what went on around it, especially in the Southwest and California; hence these regions are also identified. The Wasatch Front of Utah is depicted because it provides a perceptual anchor to the narrative and serves as a springboard into the region's deep past.

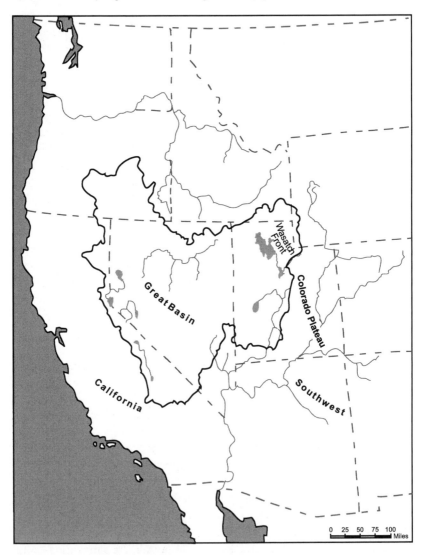

whether they arise from religious conviction, ethnic identity, politics, folklore, or written history originating in the blink of the past two centuries, must be evaluated against empirical evidence that actually originated in that past. Why? Ancient times are too large to know if we are armed only with our modern understandings. To know a past different from our present requires a fundamental acknowledgment: Regardless of what one believes happened in the past, and no matter how strongly one's convictions are held, something did happen . . . and this reality may hold little resemblance to modern people's beliefs or perceptions. The only way to navigate the diversity of stories and the inevitable contention among people's beliefs is to appeal to the evidence no matter how fragmentary, while acknowledging the vagaries of the scientific process.

The second premise of the book evolves from the first. The main reason for studying the past is because it is relevant now. The past is with us in the present. It is, as the historian Barbara Tuchman called it, "A Distant Mirror," or as the anthropologist Clyde Kluckhohn preferred, a "Mirror for Man."[2] The images in the mirrors are our selves. Knowledge about a past that might not conform to our initial perceptions or to our traditional knowledge challenges us to see the modern world differently.

Even after practicing archaeology in the Great Basin and the Colorado Plateau regions for 35 years, I still find excitement in a landscape that I like to say is "a study in pastels." I continue to find intrigue in archaeological remains that are often so subtle, visitors wonder what it is we are looking at, let alone finding. Over the years of teaching, I realized that audiences want the past interpreted and explained, not just described. Even for those whose initial interest in archaeology arose from the mere collection of objects, the deeper desire is to climb into a time machine and find out what these distant peoples and cultures were like. Finally, I believe there are educated readers seeking to go deeper into the Ancient Desert West but who don't want to work through the highly specialized and technical articles in professional journals.

At some risk of bringing too much conclusiveness to the story, I try to strike a balance between breadth, depth, scientific responsibility, and audience sensitivities. To facilitate this goal, I employ the notion of place as a vehicle for the narrative. The cultures of the Basin-Plateau conceptualized sense of place in vastly different ways, not only from us but among themselves. And sense of place changed fundamentally over the centuries and millennia. At times place was plural among different peoples of the region. As the writer Eudora Welty observed: "Location is the ground conductor of all the currents of emotion and belief and moral conviction that charge out from the story in its course."[3]

My goal is nevertheless to tell a story that is scientifically responsible, and thus one that can be supported with observed evidence. Extensive end notes are a significant element of this book. They constitute a book within a book for those who want to know what supports my interpretations. They offer avenues for further reading, and on many topics they are a subtext under the narrative. The book can be read with them or without them, and in this way I hope it can find accessibility for the educated lay reader, students, and perhaps colleagues.

The story is bigger than we think in two ways. First, the temporal scale is staggering. People have called the Basin-Plateau home for over 13,000 years. Although this number rolls easily off the tongue, to translate it into human terms requires us to consider a genealogy of over 430 generations; over five times as long as the history of Christianity. The resulting temporal cavern houses a staggering diversity of behaviors, cultures, and historical circumstances that beg not to be homogenized as "prehistory."

The past is also bigger than we think in terms of space. I start small by using the Wasatch Front of northern Utah as a source of examples and as a point of departure into a much larger region. My colleague David Madsen likes to say that the Wasatch Front was the most populous part of Utah in ancient times, just as it is today. The urban strip anchored by Salt Lake City is known to many people who do not live there, and I hope this familiarity will help the reader gain purchase on the larger but less known region. The Wasatch Front also houses much of the diversity that we find across the Great Basin and the northern Colorado Plateau.

Most of the story, however, is about the larger expanse of the Basin-Plateau. But even that is not enough. Archaeology is so specialized that we sometimes unwittingly expect the answers to our questions to be found within our "study area." I think this often misleads us, much like the drunk looking for his keys under the lamppost. Significant cultural and historical trajectories in the ancient Basin-Plateau were shaped by what happened elsewhere on the continent, especially the Southwest and California. For this reason, the narrative moves repeatedly from the local of the Wasatch Front, to the scale of the Basin-Plateau, and outward to continental levels. I call this "a spiral of contexts," and I choose this metaphor because all cultural contexts

FIGURE P-2

Examples of past cultures and landscapes are drawn from the Wasatch Front as a point of departure into the region. The Wasatch Front is now one of the most populous areas of the Basin-Plateau and is thus familiar to many people who do not live there. It also houses much of the variation we see elsewhere in the region, from alpine mountains to salt flats, enormous wetlands, and craggy desert mountains.

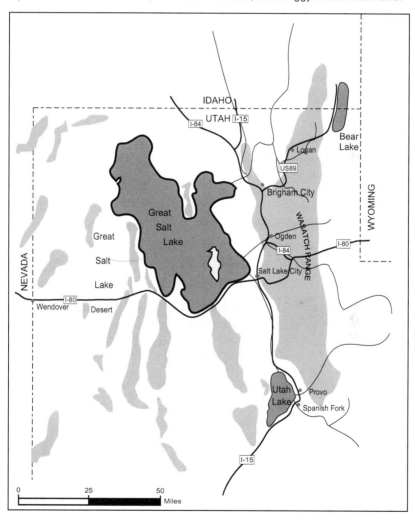

are linked to others, not only in space but through a "spiral" of time that swirls cultures together to create new contexts.

Each of these ascending scales of geographic and temporal space was important to the unfolding of prehistory. Rather than being isolated "Robinson Crusoes," ancient peoples inhabited a social tapestry on an occupied landscape. We are unaccustomed to using the term "cosmopolitan" to describe ancient Native America, but America before the arrival of the Europeans was a cosmopolitan place. It was a fully occupied, socially integrated, multicultural fabric. Humans were a driving force in the nature of America's ecosystems. What people did in one place mattered for those in other places. If an area became overhunted, demands were placed on others. If farmers immigrated to a place previously occupied only by foragers, the lives of both peoples changed. If a place became overpopulated, it sent ripples and even waves of change into the rural areas around it. In the ancient past, just as today, to know the local, one must know the regional and the continental.

I begin with a fictional Prologue to set the stage for an excursion into a life that was far more expansive, more diverse, and deeper in time than granted by our modern images of Indians riding horses and living in tipis.

Chapter 1 provides a baseline for the Ancient World of the Basin-Plateau by emphasizing variations on themes that help us imagine

FIGURE P-3

The Deep Creek Mountains located on the Utah-Nevada border rise above the floor of the Bonneville Salt Flats. This view is from Floating Island Cave, first occupied over 8,000 years ago. (Courtesy of David Rhode)

a past that can be gleaned only from the archaeology. We will find that to understand the past, we need to abandon the stereotype of a single type of society called "hunters and gatherers," or "Indians." This chapter relies on knowledge of the world's foraging societies and on knowledge gained in the past century or two of the "old ways" of Basin-Plateau Native Americans. I introduce some basics about the kinds of societies that constituted most of the region's past and organize these into interconnected themes of mobility, settlement patterns, subsistence, social organization and politics, and ideology.

Chapter 2 is an excursion into ancient environments that become more and more foreign as we press deeper into time. It provides some examples of how past environments and climates are known and explores climate and ecosystems as never in "balance," never "pristine," but as a relentlessly dynamic tyranny of circumstance for the people who lived here.

Chapters 3 through 6 make up the shank of the story and describe what happened during different periods. Each chapter presents selected archaeological data to illustrate the past. We move chronologically from the Paleoindians, America's first colonists, to the diverse foragers of the Archaic period, to the Fremont farmers, and finally through the Late Prehistoric period to the edge of "contact" with Europeans that brought disease, metal, horses, guns, and change.

The chapters are subdivided into topical sections, but no chapter forms a neat chronological unit. They overlap, because past life was not neatly cut up into blocks of time. Nor are the past cultures best understood as insular packages spinning like billiard balls across a playing table. Each chapter intentionally overlaps categories traditionally kept separate by archaeologists, because I think the processes that caused the changes we observe run among those artificial categories.

Throughout the book, Sidebars on particular topics are provided to amplify themes and isolate topics. A central feature of the book is a portfolio of artwork by Eric Carlson and Noel Carmack. Each illustration is an original, achieved through collaboration. Many represent artistic interpretations of actual archaeological finds, and expansive captions accompany each one. These reconstructions are the artist's conceptions, and mine, too, with the intent of faithfulness to the empirical record.

An Epilogue returns to some of the basic themes: that the past is with us in the present and that we can transcend the differences engendered by identity politics, religious dogma, and other differences in perspective only through empirical investigation. To have the latter we have to have the archaeological record. Yet it is under assault from urbanization, all manner of rural development, and from us—the general populace collecting arrowheads and flakes of chipped stone, and doing illegal digging. Our window into the past is a nonrenewable cultural resource. It is more fragile than an endangered species because it does not reproduce. When we allow its destruction, then we truly will be able to fictionalize any story our modern impulses desire.

ACKNOWLEDGMENTS

If I were to thank everyone for his or her contribution to this book, my list would include dozens of teachers, professors, family, friends, students, and colleagues from the 35 years I have been doing archaeology. The following is too selective, but recent enough to be appropriate. Money is the engine to have time for research, and it supports the creation of the beautiful artwork by Eric Carlson and Noel Carmack, as well as the preparation of maps by Nancy Kay Harrison and sketches by Jennifer Hulse. I thank Utah State University alumni Boyd Hayward and Richard Shipley for their generous support of archaeology. Utah State University has likewise supported me the whole way, with a sabbatical leave to get the research and writing off the ground, and abundant curiosity and encouragement from colleagues in many campus departments. Special thanks to Leticia Neal and Kate Toomey, who read early drafts. Their efforts dovetailed to provide the crucial vantage of readers with sharp intellect who represent different audiences. Mark Stuart not only wrote one of the sidebars in the book but also has taught me a great deal over the years about the archaeology of Utah. Colleagues Mark Allen, Joel Janetski, Robert Kelly, and Matt Seddon made astute comments and recommendations on a later draft. They not only raised the quality of the content but further stimulated me to convey a bit of the wonder that makes archaeologists love what they do. Thanks also to Bryan Hockett, David Madsen, Duncan Metcalfe, Dann Russell, Rich Talbot, and David Zeanah. Mitch Allen and Stacey C. Sawyer of Left Coast Press were the critical shepherds who led this work to publication. Sincere thanks to each of you.

Prologue

A smoky haze rises among five domed huts constructed by placing mats of cattail and bulrush over willow frames. There are many more people here than usual, and perhaps four dozen men, women, and children temporarily increase the size of the settlement. At least a dozen people shuffle across a patio sheltered by a thatched ramada, swaying gently in rhythm and chanting softly. Inside a nearby reed-covered house, a woman hovers over another woman who is reclined motionless on a woven mat. She bobs a sucking tube near her mouth, pushing it toward her patient and then back toward her lips. Her head, shoulders, hips, and knees synchronize a mime of spirits moving from the body of the ill woman. This is a curing, and this shaman from another valley was summoned because she is known to be the best. (See Art Portfolio, Illustration 1.)

The year is A.D. 1304, and the tiny village sits along a mildly saline and murky stream that meanders through a maze of ponds and sloughs in a convoluted effort to reach the open waters of the Great Salt Lake. A chilly October evening is deceptively darkened by an approaching storm. Musty smells of the marsh hover in the heavy, still air. In a living space burned into a clearing among the dense saltgrass and bulrushes, aromas of human, dog, and fermented fish mingle with the strong scents of burning driftwood.

This shaman is a woman. Both women and men could become shamans. Status and role are plastic and allocated by experience, ability, and charisma. If the shaman fails tonight, her reputation may be harmed, at least within this camp group of families. There are kin relations among most of the people here, some by blood and some by marriage. The kinship extends broadly outward, geographically linking villages, camps, valleys, and even regions with a set of memorized calculations. Should this curing be successful or go poorly, the word will be out, but the status and abilities of this famous woman shaman will be gauged according to those kinship calculations. That is how it worked.

The patient is a middle-aged woman, perhaps 35 years old, and the most respected basketmaker in the valley. Her family believes that a foreign matter, a force of some sort, has intruded upon her body and her being. Mind, body, soul, spirit, and all the things of the earth; they are the same thing. Animation and intent can arise from all things, including animals, plants, and rocks. They can be found in weather phenomena such as dust devils and especially in topographic features such as lakes, rock outcrops, springs, prominences, and even parts of canyons. There can be no distinction of church and state, because these things do not exist. There is no difference between the sacred and the secular. All things are entwined not only in people's minds but in the unfolding of everyday events of people, animals, plants, and even weather.

The shaman uses a sucking tube as part of the ceremony and to aid the healing. Tubes like this are used by indigenous curers in many societies around the world throughout history. This one is made of exotic stone from far beyond Utah and has been handed down among shamans living near the Great Salt Lake. Not all curing can be done this way, and shamans often specialize in the kinds of maladies they treat and in the methods of treatment they use.

The curing ceremony brings together two camp groups. Camp groups are associations of people bound by the daily demands of life and reflecting a variety of social networks. Camp groups can be amalgamations of people with contrasting life histories. The membership in camp groups can be fluid and is not strictly synonymous with boundaries of family, band, or tribe.

In the group assembled tonight for the curing, there are five or more extended families represented, two bands marking two extended lineages, at least four food-named groups, and there are several people

FIGURE P-4

This sucking tube was found many years ago at a Fremont site west of Ogden, Utah. Because it is part of an anonymous private collection, not much is known other than what we can glean from the object itself. Sucking tubes are used in curing ceremonies in many societies around the world. This one is made of a steatite reputed to originate near Spokane, Washington. The long distance movement of raw material used in such a powerful object is not unusual. (Photo by Laura Patterson and courtesy of Mark Stuart)

who speak more than one language. One way people keep track of who is who in a camp group is to refer to a *tebiwa* (in Shoshone), which means a living area or homeland. These are sometimes labeled according to distinctive features and have sometimes been called "food-named groups." They are common in the Great Basin but are also found among foraging societies elsewhere, such as in Australia. The Cattail-Eaters, the Pine-Nut Eaters, and the Ground-Hog Eaters are examples of food-named groups. Even if life takes a person across many valleys, across other food-named groups, across kin and band lines, and even across language boundaries, people know where they are from.

Men and women recognized as leaders among several different lineages are here tonight. Politics are founded on kinship ties, and power, like status and role, is plastic and achieved. This means that the decisions of everyday life, such as those involved in food-getting, the collection of raw materials, whether to move or stay, and whether to break into smaller groups, are distinct from the larger networks that might be called political organization. The larger the group and the more settled the people, the stronger the influence of political organization on their lives.

If this curing goes well, the way is paved for marriages, greater alliance among camp groups, lineages, and bands, and even perhaps the sharing of risk by pooling valuable resources or sharing stored food. Marriages are often arranged or completed at such gatherings because individuals must marry outside the lineage and preferably across band lines. In a place of few people, living in shifting groups, opportunities for marriage are intermittent and must be exploited when an event such as this curing brings people together.

For these people, alliances are paramount for sharing information about where to find the best food and where other groups are camped, and for ensuring that networks of reciprocity provide support to those in need.

If the curing does not go well by tomorrow or the next day, distrust, conflict, and separation could arise. Scores may have to be settled in the future. This could pose difficult choices, because in a dispute, an individual's decision to align with one part of the family may strain ties with another. Cooperation and conflict are not distinct states of being but are entwined representations of a social ecosystem.

The past few generations brought change. Stories the elders tell to the young speak of a past, a spirit time when people lived by farming, and the stories suggest that these ancient farmers may have been a different people. The stories imply both connection and distance. They describe people moving away and others moving in. The 14th century was a time of upheaval across what is now the western United States. Warfare in California and mass migrations in the Southwest jostled the continent's populations and created new social networks. Immigrants were flung from once-successful places and now encountered strife and overpopulation. Even though northern Utah and the rest of the Great Basin and Colorado Plateau were far from the epicenters, ripples were felt.

The curing is just beginning as evening approaches, and it may last all night. Six men approach across the salt grass meadow, each with a string of muskrats dangling from his waist. The trap lines of snares and deadfalls are checked daily and the struggling animals retrieved for meat and fur. Today it was muskrats. Another trap line set for meadow mice will be checked tomorrow. Several women set off that morning to catch fish for the event, and a pile of Utah sucker are now baking in rock-lined earth ovens. Baskets of bulrush seed and piles of starchy cattail roots will provide the foundation for a vegetable stew laced with tidbits of meat and spiced with tiny seeds of peppergrass.

A group of the younger men are not here tonight. They are in the mountains hunting bighorn sheep and mule deer. It is fall, and the animals are fat. Rutting season is about to begin, and this presents opportunities to exploit the animals' natural behavior. The people hunt in all seasons, but in the larger scheme of things, meat from large game constitutes a small fraction of the diet. The short, sinew-back "self" bows and cane arrows have an effective range of about 20 meters, and hunting requires persistence, skill, and remarkable stamina. Encounters with the animals may be few and reasonable shots hard to come by. Or, the hunters may simply miss. Large animals, however, are always sought, and when a bighorn sheep is brought into camp, the moment of plenty is shared widely, another process that knits people together through obligation.

The people are the main predators in this landscape. They are not like wolves who take only the young, old, and sick—people take what they need. The female sheep and deer are favored for their fat and hides unblemished by the fights common among males. If a pregnant female deer is taken, the fetus is a delicacy not wasted. Sometimes the people along the Wasatch Front could kill a bison. They are difficult and dangerous to hunt on foot, but if the opportunity arises, it will not be missed.

Winter is approaching, and clothing is being made and repaired. Large animal hides are valuable for clothes, bags, wrappings, and so much more. Hides are only one source of fabric, and most people wear fiber clothing as does the shaman at the curing. Skirts and breechclouts are woven from grass and bark. Long dresses, leggings, and thick, warm shirts are made of sagebrush bark. Woven cattail and bulrush leaves and stems provide another substantial fabric. Rabbit skin robes, made of strips of fur individually wrapped around strands of milkweed cordage and then sewn together, make thick, pliable, and very warm cloaks. These are the most coveted garments and are passed down among generations.

For an important event such as this curing, people will find enough food to sustain everyone for awhile. When an area is used up, families relocate to exploit a different part of the wetlands. They might split into smaller groups, but when there is enough food they congregate as long as it lasts. Some times of the year, large groups assemble: during the spring sucker spawn, the fall pine nut trip, the biannual pronghorn migration, and the famous rabbit drives of early winter.

Firewood is collected relentlessly, and fires burn throughout the camp, because heat and fuel are constant needs. Fire is part of life and not restricted to the hearth. In summer, burning keeps insects at bay and is used to open up space for living. The people employ fire across the landscape to improve hunting, to improve seed bearing, and to maintain prime raw materials for basketmaking. The landscape is a mosaic of burned and less burned areas, which works for the people, because, unlike us, they are not fully settled. This landscape is burning and burned, but it is not denuded or even dangerous. Fire is part of everyday life.

The people move within their ancient Utah wilderness with the nimbleness of long familiarity. They have lived in the wetlands, deserts, and mountain valleys of northern Utah all their lives, as did their parents, grandparents, and all the people before them in a past they can only imagine. In their language, there is no word for "wilderness." They mark no separation between humanity and nature, and cannot conceive of our juxtaposition of humanity versus nature. There is harmony and balance, but these are not static. The people are shaping their wilderness. They use and even exhaust the resources. The balance they achieve is not a final state but rather an unsteady relationship between the impact of the people and the difficult realities that determine their choices. For the past 13,000 years, the wilderness of the Ancient Desert West was a human wilderness.

1

The Ancient World of the Basin-Plateau

The slice of time fictionalized in the Prologue belongs to a world obviously different from our own. It is different not just because people were "hunters and gatherers" and did not have automobiles, shopping centers, health care systems, armies, and schools. The differences are more fundamental and found in the arrangements and meanings of kinship, in the workings of politics and economics, and in worldview itself. The differences are not specific to comparisons of American Indians vs. modern Americans but are found in every comparison of simple and complex societies across the planet.

Life was not necessarily hard in small-scale ancient societies, and the word "primitive" is inappropriate, because depending on your point of view, aspects of modern American culture might just as easily be dubbed "primitive." Nor was life in foraging societies a relentless and desperate quest for food. The people's work patterns were deliberate, informed, and structured. They had in some ways more free time than we do and like us, they had their trials and failures. Like people today, the ancient foragers of the Basin-Plateau shaped the world around them and in turn were shaped by the consequences of their choices. Like today, the "environment" consists of other people and the organizations of their behavior, not just the physical and nonhuman environment. Human culture is shaped by the twin forces of material circumstance and the historical hand we are dealt by those who preceded us.

The goals of this book are to describe what ancient life in the Basin-Plateau was like and explain why it happened the way it did. To do this, we need to "let the present serve the past" by employing a modern baseline of native cultures.[1] Baselines must begin somewhere; hence the idea of "contact" between the indigenous Native Americans and the Europeans to mark a beginning. In space, our baseline is anchored by the Wasatch Front of northern Utah.

Identifying a baseline risks casting precontact cultures as monolithic and changeless before the intrusions of history altered them from their "pristine" state. We will find that the economic moniker "hunter-gatherer" takes many forms and that it includes a great deal of cultural diversity. Moreover, for more than 1,000 years, over half the Basin-Plateau region was dominated by farming societies, not hunters and gatherers. Despite the utility of a cultural baseline, it is impossible to know the ancients by simply projecting historically known cultures backward in time. This chapter provides some guidelines for knowing the peoples of the past as diverse, dynamic, and sometimes quite different from the native cultures of the past two centuries.

Finally, we extend our baseline from the Wasatch Front outward, not only to the region but to surrounding regions and the continent as a whole. This is important because in order to know why things happened in the Basin-Plateau, we need to know what happened elsewhere. Despite the seeming remoteness of the mountains and the deserts, the Great Basin and the northern Colorado Plateau were part of a "spiral of contexts"—an interconnectedness of local, regional, and even continental contexts, historically linked through vast amounts of time.

NATIVE CULTURE BEFORE THE HORSE

All of us are familiar with images of horse-riding Indians who lived in tipis, hunted bison, shot bows and arrows, and wore buckskin clothing. These images are steeped in history and are based on the eyewitness documentation of Native American life by Euro-American explorers, pioneers, writers, and scholars. This knowledge is rich and vivid, and it is part of the traditions of contemporary Native Americans in the Great Basin and on the Colorado Plateau.

Horses were introduced to the eastern Ute in Colorado in the A.D. 1600s via the Spanish *entradas* to New Mexico. Horse adoption likely preceded the direct arrival of European visitors to the Northern Ute and Northern Shoshone, diffusing among the native Utah groups as early as A.D. 1700 and clearly by the mid to late 1700s. The horse reached the Wasatch Front before A.D. 1776, when the Dominguez-Escalante expedition visited villages of Utah Lake Ute near modern-day Provo. They had no horses but told the Spaniards that they feared the "Cumanches," horse-mounted peoples to the north. The Spaniards did not see the Salt Lake Valley, but the Utah Valley Ute described a "peaceful" people living around Great Salt Lake (Shoshone), with a lifestyle similar to their own and owning no horses.[2]

Horses brought fundamental change to how people obtained food, where they lived, and how they associated, married, led, and fought. Horses symbolized a suite of other changes brought by the associations of Europeans and natives, and natives with or without horses. The changes fall into three conceptual categories: sociopolitical, epidemiological, and demographic.

The effects of sociopolitical change are well documented, and for the Northern Ute and Shoshone they involved trading, especially the slave trade and raiding introduced by the Spanish. The new markets changed the organization of labor, leadership, and the interactions among tribes. The Ute of Colorado raided the more remote western groups of Ute in northern Utah, and by A.D. 1750, even Plains tribes were getting involved.[3]

These contacts provided vectors for European-introduced diseases, such as smallpox and measles passing among concentrations of indigenous groups. Since using horses promoted mobility and periodic large gatherings of people, the effects of disease were likely

significant, albeit difficult to fully document, because they appear
to have occurred prior to direct European visitation and eyewitness
accounts.[4]

The adoption of horses changed basic patterns of Indian life in
only a few years, but we must remember that individual elements and
strongly connected patterns of the previous life remained. Cultural
change may tear the fabric of a society but rarely dissolves it completely. For instance, the people continued to harvest native plants,
but those filled a different niche in the diet. The native pharmacopoeia
was surely the same. Many of the same places were used, albeit in different ways. Time depth is apparent in some of the themes and characters of folklore.[5] Characteristics of social organization among the
historic native cultures also give us some connection to a deeper past,
or at least some analogies to point the way.

By the 19th century, only pockets of people remained who
could help us glimpse the old world, and even in those cases, they
had firearms and had been forced into the most marginal areas by
Euro-American encroachment or by other Native Americans. By the
early 20th century, when anthropologists set out to systematically
reconstruct the precontact cultures, the memories of the few old
people living in small enclaves of indigenous culture were fading. The
extent to which these glimpses of life before the horse and tipi apply
to the deep past is a matter of debate, but the classic ethnographies
provide a rich accounting from informants who lived the "old
ways."[6]

Anthropology extends this record by contributing evidence
from hundreds of foraging societies and simple farming societies
documented around the world in recent history. Many of these
societies are classified as bands and tribes by anthropologists. Bands
are the simplest form of human society. A band comprises a small
group of kin related by blood and by marriage, often formed into
clans that trace descent to a perceived common ancestor. Leadership
is based on skills and charisma, bands have little economic
specialization, and their population typically numbers a few hundred
people often scattered over large areas. Tribes are associations of
bands and signify that hunter-gatherer societies did exhibit complexity at times—greater economic specialization and differences in
wealth and power among individuals, families, and clans.

The world's cross-cultural sample reveals that there are strong
regularities in the way band and tribal societies are organized
socially, politically, and in worldview and ideology. This knowledge

complements the information we have from our local historical and ethnographic records that describe the Native American cultures of the Basin-Plateau region.

The following sections of the chapter break native life before the horse into categories often used by anthropologists. We begin with tangible things such as technology and economics. These things shape people's food choices and how people moved across the landscape—two things archaeologists can usually see. The material foundations of cultures shape the abstractions of social life and the life of the mind; hence, these sections follow. They are more difficult to find in the archaeological "record."

The archaeological record includes the artifacts, their context, the remains of houses, hearths, refuse dumps, burials, and places where they hunt, collect plants, and find toolstone—places of resource extraction. Each of these kinds of places is a signature of the past. Mostly though, the archaeological record consists of the *patterns* created when thousands of sites and tens of thousands of artifacts are studied in systematic ways. Our excursion here, then, through the ethnographic and historical evidence for native life, is taken with an eye for what might be relevant for the archaeology. The following sections provide some analogies to help us step into a foreign past.

TECHNOLOGY

Technology determines how people get their groceries and their raw materials, and this fact holds regardless of whether food is taken with bow and arrow and nets or is dependent on the flow of oil that fuels modern agriculture around the world. The suite of food options that Mother Nature presents to foraging cultures, and the seasonal availability and their cost of acquisition, shapes where people live and in what size of a group. The patterning of settlements, where they are, their size, and how long they are used between moves are crucial to shaping human interactions—kinship, status, role, and the politics of alliance and conflict. Technology, subsistence, mobility, and settlement are thus entryways to describing the ancient lives and cultures.

The indigenous technology of the Basin-Plateau region is ingenious, and it is one of the most simple found anywhere in the world. For the first few thousand years after the first people arrived to the region over 13,000 years ago, the stone-tipped thrusting spear was the primary large weapon. It is not known if the earliest spears were assisted by the atlatl, or spear thrower, but by 8,000–9,000 years ago, the atlatl was clearly present and caused a shift from large tipped spears to smaller tipped "darts." This technology persisted for millennia until the bow and arrow entered the region between A.D. 0 and 500. These were the primary changes in weapon technology in the prehistory of this area until the introduction of firearms.

Atlatls and darts, and the bow and arrow, are only the most obvious food acquisition technologies. An array of gear aided the capture of

FIGURE 1.1

Map of the Basin-Plateau region showing historical tribal-linguistic boundaries.

small or specialized prey, including snares and traps, nets for fish and rabbits, throwing sticks, and slings. There were decoys, such as woven cattail duck decoys covered with duck skins. Pronghorn (antelope) head-dresses served the dual purpose of decoying these curious animals while enhancing the power of the shaman who "charmed" the creature into proximity.

Chipped-stone technology varied in style and specialization over the millennia, but the tool kit always included knives, drills, gravers, chisels, and scrapers; many of these objects were hafted to handles. There was a variety of handheld or hafted tools designed for wood and bone working, hide preparation, plant harvesting, and fiber cutting.

Wooden and bone tools were also used for wood shaping, for burnishing, and as wrenches and digging tools. Perhaps the single most utilized tool in the region's prehistory is the wooden digging stick, necessary for the many kinds of roots taken. Tools for grinding were just as important as the chipped-stone dart tips or arrowheads, because plant foods were the foundation of the diet.

Flat grinding stones called *metates* and handstones called *manos* were made of basalt, rhyolite, quartzite, and even soft rocks, such as sandstones. These tools were used to mill seeds into flour, hull pine nuts, pulverize roots, and puree vegetables. They also served to grind medicinal roots, minerals, and pigments. Mortars and pestles, long cylindrical hullers, shaft straighteners, stone balls, and v-edge cobbles were some of the other forms in the ground-stone tool kit.

One of the most important technologies was the fiber industry. Without looms, all cordage and fabric had to be twisted by hand, and woven, largely with awls. Most clothing was likely made of fiber. Basketry was fundamental to life from the earliest occupants of the region to historic times. Basketmaking requires astounding skill that could be transmitted only by a master teaching an apprentice, and this skill was passed down over generations. Basketmakers knew the proper cultivation and harvest of willow and other raw materials, skill in the manufacture of basketry, and they made special tools required by the industry. Both twining (woven) and coiling (wrapped) construction techniques were richly developed in the Basin-Plateau region, with coiling increasing in frequency after about 10,000 years ago. Coiled baskets improved the mass processing of small seeds and the transport of water in pitch-lined jugs. In later periods, a special basketry tool, the seed beater, was introduced to intensify the harvest of seeds beyond previous levels.[7]

The technology was ingenious in its simplicity and practicality. Compared to the constant change and complexity of modern technology, it seems stagnant. We will find, however, that significant changes occurred in technology, and these changes shaped where people lived and for how long, what they ate, and how their societies were organized.

MOBILITY AND SETTLEMENT

Many writers observe that a simple tool kit is appropriate to a mobile society; but much of the technology found in foraging societies was actually cached at key locations, creating a "built environment." The lifestyle was a traveling one, but like the high mobility we often observe in modern America, the mobility of ancient foragers was not aimless. In fact, the degree of mobility found in different places over the millennia varied greatly. The tempo, or the elapsed time between each move, also varied. During most periods, travel in the mountains and the deserts of the ancient American West is best described as intermittent. Some stops lasted weeks and months. Others lasted only a few days. It all depended on the circumstances.

Mobility is an aspect of settlement patterns—where people lived, how long, and with how many other people. Settlement patterns may have been altered by the introduction of the horse more than by any other cultural influence. Before horses were used, all transportation, whether it was the movement of people or goods, had to be done on foot—and horses changed all that. The settlement pattern among prehorse foragers of the Basin-Plateau can be generalized into two forms, each with its own themes and variations: the desert-mountain settlement pattern and the wetland settlement pattern.[8]

The desert-mountain pattern is the classic description of foragers of the Desert West: small groups of a single family, or extended families and perhaps some non-kin, moving among ecosystems ranging from valley bottoms, to foothills, and on up into the alpine zones of the highest mountains. A central feature of this pattern is that for much of the year people "mapped on" to their environment. The term "mapping on" signifies moving people to the resources rather than moving resources to the people, which is so familiar to modern people. Mapping on distinguished the desert-mountain pattern.

FIGURE 1.2

Schematic depiction of the Desert-Mountain Settlement Pattern. In this pattern, people tend to "map on" to resources and caches of food. This pattern did not have permanent villages, but it was not highly mobile either. Stays could be weeks at a time at a spring fish drive or a summer root-collecting camp, or for a special event such as a pronghorn drive or rabbit drive. Group size at special events could be large (100+ people) if the food take was large enough to support them. Smaller camps were established to collect seeds and upland roots, to run trap lines, and to hunt large game. Stays in winter villages could be several months, and they were placed near stored food, especially pine nuts. When the supply was gone, another winter village was used. People moved through the landscape in stops and starts, adjusting the group size and composition through the year. But each year was different, and there was no set pattern, nor was the cycle limited to only one valley or place, because kinship networks were far flung, enabling individuals to cycle across the landscape over the course of their lives.

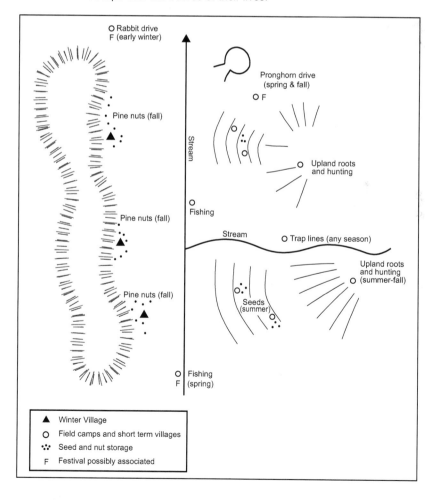

However, these people were not ever-wandering nomads. In fact, of all the foragers in the world, the peoples of the Basin-Plateau were in the middle of the variation, and are best labeled semisettled foragers.[9] Further, movement was highly structured, and the people knew the camps and caches they could rely on. They knew where to find stone for tools, salt, plants for fiber, and other necessary nonfood resources at a more intimate level than many Americans know their own communities. Knowledge of the environment and information gleaned from other people enabled foragers to predict where food resources would be. Indeed, information about the condition of the environment and where the best food could be found may have been the most traded commodity when people got together. The mobility of ancient people was as deliberate as the routines of our modern lives.

Foragers of the desert-mountain pattern moved intermittently in stops and starts in response to a patchy distribution of food and nonfood resources. Food was "patchy," not only across space with different places offering different foods but also through time, with most foods at their peak only for a brief period. These circumstances determined the number of people who could live together and the length of their stay.

Some camps might consist of a family or two and last a few days or a few weeks. Others may be special task groups of men, or women with older children, while the older women and young children remained at a base camp. Larger groups of dozens, and occasionally over a hundred people, might have created a village for an event such as a fish drive, a pine nut harvest, a rabbit drive, or a pronghorn drive. These gatherings became significant social events attended by members of several extended families in a band, as well as people from other bands and places—even surprisingly far-flung places. Such events might last for a month. Winter camps range in size from a few families to over a hundred people. Winter camps required a wood supply, which was a significant determinant of camp location in a landscape of sparse timber and frigid winters.[10] People might move among several camps over the course of winter, each occupied a few weeks to a couple of months.

Movement in the desert-mountain settlement pattern was also determined by the need to store food to prepare for winter. Transportation costs were high, so people tended to store food close to where it was gathered. Dried meats and prepared foods may have been exceptions, because they were light and easily moved.[11] Storage may be strategically placed to be near several kinds of foods, or near where people intended to camp for the winter.[12] In contrast to the summer settlement pattern, the winter pattern included a logistic component that relied on the extra cost of moving resources to a central location to be near the people and their wood supply.

The many variations and fluidity of this settlement pattern led anthropologists to use the terms "camp groups" or "kin clique," instead of more fixed terms such as family, lineage, band, and tribe, to refer to the composition of the group who occupied a place at any given time.[13]

The wetland settlement system contrasts with the desert-mountain pattern in significant ways. It characterizes areas where concentrations of food and other resources caused more settling and greater reliance on a logistic system that transported food and materials to the people. The wetlands along the base of the Wasatch Front in Utah are a prime example, but many others exist where springs once flowed at the surface to create wetlands, or where mountain streams flowed year round and spread out into ponds and sloughs once they reached the broad valleys of the region.[14] Base camps and villages were typical of the wetland pattern. They were placed in different areas according to the seasons, and stored food was important. The greater concentration of habitats required less movement to exploit a variety of resources, a necessity when the logistic system is borne on people's backs instead of trucks and trains. Too, the built environment, consisting of camps, caches, and installations such as fish traps, was more concentrated in the wetland pattern, as was the human population.

Nevertheless, camps and villages were not permanent in the wetland pattern. Group size and the place of settlement still varied with the seasons and with the need to move around wetlands to exploit different resources. Camps and villages also had to be moved every now and then as local areas became depleted by concentrated human use.

People still needed to travel outside the wetlands for additional resources, such as particular toolstones, special woods, fiber, and medicinal plants that do not grow in the lowlands. Large game could be had at the wetland-valley margins; however, trips to the higher country were required to fully exploit these resources. Thus, the high country and more remote areas around the patches of concentrated resources in the Basin-Plateau wetlands remained linked by a logistic system.

FIGURE 1.3

Schematic depiction of the Wetland Settlement Pattern. In this pattern, the resources are moved to the people, using a logistic system. Even this pattern is not necessarily sedentary with permanent villages. Several villages might be used in any one year and over blocks of years. Lowland villages, however, formed the nexus of a logistic system. Task groups went out for days or weeks at a time, temporarily decreasing the village size. The groups returned with processed resources when the task locations were nearby. The logistic approach works because Great Basin wetlands offer concentrations of diverse resources. But longer trips were needed, too, and, some groups moved to the high mountains and upland lakes for the summer. The Desert-Mountain and Wetland patterns are not mutually exclusive, and people could live in both during their lives. Nor do they necessarily match tribal and linguistic boundaries. They do, however, mark distinctions in the conception of place.

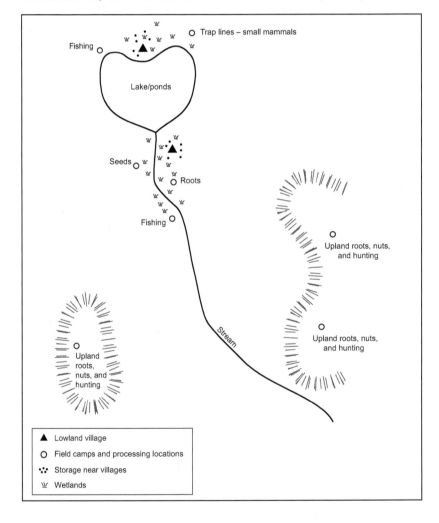

The wetland settlement pattern contrasts with the desert-mountain pattern in population density, degree of residential stability, group size, and in the role of the logistic system. Variations on these two settlement themes are present during much of the region's ancient past.

SUBSISTENCE

Subsistence is part and parcel of technology and settlement, and classic images of ancient Native American diets range from noble hunters feasting on venison to starving savages nibbling on insects and leaves. Like mobility and settlement, subsistence also took different forms depending on the place and especially the period in prehistory.

The range of foods available to ancient foragers was staggering, with at least 150 vegetable foods and dozens of meat items available.[15] The variety of foods eaten through the year easily exceeded what modern shoppers see on any given day in their grocer's vegetable and meat sections. The availability of wild foods was, however, strictly determined by the seasons. This presented the people with an annual cycle and structured their food ways. Decisions had to be made whether to take or ignore particular foods. These decisions were neither random nor capricious and cannot be explained by appeals to personal or cultural preference, which beg the question of what caused the "preference" in the first place. Furthermore, there are broad patterns of subsistence choices across the region, and across cultures, and there are food trends that span millennia, transcending the lives of individuals.

One way to consider patterns in subsistence is to contrast broad with narrow diets. This is an important distinction that helps us describe the composition of diets, not only with lists of foods but also with attention to the roles different foods played in diets and economic systems. Distinguishing between broad and narrow diets helps us to understand why some foods were taken and others ignored, why some foods were keystones in the economy, and why cultural conventions, such as food taboos and food folklore, are built around these decisions. The large-scale "decisions" that led to subsistence systems revolve around the relative merits of alternative foods, including the cost of their acquisition, their nutritional benefits, transportability, and storability. These things mattered just as they do with modern, large-scale patterns of food use.[16]

During most of prehistory the diet of the Basin-Plateau region was astonishingly broad, and this pattern persisted in historical times. The classic ethnographies done by anthropologists in the early 20th century show an economy anchored by gathered plant foods. Meat was always sought but constituted a minority of the diet.[17] Indeed, while conducting fieldwork in the Great Basin in 1935, the anthropologist Julian Steward wrote to his professor, Alfred Kroeber: "This comes near to being a woman's economy."[18]

The annual cycle began in the spring, when the first shoots and greens could be gathered and small mammals emerged from their burrows. Migrating waterfowl were taken individually, and their eggs were sought. In scattered places, plant growth around hot springs enabled the gathering season to begin a few weeks early to ease people out of winter.

A major attraction in the late spring was spawning fish, driven into weirs made of brush and sticks, where they were scooped up with nets and by hand. Several species of suckers were harvested in huge numbers as they swarmed upstream, and eyewitness accounts describe these spectacles occurring on the tributaries of Great Salt Lake and Utah Lake.[19]

In the desert foothills and flats, some types of roots fleshed out early and large stands such as bitterroot produced their edible roots every year, sometimes for centuries. These stable sources attracted people each year in significant social gatherings. Marilyn Couture described Northern Paiute "root camps" in southeastern Oregon that attracted different bands and even language groups to a single location. These people often communicated by "sign language"; the root camp phenomenon is a good example of people being tethered, even if only temporarily, to predictable resources and the fluid social networks that accompanied this pattern of movement.[20] The biological persistence of root stands over lifetimes, and even centuries, fostered traditions, and, as we will see, when we examine social organization, provided a mechanism for both territorial identification and for networks across territories.

Spring presented an opportunity to drive pronghorn into enclosures as they migrated from the low flats toward the foothills. Pronghorn had to form large enough groups to make a group hunt feasible, and traps were positioned differently for the spring hunt versus the hunt during the fall migration. The location of drives had to be moved widely across the landscape among years. Thus, pronghorn hunting required large foraging ranges and often brought together people from different places, families and bands. Pronghorn drives are known along the Deep Creek Mountains on the Utah-Nevada border, and there are driving fences in Park Valley, northwestern Utah. Many others are known from northeastern Nevada all the way to eastern California.[21]

Spring signaled the end of winter, but in many ways was a difficult time of the year. Most of the stored food from winter was gone. It was too early for many foods, and the starchy filler foods, such as roots, had yet to flesh out. The high protein and fatty grass and shrub seeds had yet to come on. Large animals were scrawny and moving upslope into the high country. Spring started off sparse but became richer and richer as it unfolded.

Summer brought the seeds. Wild seeds provided the most storable food available, and they contained more fat and protein than did modern domesticated seeds such as wheat and rice. In the desert habitats, people gathered seeds in succession as they ripened, storing them close to the point of gathering, but in strategic locations to be available for winter.

Small and medium mammals put on weight and were constantly hunted, trapped, skewered in their holes, or flushed and clubbed. The archaeology of the Basin-Plateau region is clear that cottontail rabbits and especially jackrabbits were the most consumed meat through virtually all of prehistory.[22]

Periodic superabundance occurred when grasshoppers and crickets emerged. These were taken in a variety of ways, such as driving them into a hole full of brush and igniting it. An intriguing image comes from the Great Salt Lake where grasshoppers were sometimes blown ashore, leaving windrows of salted, dried grasshoppers many kilometers long.[23]

In August and September, the larvae of brine fly could form windrows that ringed the shorelines of Mono Lake in eastern California, Great Salt Lake, and many others in between. One early observer described the masses of larvae as "about two feet high by three or four in thickness, (it) extends like a vast rim around the shore of the lake." And an observation about brine-fly larvae by none other than Mark Twain: "If you dip up a gallon of water, you will get about 15,000 of these."[24] Word of such bounty could travel quickly, bringing people of various bands, and perhaps speaking different languages, from many miles away to feast and process for transport these short-term bounties for as long as they lasted, or until some other opportunity drew them away.

Summer presented other meat options, too, and the people hunted such large game as mule deer, bighorn sheep, pronghorn, and elk. These were always sought when trips to the higher country were made to obtain roots, berries, and raw materials such as stone for chipped stone tools. Thus, large game hunting surely was important, and the animals were always sought, but during the summer, big

FIGURE 1.4

This is a bighorn sheep and deer trap in the Jarbidge Mountains in extreme northern Nevada. Animals were driven from the right onto the talus slope and contained by the wooden fence. Blinds were dug into the talus on the facing slope opposite the base of the trap. Rocks were arranged to create a circular, relatively flat area for processing the animals; this is visible inside the corral at the lower left. A rock foundation for an earlier version of the fence was found lower in the ravine at the base of the trap; it was situated to improve the trajectory of darts propelled by the atlatl. The wooden fence in the photo is only a few centuries old and used with the bow and arrow as well as guns. Shells from 19th-century Henry rifles were found in the blind pits. (Photo by Steven Simms)

game hunting was likely embedded in other activities. Bison were variously present in the region but are strongly represented in the archaeological record only in a few times and places. Bison are mobile and not always available, and they were dangerous to hunt on foot, relative to other food options. Meat from large animals was available intermittently, and when one was killed, its meat was likely shared widely and was a source of power and social prestige—at least this is a pattern found in many foraging societies.[25]

Summertime in the wetlands offered different choices than did the valleys, foothills, and arid mountains. Waterfowl were taken by drives in the summer when the birds were molting and less prone to flight. Small mammals such as muskrat, gophers, mice, and beaver occurred in greater densities in wetland habitats than in drier areas. Freshwater mollusks were gathered. Bulrush and cattail roots fleshed out in stupendous abundance and were excavated in huge mats. For a few weeks, cattail pollen was plentiful and made into one of the few breadlike foods available.

Gathering remained the central activity through the summer, not only for storable seeds but also for summer roots such as sego lily, bitterroot, biscuitroot, and many others. By late summer, gooseberries, currants, and serviceberries, to name a few, came on.

Fall was a prime hunting time and conjures up images of fat deer, bighorn sheep, and elk. Animals were more likely to be in good condition, and rutting season expanded the opportunities to take these animals, because their mating behavior could be exploited. For instance, hollow logs were beaten together to simulate dueling bighorn rams and to attract more females for the kill.[26]

The pinyon nut harvest was the most significant event of the year for many people.[27] Pine nuts attracted large groups of people, and the harvest lasted weeks. Caches containing pine nut hooks, grinding stones, hullers, and various kinds of baskets were kept in the best pine nut groves. Pine nut hooks are long poles with a wooden spur attached to pull down branches and clusters of cones. The harvest began with green cones that were processed in large roasting areas to open them. In another two weeks, the brown cones were taken, but by then competition from squirrels and pinyon jays could become significant. Finally, trees could be shaken to knock down the fully ripe nuts onto mats.

The point is that the harvest was long, and processing the nuts into usable meal was labor intensive, but the production of a high-calorie, fatty, and protein-rich storable product was enormous.

Further, the productivity of specific groves could be predicted up to two years in advance, ensuring that people who had not seen one another for awhile could arrive at the right places. Pine nuts were cheap to acquire relative to the many smaller seeds that also could be stored. They were costly to transport but important enough to be moved across the landscape to a limited extent. Accounts show that people living along the northern shores of Great Salt Lake might make several trips to the Grouse Creek mountains near the Nevada border to retrieve pine nuts for their winter villages along the Wasatch Front.[28] As we will see when we step into prehistory, the pinyon pine tree did not always live as widely in the Basin-Plateau region as it does today. But the spread of this botanical migrant over the past few thousand years shaped how people lived.

By early winter, stores had to be laid in to make it through the winter in a region that offered few groceries over a several month

FIGURE 1.5

The Bustos wickiup site included the slumped remains of five conical structures made of juniper logs. The logs were obtained by lighting trees on fire and using a stone ax to chop away the charred wood. The small village was used as a pine nut camp in the early 19th century. Eight circular stone rings were used to store the nuts, and fire hearths outside the doors to the structures contained charred pine nut hulls. (Photo by Steven Simms)

period. The early winter jackrabbit drives were the last large-group activity of the season and could attract more than a hundred people. Carefully maintained nets passed down among generations were strung together and drivers sent out. Rabbits tend to herd as the weather chills, and they could be driven into the nets and clubbed by the hundreds and even thousands. Rabbit drives were significant feasts and the last large social event before people broke into groups of perhaps ten to several dozen people and headed to their first winter village.

These descriptions are of the classic broad diet of the Basin-Plateau region and refer to activities common to both the desert-mountain and the wetland settlement patterns. In contrast, there were some periods and places where the suite of foods taken from the potential array was narrow. The earliest period of human occupation over 10,000 years ago may be one of these. When the first colonists arrived on the continent, meat may have constituted a larger share of the diet than in other times and places. Roots and vegetables were part of the diet, but ignored more often. Seeds were eaten but had not yet become the economic keystone they would be millennia later.

Another time of narrower diets would be the period of agriculture in the eastern Basin and on the Plateau between A.D. 0–1300. So much investment was placed on the farming of maize, beans, and squash that this triad became the staple for many people, even though the diet was always supplemented with wild foods, and hunter-gatherers continued to occupy the region.

The notion that a diet is "narrow" does not mean that people ate only a few things; rather, it means that the keystone resources were different, the orientation of subsistence effort was different, and the bulk of their food intake comprised fewer things.

There is much more to the idea of wild subsistence than a simple list of edible foods. Decisions about what to harvest and what to ignore varied, and the people had an intimate, practical knowledge of the trade-offs. There were trade-offs involved in moving camp to acquire a certain resource, because that might mean foregoing the opportunity to acquire something else. The time to travel to places had to be taken into account. Decisions had to be made about which foods to store and how their retrieval was to be accomplished. Having information about where certain foods were abundant, or ready for harvest, was a constant influence on how people lived. And people's decisions were shaped by knowledge of what other people were exploiting. Thus, food and settlement choices were shaped not only

SIDEBAR: FORAGER CUISINE

Stories abound of foragers eating strange and even disgusting foods. Descriptions of how food was acquired are often equally rustic to a modern people who have little idea of how it was produced. Accounts describing the indigenous food of the Great Basin as it appeared around a campfire are few, fragmentary, and often ethnocentric. Despite graphic images of Indians eating grasshoppers, larvae, bone marrow, and seeds, the cuisine of ancient Utah was for the most part simple and probably not as strange as the more grisly stereotypes lead us to believe.

Daily cuisine revolved around the stewpot. For most of antiquity this was a basket with the contents heated by hot stones transported from the campfire on a special implement called a *rock lifter*. A basket of water can be boiled this way in less than five minutes. The ingredients varied through the year, often using a base of flour made from seeds such as Indian ricegrass, blazing star, saltbush, and native bluegrass, to name just a few. The mush might have been laced with bits of meat, perhaps rabbit. Greens and seasonings may be added, such as peppergrass or tansymustard seeds, to produce a mild spiciness. In the fall, the stews might have been based on pine nuts, one of the delicacies of the year. With several dozen varieties of seeds, meat from small and medium-sized mammals, and many kinds of greens and sources of spice, there were endless variations on the theme of the stewpot.

Starchy roots could serve as the basis for a stew, but roots were also baked in the sand at the bottom of a campfire, or in a rock-lined earth oven. Roots can be baked in their skins like a potato, or wrapped in leaves. Some roots were best eaten raw, like our modern carrots. In fact, many foods were considered best when eaten raw, and surely people ate these as they picked.

Bread as we know it did not exist, but some roots are reported to be breadlike after being baked. The seeds from curly dock were pounded, soaked, and ground into a dough that was baked in coals. Cattail pollen was formed into cakes and cooked on a stone slab or on coals to make a breadlike concoction.

Not all cooking was for immediate consumption. Desert fruitcake was a mix of whatever dried berries, meat, and seeds were available and formed into loaves. Roasted grasshoppers and brine-fly larvae constituted the base of fruitcakes to make storable the superabundance of these highly nutritious foods that could be harvested only a few weeks a year. Desert fruitcake was surely a highly concentrated form of energy and protein—an early version of the energy bars of today.

When not used in a stew, many meats were simply roasted. Sometimes a whole animal, such as a marmot, might be placed on hot coals after the fur had been singed off. Smaller animals were gutted by squeezing them and then made into a convenient kebab by inserting a stick into their body. Pieces of meat from larger animals were barbequed much like today. Jerky was an important meat preservation option.

Foragers around the world seek sources of fat. Despite the variety of meats and the relatively high fat content of wild seeds and pine nuts, the indigenous diet was so low in fat that this essential ingredient was actively sought. Wild game is extremely lean, but there is fat under the skin and in the bones. It was boiled from the bones and scraped from the skins for consumption. It was an essential binder for desert fruitcake. Bone grease skimmed from a boiling pot of bones might get a person through the worst days of winter, and it certainly richened the stew.

The overall diet was high in protein, low in fat, and high in nutrients and fiber—satisfying the recommendations of modern nutritionists, doctors, and mothers. The diet was also short on sweets. One of the few sweets reported is "honey" deposited by aphids on plants such as cattail. This was scraped off and eaten. Occasionally, honey from wild bees could be found.

On the one hand, the diet would strike modern Americans as strong and bitter; on the other, it might taste bland to modern sensibilities because of a lack of fat and sugar. The passage below gives some sense of this. It is from a story called *The Pickleweed Winter* and was told to the linguist Wick Miller by Maude Moon, a Goshiute Shoshone born in the late 19th century somewhere south of Wendover, Nevada.

Long ago Indians had everything they needed. They ate these things which grew on this earth . . . all kinds of seeds. This pickleweed, and also ones such as sunflower seeds, bunch grass seeds, rye grass, and just any kind like keppisappeh, like wild onions, like Indian balsam, like carrots, like wild potatoes, like thistle . . . During the winter, one ate all he wanted. It was over there at Big Springs (Blue Lake, between Wendover and Goshiute), they called it the pickleweed winter. They ate it with pine nuts they say. They ate it with jack rabbits. Times were good, they say . . . But now you modern people, girls and other modern Indians: they don't know anything. If they were gathered, they wouldn't eat them. They taste bad, they say. The sweetness has killed their mouths. They eat and drink canned sweet things. Only these taste good (to them today). Indian food doesn't taste good anymore. It tastes too strong. It just tastes bad. It can't be swallowed. This is how it is.[a]

by where the food was but also for the benefit of sharing information; the "information age" began long ago. There is much more to looking back at ancient subsistence systems than a romantic nod to "living off of the land."[29]

SOCIAL AND POLITICAL ORGANIZATION

Sociopolitical organization shapes people's behavior by structuring the relationships among people and defining the approaches to cooperation, competition, and the use of power. The social matters of ancient cultures are a source of wonder because these things are so human, yet the archaeological past is so dim and difficult to know. Artifacts, campsites, food remains, human remains, and houses can be preserved directly, but kinship terms, rules of civility, and group relationships exist through the selective filters of memory and folklore.

Fortunately, social organization can be gleaned from ethnographic and historical accounts as well as from anthropological knowledge about the patterns of social organization among the hundreds of foraging and simple farming cultures documented around the world in recent centuries. Together, these enable a glimpse of past social organizations in the Basin-Plateau, because the general features of social organization vary in patterned ways with the things archaeologists do see—settlement, mobility, economics, the organization of technology and such.

In the early 20th century, anthropologists and ethnohistorians began interviewing old people and culling documents in an attempt to reconstruct "precontact" social organization for the Basin-Plateau region. Scholars debate whether the late 19th century, and historical accounts from even earlier times, are an accurate reflection of life before the influence of Euro-Americans.[30] Rather than dwell on whether our description represents the truly "pristine" indigenous culture of the region, we should remind ourselves that no culture exists in isolation—all people have lived around other people and were thus in "contact" with others since the planet was fully colonized over 10,000 years ago. Nor do anthropologists continue to labor under the naive illusion that there is some fundamental foraging, or "primitive," society that is static and timeless.[31] Anthropologists such as Julian Steward argued decades ago that defining particular culture types is less productive than seeking an understanding of the processes that cause different forms of social organization.[32] This interest in process signals our concern here not with basic types but with variations on themes.

Our goal is to describe the themes of prehorse societies to glimpse the circumstances under which sociopolitical organization varies.[33] This prepares us to step into a large past where there was no single

"Indian" sociopolitical organization that covers all of antiquity, but rather different expressions of social organization depending on the circumstances of place and the historical trajectories established in previous times.

Sex roles defined many activities, with women managing most wild plant gathering and playing a significant role in farming during the agricultural periods. Women and, to varying extents, children also hunted small and medium-sized mammals and participated in fish, rabbit, and waterfowl hunting, especially in mass catches of these animals. Men hunted larger game, which required weapons, and hunted ducks with nets and set trap lines of snares and deadfalls. Men also participated with women and children in gathering activities such as egg-hunting in the marshes and pine nut harvesting.

Most public leadership was in the hands of men, but women's voices were strong on matters of daily concern in the household and camp group. They were influential in decisions about gathering, the lynchpin of the economy. The female shaman depicted in the Prologue signals that power and leadership occur in many contexts.

A significant difference in sex roles is found in the mobility of men and women. Aside from the contrast in mobility between the desert-mountain and the wetlands settlement patterns, men's mobility was likely higher than women's was for most of prehistory. The demands of hunting, but perhaps even more the demands of public leadership in decisions about where a group should move next, required knowledge of vast areas.[34]

Knowledge was also important to women's roles, and their knowledge of plant gathering was a key to the economy. The demands of child rearing and the limitations of small children on women's mobility among foragers were also significant. While parenting chores could be allocated to older, less mobile females, young children placed limits on moving households, on foraging ranges, and probably on where people lived after they were married.

Next come marriage and kinship, the most relevant elements of social organization for people inhabiting the ancient Basin-Plateau region.[35] Polygamy was common in most cultures through history, and the Basin-Plateau region was no exception. The marriage of two sisters to a man is frequently mentioned in informant accounts, a practice called sororal polygyny. A related practice was the levirate, in which a man's widows are kept in the group by marrying them to a deceased husband's brother. This practice maintained alliances among two kin lineages that were created by the first marriage.

Structured marriage arrangements such as these were more frequent in societies where group sizes were small and population density was low—factors leading to a shortage of marriage partners and uneven sex ratios within groups. Polyandry, the marriage of multiple men to one wife, was also known for the Basin-Plateau but appears to have been as rare as it was among foraging societies in general.

Plural marriage was practiced, but many unions were monogamous, as necessitated by factors such as wealth, age, the death of a spouse, and the availability of partners. Marriages could not be made among close relatives, but the definition of kin relations was, as we shall see, subject to considerable variability. Under more mobile, small group circumstances, such as the desert-mountain settlement pattern described previously, marriage had to be outside the extended family, lineage, and ideally even the band, that larger entity of several lineages that extended kinship into the past to a common ancestor and affixed kinship to place.

Under more settled circumstances, such as the wetland settlement pattern, marriage among cross-cousins (for instance, a child of a father's sister or a child of a mother's brother) might have been more frequent. The practice of cross-cousin marriage was known in many foraging societies and continued the exchange of brothers and sisters into the next generation in a way that did not violate incest rules. Such marriages contributed to the identity and the maintenance of alliances within a corporate community group.

Anthropologists use the term "corporate group" to signal the differences in society when people live more settled lives and in larger groups. Corporate groups assign statuses and roles that regulate each member's relation to other members. They have common purposes, such as administering property or defending against attacks. Corporate groups have clear rules of membership and, because they are more stable, persist beyond the lifespan of their members. As our story of the past unfolds, we will see the importance of the distinction between corporate and fluid group structure to comprehending diversity in ancient social life.[36]

Kinship consists of two components: affinity and descent. Affinity defines relationships through marriage. Descent defines relationships of parentage, regardless of whether descent is biological or fictive. Descent is traced in a variety of ways across the world's cultures, but the three forms germane to the Basin-Plateau are, in descending order of frequency: bilateral (tracing through mother and father), patrilineal (tracing through father), and matrilineal (tracing through mother).

Bilateral descent is common among the world's foragers and enables the creation of broad networks. Bilateral descent is also flexible, because more narrow forms of descent, especially patrilineal, can be practiced in some circumstances, while tracing lineage through either the male or the female line can be applied to other circumstances. Bilateral descent with patrilineal descent embedded within it was likely the most common among foragers in the ancient Basin-Plateau.

It is possible that matrilineal descent existed during periods in prehistory when agriculture was present on the Colorado Plateau and in the eastern Great Basin. Matrilineal descent is found among some dry-farm and hoe agriculturalists around the world and is the pattern of descent among some Puebloan groups, such as the Hopi, who are one of several Southwestern descendants of the prehistoric farmers that occupied Utah and southern Nevada from about A.D. 0–1300.

The rules and behaviors for postmarital residence were related to kinship but did not mirror it in all cases. Postmarital residence was important because it linked kinship with where people lived and with whom; thus it was fundamental to understanding group composition. Postmarital residence in the ancient Basin-Plateau region was likely fluid, with newlyweds possibly residing with the wife's family, the husband's family, with both in succession, or just setting up a residence of their own. Decisions about where to live depended on considerations inherent in the sexual division of labor. A woman's familiarity with food-gathering territories was important, as was her social network for child rearing. Men, in contrast, needed to maintain familiarity with a hunting area and maintain a teamlike association with their hunting partners. Men's relationships with trading partners were important for shaping political alliances. The potential for families to eventually set up an independent residence added flexibility and, coupled with bilateral descent, made kinship responsive to the problems of life.

Beyond the kinship relationships of the nuclear and extended family, there is the band. Descent in the Basin-Plateau region was often reckoned through memory for about four generations, with fictive references beyond to cement band identity.[37] The band was likely the largest sociopolitical unit relevant to everyday life, although even the band probably did not matter in many daily decisions as much as the camp group did. People foraged and married across band lines, members of different bands camped with one another, and so on. In the Basin-Plateau bands were generally a group of a hundred to several hundred people who traced ancestry directly and fictively to a single ancestor. In this way, bands provided one way for people to identify themselves and their place in the landscape.

The concept of tribe was a realization that several bands had a common bond of region and language. The presence of tribes in the Basin-Plateau region has long been debated, and although the concept of tribe was likely real, it was not always relevant to everyday life.[38] Tribal affiliation might be invoked when the demands of large-scale relationships called it into play. Such circumstances could include encounters between people speaking different dialects or languages, especially during group activities of root and pine nut collecting, and pronghorn or rabbit drives. The foraging ranges used by people over years and decades usually overlapped linguistic variation, sometimes bringing distinct tribal identities into proximity.[39] Heightened tribal affiliations might occur when migration brought unfamiliar people into a region over decades and even centuries, creating tension when immigrants came to stay rather than merely visit.

Other aspects of social organization in band societies are also important to our description. Fluidity in group size and composition are important to understanding the relationship between the cultural rules of kinship, band, and tribe and the daily patterns of behavior. Also, there are significant distinctions between the concepts of territoriality, the home district, and the foraging ranges used by people during their lives.[40] Finally, the nature of leadership is important to understanding political matters.

The family and band provided the calculus of social organization, but it is a mistake to assume that the rules of kinship equate with actual behavior (one need only examine our own culture to see this is true). To bridge the gulf between the calculations of kinship and the day-to-day behavior of people in Great Basin prehistory, we can appeal to the concept of the camp group (also known as the kin-clique). The description of the camp group by Catherine Fowler for the Northern Paiute of Nevada illustrates the beauty of the pragmatic.

> The camp group consisted of from three to four to as many as ten families that habitually foraged together during most of the year but at a minimum wintered together at some fixed location within its *tibiwa* or home district. Such units were

FIGURE 1.6

Map of the western Great Basin showing food named groups or home districts of the Northern Paiute (after Wheat 1967). These served as an identity and for many as a place of residence. They do not refer to tribes per se but are references of place. A person would always know he was from the "Cattail-Eater" area, even if he no longer resided there. Home districts can refer to geographic space, but symbolically they also represent identity.

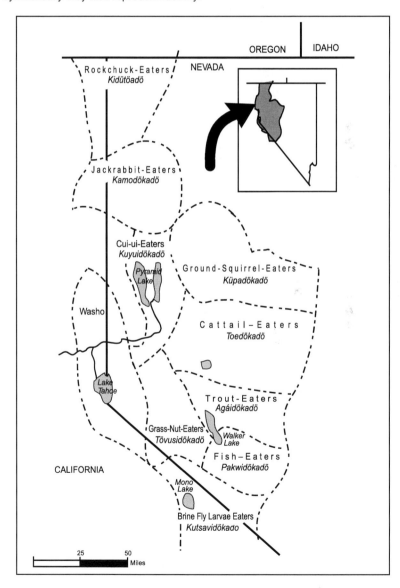

generally kin based, although non-kinspeople and visitors were often included. Each *nogadi* (camp group) moved several times during the year, following a foraging round suggested by the character of the local terrain. Each camp was also more or less independent of all others, being free to move about and affiliate or disengage with others according to its needs. All maintained a wide network of bilateral kinship and visiting ties to camps both within and outside their home districts.[41]

Note the fluidity in size and group composition that is possible in camp groups. This creates a seamless match with the patterns of mobility, settlement, and subsistence described in the previous sections. For instance, a camp group would be large for a fishing event during the spring spawn of sucker fish along the Provo River of northern Utah. Or a large group might gather for an early winter rabbit drive in Surprise Valley, northeastern California. Smaller camp groups might winter together, as did summer grass-seed collecting and hunting groups. Villages in the wetlands along the Wasatch Front, termed *rancherias* by Spanish explorers, were a variation on the theme of camp groups by being a specific place attracting varying numbers of people of diverse kin compositions depending on the season and the activities.[42]

The concept of home district is relevant, too. As described in the Prologue, all people had a home district, a *tebiwa* that provided identity, and, for many, it marked a place of residence. These were often labeled by reference to a particular food, such as the "Cattail-Eaters" or "Pine-Nut Eaters," and reference to the food could also denote there was food to share—a political bond of reciprocity. Home districts served as a reference to one's kinship and band relations, and they denoted sense of place, even if it was not the only place one lived.[43]

Foraging range is a broader, more secular concept than home district, and when paired with the fluidity of the camp group, foraging range identifies the traveling area of a person or group of people. Foraging ranges may encompass a home district and parts of others, and a camp group could include members from different groups or extend kinship ties across home ranges via bilateral reckoning through male or female lineages. Foraging ranges could overlap band lines, and even linguistic boundaries. This is because in practice, boundaries were broad zones of land, rather than lines in

FIGURE 1.7

Map of the eastern Great Basin showing food named groups or home districts of the Western Shoshone (after Steward 1938). Home districts harbor a strong element of kinship and band—who is related to whom. Home districts also embrace the intricate and ever-changing composition of camp group; who is living with whom. This is apparent in some of the home districts along the Wasatch Front. The Hukundüka and the Tubadüka living north of Great Salt Lake were both of the Shoshone tribe and language. They married each other and visited each other to harvest foods unique to each place. The membership within each home district was likely fluid, but everyone knew where they were from and that the distinction referred to place as much as it referred to any particular place.

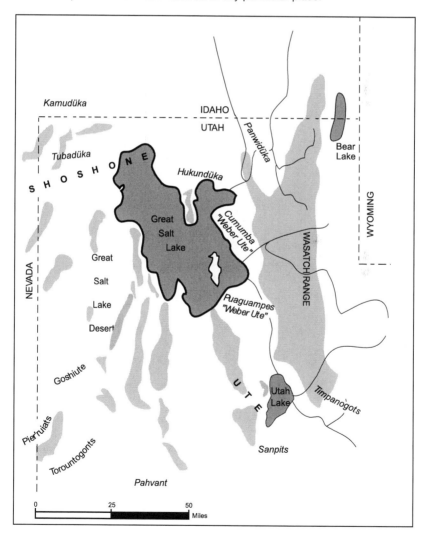

the sand, and there was joint use depending on who was present at any given time.

A standard method among ethnographers of the early 20th century for describing foraging activities is the annual seasonal round. But note from the previous discussion of subsistence that foraging ranges do not remain static over time. Amoeba-like, a foraging range changes in extent, size, and shape over years, decades, and even centuries. Transition and fluidity demarcate landscapes rather than strict boundaries among bands, tribes, and language groups.

This brings us to territories. The degree of territoriality and ownership as modern people might recognize it varies considerably in foraging societies. Personal items were owned, such as a man's bows and arrows, and costly possessions such as baskets, rabbit nets, and rabbitskin robes might be passed down among generations. The ownership of land was for the most part based on right of use—usufruct rights—rather than the legally hard and fast way that we understand land ownership. If a group habitually exploited an area such as a set of rocky ridges with abundant bitterroot, they would have expected to do so in the future. If another group wanted to move there for the roots, they might have had to ask for permission.

Similar patterns, but perhaps with a tendency toward stronger territoriality, are recorded for concentrated resources such as fish-spawning streams or the use of pronghorn drive fences and pine nut groves near large concentrations of population. Territoriality tends to increase among the world's foragers where there is a combination of concentrated resources, a predictable abundance of a specific resource, an investment in infrastructure, and increased human population density with decreased mobility.[44]

Leadership in foraging societies is primarily an achieved status and is applied to decisions about camp movements, foraging choices, disputes, and problem solving. There might be several chiefs or "captains" in a group, with some serving as spokesmen, while others rise to prominence during specialized activities such as a pronghorn or rabbit drive. Leadership and power could be gained through one's ability as a persuasive speaker, through a particular hunting skill, or through a history of successful encounters in conflict and mediation. The latter certainly seems to be the case for the Ute leaders who met the Escalante Expedition in Utah Valley in A.D. 1776. The Spaniards heard frequent references to "blood" and "battles" as a reason behind the status of several chiefs.[45] Whether this particular form of leadership was in response to the fact that the Utah Valley

Ute were horseless, but raided by horse mounted peoples, is unclear. We can be sure that conflict is possible in all cultures and that status can be gained by expertise in conflict as well as skill in negotiating its resolution.[46]

The power of leadership was likely derived from a variety of sources stemming largely from charisma and skill. This is consistent with patterns found in many foraging societies in the world who live in low population densities, are semisedentary, and have fluid social organizations to match fluid settlement arrangements. Despite the temptation to label these societies as egalitarian, in practice there was an inertia that often maintained leadership within family lines.

During some periods of more settled life and larger population sizes, leadership may have intensified and been transferred among relatives more readily. There were surely more levels of leadership than among the sparse desert peoples, but as we will see there is little evidence for kings, despots, and aristocracy in the Basin-Plateau region even during the height of agriculture.

As with other aspects of social organization, no single form of leadership describes all of prehistory. Leadership and political organization ranged from ephemeral status with only diffuse power to the existence of selected chiefs who amassed power over time and perhaps to chiefly power sufficiently concentrated to transmit to the next generation at least once before the power dissipated.

The ancient Basin-Plateau region thus exhibits a generalized pattern of sociopolitical organization expressed along a continuum. During many periods and places it was "family level," with few organizational complexities beyond the band. Every adult knew of larger social arrangements and who was affiliated with whom, but large-scale political interactions were probably not an important part of daily life. Camp groups were the organizational unit most relevant to daily living, and although these probably consisted mostly of kin, non-kin could move in and out of these associations. The fluidity of this system fostered extensiveness and inclusiveness in the social organization. Marriage ties and lineage membership were extended outward via bilateral kin reckoning and a situational approach to postmarital residence rules. This system ensured a network of information about resources and people, ensured a supply of marriage partners, and moderated the uneven sex ratios that are a statistical fact of living in small groups. Importantly, this system was not just sociopolitical but had a geographic aspect, because it was a network across a landscape.

In some places, such as in the wetlands and during the period of agriculture, society responded to larger group sizes, less mobility, and the organizational demands of moving resources to concentrations of people rather than moving a diffuse people to scattered resources. In those situations, there surely was a higher frequency of chiefs who could sustain influence and coerce people through control over stored surplus production. Territoriality was intensified. Camp groups were tethered to specific places by a logistic system. The social organization in these systems had to emphasize maintenance of the community. Among the world's foragers a common way to accomplish this was through cross-cousin marriage, a practice that promoted reciprocity and marriage bonding between two domestic groups. These and other practices strengthened the larger communities and increased the sense of who was a member of the group and who was not. This social organization also had a geographical aspect, not just a social one. The two systems were not polar opposites, one with an outward-looking social organization and the other inward-looking, but, rather, variations on a theme. When they occurred together, as they often did, they constituted a social landscape—one that I judge as more cosmo-politan than we typically allow for the peoples of the Desert West.

IDEOLOGY

Native ideology is also important to constructing a baseline to help us more fully describe the cultures in prehistory. Ideological systems, or "worldview," include beliefs in the supernatural and its influence on life, ritual, shamanism, and oral traditions. These things are the most difficult of all to interpret from the archaeological record, and hints may be all we can ask for, because it is impossible to extend the particulars of ritual and practice into deep antiquity. There are, however, variations on themes that help us step into a past where no single "Native American religion" can cover the expanse of prehistory.

First, some patterns in Basin-Plateau ideology match those described for settlement, subsistence, and social organization—a match that reflects the symphony of culture. We can thus gain a sense of how past ideological systems varied as the economic, social, and political circumstances varied.

Second, there is a degree of uniformity in the ethnographically and historically known Basin-Plateau cultures in terms of practices and stories.[47] The Basin-Plateau has its own ways compared to other major culture areas such as the Puebloan Southwest and the Plains. The unity across the historically known peoples of the Basin-Plateau is not pervasive through all details but illustrates a connection among traditions over a large area. Despite the seemingly local nature of the foraging life, the networks and the travels of people were more extensive than we often imagine, especially when we consider the time spans of human lives and many generations.

Third, there are limits to the time depth of ideological patterns once we step into the scales of time that archaeology brings. There are times in the past when extensive ideological connections over large areas were promoted, and other times when group maintenance, community, and competition fueled the importance of boundaries and inward-looking values. Accordingly, no single ideological thread connects the modern indigenous peoples of the region to the whole of the prehistoric past.

The worldview depicted in the Prologue illustrates the integration of all aspects of life. Even the most mundane aspects of people's daily routine were ideologically charged. The "actions" of people, plants, animals, rivers, and weather were directly connected to the past and constitute a flowing river of meaning. This notion of integration cannot be overemphasized to us, a people who live in a highly specialized, secular society, in which aspects of culture are segregated from one another in terms of behavior, thought, values, and law. A central theme about ideological systems found among foraging cultures is that all things and phenomena past and present are of the same fabric.

One concept to illuminate this fabric is power. Power is not static, but kinetic and is thus a life force in constant motion.[48] It resides in all things, regardless of whether these are astronomical, such as sun, moon, and Milky Way; terrestrial, such as rocks, springs, caves, and mountains; or plants and animals, or human things. Power not only accounts for things and actions but also helps people understand their place in the world. It also mediates human relationships and is central to accounting for birth, illness, curing, and death. Power connects different times and is the means by which the past remains "alive" in the present.

Ethnographically in the Basin-Plateau region, power was a personal relationship between an individual and everything else. No central authority certified a person's religious interpretations. Power in humans came from nonhuman things and could be actively sought or passively acquired. A young man might seek power to prepare for marriage—or a deer hunt. A shaman's power was expressed during a curing and represented different forms of power, depending on whether the curing was successful or not. A chief's power was evident when a public speech motivated people to action or successfully mediated a dispute. The power of nonhuman beings might be evident when someone fell ill, or a child was born, or someone died, or a person returned after a long absence. The opening of pine nut cones, the migrations of pronghorn and waterfowl, the plumpness of sego lily bulbs were expressions of the power within them and, importantly, of their interactions with people.

Ideology varied in subtle ways with the ebb and flow of group sizes. When people assembled into larger groups they had a common bond, even without a formal religious society with well-defined membership. Since camp groups were kin based, and the connections among people well established, the degree of individual variation in ideological perceptions and the amount of personal power that could be amassed were always constrained. The repetition of stories, with characters behaving mostly as expected, and themes revisited a thousand times spun a blanket that touched everyone differently even as it enveloped the group. The fundamental, baseline ideological system of Basin-Plateau foragers is cogently described by the legendary ethnologist Ake Hultkrantz: "Religious ideas and practices were diffused throughout the culture, but did not constitute a set of defined beliefs, values, and rites."[49]

Ideology changes in concert with settlement, subsistence, and social organization. It mirrors the more complex social organization found in the more stable residential system of the wetlands pattern, and those during the long period of Fremont agriculture. Under those circumstances, more specialization and persistence of power might have existed among shamans. Chiefs could intensify their relationships with the supernatural to help cement their positions. Chiefly power would more often be passed among generations, concentrating power within lineages and fostering inequality across the society. In the largest communities, ideological boundaries might be extended to corporate kin groups, as with some of the historically known Southwestern groups such as the Hopi. When ideology certifies the interests of corporate kin groups, sharper boundaries are drawn among people, and the way is paved for more entwined relationships of alliance and conflict. Once again, these variations on the theme depended on the context of time and place in prehistory.

When ethnographers recorded the stories of Native American elders, they noticed broad patterns across the region.[50] Themes and character representation in the stories of the Northern Paiute, Shoshone, Southern Paiute, and Ute show unity despite significant differences in lifeways among these groups during the historic period. The stories of the horse-mounted, "Plainslike" Northern Ute, for instance, suggest far deeper cultural bonds with the nonhorse foragers of the Great Basin to the west than with other Plains Indians groups.[51]

These are important points, because the folkloric element of ideology illustrates some of the behavioral patterns described in previous sections of this chapter. Fluidity in group composition, an extensive, bilateral kinship network, and rules of exogamy among the predominantly desert foragers of the region produced broad cultural ties over time, ties that are not appreciated by a perception of destitute Indians living with the same family group in a single, unchanging homeland for their entire lives, essentially unaware of the larger social picture.

On the one hand, folklore seems timeless in terms of human lives. But on the other hand, on archaeological time scales, folklore becomes mythological time and eventually becomes useless as historical narrative, or at least impossible to support with evidence. Indeed folklorists note that it is mostly the temptation of modern Euro-American civilization to employ folklore as narrative history, whereas the significance of folklore lies actually in other realms. Native peoples created, transmitted, and interpreted folklore in their own ways and for their own reasons.[52] Glimpses of narrative history can surely be gleaned, but folklore can also be a chimera of what we wish or dream the past to be. These beliefs may be real, but that reality applies only to the present.[53]

The time span of folklore as narrative history surely varies. Great Basin linguist and folklorist Sven Liljeblad conducted a great deal of first-person fieldwork in the region from the 1930s on, and he suspects the limit is roughly the age of the grandparental generation of the speaker.[54] This might be about 150 years, an estimate that squares with others.[55] As previously mentioned, ethnographic accounts suggest that kinship reckoning tends to become fictionalized after about four generations. It may be at this point that the reliability of stories as historical narrative is severely strained.

However, some elements of stories hint at previous events. Stories of the Southern Paiute suggest why they had conflict with the Hopi

in the early historic period and before. Southern Paiute stories can
be cross-referenced to migrations, physical differences, subsistence,
and artifacts that distinguish them from the earlier Fremont people.[56]
David Whitley's extensive research on rock art in the western Great
Basin and California finds that a great deal of rock art less than about
1,000 years old can be explained in terms of ethnographic evidence.
Before that time, the ability to empirically support a connection
becomes difficult. Thus, some elements of rock art may also be a
window into the archaeologically recent past.[57]

Ideology is indeed difficult to extend into the deep past, but we
must remember that some elements of ideology are more resistant
to change than are many of the plastic aspects of culture, such
as the composition of a camp group or the complexity of political
organization. Regardless of the temporal limitations of ideology, one
thing remains instructive: The prehistory of the desert and wetland
foragers who inhabited the Basin-Plateau region for over 13,000 years
and that of the Fremont farmers who coexisted with foragers for a
millennium is a more complex, textured, and, in a sense, cosmopolitan
one than typically allowed for—even by archaeologists.

FROM HISTORIC BASELINE TO THE DEEP PAST:
A SPIRAL OF CONTEXTS

The metaphors of wilderness, nature, and pristine harmony have
been applied to Native Americans since the days of Columbus and
go hand in hand with romantic images of Indians living in isolation.
Ever since the advancing wave of first colonists crossed the continent
over 13,000 years ago, the North American wilderness included
humans. As people filled in the spaces behind the advancing wave,
a process began that quickly built constellations of human social
networks that formed a spiral of contexts—connections across space
and through time. We must remember this notion if we are to employ
the baseline of lifeways, social organization, and worldview described
in this chapter to know what the past was like at different times and
places in the ancient Great Basin and northern Colorado Plateau.

American Indians were not campers in a designated wilderness
area. America was full and had been for many millennia. We
cannot understand these societies as super-rural isolates, living
independently, but always on the edge of death with only a harsh
environment to confront. In the occupied landscape that was all

FIGURE 1.8

This map shows recorded rock art sites near the Wasatch Front as an example of just how common this form of expression was. Similar densities are found across the Basin-Plateau, although certain places seem to carry greater significance over the millennia. Examples of such places might be the San Rafael Swell and Canyonlands of Utah and the Coso Range and vicinity of California. (Courtesy of Mark E. Stuart)

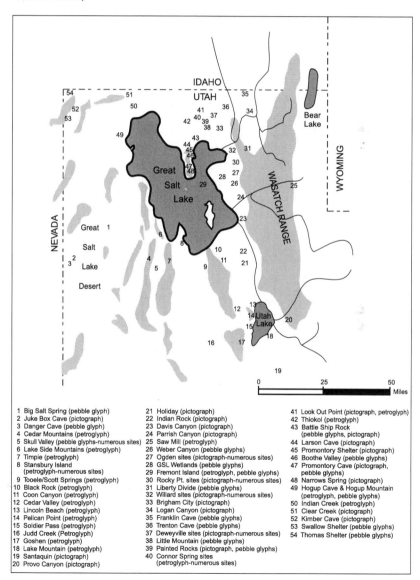

1 Big Salt Spring (pebble glyph)
2 Juke Box Cave (pictograph)
3 Danger Cave (pebble glyph)
4 Cedar Mountains (petroglyph)
5 Skull Valley (pebble glyphs-numerous sites)
6 Lake Side Mountains (petroglyph)
7 Timpie (petroglyph)
8 Stansbury Island
   (petroglyph-numerous sites)
9 Tooele/Scott Springs (petroglyph)
10 Black Rock (petroglyph)
11 Coon Canyon (petroglyph)
12 Cedar Valley (petroglyph)
13 Lincoln Beach (petroglyph)
14 Pelican Point (petroglyph)
15 Soldier Pass (petroglyph)
16 Judd Creek (Petroglyph)
17 Goshen (petroglyph)
18 Lake Mountain (petroglyph)
19 Santaquin (pictograph)
20 Provo Canyon (pictograph)

21 Holiday (pictograph)
22 Indian Rock (pictograph)
23 Davis Canyon (pictograph)
24 Parrish Canyon (pictograph)
25 Saw Mill (petroglyph)
26 Weber Canyon (pebble glyphs)
27 Ogden sites (pictograph-numerous sites)
28 GSL Wetlands (pebble glyphs)
29 Fremont Island (petroglyph, pebble glyphs)
30 Rocky Pt. sites (pictograph-numerous sites)
31 Liberty Divide (pebble glyphs)
32 Willard sites (pictograph-numerous sites)
33 Brigham City (pictograph)
34 Logan Canyon (pictograph)
35 Franklin Cave (pebble glyphs)
36 Trenton Cave (pebble glyphs)
37 Deweyville sites (pictograph-numerous sites)
38 Little Mountain (pebble glyphs)
39 Painted Rocks (pictograph, pebble glyphs)
40 Connor Spring sites
   (petroglyph-numerous sites)

41 Look Out Point (pictograph, petroglyph)
42 Thiokol (petroglyph)
43 Battle Ship Rock
   (pebble glyphs, pictograph)
44 Larson Cave (pictograph)
45 Promontory Shelter (pictograph)
46 Boothe Valley (pebble glyphs)
47 Promontory Cave (pictograph,
   pebble glyphs)
48 Narrows Spring (pictograph)
49 Hogup Cave & Hogup Mountain
   (petroglyph, pebble glyphs)
50 Indian Creek (petroglyph)
51 Clear Creek (pictograph)
52 Kimber Cave (pictograph)
53 Swallow Shelter (pebble glyphs)
54 Thomas Shelter (pebble glyphs)

parts of ancient America, the actions of people held consequences—
whether their impact was on habitats or were the effects of one group
of people on another.[58]

A recurrent theme in this chapter is that variations existed
among cultures of foragers—there is no single pattern of "hunters
and gatherers." These variations ensured that the actions, histories,
traditions, and interactions among people were often conditioned
by contrast and conflicts of interest. Prehistoric life was not just a
matter of foragers living around other foragers in a pattern of benign
harmony.

For instance, the contrasts between a desert-mountain settlement
pattern and a wetlands settlement pattern were contexts guiding
people's lives. The Ute of the Uinta Basin lived differently from the
Ute around Utah Lake, even though they saw themselves as one
people and traveled among camp groups and villages. When Ute
travelers came to Utah Lake in the spring for the fish harvest, the
heightened territoriality among the more settled Ute of Utah Lake
surely conditioned the nature of the interactions.

John Fremont glimpsed this contrast when he visited Pyramid
Lake in western Nevada in 1843. His party encountered some
Northern Paiute living a desert lifeway prior to his arrival at the
rich trout fishery at the lake where other Northern Paiute lived. "I
remarked that one of them gave a fish to the Indian we had first
seen, which he carried off to his family. To them it was probably a
feast; being of the Digger tribe, and having no share in the fishery,
living generally on seeds and roots."[59] The fish mentioned in this
event were shared, even if there was a sense that the territory was not
shared equally. It seems possible that the desert dweller also spoke
Northern Paiute and perhaps even was an individual known to the
lake dwellers. Nevertheless, the impact of neighbors on people's lives
is unmistakable.

These examples illustrate that regardless of whether relationships
are harmonious or acrimonious, the presence of neighbors always
shapes the outcome. The people of the Basin-Plateau had neighbors
for over 13,000 years![60]

Archaeologists divide the prehistory of the region into four basic
categories. The first is the Paleoindian, a period remote in time
beginning over 13,000 years ago, when humans were colonizing
the region, and ending somewhere around 10,000 years ago. The
Archaic period spans the next eight to ten millennia and harbors an

FIGURE 1.9

Timeline showing the major cultural periods of the Basin-Plateau.

Major Periods and Archaeological Cultures
Time B.P. (A.D./B.C.)

15,000	13,000	11,000	9,000	7,000	5,000	4,000	3,000	2,000	1,000	500	present
								A.D. 0	A.D. 1300		

? — — — Paleoindian —

        – Early Archaic – Middle Archaic –   Late Archaic – –
                                                  (western Basin)

                                    – Late Archaic – Fremont – Late Prehistoric
                                      (eastern Basin – Plateau)

enormous amount of history ranging from fundamental change in social organization, politics, and ideology to important changes in technology, such as the introduction of the bow and arrow. The third is the Fremont of the northern Colorado Plateau and eastern Great Basin, and it marks the arrival of maize agriculture, immigrants, pottery, and connections with the Southwest about 2,000 years ago. The last millennium is the Late Prehistoric, and it brings more immigrants, social upheaval, and connections with California.

These categories are conveniences, and in some ways mere appendages to our story. The narrative of ancient peoples and place is more of a spiral of contexts than a set of discreet historical events. And the story is about people, not the things that archaeologists dig up.

2

Ancient Climate and Habitats

The world of ancients was a wilderness that was lived in, not just visited. Their wilderness was a human landscape more akin to our notion of neighborhood and the idea of "place."[1] The landscapes, the neighborhoods, if you will, of ancient peoples are many. We have already seen how people's lives were as different as the "desert-mountain" and "wetlands-lakes" patterns and that these depended on location. We thus need a sense of space to aid our sense of place, and providing that is the goal of this chapter.

The landscapes and climates of the past cannot be captured directly by a modern "wilderness experience," regardless of the myth that ancient peoples lived in the wilderness before it was destroyed by the white man. Our need to protect areas from development leads to a tacit hope that wilderness is pristine or, at least on our time scale, unchanged. This view may be appropriate to wilderness protection in the modern world, but it ill prepares us for comprehending landscapes and environments of the past that are fundamentally different from anything we see in the region today, wilderness or otherwise.

Some of the species that convey place in our modern landscape were not present thousands of years ago. It was too cold 10,000 years ago to sustain the scrub oak thickets found in the eastern Great Basin. There were no pinyon pine forests in many places there are today. Limber pine, bristlecone pine, and even spruce forests existed where scrub oak, pinyon, and juniper dotted with sagebrush flats are found today. Vast areas of the low shrub called winterfat covered many valleys where nonnative cheatgrass dominates today. The dense sagebrush "ocean" that characterizes the Great Basin today was a much more open landscape only a few centuries ago, sprinkled liberally with clumps of bunchgrasses among more widely spaced sagebrush. Springs and marshes were present where only stark desert is found today, because we have pumped the water table lower with wells even in some of the most remote places in Nevada and southeastern Oregon, and in the isolated canyons of the Colorado Plateau.

Climate is also part of people's environment, and most appreciate the fact that there were times in the past that were cooler, more moist, wetter, or drier than today. But there is more to climate than these things, and seasonality is an example. There were periods when the differences between the seasons were smaller, and other times when they were greater than today. There were times when summers were cloudy and cool. In some centuries, the rain fell primarily in the winter, and in others significant amounts fell in the summer. Climate can change rapidly, and there were periods when drastic climate change occurred during the lifetime of individuals.

Our sense of place then, refers to the neighborhoods of ancient peoples, places that changed among seasons and among years, but also on the scale of people's lives. Our sense of place also refers to the transformation of landscapes as we extend our gaze across the millennia. Finally, our sense of place centers not on a description of nature per se but on the way nature shapes the choices and decisions of people who inhabited this human wilderness in all its guises over the past 13,000 years.

Our story here breaks with the convention of describing the oldest environments first. Instead we build a baseline by starting with the landscapes at the dawn of history and then move backward in time. Examples are drawn from the Wasatch Front of the eastern Great Basin and move geographically outward across the Basin-Plateau. In this way, we work from the familiar to the strange and begin to see how much has changed, and not changed, even in the past century and a half. As we proceed into the deep past, we will find places less and less familiar and begin to realize that there is more to prehistory than a description of Native Americans living "the old ways" as we saw them in the 19th century.

THE GREAT BASIN AND THE COLORADO PLATEAU

The Wasatch Front lies in the Great Basin at the interface of the "Basin-Plateau" regions. The Great Basin is a vast land stretching from western Utah to eastern and southern California, where all the rivers drain into the ground. This huge bowl, however, is strewn with towering mountain ranges all aligned like "warships" in "an ocean of loose sediment with these mountains standing in it as if they were members of a fleet without precedent."[2] The mountains are high, often over 10,000 feet, and include gems such as the Ruby Mountains near Elko, the towering White Mountains on the California-Nevada border, the Toiyabe Range near Austin, Nevada, and the Snake Range on the Nevada-Utah border.

The Great Basin is "half wet" because the valleys trap all the moisture that falls primarily as winter snow in the mountains and "half dry" because sparse rainfall over the rest of the year produces a desert over much of the region.[3] Many valleys harbor riparian ribbons and patches of wetlands. The surrounding terrain ascends through shrub deserts on the valley slopes and up the lower flanks of the mountains into pinyon-juniper forests. The higher terrain is a discontinuous patchwork of sage parks, meadows, and stands of fir, pine, and in the eastern Basin and Plateau, quaking aspen. The better watered mountains house more forest, but quite a few ranges are barren. Alpine environments, frequently expressed only as high altitude sagebrush parks, top many Great Basin mountain ranges.

Everything is within reach of a long day's hike, but more importantly, fantastic ecological diversity is stacked in vertical zones and then repeats itself valley to mountain and valley to mountain across the breadth of the Great Basin.

In contrast are the high tablelands of the Colorado Plateau, dissected by eons of erosion often exposing sinuous strands of cliffs and the colorful "red rocks" of central and southern Utah. Rivers seem to flow every which way, and, along their courses, small wetlands can form. But there are none of the large entrapped wetlands like those

FIGURE 2.1

The Great Basin and the Colorado Plateau showing key locations referred to in Chapter 2.

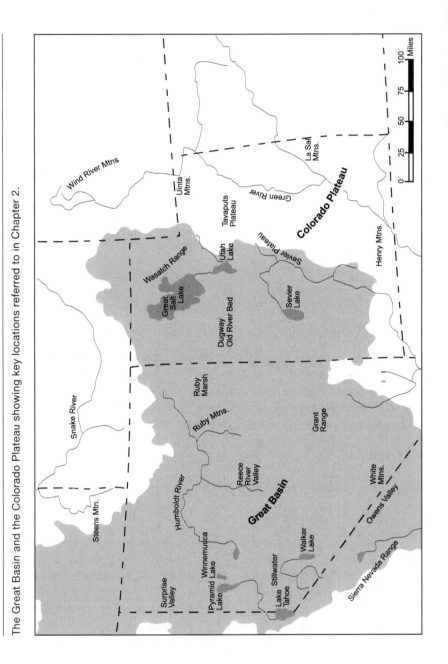

in the Great Basin, because all the water on the Colorado Plateau flows into the Green and the Colorado rivers and on to the sea. The Colorado Plateau is also a landscape of stacked life zones, from lush riparian strips and springs hidden within canyons to stark, open desert, to forested mesas, mountain forests, and alpine meadows. The Plateau exhibits less of the structured repetition of the Great Basin but is lifted in long stretches of high tablelands such as the Tavaputs Plateau in central Utah and poked upward by massive but isolated monoliths such as the LaSal Mountains near Moab and the Henry Mountains near Hanksville.

The Colorado Plateau is flanked on the north by the Uinta Mountains and separated from the Great Basin to the west by a near continuous chain of north-south trending mountains, including the Tushars, the Sevier Plateau, and the Wasatch Range. All exceed 10,000 feet in elevation. The Colorado Plateau presented a diverse but tangled web of environments to the people in prehistory.

THE WASATCH FRONT

The Wasatch Front occupies the northeastern rim of the Great Basin and marks the boundary with the Colorado Plateau to the southeast. Great Salt Lake and Utah Lake spread out along the Front and symbolize the half-wet character of the Great Basin. The Wasatch Mountains loom to the east and present the full array of biotic zones within a dozen miles of the lakes.

The deserts to the west are, of course, the half-dry part of the Basin. The Great Salt Lake Desert is the bed of ancient Lake Bonneville, which occupied most of western Utah 15,000 years ago. For humans who lived along the Wasatch Front, the Great Salt Lake Desert is less important than the desert mountain ranges and uplands that protrude from the ancient lakebed and bound it on all sides. These ranges are anything but diminutive, and most top out well over 9,000 feet.

The "Front" is a microcosm of the Great Basin; it is truly half wet and half dry. Let's imagine this place as a wilderness and begin the process of stepping into a remarkable past across the Great Basin and the Colorado Plateau.

FIGURE 2.2

The Wasatch Front showing key locations referred to in Chapter 2.

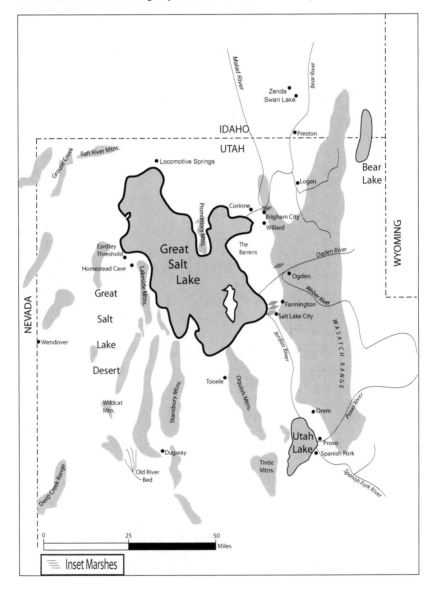

JUST BEFORE HISTORY

The year is A.D. 1800 at the site of Salt Lake City. No cities, roads, power lines, dams, or reservoirs. Ah, wilderness! Removing these overwhelming visual intrusions may wipe the slate clean, but what shall we put in its place? At a distance, the Wasatch Range would appear much the same, and the list of plant and animal species in the 18th century would be familiar. During the 19th and 20th centuries the effects of logging, mining, fire suppression, water use, grazing, and the invasion of nonnative, often weedy plants would drastically alter the composition of habitats—the things up close and most important to people who lived off the land.

Some species of animals that are rare now, such as bighorn sheep, were a more frequent sight. Elk were abundant, and large numbers of them wintered in the thickets along streams, such as those observed by fur trapper Osborne Russell along the lower Weber River in 1840. A Ute Indian told Russell that bison once roamed on the flats west of Ogden and Brigham City.[4] Deer are the most common ungulate seen today, but their ranges are severely restricted by urbanization. Ancient humans had a significant role in past ecosystems and surely shaped deer population structure, numbers, and behavior.[5]

Vegetation also changed. Repeat photography along the Wasatch Front shows that the scrub oak and maple stands along the foothills are more extensive now than a century or more ago, a function of climate and fire suppression. In our mind's eye, we might envision a sagebrush plain replacing Salt Lake City. We would be wrong, unless we opened up the sagebrush and peppered it with perennial bunchgrasses such as Great Basin Wild Rye and Indian Rice grass. The lower parts of the Salt Lake Valley may have been extensive flats of low shrubs such as winterfat and goosefoot. Stands of these are rare now, because they were favored by cattle and were among the first to disappear from the landscape.[6]

The marshlands along the Wasatch Front and elsewhere across the Great Basin are modern places of wilderness "refuge" where we are transported to a nature unleashed from civilization.[7] The flat, open margins east of Great Salt Lake and Utah Lake were lush grass-lands, interrupted by mosaics of streams, ponds, and sloughs where fresh water from the mountains crossed them as they made their way to the lakes. Trees and willows bound these streams and further out onto the lakebed, these give way to walls of cattail and bulrush as the alkalinity increases. Early settlers called the extensive flats west

of Ogden "The Barrens." The name signals the attitude of the time
that this land was too alkaline to farm, but the grasslands and trees
along the stream margins were said to extend halfway to Fremont
Island from the Weber River delta that protrudes west from Ogden.[8]
These lands may have been "barren" of cultivation potential but were
nevertheless valued as grazing land for enormous herds of sheep and
cattle. Bison roamed these areas in prehistory and are also known
north and west of Great Salt Lake, and even well into Nevada.[9]
Ancient people lived there in huge numbers, and the area is a near-
continuous archaeological landscape.

The narrow strip between the barrens and the sharply rising mountains harbors another set of wetlands, a series of "inset" marshes. The
Wasatch Fault extending along the base of the mountains distorts
the flatlands to the west, creating pockets of lower ground abutting
the base of the steep mountain slopes. These pockets are isolated
from the saline bed of Great Salt Lake by a low threshold to the west,
and when supplied with fresh water from streams and the numerous
springs along the base of the mountains, inset marshes of fresh to
brackish waters form. Most of the inset marshes are now obscured
by the urbanization that hugs the mountain slopes, although some of
the people living in these areas are reminded of the former state of
things whenever their basements flood.[10] Inset marshes occur at the
foot of many Great Basin mountain ranges.

The habitats bordering the eastern shores of Great Salt Lake and
Utah Lake supported a wide range of plants and animals, but the
astonishing quantity of waterfowl captured the attention of the first
Euro-Americans, just as the appreciation of birds and the preservation
of migratory bird flyways and habitats are of paramount concern
today. The explorer John C. Fremont wrote: "The whole morass was
animated with multitudes of waterfowl, which appeared to be very
wild rising for the space of a mile round about at the sound of a gun,
with a noise like distant thunder. Several of the people waded out into
the marshes, and we had tonight a delicious supper of ducks, geese
and plover."[11] The same could be said of the marshes at Harney
Lake, Oregon, Stillwater, western Nevada, and the Owens Valley of
California.

Animals that hardly come to mind when we think of the wetlands
today are fish. Utah Lake is perhaps the best documented fishery along
the Front, because the lake sits about 300 feet higher than Great
Salt Lake, and its open waters are essentially fresh, even before the
outlet was dammed in 1872. Utah Lake was home to a dozen species

of fish, including Bonneville Cutthroat trout and a host of suckers, such as chub, whitefish, and sculpin.[12] Secondary perhaps in abundance to the Utah Lake fishery are the marshes and the tributaries along the eastern shores of Great Salt Lake. The saline lake itself could not support fish life over much of prehistory, but the larger tributaries, including the Bear, Weber, Ogden, and Jordan rivers, and dozens of smaller streams fed huge tracts of fish habitat where the water crossed the flatlands or ponded in the inset marshes along the base of the mountains.

Images of fish spawning in the waters of the Wasatch Front are essential to our excursion into the past. Joel Janetski has studied the fish resources available to native peoples of the region, and he compiled ethnohistoric accounts of fishing, including remarks about sucker fishing made in an 1849 letter by the early settler Parley Pratt: "I was at Utah Lake last week and of all of the fisheries I ever saw, that exceeds all. I saw thousands caught by hand, both by Indians and whites. . . . They simply put their hand into the stream, and throw them out as fast as they can pick them up."[13] Similar images could be offered from Pyramid Lake, western Nevada.

Our understanding of the Wasatch Front before history must also consider the effects of urbanization, irrigation, and dams. Much of the water consumed by agriculture and increasingly, urban life, evaporates before it reaches the wetlands and Great Salt Lake. A rule of thumb for imagining the past is to add about 5 feet to the level of Great Salt Lake to account for this effect. The difference can be significant. During the flooding of the late 1980s, when Great Salt Lake reached its historically recorded high, the "natural" level of the lake would have caused it to flood part of the Salt Lake City airport and even overflow into the Great Salt Lake Desert without the massive pumps near Lakeside. Of course, thousands of acres of subdivisions and businesses would also have been flooded under "natural" conditions!

Dams large and small were built over the past century and a half to store water for farming and later for drinking and watering lawns. Dams control flooding by leveling the flow of water through the seasons, and this makes our modern images poor analogies for the wetlands of the past. Before the dams, streams jumped their banks in the spring, spreading water over tens of thousands of acres where farms and subdivisions now stand. The flow would subside by early summer. By fall, many streams and wetlands that we see flowing today would be mere trickles in the days "before history."

Great Basin wetlands also changed on the scale of years and decades. If some wet years raised water levels, enormous landscapes of wetlands died, leaving a featureless moonscape when the waters receded. But even as floodwaters killed one wetland, other wetlands would form to take their place. The wetlands we see today across the Great Basin, even in rural places, are largely artificial.

As lush as the wetland habitats may have been, and regardless of their importance as grocery and hardware stores, people were still attracted by and needed resources from the deserts and mountains. These, too, have changed, and we need more than an image of stark desert to take us into the past. Bunchgrasses were more common before grazing, although some areas have recovered in recent decades from the peak of grazing reached in the first quarter of the 20th century. Pinyon and juniper forests may have expanded slightly in the past century, but the plant life found in their understories is more impoverished because of fire suppression and grazing. In some areas, though, the pinyon and juniper forests have probably been much the same for the past 2,000 to 3,000 years. Extensive stands of roots, such as the bitterroot found today on the rocky ridges, may have been present for centuries.

The deserts and the mountains were also important for their nonfood resources. Stone was needed for chipped stone tools such as knives and drills, and for grinding tools such as *manos*, *metates*, hullers, and pestles. Stone was the steel of the day, and it was virtually absent in the wetlands, except for a few outcrops of slate that could be used to make rough knives. Trips to the mountains, but especially the rocky outcrops found in the desert, were as essential as our trips to the store. The need for wood to make tools could not be fully met without going out of the wetlands. Large shrubs from the mountains, such as serviceberry, provided wood for bows, as did the desert trees, such as juniper and mountain mahogany.

The mountains and the deserts west of the Wasatch Front and surrounding the many other wetlands from Utah to California were also the full-time home of some people throughout prehistory—people who did not routinely include the wetlands in their lives. Whether these people of the desert were networked to the wetland dwellers by kinship, or perhaps experienced life in both places, or were second-class rural dwellers, probably depends on which period in prehistory we consider. Like the dynamic environments, the activities of daily life, group structure, and social associations varied as we press deeper into time.

STEPPING INTO A DEEPER PAST

So far, we have traded a moment from the present for a moment "just before history." As we step deeper and deeper into the past, the moments quickly multiply to unmanageable proportions. It is impossible to know dynamic environments as an infinite series of moments. Instead, scholars who study the past tend to describe processes that transform environments and climate, and trends of change over time. This convention derives in part from the fact that reconstructing environments depends on the kind of evidence available. One place may yield information on the plants, whereas another may report on animals, and yet another reveals fluctuations in the level of lakes. Sometimes the different kinds of evidence are contradictory, because they represent conditions in nearby but distinct habitats, or slightly different times that appear to be contemporary only because the dating is not precise.

The familiar convention of A.D. is used for the most recent centuries and then followed by increasing use of the shorthand B.P., before present, to signal how much time has really passed. There is also the problem of correlating absolute time with the measures of time scientists use to chart the past. The two are not the same, and when reading about the past we must be careful to know whether an author means "years ago" in the literal sense or if he or she means years ago in terms of a measuring stick such as radiocarbon time.

Our reconstruction of past environments and climates across the expansive range of the Great Basin and northern Colorado Plateau employs the Wasatch Front as a point of departure. The contrast between Great Salt Lake, and the adjacent mountain and desert environments is one found often across the entire region. Further, the environmental records of the Great Salt Lake region have long been important to understanding past climate and habitats in the northern hemisphere. The Wasatch Front is thus a stepping stone into the region's past.

Fluctuations of Great Basin lakes leave their mark, and since water levels and the amount and timing of precipitation are crucial to the formation of adjacent desert and mountain habitats, we can go a long way toward tracking past environments by tracking the lakes. Like all Great Basin lakes, Great Salt Lake has no outlet to the sea, meaning that the lake levels are a handy measure of effective moisture in the region.

In the following historic referents to gauging the level of our inland sea, the levels of Great Salt Lake are reported in feet above sea level.

FIGURE 2.3

These charts depict changes in temperature (*top*) and levels of Lake Bonneville/ Great Salt Lake indicating moisture (*bottom*) over the past 15,000 years. Note that warm periods such as the one about 9,000 years ago (*top*) can occur during wet periods (*bottom*), and cool periods such as the one about 4,500 years ago can occur during dry periods.

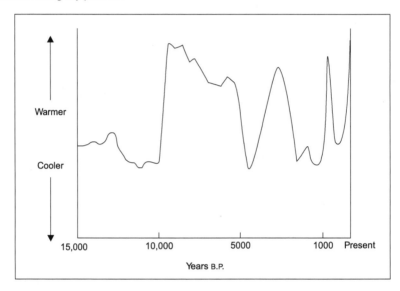

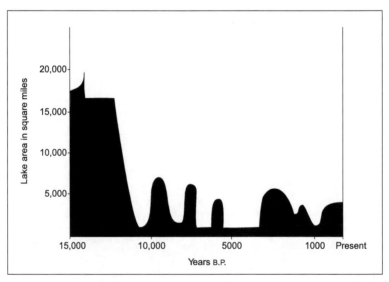

FIGURE 2.4

Basin-Plateau climate: Characteristics and trends.

Modern Times
- Human caused warming superimposed on other factors shaping climate. Effects apparent since late 18th century and increase dramatically in 20th and 21st centuries.

The Little Ice Age: A.D. 1300–1800
- Cooler than today from A.D. 1300–1650 with dips in mid 18th, 19th, and early 20th centuries.
- Winter dominant rainfall. Periods of great storms. Cloudier summers.
- Great Salt Lake floods Great Salt Lake Desert in early 1600s.
- Rapid cooling trend in 14th century; then variable but cool/moist climate punctuated by spates of storminess.

Medieval Warm Period: A.D. 0–1300
- Cooler than today at first, but warming similar to 20th century toward end of period.
- Summer dominant rainfall by A.D. 1000.
- Great Salt Lake near historic levels.
- Decades of drought staggered with decades of abundant precipitation.
- A slow warming until A.D. 900; then rapid warming with summer rainfall.

The Neoglacial 4500–2000 B.P. (A.D. 0)
- Cooler than today. Increased storminess. Cloudier summers.
- Winter rainfall dominant, some summer rainfall.
- Great Salt Lake extends to Nevada. Pyramid Lake rises.
- Expansion of glaciers in Sierra Nevada and Wasatch ranges.
- New wetlands and high desert productivity. Pinyon pine spreads to western Great Basin.
- Return to Pleistocene like conditions, but with modern plants and animals.

Middle Holocene Warming and Change 8000–4500 B.P.
- Variable period with periods cooler and warmer than today.
- Possible summer dominant rainfall.
- Great Salt Lake close to drying up just before 6000 B.P. and may have done this two or more times.
- Wetlands expand and contract often.
- Pinyon pine expands in eastern and central Great Basin. Utah juniper spreads. Hybrid oak brush arrives on Wasatch Front.
- Large scale fluctuations in only a few millennia.
- Modern flora and fauna established by end of period.

Early Holocene 10,000–8000 B.P.
- Cooler than today at first, but by 8000 B.P. may be warmer than today.
- Possibly winter dominant rainfall.
- Stronger seasonal variation more like today.
- Many lakes remain, but are shallow with extensive wetlands.
- Megafauna mostly gone. Small mammals isolated as tree lines move up.
- Lakes shrink and wetlands expand.
- Steady warming trend.

Late Pleistocene 16,000–10,000 B.P.
- Cloudy and cool summers but less variation among seasons. Winters not much colder than today.
- Many Great Basin lakes and some large wetlands, but fewer wetlands than early Holocene.
- Larger glaciers in mountains.
- Megafauna and small mammals. Modern ungulates present. Possibly large animal ranges.
- Sagebrush; no Utah juniper or pinyon pine, but shrub zone instead. Bristlecone and limber pine at much lower elevations. Many grasses and forbs. Long steady growth season for cool-season plants.
- Warming trend by 13,000 B.P.
- Younger Dryas Event 12,700–11,700 B.P. Return to glacial conditions within a few decades.
- Slow warming; still cooler than today.

SIDEBAR: HOW DO WE KNOW ABOUT PAST ENVIRONMENTS AND CLIMATE?

A crime is committed; the police seal the site and call in the investigators. Here come the scientists with their tackle boxes of chemicals, sensors, vials, bags, tags, and their secrets of the trade. They comb the scene for evidence to solve the crime. When this process is depicted on television, the evidence falls into place, and despite setbacks, the case is almost always solved. In the real world of criminal investigation, the term "solve" has a different meaning. The evidence is really just bits and pieces, glimpses of a variety of things that happened. Some of the pieces somehow fit into the crime, although it may not be clear how, and other finds have nothing to do with it.

Figuring out what happened becomes a challenge in the under-rated art of asking the right questions of the evidence, knowing what the evidence can and cannot tell you. The result usually has much more to do with probability than with the seductiveness of absolute truth. If investigators already think they know the truth, and they merely find evidence that supports their beliefs, they will be picked apart by the lawyers, doubted by a cautious jury, and dismissed by the judge. In the end, the evidence will reveal some of what happened, perhaps enough to convict, but there will always be more to know and, in many cases, an abundance of reasonable doubt.

The sciences of the past, whether geology, archaeology, paleontology, paleoecology, paleoclimatology, evolutionary biology, or even astronomy, are strikingly similar, because in the investigation of anything that already happened, being there is no longer possible.

The tool kit for knowing past environments and climates is everywhere, but Mother Nature and the hand of humanity destroy the evidence every day. As at any crime scene, the quality of the data is paramount. As we build houses on the ancient beaches of Lake Bonneville, we destroy evidence. Our recreational vehicles tear apart the landscape and destroy evidence. The evidence comes in many forms, and each tells us about a different aspect of the past.

Some kinds of evidence, such as the nests of the wood rat, Neotoma, also known as middens, provide a remarkably accurate, close-up picture of the past. Wood rats faithfully sample everything in their environment for about 100 meters around their nests. Leaves, twigs, bark, seeds, nuts or berries of every plant and tree, bird feathers, animal feces and fur are just some of the items found in wood rat middens. They pile it up, urinate in the nest, and effectively seal these treasures in. The middens accumulate in layers, sometimes over tens of thousands of years, and the organic contents can be radiocarbon dated. Wood rat middens are perfectly preserved crime scenes, but only for a single, small area. They are useful for locating the elevation of tree lines, and with hundreds of them now investigated, they provide a picture of regional vegetation and climate.

Other lines of evidence provide a larger picture. Lake levels are sometimes recorded in old beach lines. Sometimes driftwood might be found in them, or archaeological sites are on them, enabling dating. But often the dating is ambiguous. Also it is difficult to know how much time a beach represents and whether lake fluctuations were sustained or only brief events. Drill cores can be taken from lake beds, marshes, and spring bogs across the Basin-Plateau region to record the pollen, chemicals, and isotope signatures deposited over thousands of years. Such things can identify lake levels and the salinity or freshness of the water and together provide a general measure of plants growing in a region, such as the ratio of sagebrush pollen to pine pollen.

The bristlecone pine are the longest-lived organism in the world. Their rings contain a record of climate and the precise age of each change. The sequences from living trees are in some cases connected to those of dead trees essentially freeze-dried in the high-altitude air, extending this record back over 7,000 years. The bristlecones provide an accurately dated record of climate, but at high altitude. Since the trees occur on the highest mountains widely scattered from California to Utah, they provide a large-scale climatic picture.

Homestead Cave enables mention of a fascinating line of evidence found at only a few places in the Basin-Plateau region. Located near the tip of the Lakeside Mountains on the Hill Air Force Base Test and Training Range, Homestead Cave contributes significantly to our understanding of the Wasatch Front. The cave was not occupied by humans but was home to owls for nearly 13,000 years (about 11,500 radiocarbon years). The owls deposited prey and fecal pellets in thousands of layers over 2 meters deep. These deposits record times when fish were living nearby, and the changing frequencies of small mammals such as mice and pikas, which are sensitive indicators of vegetation and climate. Further, the trace chemicals in the fish bones can identify the signature of the tributaries draining into Great Salt Lake at the time the fish was alive. This enables the flow patterns and hence climate to be compared among the various rivers that supply the lake.

These and the other lines of evidence contribute to the task of reconstructing past environments and climates, but each source of evidence has its strengths, weaknesses, and its specific application.

FIGURE 2.5

Map of the Basin-Plateau showing just a sample of the study areas that yield the many lines of evidence used to reconstruct past climate and ecosystems.

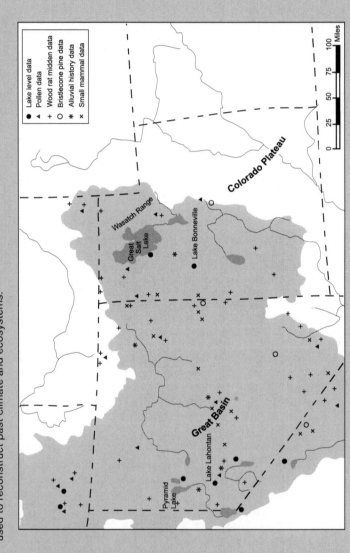

SIDEBAR: DATES OF THE PAST AND HOW TO READ THEM

Radiocarbon dating and tree ring dating are the most valuable tools for documenting the ages of past environments and archaeological sites in the Basin-Plateau region. Both have proven their accuracy and utility over and over again, but, as with all tools, they are more powerful in the hands of a craftsman than in the hands of a novice. Each tool is applicable to different jobs, and each has strengths and weaknesses.[a]

Tree ring dating, or dendrochronology, is especially important in the region, because the annual growth rings of bristlecone pine provide a precise record of climate for the past 7,000 years. The precision of tree ring dating also provides an important check on radiocarbon dating.

On the down side, tree ring dating is largely limited to climatic reconstruction in our region. Unlike the American Southwest, where ancient peoples constructed houses and other buildings using large pine and fir

FIGURE 2.6

Radiocarbon calibration chart adjusting for the differences between radiocarbon time and calendar time as known through comparison to the tree ring record, Greenland ice cores, and Caribbean coral. To determine the calendar age of a radiocarbon date, run a straight edge horizontally from the age at the left to the calendar time line. Read the calendar age below the point of intersection; example: 11,500 ^{14}C years = 13,200 B.P. calendar age.

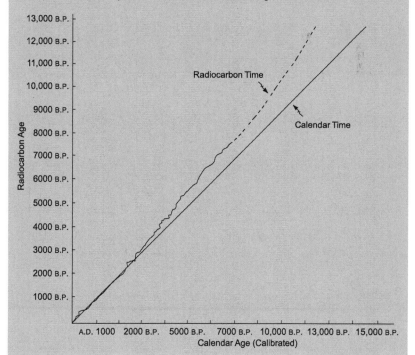

logs, large wood was not frequently used in the Great Basin and is thus not often found in archaeological sites. For this reason, there has been little stimulus to extend tree ring dating sequences northward from the Southwest, although the relevance of climate research is causing this to happen.

Radiocarbon dating is by far the most common tool for dating past habitats and the activities of people. Anything that was once alive can theoretically be radiocarbon dated back to about 50,000 years, easily covering the spans of time we study in the Americas. A charred chunk of pinyon pine or juniper wood from an ancient campfire, a stem of grass embedded in a wood rat midden, a fish bone encased in an owl fecal pellet, a chunk of the coral-like tufa deposits that form on the margins of alkaline lakes such as Great Salt Lake, and even the shells of snails embedded in the sediments of ancient wetlands, are just a few examples of objects that are radiocarbon dated in our region.

Radiocarbon dating is less precise than tree ring dating because it relies on a sample of an ongoing process of radioactive decay. Some of the imprecision in radiocarbon dating results from the same problem encountered by a political pollster estimating how people will vote in an election. The pollster must identify a representative sample and consider the effects of sample size. He or she must control for various sources of bias. The results will have a margin of error, typically expressed as one standard deviation, or about a 67% chance of being accurate within a certain range.

Like the political pollster, the radiocarbon craftsman must select the proper sample. The differences among wood charcoal, bone, and shell are significant because their chemical compositions can produce different radiocarbon ages.

Even more important, the craftsman must know how the sample is related to what she wants to date. The radioactive decay that is the essence of the dating method begins only when an organism dies, and this is not always what we want to know. For instance, wood from a fire hearth may have lain on the ground for centuries before someone used it to cook dinner. Radiocarbon dating will faithfully estimate when the tree died, but not when the dinner was cooked. A piece of driftwood in an ancient beach of Great Salt Lake may have been deposited not when relentless waters carved the land into a beach but by a later brief flooding event. Radiocarbon dating estimates the age of the wood, which may have nothing to do with the formation of the beach. The craftsman must decide what the date means.

When you read radiocarbon dates, keep two things in mind. First, the date is an estimate with a range of error. Do not be tempted to simply split the difference and believe that the average between the extremes is the "true" age. The average is a central tendency. Second, error is reported as a 67% chance of being correct (one standard deviation), or as a 95% chance (two standard deviations). Unless it is stated that the error reported is in the 95% category, assume the estimate has a 67% chance of being correct. Of course, we would prefer to be 95% confident, but this luxury will cost us a healthy dose of precision. A standard radiocarbon estimate of 550 B.P. ± 50 years comes with only a 67%, or two-thirds, chance of being from 500–600 years old. If we want to be 95% sure, the same date becomes 550 B.P. ± 100 years, a range of 450–650 years. A lot can happen in 200 years! These things are just the reality of statistics, but in the hands of a craftsman, each date adds in some small and imperfect way to the picture of the past we build.

Perhaps the strangest thing of all is that radiocarbon dating is its own clock, a clock that records radiocarbon time. Researchers noticed decades ago that when radiocarbon samples were compared to samples from historic buildings of known dates, and eventually to radiocarbon dates from individual tree rings of known age, the dates did not always match. Some periods matched well and others did not. It turns out that radiocarbon time does not proceed in a straight line as "real" time does. Instead, it wiggles, because past changes in the composition of the earth's atmosphere alter the rate at which the radiocarbon clock runs. The radiocarbon record can now be calibrated for the entire span of human occupation of the Americas by comparison to the tree ring record and recently to the records of ice cores from Greenland; deep sea and lake cores from the Atlantic, Japan, and Europe; and coral reefs in the Caribbean Sea.

The chart illustrates that for some spans of time, the difference between radiocarbon and calibrated ages hardly matters, but for other times it matters a great deal. Unfortunately, the most significant departure between radiocarbon and calibrated time is the earliest period of human occupation in the Americas. For instance, a radiocarbon date of 11,500 B.P. ± 95 B.P. may be a highly accurate estimate of radiocarbon time but in fact is about 2,000 years too young.[b]

Our story here is reported as years ago or B.P., and adjustments for calibration are made when necessary and so stated. The chart here shows you the periods when you must be aware of the need to consider radiocarbon calibration.

The historic low of Great Salt Lake was reached in 1963, when it regressed to 4,191 feet. The lake was then very shallow, and one could walk from Salt Lake City to Antelope Island, or from Willard to Promontory. In contrast, the historic high in 1987 reached 4,212 feet and flooded an enormous area between Brigham City and Salt Lake City. Although there is no normal level of Great Salt Lake, during much of the historic period the lake resided between 4,198 and 4,204 feet.[14]

When Great Salt Lake exceeds 4,215 feet, it flows west into the Great Salt Lake Desert and creates an enormous lake almost reaching the Nevada border. The overflow point is the Eardley Threshold, located north of the Lakeside Mountains, and this is where the state

FIGURE 2.7

Direct measurements of historic fluctuations of Great Salt Lake provide a great deal of precision about short-term change but very little understanding of the long term dynamics of the lake.

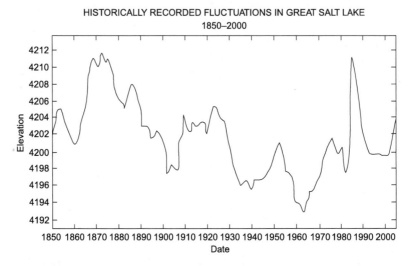

HISTORICALLY RECORDED FLUCTUATIONS IN GREAT SALT LAKE
1850–2000

of Utah placed pumps in 1987 to remove waters from the rising lake. Without the pumps, the lake would naturally rise to the Eardley Threshold, but it would also begin to flood the urban areas of the Wasatch Front. The lake breached the Eardley Threshold repeatedly in the past.

Our story, then, is based on the history of a dynamic Great Salt Lake, but other lines of evidence are available to complement the story: glaciers and spring bogs in the Wasatch Mountains; caves full of owl fecal pellets providing a record of vegetation, small mammals, and fish spanning 12,000 years; wood rat middens in the mountains sprinkling the Great Salt Lake Desert; and pollen from caves and lake bed cores. There is also a climatic record from the mountains in Utah, Nevada, and California embodied in the long-lived bristlecone pine trees. These and other kinds of evidence of past environments found near the Wasatch Front are complemented by similar sources of evidence from across the Basin-Plateau to gain a larger sense of place.

THE LITTLE ICE AGE: A.D. 1300–1800

We need not step far into the past to encounter a significant departure from what we might recognize as the Basin-Plateau "just before history." The Little Ice Age lasted nearly 500 years, affected the entire northern hemisphere, and in our region exhibited diversity that reminds us there is much more to describing climate than a simple dichotomy of hot and dry versus cool and moist.

The Little Ice Age is well known to European history and had direct consequences for human lives. As climate cooled and storminess increased in the North Atlantic between A.D. 1300–1500, the Norse abandoned their settlements in Greenland and Newfoundland, and wine grape cultivation failed in England and in the foothills of the Alps in France and Switzerland. Glaciers advanced in the European Alps in the A.D. 1700s, constraining agriculture there, and the cod fisheries of the north Atlantic failed.[15]

Not all areas express climate change in the same way. There is clear evidence of cooling across the Basin-Plateau, and along the Wasatch Front there seems to be a long decline in the size of Great Salt Lake beginning prior to A.D. 1300 and continuing after that. This decline is due in part to cooler temperatures, but there was also a drying trend, exactly the opposite of the commonly held view that if it is cold, it must also be wet.[16]

Cooler temperatures prevailed, and the tree ring record shows that from A.D. 1650 to almost 1900 there were troughs and spikes every decade or so—a faster-paced variation than in the 20th century. Precipitation during the same period also spiked and dipped, but the wet periods were farther above average than the droughts were below.[17] The seasons became more equable in temperature, but there were periods when the rain shifted from summer dominant to more rain in the winter and spring. Cooler temperatures caused what water there was to be locked up in summer snowfields in the mountains.[18]

The cooling may be associated with a southern shift in the jet stream that increased storminess in the Great Basin. The combination of year-round snow at high elevations, cooler temperatures, and increased storminess shortened the growing season in the wetlands and the desert habitats of the Wasatch Front, even when these factors did not cause the lakes to rise. The frequent swings in this pattern did not equate to one long, stormy deep freeze but ensured assaults on the habitats every decade or two. This would have caused greater mobility in the location of villages and probably significant changes in life between human generations. Cooler temperatures might have caused people to put more time and effort into food storage to prepare for longer winters. The period from A.D. 1300 through at least the 1600s was not friendly to native farming, because the frost-free season was shorter and rainfall was more variable, and it fell mostly in the winter—the wrong time of the year for a dry farmer in the eastern Great Basin and northern Colorado Plateau.

During some decades of the Little Ice Age, Great Salt Lake expanded, and it may have overflowed into the Great Salt Lake Desert

FIGURE 2.8

The elevations and extent of Great Salt Lake during significant episodes in the past.

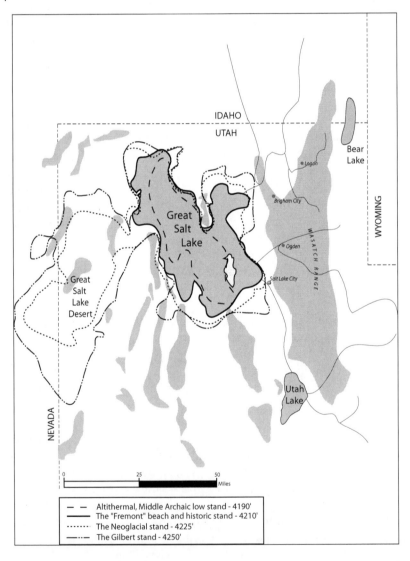

- – – Altithermal, Middle Archaic low stand - 4190'
- —— The "Fremont" beach and historic stand - 4210'
- ······· The Neoglacial stand - 4225'
- —··— The Gilbert stand - 4250'

in the early 1600s.[19] The dating of this transgression is sketchy, but the tree ring record for the Great Basin shows a spike in precipitation at A.D. 1610, a slight dip (still above the long-term average), and a stronger spike at 1620. At the same time, temperatures were spiking well above average at A.D. 1610, dipping, then heading upward again at 1620 and after. This combination may have melted mountain snow and contributed to the lake rise.

To gain a sense of the effects of rising water in Great Basin wetlands during the Little Ice Age, we can again look at the 1987 flooding of Great Salt Lake. If we take into account the water lost through evaporation from urban and agricultural use, we would say that the flooding probably would have spread into the Great Salt Lake Desert in spite of the pumps near the Lakeside Mountains. Without the pumps, an even larger area would have been inundated and destroyed. Instead of homes, businesses, and infrastructure, the prehistoric flooding in the early A.D. 1600s would have destroyed wetlands that fed the people and provided their raw materials.

To understand why the lake might have risen only at certain times during the period known as the Little Ice Age, consider events of the early 20th century. There was a strong increase in precipitation between 1910 and 1920, but Great Salt Lake rose only moderately because temperatures were well below average, preserving moisture in the snowpack and in the ground. Also, the rapid pulse of climate during the Little Ice Age reminds us that we should allow for more than one lake transgression. After all, Great Salt Lake took only 10 years to climb to a historic high in 1987 before falling back to more familiar levels by 1992.

Wherever wetlands existed across the Great Basin, periods of rapidly rising waters could have occurred so suddenly that people's lives, then as now, would have been strongly affected. The waters may have receded just as quickly, with huge wetlands dying while new wetlands became established in a few years. The frequency of climate change was probably one of the greatest impacts on human life, as people were pushed and pulled across landscapes every few years or decades. The northern Colorado Plateau has few expansive wetlands like the Great Basin, but the rapid pulses in climate change would have reshaped local habitats there, too. Again, it is often the tempo of climate change that is most significant to people who make a living by foraging. The effects shaped much more than where people lived and what they ate; they also caused rapid changes in social landscapes and place.

WARMING, VARIATION, AND THE MEDIEVAL WARM
PERIOD: A.D. 0–1300

This period, too, is more multifaceted than the title suggests, but the term "warm" is appropriate for a period ending when prehistoric agriculture reached its peak. The Medieval Warm Period is, like the Little Ice Age, well documented in European history.[20]

Modern vegetation patterns were well established in the Basin-Plateau, but following centuries of slightly cooler temperatures, a warming trend peaked in the A.D. 1000–1100s that was perhaps not surpassed until the second half of the 20th century. It is also a period when these long trends were punctuated by climatic swings and possibly shifts in the seasonality of precipitation. This was the period of farming among the Fremont peoples of the eastern Great Basin and northern Colorado Plateau, as well as the Southwest Puebloan peoples. In the rest of the Great Basin, forager populations had peaked by the end of the Archaic period, and the Medieval Warming Period would stir the pot in a region that had been undergoing social and demographic change for several millennia.

The warming trend is evident by about A.D. 300. For instance, cores drilled into Swan Lake, north of Preston, Idaho, reveal an increase in sagebrush pollen and less pine pollen. Wood rat middens near Wendover, Nevada, show that the desert-loving Utah Juniper tree had replaced the Rocky Mountain Juniper even before this time. An expansion of grasslands may indicate a summer dominant rainfall pattern, the late summer monsoons we recognize today, especially on the Colorado Plateau.[21]

Evidence of greater moisture is indicated by fish remains at Homestead Cave on the Hill Air Force Base Test and Training Range, where the contents of owl pellets show an increase in these and also in bushy tailed wood rats, voles, and pocket mice.[22] Great Salt Lake levels suggest the lake fluctuated within the historically known range during this period.[23] The bristlecone pine records show that at high altitudes, despite the evidence for a long-term warming trend, there were significant fluctuations in high-altitude tree growth that exceeded any variation we know during the historic period. What are we to make of this period that seems to have a little bit of everything?

Prior to the warming trend, Great Salt Lake flooded all the way to the Nevada border, and the climate was just recovering from semiglacial

FIGURE 2.9

These charts depict different aspects of Great Basin climate change using the bristlecone pine record. The top chart (after Madsen and Schmitt 2005:31) shows the growth index for trees in the Grant Range, south-central Nevada. Growth responds to effective moisture: temperature, precipitation, and evaporation. The lower chart (after LaMarche 1974) is from the White Mountains, eastern California. The solid line shows the growth of trees near the upper tree line. This indicates temperature, because tree growth at these elevations is temperature limited. The thick dashed line shows the growth of trees near the lower tree line. The lower tree line is drought sensitive, hence an indicator of moisture.

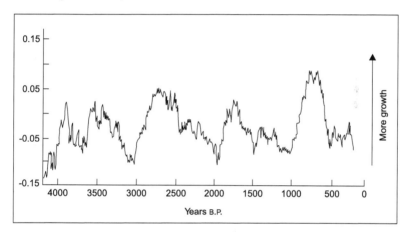

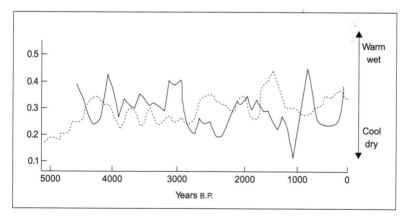

conditions. Grasslands expanded during the early centuries A.D., and lake levels lowered. Once the lake receded to its historically known levels, conditions became similar to today, when climate can change radically year to year, or over short spans of years.

During the A.D. 800–1100s along the Wasatch Front, temperatures were likely as warm as in recent decades, and the frequency of summer rainfall may have been greater than today; a boon to prehistoric farmers. Many archaeological sites on the Wasatch Front and dating to these centuries cluster along a shoreline that formed at 4,210 feet, suggesting that this was a feature with some stability. This elevation is also a diffuse boundary where people can be somewhat protected from flooding, because the gradient increases above 4,210 feet in contrast to the skillet-like character of the wetlands to the west.

The term "Medieval Warm Period" runs the risk of painting too much stability. Dates on archaeological sites show at least one period before A.D. 600 when the lake was likely well below 4,210 and at least one period after that time when the lake was higher, and perhaps high enough to overflow the Eardley Threshold into the Great Salt Lake Desert.[24] Although archaeological sites do cluster along the shoreline at 4,210 feet, there are many sites of this general period below that level, including substantial village sites with houses and such at elevations of 4,206 feet and possibly lower. Even this small difference in elevation meant that the lower villages were many miles farther out on the bed of Great Salt Lake.[25]

The centuries of perhaps greatest significance for people are those between A.D. 800–1200. This was a time of population growth brought by agriculture that peaked by the late A.D. 1000s and early 1100s. It was not only warmer, but spring rains brought the crops up, and late summer rain brought them to fruit. This may have changed in the mid-1100s, when drought or perhaps a shift away from the crucial summer precipitation placed stress on farming economies. Bristlecone pine tree-ring records from the White Mountains in eastern California and from central Utah show drought and warmth at this time, as do the tree-ring records from the Southwest.[26]

The Late Archaic foraging societies of southeastern Oregon, eastern California and the Mojave Desert, and most of Nevada were also experiencing massive changes during this time. Population growth that began before the Medieval Warm Period yielded societies that now had to face the warming trend. Warm periods can be good, if the rains come at the right times. But it was the abrupt changes in the climate during the Medieval Warm Period that, like abrupt climate change today, created social and demographic upheaval.

COOLING AND THE NEOGLACIAL PERIOD:
4500–2000 B.P. (A.D. 0)

This period is aptly named because virtually all lines of evidence show that it was cooler than the times before and after. But note that as we move farther into the past, the duration of each period increases. This results from the coarseness of the evidence and the difficulties of dating. Keep in mind that in human terms, a lot can happen in 2,500 years!

The first part of this period, from 4,500–3,000 years ago, marks an initial slide to cooler times. In several places across the eastern Great Basin, heat-tolerant shrubs such as shadscale gave way to the cool-loving sagebrush, and in the uplands of southern Idaho, sagebrush yielded to conifers.[27]

Around 3,500 years ago, Great Salt Lake breached the Eardley Threshold and spread a sheet of water west toward Nevada. Shallow-water ducks returned to Homestead Cave, and the overall number of bird species suggests a diversity of habitats around the Lakeside Mountains.[28] However, the bristlecone pine record shows that the high-altitude growth index was fluctuating considerably between 4,500 and 3,000 years ago, creating a pattern of dips and spikes similar to those in the centuries leading up to the Medieval Warm Period.[29] This means that although there was a cooling trend relative to the previously warm and dry period, variation remained high. This all changed about 3,000 years ago, when one of the most significant climatic variations in the prehistory of the region began to take hold.

After about 1,500 years of a bumpy road toward an environment that expressed itself as "cooler," the relationship between coolness and moisture began to change. Storminess increased, and evaporation decreased, and the period between 3,000 and 2,000 years ago, called the Neoglacial, was a time when moisture was preserved not only in the lakes and wetlands but also in the desert soils.

This period provides an excellent lesson that temperature and moisture do not always work in concert. The Neoglacial brought more storminess, and winter dominant precipitation. Increased summer cloudiness may also have been part of the picture, keeping temperatures and evaporation rates down. Mountain snowpacks survived the summer and fed the aquifers for lakes, springs, wetlands, and even once-desert valleys. Despite the name "Neoglacial," winter temperatures may have been similar to those of the last two centuries. The

bristlecone pine growth index suggests that times were good for these
denizens of the high mountains. The summers were likely cooler than
today, and along with similar winters, they gave the Neoglacial period
a feeling of moist coolness.

Great Salt Lake remained engorged for nearly a thousand years
to a high stand of 4,222 feet.[30] Homestead Cave, located on the west
side of the now dry Lakeside Mountains, yields Utah Chub, showing
that the lake became fresh enough to support at least the salt-tolerant
suckers. Isotope records from cores into the bed of Great Salt Lake
also indicate a freshening of lake waters during the Neoglacial.[31]

The modern suite of vegetation was essentially in place, except
the now common Mormon Tea may have arrived during this period.
Wood rat middens show that the tree lines of junipers were lower by
150 to 300 feet. The pinyon pine tree was present across the region
but seems to have expanded to its modern limits during this time.[32]

The Neoglacial was a major cooling event in the northern
hemisphere. A wealth of data across the mountains of the western
United States show cooler times and increased snowpack, including
changes in forest structure and glacial activity in the Wind River
Mountains of Wyoming and the Sierra Nevada range.

Cooling in the Mojave Desert of southern California permitted
moisture to be retained in streams and sediments, increasing plant
foods and small mammals used by people. True lakes did not return to
most of the Mojave, but Owens Lake exhibits several fluctuations. The
timing was different from that of other places in the Basin-Plateau,
reminding us that the various lake basins do not respond in strict
concert across the region.[33]

The significance of this period for humans is perhaps even greater
than the Medieval Warm Period that was so important to the brief
success of prehistoric farmers in the eastern Basin and Plateau. As
with all environmental change, the faces of Neoglacial expression are
several. As water was trapped in Great Salt Lake, over 100,000 acres of
wetlands along the eastern shores would have been inundated. As the
lake rose, the land sandwiched between it and the mountains became
steeper, leaving less land available for the growth of new marshes.
New marshes would have formed elsewhere, however, such as in the
area west of Corinne and along the Bear River below Cache Valley,
and over much of the northwestern portion of Salt Lake Valley. The
flow of springs increased, creating new, spring-fed marshes.

Increased marshland is documented at various places in the
Great Basin, such as the Ruby Marshes east of Elko, Nevada. Small,

spring-fed marshes may have dotted the desert areas west of the Wasatch Front and other, now dry valleys in the Great Basin, peppering a landscape that previously, and more recently, was nothing but desert shrubland.

Despite the loss of productive marshland to rising waters along the eastern shores of Great Salt Lake, the influx of fresh water likely created a fishery more akin to that known historically around Utah Lake. The antiquity of Utah Lake is obscure, and possibly it formed only sometime after 5000 B.P. when tilting of the landscape known as *isostatic rebound* isolated Utah Valley from the Salt Lake Valley.[34] After that, the levels of Utah Lake came under the control of its outlet to Great Salt Lake, and the level of this outlet changed over time. During the Neoglacial, Utah Lake rose to a peak well above its historic level.[35] Well-watered Utah Valley contained a variety of riparian and wetland habitats regardless of whether Utah Lake was present, but once the lake formed, it became the astounding fishery we know in historic times. Utah Lake reminds us that the local circumstances of lake basins and wetlands shaped the particular habitats that ancient humans faced, whether these places are in northwestern Utah, western Nevada, or the Owens Valley and Mojave Desert of California.

Just as important as the lake levels is the preservation of moisture in the surrounding landscape. The valleys, whether they be the Salt Lake Valley, Utah Valley, or the dozens of desert valleys encountered across the breadth of the Neoglacial Great Basin, likely produced more grasses and forbs, the small herbacious plants that grow among shrubs.

Even the Mojave Desert fared better during the Neoglacial, as populations returned after extreme drying in this frequently parched portion of the region. A period known as Gypsum Complex correlates to a time of expanding populations and changing social organization in the western Great Basin.

Neoglacial moisture increased seed productivity, a resource important to foragers at this time. Root plants, too, would benefit from the increased moisture. Changes in vegetation provided an enormous stimulant to animal populations large and small. It is possible that high water tables in previously dry valleys promoted grasslands in places where only sagebrush and shadscale are found today. Even briny salt grass meadows increased animal productivity with larger numbers of rodents, reptiles, and birds, their predators, and the ungulates that browse such areas.

Human numbers grew across the Basin-Plateau, and the many wetlands, as well as improved conditions in the harsher desert areas, all anchored expanded human activity. If any period fostered a wetlands-lakeside mobility, settlement, and subsistence pattern, with concomitant increases in human activity in surrounding upland areas, it was the Neoglacial between 3,000 and 2,000 years ago.[36]

TWO SPIKES OF WARMING: 8000–4500 B.P.

Once known as the "Altithermal," the period between 8,000 to nearly 4,000 years ago was a time of increased temperatures and decreased water budgets, relative to the periods before and after.[37] But as with the other periods, it is difficult to stereotype such vast expanses of time. This was not a single, long span of unrelenting heat and drought; the period is better characterized as one of wild fluctuations in climate and consequent habitats within a large-scale theme of aridity. In this regard, this period contrasts with the Neoglacial, not because that period was cool and this period was warm, but because the Neoglacial was a relatively stable period of high moisture levels, whereas this previous period of warming seems frequently punctuated.

The period opens with a drying trend that resulted in what were likely the lowest levels ever of Great Salt Lake. Between 7,000 and 6,000 years ago, the lake was reduced to an elevation as low as 4,180 feet. This is 13 feet lower than the historic low recorded in 1963, and it left the lake a mere puddle. This substantial regression is attested to by submerged sand dunes off the eastern coast of Stansbury Island and an area of mud cracks in what is now the deepest part of the lake in the northwestern arm.[38]

Other evidence from around the region also indicates aridity. Pollen core samples from the Ruby marsh in eastern Nevada show that between about 6,800 and 4,500 years ago, the marsh largely disappeared and was replaced by a shadscale shrub community. Sagebrush increased at the expense of grass in southeastern Oregon and at Swan Lake in the uplands of southeastern Idaho. Treelines in the White Mountains on the California-Nevada border migrated upslope as much as 500 feet between 7,500 and 4,500 years ago, and in the drier ranges, such as the Jarbidge Mountains in northern Nevada, sagebrush and juniper replaced subalpine vegetation. The desert-loving Utah Juniper began to expand into the region during this period. Turbinella scrub oak typical of Arizona and southwestern Utah pushed north and hybridized with Gambel oak to produce a unique drought- and cold-tolerant scrub oak hybrid on the flanks of the

Wasatch Front. The southern Great Basin and Mojave Desert became so dry that human population density dwindled as the hot deserts were used sparingly after a long period of full use by foragers.[39]

Perhaps the most significant vegetation change however, is the migration of the pinyon pine into the region. For tens of thousands of years, pinyon occupied the Southwest and northern Mexico, reaching north only as far as southern Nevada. Pinyon migrates primarily through the aid of nut-transporting birds such as Pinyon Jay, but its spread to the northern Great Basin and Colorado Plateau may be due in part to the people who harvested, stored, and transported the nuts. Pinyon nuts were used by humans at Danger Cave near Wendover between 7400–6700 B.P. It was growing in the Onaqui Mountains of western Utah by 6,600 years ago (4600 B.C.).[40] Imagine how the notion of place would be altered for those of us who associate a pristine Basin-Plateau with pinyon-juniper woodlands. This period is significant because it is the first time in our excursion into the past when we must envision a very different place—one where some of our most familiar vegetation was not present.

High in the Wasatch Mountains, the Snowbird bog pollen record shows warmer than average temperatures after 8,000 years ago, but the area continued to be vegetated by coniferous forest, showing that some landscapes persist even as change swirls around them. In the deserts west of the Wasatch Front, however, sagebrush was replaced by drought-tolerant shadscale. The cover of herbacious plants was so low in the deserts that even populations of mice and other small mammals declined, and there surely must have been a decline in large game populations. The trend during this period was toward a reduction in the species diversity of animals, and probably plants as well.[41]

A millennium-long period of conditions perhaps as dry as those of the late 20th century conjures up dire images of a super drought. But closer examination of the evidence suggests that within this large-scale warm and dry theme, short-term variation was high. Thus, the mud cracks in the northwestern arm of Great Salt Lake may represent only a few years or a few decades before the lake rebounded. The pollen charts depicting the battle between grasses and sagebrush look more like an ebb and flow of tides than a capitulation. Indeed, there is evidence for a transgression of Great Salt Lake to perhaps a healthy 4,208 feet around 5,900 years ago (3900 B.C.), and the Snowbird bog suggests cooling at this time. Nevertheless, the overall theme of warmness during this period persists, with another regression of Great Salt Lake after 5,300 years ago.[42]

The impact of all this on humans has long been debated. Images of an Altithermal super drought combine with a very spotty archaeological record to suggest that overall population density in the Basin-Plateau region declined. The contraction of wetlands, the vanishing of small marshes around desert springs, low soil moisture, deepening water tables, fewer plants, and a reduction in animal species diversity surely had strong effects on how people lived and how their societies were organized. In the hot deserts such as the Mojave of the southern Great Basin, large areas seem to have been virtually abandoned by foragers, probably used so lightly that archaeologists can barely see it.[43]

However, many places saw ample activity, and the archaeology of the wetlands and the uplands of the Wasatch Front attest to this. The enormity of the wetlands along the Wasatch Front was clearly diminished, but even when Great Salt Lake was at an all time low, fresh water tributaries continued to flow across the broad, skillet-like floor of the lake, surely creating wetlands of substantial size. Perhaps more important than overall size and total productivity of regions or the habitats within them is the variability in climate and habitat during this time. Rapid change can be just as important for shaping peoples' choices and decisions as categorical and static images of "good" times and "bad" times.

The lives of the people and the form of their cultures during this time were likely significantly different from anything described in the histories and ethnographies of the past two centuries. The Middle Holocene is a watershed in our excursion into the past because we are beginning to see our modern environmental analogies breaking down. The habitats before this time were vastly different from anything we see in the region today.

THE EARLY HOLOCENE AND WATER IN THE DESERT: 10,000–8000 B.P.

The oldest expression of Great Salt Lake dates to this time; earlier versions are considered to be Lake Bonneville. The initial centuries of this period may have been extremely dry, and by the end of the period, temperatures were again warming. There were surely fluctuations in effective moisture in the early Holocene, but in contrast to historic times, this period was significantly wetter and then dried out catastrophically.

At first, lakes and wetlands were scattered across the Great Basin, often in locations where only dry lakebeds are found today. The differences between now and then are perhaps best shown in the Mojave Desert. One of the harshest deserts in the world today, the Early Holocene saw significant human activity that helped define early human occupation of the Great Basin—the stemmed projectile point complexes such as Mojave and Pinto. These reflect a time when springs dotted the southern Great Basin, and wetlands and streams came and went in rapid succession. The tempo of change fostered a high degree of residential mobility, but the overall environment supported an archaeologically significant human population.[44]

In the northern Great Basin, near Elko, Nevada, the Ruby marshes were inundated by Lake Franklin in the early Holocene. In other places, the modern lakes or lake beds we know, such as Sevier Lake in western Utah and Pyramid Lake and the Winnemucca Lake bed in western Nevada, were significantly larger. Great Salt Lake was for a time larger than it has been ever since. Around 9,700 years ago, Great Salt Lake extended to the Nevada border. The waters lapped at the site of downtown Salt Lake City and flooded much of the area around Brigham City and virtually all the land in between west of Interstate 15.[45]

Another wetland was present in the Wasatch Front region at this time, one we have not yet encountered. A vast area of salt grass meadows, and a maze of bulrush and cattail-walled ponds and sloughs, occupied the Dugway Proving Ground, where only salt flats and harsh greasewood playas are found today. This is the Old River Bed, a name derived from the fact that this is where the Sevier Desert arm of Lake Bonneville drained northward into the Great Salt Lake arm. The Old River Bed persisted as a large wetland until 8,800 years ago.[46]

As we step back in time, the landscape that constitutes our modern sense of place seems to be losing species. No modern oak hybrids, no pinyon pine, no Utah Juniper, no Mormon Tea, and so forth. What grew in their place? Instead of pinyon and juniper woodlands along the lower flanks of the mountains, we would find forests of limber pine and bristlecone pine. These trees grow at high elevations today, especially the bristlecone, which typically occur above 9,000 feet. In the Snake Range along the Nevada-Utah border, wood rat middens show that limber and bristlecone pines grew as low as 6,000 feet as late as 7,350 years ago. Limber pine was present in Danger Cave near Wendover between 7,000 and 8,000 years ago.[47] Today, only a few lonely juniper cling to the rocky slopes near Danger Cave.

FIGURE 2.10

Dugway Proving Ground, Utah, looking west toward the distant Deep Creek Mountains and the Nevada border. The white, flat area from the center of the photo and extending to the left marks the location of the Old River Bed, an enormous wetland and marsh system during the Late Pleistocene and Early Holocene periods. (Photo by Steven Simms)

Sagebrush occupied the lower slopes and desert valleys, but it was giving way to saltbush and other desert plants. Nevertheless, there is evidence from wood rat middens in the foothills of the Deep Creek Mountains that instead of the monotony of pinyon and juniper so familiar today, we must imagine a mosaic of habitats. Some places were occupied by shadscale and horsebrush, while others were sagebrush parks dotted with Rocky Mountain Juniper, occasional limber pine, and a host of shrubs such as squawbush, chokecherry, hackberry, and elderberry, indicating a cool-moist habitat.[48]

Glaciers survived in the mountains, and in the Wasatch, small glaciers survived in the upper reaches of the Alta ski area at 9,500 years ago. Glacial till deposits from a minor advance of the ice shows that the glaciers grew and shrank between 9,600 and 7,500 years ago.[49]

Animals we rarely see today, even at high altitudes, such as marmots and pikas, were present along the valley edges. The deserts were home to now endangered pygmy rabbits and species of voles, rats, and mice that are gone from those elevations or extinct altogether.[50] Modern species of large mammals were present, with bighorn sheep being far more common than the mule deer we expect to see today.

The climate also requires us to stretch our imaginations. The now desert valleys west of the Wasatch Mountains would have had summer temperatures like those we expect when we visit the ski resort town of Park City. Summer at the Stillwater Marsh east of Reno, Nevada, might have felt like the resorts at Lake Tahoe today. The Mojave Desert of southern California harbored wetlands in what are some of the hottest places on earth today.

Precipitation was apparently strongly winter dominant and, together with the cool summers, suggests that the jet stream shifted south more frequently and strongly than anything we know from recent history. The Basin-Plateau was a cloudier place with perhaps more equable temperatures among seasons, but with contrasting moisture between seasons. It is possible that the cool summers and inadequate summer precipitation kept pinyon pine out of the region, or locked up in a few places of refuge.[51] All this changed, and by 8,000 years ago, the climate was warming, tree lines were going up, and the valleys were drying out.

Once again, our penetration into the climate and the habitats of remote time present a landscape occupied by ancient peoples that was substantially different from anything documented among the modern Native Americans of the region.

THE WILD RIDE OF THE PLEISTOCENE-HOLOCENE TRANSITION: 13,000–10,000 B.P.

In the parlance of paleoscience, this period is known as the PHT, shorthand for the Pleistocene-Holocene Transition. Variation is found in every period, but this was a time characterized by repeated and rapid climatic change from full glacial, "ice-age" conditions to climates familiar to us now. These changes happened quickly, often in a decade or two and clearly within the experience of people living at the time. Such rapid climate change probably played havoc with many habitats but passed so quickly that some ecosystems were likely able to weather the change.

As the planet emerged from the ice ages of the Pleistocene period about 13,000 years ago, the remnants of Lake Bonneville shrank to levels familiar to Great Salt Lake in the historic period.[52] The end of the ice age did not last long, and around 12,700 years ago, the Younger Dryas marked an abrupt return to nearly full glacial conditions in the northern hemisphere. Lake Bonneville was reborn and rose to the Gilbert level, a shoreline at 4,260 feet. At this elevation, downtown

Salt Lake City was under water, and the lake again supported an array of fish life from suckers to trophy-sized lake trout all the way to Wendover, Nevada.[53]

The deserts west of the Wasatch Front were a vast treeless, sagebrush steppe flanked on the valley slopes by a mosaic of large shrubs that we expect to see today only in watered canyons and on protected slopes. Forests of limber pine, spruce, fir, and bristlecone pine covered even the desert mountain ranges that today are barren or occupied largely by juniper. The Wasatch Mountains were heavily forested and capped by perennial snowfields and even a few small glaciers.

The wetlands are a major feature of all the periods we have visited in our excursion through time, but things were different during the Pleistocene-Holocene Transition. Despite the repeated episodes of cool, moist weather, the preservation of water in the closed basins may have been too much of a good thing for many areas where we expect to see wetlands today. During much of the PHT, wetlands may have been restricted in size and hampered by rapid climatic change. When Lake Bonneville reached the Gilbert level, the gradients along the shoreline steepened significantly, transforming the skillet-like shape of Great Salt Lake into the steep-sided bowl that is Lake Bonneville.[54] This left little ground suitable for wetland development and essentially traded the diverse plant and animal productivity of wetlands for the fish in a relatively freshwater lake. To be sure, other areas that are now only desert were opened up for wetland plants and animals, and across the Great Basin region there were many wetlands at this time, in locations sometimes quite different from those of today.

The effects of topography are only part of the reason why wetlands during the PHT were different from our modern analogies. The rapid-fire changes in water levels and climates of the Younger Dryas perhaps altered the vegetation succession patterns that occur as wetlands are exposed to fluctuating water levels. The locations of wetlands may have changed often, and some wetlands may not have had time to develop into mature biotic systems before fluctuating water either dried them out or inundated them. Thus, we should keep in mind that although there may have been "many" wetlands in the early Holocene and the Late Pleistocene Great Basin, their location and their stability were different from those of the historic period.

The Younger Dryas lasted over 1,000 years but is most astonishing because this cold snap came on quickly and did not rest; "early Great

Basin foragers were being whip-sawed from one climatic extreme to another, often within periods of less than a decade."[55]

The significance of rapid habitat change for animal populations during the PHT is suggested by the fact that none of the Pleistocene megafauna, such as the mammoth, musk ox, camels, and horses that lived along the Wasatch Front in the Pleistocene, survived the volatile Younger Dryas times. The habitat change was simply too much, too fast for these animals. It is possible that the animals that did persist, such as bighorn sheep, elk, deer, and pronghorn, were reduced in number by the same environmental challenges.

Another significant feature of the PHT was the seasonal equability of the climate. Although equability is found at times during more recent periods, it was a major feature of the terminal Pleistocene and contrasts markedly with the strong seasonality that is part of our sense of place in the historic period. The characteristics of the PHT produced a unique set of circumstances faced by early Native Americans that was never encountered again.

LAKE BONNEVILLE AND THE PLEISTOCENE: 16,000–13,000 B.P.

Many people are aware that an enormous lake once resided in northern Utah, leaving the familiar land formations known as the "benches" in Salt Lake City and indeed all along the Wasatch Front. These are beach terraces of ancient Lake Bonneville, a restless inland sea that grew to mammoth proportions about 16,000 years ago. When the shoreline of Great Salt Lake is at 4,200 feet, our modern lake covers about 1,700 square miles and is at most 35 feet deep. When Lake Bonneville peaked, it covered nearly 20,000 square miles and was 1,220 feet deep—about the size of Lake Michigan.[56] The western Great Basin was home to Lake Lahontan, another massive lake nearly as large as Bonneville. Although the histories of these and other Pleistocene Great Basin lakes vary in specifics, the general patterns of Late Pleistocene climate are found in the example of Lake Bonneville.

Two of the Bonneville beaches are strongly apparent along the Wasatch Front, and although there are others, these two are most significant to our story. The highest is the Bonneville terrace, at about 5,100 feet, a level marked in Salt Lake City by the University of Utah Medical Center and along the Wasatch Front by expensive

FIGURE 2.11

The maximum extent of Lake Bonneville in comparison to lakes of the historic period.

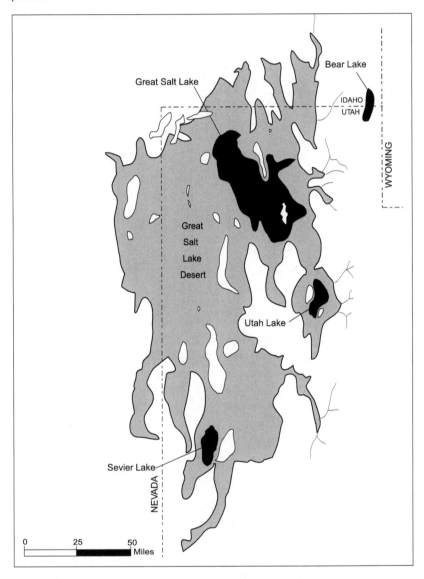

homes. A few hundred feet below is the Provo terrace, at about 4,700 feet, the bench on which all the universities along the Wasatch Front are built. The lake stretched west into Nevada and fingered south across the Sevier and Escalante deserts to a point northwest of Cedar

City. It was dotted with tree-covered islands and was a cool but lush landscape of coniferous forests and sagebrush vistas. Lake Bonneville was probably deep blue on clear days, and innumerable shades of steely grays on the frequent cloudy and stormy days during the Pleistocene. Steep, rocky coastlines largely bound the shores, and glaciers resided in Little Cottonwood Canyon not far from the lake. Lake Bonneville was a freshwater inland sea, with ocean-sized waves and ocean-sized fish.

Over several thousand years, the lake grew to its maximum size and by 16,000 years ago began overflowing into the Snake River in Idaho. The outflow stabilized the lake and led to the formation of the Bonneville shoreline. The lake subsequently receded a little, only to rise again at 14,500 years ago. This time the natural dam containing the lake at the Zenda farm, about 23 miles north of Preston, Idaho, gave way in a spectacular flood that literally overflowed the Snake River gorge and scoured its way down the Columbia River all the way to the Pacific Ocean. Over the course of perhaps only months, or at most a few years, the lake receded several hundred feet downslope to the Provo level when the outlet in southern Idaho reached hard rock, stabilizing the lake once again.

The initial demise of the lake was a matter of geographic fate, and the result was catastrophic, but the death knell of the lake was climate change. After resting for a century or two at the Provo level, the lake continued downward at the end of the last Pleistocene ice age. By perhaps 13,200 years ago and for the next 500 years, the lake was similar in size to the historic Great Salt Lake and for a brief time may have even dried up.[57]

There is no direct evidence that humans were present to see the lake at either the Bonneville or the Provo levels, so we can only fantasize about ancient Native Americans pulling 30-pound lake trout out of icy windswept waters against a backdrop of glaciers fingering down the canyons of the snow-laden Wasatch. However, humans were in the hemisphere over 13,000 years ago, and their presence on the Wasatch Front was soon to follow. People could have been here, but their presence must remain only a possibility for now. Or, they may have just missed the days of Lake Bonneville, only to arrive during the drought that was prelude to the climatic roller coaster of the Younger Dryas.

3

The First Explorers, Colonists, and Settlers

The Dominguez-Escalante expedition in 1776 is often labeled the first exploration of the Great Basin, followed in the subsequent century by the colonists and settlers. All these groups encountered Native Americans. Thus, we have to step far back in time to find the first true settlers, and we must journey even farther back to find the first colonists. Then there is the matter of who the first explorers were. Such distinctions are important to expanding the scale of time we must use to comprehend what was a multifaceted process of peopling the Americas.

The Paleoindian period is a murky past and known first and foremost by a distinctive technology—a type of spear point. The two main types are Clovis and Folsom, and they are sought after by collectors around the world. Mundane as these stone points might be to those of us who do not collect artifacts, they are a window into one of the most fascinating times in America's past. But the intrigue of being the first Americans over 13,200 years ago pales in comparison to the real fascination; Paleoindian times were unique and unlike anything since.[1]

People were colonists and settlers in the Basin-Plateau during Clovis times, yet we know the Americas were explored even earlier. The Monte Verde site in Chile yields clear evidence of human residence and firm dates between 11,800–12,800 radiocarbon years ago—that is, over 14,500 B.P.[2] It is highly likely that Meadowcroft Rockshelter in Pennsylvania was occupied at about the same time as Monte Verde.[3] Slowly but surely, other early sites in North and South America are being carefully excavated and dated, and cumulatively they are leading more archaeologists to suspect that human colonization of the Americas exceeds 15,000 years ago, and may press beyond 20,000 years ago.[4] Sites from this murky period are rare, and there is a watershed between the largely unknown but possibly long period of pre-Clovis exploration and the strong presence of Clovis colonists.

The record of pre-Clovis explorers is scant everywhere in the hemisphere, and we probably have seen the earliest dates. Other parts of the world yield abundant remains of human activity much older than the earliest archaeology of the Americas, and it appears that humans came here only near the end of the Pleistocene.

The arrival of humans to the Americas was a halting, at times staggered mosaic of migrations of various early Asian peoples. They moved along the now inundated Pacific continental shelf, and the Clovis technology may track migration through the interior of North America.[5] The first populations were small, and they were isolated by the expanse of an open landscape. Some lineages surely died out, causing local depopulation. Advances in the study of the ecology and the demographics of foraging societies suggest that when humans first enter new lands, they do so slowly, and they may falter. These studies also show that forager populations experience boom and bust cycles. The overall population growth rate of the pre-Clovis explorers was likely very low and may have remained so for millennia. It may be that the continent-wide appearance of Clovis by 13,000 years ago is more a matter of a population boom with people stepping into the archaeological light than it is a single abrupt colonization event.[6]

The distinctive Clovis and Folsom points tell some of the story. These spear points are often called "fluted" points in reference to the

SIDEBAR: WHO WERE THE FIRST EXPLORERS AND COLONISTS?

In less than 100,000 years, humans spread into virtually every environment on earth. At root we are all related, and in some sense we are all
immigrants. Many modern Americans identify themselves as Caucasian
and trace their roots to Europe. These connections, however, are recent.
The modern people of Europe are also immigrants, who replaced
the indigenous inhabitants thousands of years ago with the spread
of agriculture, horses, and wheeled vehicles. On the larger scale of
archaeological time, "Caucasians" did not "come" from Europe, but
this does not change the fact that many Americans see themselves as
descendents of European "Caucasian" ancestors. Similarly, Native
Americans see themselves as the descendents of all previous occupants
of the continent. They are all "Indian" and they have "always" been here.
But the origins of Native Americans are also steeped in deep time. Who
were the first American colonists, and what is the dual relationship of the
Paleoindians to living Native Americans and the living peoples of other
continents today?

For decades, the answers to these questions came from studies of
language, dental patterns, blood groups, and gross cranial characteristics.
The combined evidence points to Native Americans originating in Asia.
This conclusion is consistent with archaeology showing migrations across
the Beringian continent connecting Siberia and Alaska when sea levels
were hundreds of feet lower during the Pleistocene. People likely traveled
along the now inundated coast and through the interior. It is likely that
more than one Asian population is represented among the colonists, because there may be more than one means of transport, more than one
point of origin, and more than one migration over many millennia.[a]

Three lines of new evidence add greater detail and excitement to
the story. Cranial studies are now computer-assisted and employ over
two dozen measurements on skulls. Mitochondrial DNA traces female
lineages, and the nonrecombinate sections of Y chromosome DNA can
trace male lineages. These studies are primarily being carried out on
carefully chosen modern samples of people and to a far lesser extent
on ancient samples of DNA from skeletal biopsies. These new lines of
evidence show several things:

1. Consistency with the previous evidence of an Asian connection, and
   migration via Siberia, not via Polynesia, the Middle East, or Europe.
2. Striking differences between the cranial measurements and hence
   appearance of Paleoindians and Native Americans who lived in the
   last few thousand years. The cranial data also indicate substantial
   differences among Paleoindians and show biological affinities with
   various circum-Pacific to central-Asian populations.

3. Mitochrondrial DNA shows that Native American maternal lineages have connections to populations in a circum-Pacific arc that includes northeast and central Asia, Japan, Southeast Asia, Melanesia, and Polynesia.
4. Y chromosome DNA shows that Native American paternal lineages have connections to populations primarily in northeast and central Asia.

What are the implications of these observations?

The first is old news and shows that as evidence accumulates, it is becoming more established that Native American connections are with Asia. The lesson of time reminds us that this connection is not with the modern genetic landscape of Asia, but with Asia as it was over 15,000 years ago. It makes sense to "compare ancient people [only] with their contemporaries and predecessors in various parts of the world, not with their successors."[b]

The second observation is enlightening. Osteologists in the United States, Brazil, and Argentina observe that Paleoindians have different cranial features than recent Native Americans. The skulls of the first Americans have particular elements that are similar to populations in northeast and central Asia and in Polynesia, and with the indigenous people of northern Japan, the Ainu. There are differences, however, among the Paleoindian crania showing affinities to different Asian populations. For instance, the Kennewick skull from Washington and Spirit Cave man from western Nevada show affinities to Pacific Islanders and the Ainu, and the Buhl woman from Idaho is typically Ainu. In contrast, the Wizards Beach, Nevada, cranium is similar in some respects to modern Native Americans but also to Europeans and Polynesians.[c] Of course, all these Paleoindians are also Native American.

Observations three and four refer to fast-paced advancements in DNA analysis. Mitochrondrial DNA studies trace maternal lineages and show that the colonization of the Americas was long enough ago that Native Americans have genetic affiliations with various ancient Asian populations stretching around the Pacific Rim and into the central Asian interior. An intriguing example is the presence of a lineage found among Polynesians. At first, some geneticists concluded that early Polynesians migrated to South America. But it is important to complement modern DNA studies with samples from ancient skeletons. This was done using a 9,000-year-old Paleoindian skeleton from Colorado, revealing the same Polynesian lineage. Migration from Polynesia is ruled out because Polynesia was not peopled until well after 5,000 years ago. Instead, it shows that the "Pacific" connection is very old and is better explained as the result of a common Asian ancestor of both Native Americans and Polynesians.[d]

Analysis of DNA found on the Y chromosome identifies male lineages. Both forms of DNA analysis are important to understanding prehistoric migrations, because differences in sex ratios among small populations of foragers can cause any single line of DNA to have biases. Y chromosome DNA shows connections among Native Americans, Siberia, and the Altai area of central Asia now occupied by western China and Kazakhstan. This last area is, by the way, the eastern extent of the Russian steppes, which is important to the origins of Indo-European groups and thus "Caucasians." This is not to say that Native Americans originated from Caucasian ancestors on the Russian steppes but that in the deep past, the genetic map was quite different from today's, and these ancient roots explain why Paleoindian cranial measurements and facial characteristics appear as they do—different from modern Native Americans. Y chromosome DNA studies also show that Native American DNA varies significantly from Siberian counterparts, suggesting that once America was colonized, and rising sea levels inundated Beringia, the two populations became relatively isolated.[e]

Paleoindians are indeed ancestors of Native Americans, but a great deal of change has occurred since Paleoindian times in both the Americas and in Asia. In the same way a German (or a German descendent in the Americas) has ancestors originating from the central Asian "homeland" of modern Europeans, Native Americans have ancestors who were part of Asian populations that migrated across Beringia.

Perhaps there is a benefit to comprehending a deeper sense of time than we often allow for in our categorizations of people.

scoop-shaped channel flakes on both sides of the blade. Clovis points were shown to be associated with extinct mammoth on the plains of southeastern Arizona and eastern New Mexico in the 1950s, and they date to a relatively narrow period between 11,200 and 10,900 B.P. radiocarbon years. The Folsom type was first defined in New Mexico in 1925 in association with extinct bison, and subsequent study shows that it reflects a narrow time span between 10,900 and 10,200 B.P. radiocarbon years. Fluted points are found across the continent with regional variations.

Regardless of how long people had been exploring the Americas, with the appearance of Clovis it is as if a switch was flipped on, illuminating the human presence on the North American continent. From that time on, people left an indelible imprint that stands in contrast to whatever happened before and everything that happened since. The continent-wide ignition of the archaeological record with Clovis is characterized by an uncanny patterning that suggests certain things about lifestyle. Information about the Clovis period is abundant, relative to the dimly lit pre-Clovis explorers, and it tells a story of explorers becoming colonists, and then settlers.

AN ECOLOGICAL MOMENT AND WHY PALEOINDIAN LIFE WAS DIFFERENT

For an "ecological moment" beginning with the First Americans, humans occupied a place that was unaltered by the hand of humanity. It was an original wilderness. This could happen only once. Given the low populations of pre-Clovis explorers, the notion of an ecological moment signals a set of circumstances that makes the Clovis colonization unlike anything that came later. We reserve the term "Paleoindian" to refer to this ecological moment.

Robert Kelly and Lawrence Todd wrestled with the problem of "coming into the country," to account for some broad brush patterns in Paleoindian archaeology that seemed to transcend local explanation. They proposed that the colonists were highly mobile in terms of residence, in terms of food and raw material provisioning, and in terms of lifetime territorial ranges. Paleoindians were "generalists in relation to large terrestrial faunal resources and opportunists in relation to all other food resources."[7]

Paleoindian explorers may have been on the continent in low numbers for millennia, but Clovis colonization was rapid, occurring in about three centuries, and continued with Folsom colonization over the next seven centuries. The rapid nature of this spread suggests high mobility and the exploitation of an open ecological niche.

Fluted points occur across the continent and are remarkably homogeneous in form compared to the multitude of point styles that came later. This also suggests that the early people were relatively mobile, and over the span of people's lives, they may have ranged widely. It also means that their borders were open with deeply entwined networks to exchange materials and information. In the absence of telephones and rapid means of transportation, mobility and networks provide the only means for the general attributes of a Clovis point found in Virginia to be similar to one from California.

Paleoindian technology was geared toward portability, maintenance, and flexibility. It was suited for direct tasks and for use as tools to in turn fashion a wood and bone tool kit. It was useful regardless of whether the territory was familiar or new. The raw material, or toolstone employed, is often high quality and often obtained from sources far from where the tools are ultimately lost or discarded. In some cases, this distance can be over a thousand miles, and although it is less in most instances, the movement of toolstone was an important element of Paleoindian technology. High quality toolstone was needed, given the difficulty of manufacturing fluted points but also because Clovis, and especially Folsom craftsmen, intended to produce a long use life for their expensive, high-quality tools.

Toolstone was conserved, enabling people to enter new territories where no one lived to guide them to local resources. One measure of an intention to conserve expensive to acquire toolstone is a high edge to weight ratio. For instance, a scraper with more working edge per gram of weight is a more effective use of the toolstone if one is mobile and far from good quality stone. Compared to later periods, the tool assemblages of Clovis and Folsom times have high edge to weight ratios.

The tool kit for plant processing, such as grinding stones and hullers, is smaller than in later periods. Rather than indicating that people were ignoring plant resources, this pattern shows that plant foods requiring a high degree of processing may have been eaten but were not keystones of the diet. In other words, plants were not driving the economic system. An example might be hard seeds that require time-consuming grinding to make them digestible, a necessary step if they are to be a staple food. This circumstance is akin to that of a modern person who might snack on sunflower seeds but whose staple is the highly processed wheat flour or corn syrup found in many foods today.

There seem to be fewer Paleoindian ground stone tools in general, such as net weights and stone balls. Bone and wooden tools were common, such as the bone "wrenches" that, regardless of their function, were portable. People did not invest in heavy ground stone tools, because the opportunities to transport them were less and the need for a highly refined ground stone technology was less.

There was less food storage in this earliest period. This, too, suggests a different form of mobility than that found in later periods in which food storage was a centerpiece of the cultures across the Basin-Plateau. Storage of food by any animal, whether chipmunk or human, demands that the organism be tethered to the storage and the stored food hidden and even defended from competitors. Thus, storage is of little use unless a person is settled or has a redundant mobility pattern that ensures he or she will return to the stored food. Furthermore, the labor to prepare the food, build the storage facility, and protect the contents makes food storage costly when other options are available.

Paleoindians are sometimes stereotyped as "big game hunters." Although this phrase misrepresents the depth of their lives, there is a grain of truth to it. Large game that often roamed in groups over potentially large territories was the driving force behind Paleoindian decision making. This does not mean that Paleoindians ate only large game, nor does it mean that large game included only mammoth, extinct bison, and other megafauna. Elk, deer, bighorn sheep, and pronghorn were present in the Basin-Plateau in Late Pleistocene times. The emphasis on large game refers us back to the notion of an ecological moment of colonization. During that time, Paleoindian adaptation revolved around mobility and open, unknown territories.

There is even a certain redundancy in the sites left by Paleoindians, suggesting they did pretty much the same thing wherever they went. As long as empty land remained, there was little stimulus for change. There were few incentives for stewardship of anything but their lifestyle. It was a lifeway that skimmed the cream from a new continent, and it was geared to the exploration and colonization of an unfamiliar land.

As humans spread across the landscape, the ecological moment of colonization disappeared. The moment was brief on archaeological time scales—perhaps only a few centuries. But the landscape filled and neighbors became part of the cultural fabric. Distinct local traditions and adaptations developed, and the ecological moment of the Paleoindians passed into what archaeologists call the Paleoarchaic period in the Basin-Plateau region. The Paleoindian colonists became the Paleoarchaic settlers.

PALEOINDIAN-PALEOARCHAIC ARTIFACTS

Paleoindian campsites that yield detail about housing and all the daily activities are rare, but Paleoindian stone tools are in fact common and scattered widely over the Basin-Plateau. Thus, we tend to know this early period by their distinctive stone technologies. Clovis and Folsom fluted points are striking examples of biface lithic technology, the craft of manufacturing long, thin, two-sided implements of high-quality toolstone that can be resharpened and reworked to provide a long use life. Their bases are often ground and abraded, and they were affixed to a split shaft most likely used as a thrusting spear,

FIGURE 3.1

The Clovis dart point symbolizes the Paleoindian period; variations of this point occur across the United States. The spread of Clovis was likely the spread of a technological style, not a people. One possible means of hafting the point is shown on the left. The Clovis point on the right is from northwestern Utah. (Sketch by Jennifer Hulse; photo courtesy of Dann Russell)

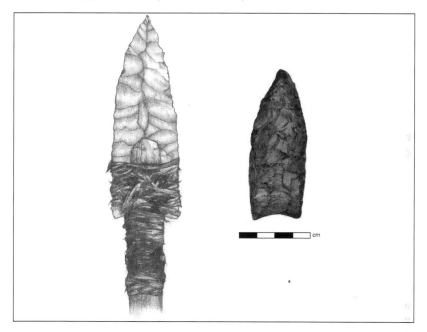

or possibly in conjunction with the atlatl.[8] Fluted points were frequently made of microcrystalline rocks generically known as chert and chalcedony. Volcanic rocks such as obsidian were also used, as were the hard, fine-grained volcanics such as dacite and andesite that are common in the Great Basin. There is more, however, to the Paleoindian period than Clovis and Folsom points.

The Great Basin Stemmed Series refers to several types of points, the most common Paleoindian and Paleoarchaic points in the Basin-Plateau region. Stemmed points were mostly made of durable but difficult to flake material such as andesite and dacite. They were also made from more readily flaked obsidian. Stemmed points are often blocky, with uneven flake scars. Like many other Paleoindian points, the bases were often ground, but Great Basin stemmed points were hafted to a shaft by socketing, directing the force of impact squarely into the shaft. Patterns of breakage and microscopic wear show that

FIGURE 3.2

Great Basin stemmed points come in myriad forms, including their original type traditions of Lake Mojave and Silver Lake. They occur across the entire region. Their manufacture begins in Paleoindian times and persists to the Middle Holocene in some parts of the Great Basin. Stemmed points are typically made of basaltic rocks that form durable working edges and tools. The Great Basin stemmed points shown here are from northwestern Utah. (Courtesy of Dann Russell)

stemmed points were multipurpose, probably ranging from use as thrusting spears or perhaps darts for use with the atlatl, to hafted knives with a variety of "Swiss Army knife" purposes.

The techniques for producing fluted and stemmed points probably reflect technological traditions and tool kits for different circumstances.[9] Fluted and stemmed forms are both suited for a lifestyle that was flexible and that favored portability. Some of the tools were designed for ease of maintenance, whereas others were made to be durable. Since so many stemmed points are found on the ground surface, the dating is vague. The manufacture of Great Basin Stemmed Series points may begin at the same time as Clovis.

The Paleoindian, Buhl burial found near Twin Falls, Idaho, is a female with a stemmed point buried underneath her head. She lived 12,500 years ago (radiocarbon 10,675 B.P.). But stemmed points continued to be made for thousands of years after the Clovis and Folsom types vanished, making them less useful as time markers. Stemmed points are common in the vicinity of the Wasatch Front and were used by both the Paleoindian colonists and the subsequent Paleoarchaic settlers.

Stemmed points were originally identified in the Mojave Desert in the 1930s by Elizabeth and William Campbell as part of their quest to demonstrate great antiquity for a human presence in the Great

Basin. The Lake Mojave Complex represents Paleoindian and Paleo-archaic residents attuned to rapidly changing habitats much wetter than the Mojave is today. The stemmed points called Lake Mojave and Silver Lake and the associated artifacts of the Complex indicate small, mobile groups of foragers moving to resources and a diverse, opportunistic diet that over the years involved extensive foraging ranges.[10]

There are many other types of large, leaf shaped, bifacially flaked points that are later than the fluted types. These are called Late Paleoindian, or Paleoarchaic, in the Basin-Plateau region and include Scottsbluff, Hell Gap/Haskett I, Lovell Constricted, Agate Basin/Haskett II, Jimmy Allen/Frederick, and Angostura among others. These Paleoarchaic point types are younger than 11,500 B.P., and most are less than 10,000 years of age.[11]

The stone toolkit of the Paleoindian period contains other tools, the most distinctive being the crescents of the Great Basin. Shaped like their name suggests, these chipped stone implements are also multipurpose. Microwear studies show they were often used as scrapers but were also employed as gravers and perhaps as transversely mounted, broadhead points useful for bird hunting. Another alternative arose incidentally from research with the Burns Paiute Tribe in southeastern Oregon in the early 1980s by Marilyn Couture and the botanist Lucille Housley. Elderly Paiute women showed Couture how to harvest roots, and Housley noted that some desert and mountain root stands can persist for centuries, and even millennia. Housley and Couture observed Paiute women occasionally finding crescents in the root stands and reusing them as a vegetable peeler to scrape the skin from roots much like peeling a carrot. Perhaps this was one way crescents were used from the beginning.[12]

Other tools such as distinctive forms of beaked gravers and spur-red scrapers suggest the flexibility of the stone tool kit; these tools are useful for manufacturing bone and antler tools, although this use is better demonstrated in the Old World Paleolithic period than in the Americas. Paleoindian tools show some distinction when they occur in an associated assemblage, but since the same tools are indeed found in later periods, isolated examples from the surface are unreliable for identifying a Paleoindian-Paleoarchaic occupation.

Paleoindian artifacts from the Basin-Plateau region are found in the mountains but are far more common in valley locations.[13] The tendency for these early artifacts to occur along the margins of ancient lakebeds was first noted in the 1920s and 1930s by researchers

FIGURE 3.3

Crescents are most often found in lowland contexts where wetlands existed. However, they are known from other locations, including areas favorable for edible root crops such as Bitterroot. Studies of use-wear indicate abrasion from several different directions, suggesting they were general cutting and scraping tools. Most were probably handheld, but hafting was an option. They were most often made from basaltic stone but were also fashioned from a variety of other toolstones, including obsidian. The Crescents shown here are from northwestern Utah. (Courtesy of Dann Russell)

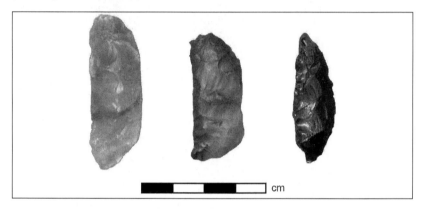

such as the Campbells working in the Mojave Desert of southern California. By the 1970s, Stephen Bedwell proposed the "Western Pluvial Lakes Tradition" by hypothesizing that early peoples hunted in the rich wetlands and lakes of the region.[14] Bedwell knew his Great Basin geography and suggested that the pattern of human migration would have followed the north-south orientation of Great Basin valleys, so people never had to leave a wetlands-lakes environment. His evidence was indirect, and his model was perhaps oversimplified as are many new ideas vying for the attention of researchers. But, as we will see, he and the other early scientists were on the right track.

PALEOINDIAN PLACES

A smattering of archaeological sites and localities, most drawn from the eastern Great Basin, can provide a gist of what archaeologists know about the Paleoindian period. Also, the archaeology of this early period is a bit different from that of most of the later periods, so in order to convey something about Paleoindian sense of place, first we need to examine a few examples of Paleoindian places.

Danger Cave, located just outside Wendover, was first investigated by Elmer Smith in 1940–1941 and was extensively excavated by Jesse Jennings between 1949 and 1953.[15] The oldest level in the cave contained six small fire hearths built on beach sands. More recent analysis of the Danger Cave animal bones by Donald Grayson reveals a very different environment than is found at the cave today. The bones of pygmy rabbit and sage grouse indicate dense stands of sagebrush, a plant not found near the cave today. The early deposits yielded bones of marmot and bushy tailed wood rat, species now limited to high mountain environments.[16]

In the early 1950s, radiocarbon dating was in its infancy, and some of Jennings' dates used the "solid carbon" method now known to be unreliable. Recent sampling of Danger Cave by David Madsen and David Rhode finds that the first occupation probably dates to about 11,700 years ago.[17] Two points were also found somewhere in the lowest levels of Danger Cave but were later lost. The cave deposits thus show that the initial occupation was not a flash in the pan but the initiation of repeated use that continued until modern times. We will find that this is a consistent theme.

Just south of Wendover is Bonneville Estates Rockshelter, where excavations by Ted Goebel, Kelly Graf, and Bryan Hockett found stemmed points, tools, flaking debris, hearths, and ashy areas dating over 13,000 years ago. The recovery of animal bones was more complete than the earlier excavation of Danger Cave and shows that young cottontail rabbits were the object of the hunt, as well as pronghorn, other small mammals, sage grouse, and waterbirds. A Clovis point was also found, albeit out of context, in much later deposits.[18]

Farther south along the Utah-Nevada border is Smith Creek Cave, in the Snake Range north of Great Basin National Park. The site was excavated in the 1930s by Mark Harrington of the Southwest Museum in Los Angeles and in the late 1960s to early 1970s by the Canadian team of Alan Bryan and Ruth Gruhn, who have so championed the search for early Americans. Stemmed points, hearths, stone and bone tools, and bits of cordage are found with a range of radiocarbon dates that may be confounded by some mixing of the deposits. The cave may have been occupied at 13,000 B.P., and a definite presence is indicated by 12,700 B.P.[19] An interesting aspect of Smith Creek Cave is that the layers beneath those bearing clear evidence of human use contained hair from now extinct camels. The layers above

FIGURE 3.4

Paleoindian sites and localities referred to in Chapter 3. The map is not encyclopedic and emphasizes the eastern Great Basin and Colorado Plateau to show that evidence of Paleoindian life comes from a variety of locations.

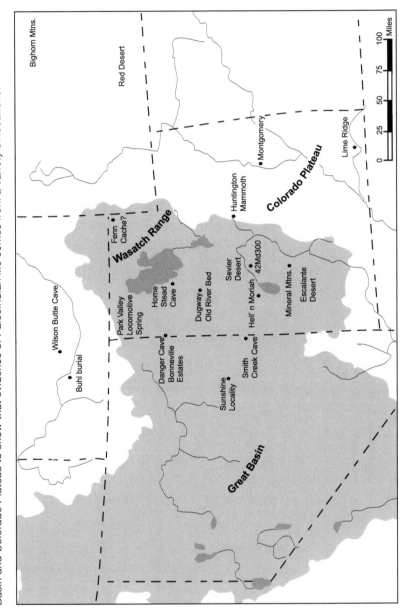

FIGURE 3.5

Bonneville Estates Rockshelter under excavation. This is the first excavation of a Great Basin Paleoindian deep cave site in decades, and the use of modern techniques vastly improves our understanding of Paleoindian chronology and life in the eastern Great Basin. (Courtesy of the U.S. Bureau of Land Management, Elko Field Office)

contained artifacts, and the hearths were associated with bighorn sheep. At Smith Creek Cave, the humans seem to follow the time of the camels, but as in the other places, once humans came to the region, they kept coming back.

The Sunshine Locality has long been known for its rich production of Paleoindian artifacts but is steadily producing hard evidence. Located in Long Valley, northwest of Ely, Nevada, the archaeology of the area has been synthesized and expanded over the past 20 years by Charlotte Beck and George "Tom" Jones. The Sunshine Locality yields fluted and stemmed points, as well as many crescents, mostly recovered from the ground surface. Persistent work paid off, and buried layers dating to 11,000–11,500 B.P. yielded stemmed points, one of which may be associated with camel bone. A fluted point similar to a Folsom was found in a slightly older layer, and a date on the camel bone itself was over 13,000 B.P. This evidence is tantalizing not only for placing humans and camel very close in time and space but also because it leaves open the question of whether fluted points and some stemmed points were contemporaneous.[20] Beck and Jones scoured other valleys in eastern Nevada over the years, enabling them to analyze large assemblages of tools and, importantly, the debris from the manufacture of tools, as well as the sources of stone. As we will see below, this kind of analysis is informative of human intentions and mobility.

The case of the 13,000 year old Huntington mammoth is an exciting but indirect instance of early human presence (see Art Portfolio). The mammoth was found at 9,000 feet above sea level on the Wasatch Plateau above Fairview, Utah, during repair work at the Huntington Dam. Cut marks on the mammoth bone appear to be from stone tools, suggesting butchering or scavenging of the mammoth meat. A Late Paleoindian artifact resembling a Pryor stemmed point was found in the deposits but was disturbed by construction workers. Analysis of sediment adhering to the point suggests that it was not directly associated with the mammoth. A Paleoindian archaeological site was found only 100 meters away, and it yielded a Cody knife and a Scottsbluff point. The artifacts and the cut marks on the mammoth bone establish that Paleoarchaic peoples were living in the high mountains, not just the valley wetlands.[21]

Geoarchaeologist Jonathan Davis liked to say: "If you want to find old stuff, you have to find old dirt."[22] The Paleoindian archaeology of northwestern Utah is a case in point; here, ancient sediments occur in patches that yield many early artifacts residing largely in private collections.

FIGURE 3.6

Paleoindian sites and localities on the Wasatch Front officially recorded but not necessarily thoroughly investigated. The point types known from each location are also shown. Very few of these have been excavated. Many other areas in the Great Basin of similar size also yield the same staggering numbers of Paleoindian sites. Some Paleoindian peoples tethered to valley bottoms near the extensive wetlands and ranged from there. Others surely lived independently of the valleys, exploiting the highest mountain environments. The entire landscape was explored, colonized, and settled in Paleoindian times. (Courtesy Mark E. Stuart)

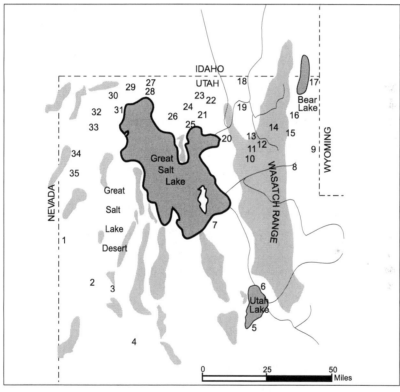

1 Danger Cave (Western Stemmed, Folsom)
2 Test Range (Western Stemmed)
3 Dugway/Old River Bed (Western Stemmed, Cody Complex)
4 Cherry Creek (Folsom)
5 Martin Site (Cody Complex)
6 American Fork (Cody Complex)
7 Black Rock Cave II (Cody Complex)
8 Echo Canyon (Mountain Plano)
9 Eagle Springs (Mountain Plano)
10 Pineview 1 (Haskett)
11 Pineview 2 (Agate Basin)
12 Big Horn (Mountain Plano)
13 Aspen Spring (Mountain Plano)
13 Ant Flat (Mountain Plano)
15 Monte Cristo (Mountain Plano)
16 Randolph (Cody Complex)
17 Fenn Cache (Cody Complex)
18 Franklin Cave (Folsom)

19 Pelican Pond (Cody Complex)
20 Willard (Cody Complex)
21 Connor Springs (Clovis)
22 Beaver Dam (Clovis)
23 Hampton Ford (Clovis)
24 Blue Creek 1 (Folsom)
25 Blue Creek 2 (Cody Complex)
26 Promontory (Folsom)
27 Deep Creek (Folsom)
28 Salt Wells (Western Stemmed)
29 Running Antelope (Haskett)
30 Indian Creek (Western Stemmed, Cody Complex)
31 Hogup Cave (Western Stemmed, Cody Complex)
32 Dove Creek Sink (Cody Complex)
33 Russell Dune (Western Stemmed)
34 Lucin (Cody Complex)
35 Newfoundland (Western Stemmed)

One of these areas is the Old River Bed (see Chapter 2: The Early Holocene and Water in the Desert: 10,000–8000 B.P.). David Madsen, Dave Schmitt, and geologist Jack Oviatt found an extensive wetland of slow moving channels and ponds that attracted Paleoindians, who camped on gravels deposited just after 13,000 years ago. The area is littered with stemmed points, and a Clovis point was found. After colonization of the Old River Bed, the occupation intensified, showing that, as in the other places, once humans arrived, they stayed on and grew in their presence.[23]

Other Paleoindian sites in western Utah, such as the Hell' n Moriah Clovis Site and 42Md300, are also associated with wetlands, similar to those all the way from the Mojave Desert to southeastern Oregon, and elsewhere in the region. At Hell' n Moriah, the seven Clovis points are so similar, they may have been made by one person but using several locally available high-quality materials. 42Md300 yields Folsom, Clovis, and stemmed points to local collectors, and it is one of the few open sites with dates showing that people were there

FIGURE 3.7

Site 42Md300 is a blow out in silt dunes located near Delta, Utah, and was embedded in a vast wetland in the Late Pleistocene and Early Holocene periods. Many Paleoindian artifacts from this site are in private collections. Limited excavations provided radiocarbon dates showing that some of the artifacts date to about 10,000 years ago. (Photo by Steven Simms)

as early as 10,500 years ago. These cases exemplify the fact that each site manages to yield at least one tidbit of information.

Wherever "old dirt" is exposed, the Paleoindian presence is apparent. During the infamous MX Missile Project of the early 1980s, we scouted private collections, and I remember seeing an astonishing number of Paleoindian points. In one memorable instance, a collector in Milford, Utah, lived in a double-wide trailer next door to his home that had been converted into a personal museum. The trailer was simply not large enough to house the material he had collected! He had mounted old wagon wheels on the walls and filled the spaces between the spokes with early points from the west deserts of Utah.[24]

Sometimes the treasures hidden in private collections make their way into the light and treat us to a striking glimpse of the ancient world. Such is the case of the Fenn Cache found in about 1902 somewhere near the juncture of Utah, Idaho, and Wyoming—the area east of Bear Lake. It consists of 56 Clovis-era bifaces weighing about 18 pounds. The collector is long dead, and the cache was passed down among the family. The cache was saved from obscurity when New Mexico collector Forrest Fenn acquired it and arranged for study by the noted archaeologist George Frison and flintknapping expert Bruce Bradley.

The Fenn Cache artifacts vary in size and shape, but the method of manufacture is similar, likely the work of one artisan. The craftsmanship is superb. Most of the items appeared unfinished, and the few finished ones were unused. The toolstone came from east-central Utah, the Big Horn Mountains and Red Desert of Wyoming, and even as far away as southwestern Idaho. This reflects the entwined network of knowledge among Paleoindian people and their mobility. The quality of the materials is very high, and other good sources of toolstone were passed over en route to these particular sources. The cache may have been carried in a bag, because the type of wear suggests that the items rubbed against one another. Perhaps the artisan walked this vast and rugged country to personally collect the stone.

The Fenn Cache is not unique, and several others are documented from the western United States, with who knows how many hidden in private collections. The objects are often rubbed with red ochre, as were most of the items in the Fenn Cache. Ochre has long been used on many continents in ritual. No one knows if the cache was left with the intention to return for it to use as tools, was deposited with a nearby burial, or was left as a ritual offering with no intent to return.

Regardless, the Fenn Cache shows the unification of a technology with artistic and ideological expression.[25]

Looking east of the Wasatch Front, the Colorado Plateau yields dozens of locales with Paleoindian points. As in the Great Basin, these tend to occur in lowland settings at an average elevation of 5,700 feet, despite the fact pointed out by Alan Schroedl that less than 40% of the Plateau is below 6,000 feet. The Lime Ridge Clovis Site near Bluff, Utah, yields Clovis points, blades, scrapers, and the industrial waste from tool manufacture that is so informative. The site was a hunting blind and camp area rather than a butchering station. The raw materials used imply that the people's movement focused on the San Juan River Valley. The Montgomery site near Green River, Utah, is another camp; in addition to two Folsom points, it yielded a Paleoindian assemblage of scrapers, gravers, and waste flakes.[26]

Southeastern Idaho produces many fluted points, and 28 of them were available for analysis by stone technology experts Gene Titmus and Jim Woods, even though many more remain hidden in private collections. Ruth Gruhn excavated Wilson Butte Cave near Twin Falls, Idaho, in 1959–1960 and made claims of extremely early occupation. Recent excavations by Gruhn have revised the dates downward but still suggest that humans arrived at the cave by 12,000 years ago.[27]

As might be expected, southwestern Wyoming was colonized by Paleoindians, and the evidence from the excavation of buried deposits in addition to surface finds illustrates another dimension of Paleoindian life. Late Paleoindian places such as the Vegan site, Blue Point, and Deep Hearth show that floodplains yielding roots, perhaps seeds, and a variety of small mammals were exploited again and again nearly 9,000 years ago. Basin hearths with fire-altered rock mark areas where biscuitroot and wild onion were baked. Rabbits, wood rats, and mice were taken locally, and local toolstone makes up the bulk of the kit. Informative excavations at a site known only by its official number, 48UT375, show that a large area of ancient dunes adjacent to broad, open basins and playas was used intermittently as were the other sites for similar activities. Each occupation was in a different locale within the dune field, and the gaps between occupations could have been long, decades and even centuries, signifying the low population densities and episodic nature of residence. Southwestern Wyoming is high country with bursts of high mountains, but in the area of these sites, it is an open, Mongolian-like steppe with wandering drainages and salty basins. It is windy and cold most of the time, and yet it offers a variety of attractions to knowledgeable foragers. Other areas of Wyoming show that big game from modern forms to extinct megafauna were taken, and this surely happened in southwestern Wyoming. Paleoindian settlement was pervasive and exploited the entire landscape, even as the overall theme of the people's lives contrasts with those who came later.[28]

WETLANDS, BIG GAME, AND A DYNAMIC CLIMATE

The period of human colonization was a time of climatic and habitat upheaval (see Chapter 2: The Wild Ride of the Pleistocene-Holocene Transition: 13,000–10,000 B.P.). Lake Bonneville was gone for a time, and ironically, the first inhabitants may have gazed on a Great Salt Lake residing at levels familiar to the historic period. But the resemblance ends there, because this was a strangely different place.

Perennial snowpack occupied the mountain peaks and some alpine basins. Treelines were lower, and even the desert mountains were shrouded with spruce, limber pine, and bristlecone pine. The lower slopes and valley edges were sheathed in a mosaic of large shrub communities we see only in pockets today. The barren vistas of the Great Basin desert so familiar to our modern eyes were inundated in a sea of sagebrush peppered with herbaceous plants and perennial bunch grasses. The climate was cooler in the summer, with winters only slightly colder than today and with less difference among the seasons. There may have been greater winter precipitation or greater summer precipitation, or both.

The large ungulates we see today in the region, such as bighorn sheep, elk, deer, and pronghorn, were present when the first humans entered the region. It is important to include these animals in our notion of "big game." They are large bodied relative to other animals found in the region, they often travel in groups, and they can occupy large territories with the potential to migrate over dozens and even hundreds of miles if habitat change forces them to do so. We will find that these attributes are important for understanding Paleoindian and Paleoarchaic life.

In addition to the modern species, there was an array of now-extinct megafauna. Mammoth, mastodon, giant short-faced bear, woodland musk ox, western camel, giant bison, horses, sabertooth cats, and even the giant gopher all lived along the Wasatch Front and are well documented. The woodland musk ox is known from 16 localities

SIDEBAR: DID HUMANS KILL OFF THE PLEISTOCENE MEGAFAUNA?

The association between humans and now extinct megafauna was first demonstrated in Europe in the mid-19th century. The connection raised the possibility that humans were responsible for the fate of these animals, and the view persists to this day. The "overkill" explanation, however, meets with strong opposition from those who find little evidence for it and considerable evidence that the extinctions were driven by changes in climate and habitat.

This is a debate that raises a mirror to our face. People on all facets of the political and ethical spectrum can find something to like or dislike. The image of Pleistocene "overkill" serves some as a lesson for our modern environmental concerns. Others think that because ancient people harmed the environment and lived through it, that we can, too. Some cannot accept that people caused the extinctions, because that presents a bad image of Native Americans; still others believe that it shows early peoples were just as human as we are. Issues such as this engender strong feelings, even among scientists.

Paul Martin of the University of Arizona was the original champion of the "overkill" model. He takes a large-scale approach and notes the general correlation of the arrival of humans with Pleistocene extinctions on many continents. From a distance, the correlations are indeed striking. Martin's case for North America depends primarily on the sudden appearance of Clovis, its rapid spread, and the fact that Paleoindian hunters took mammoth, extinct bison, and horse.[a]

Donald Grayson of the University of Washington speaks strongly in opposition and with David Meltzer, a Paleoindian specialist from Southern Methodist University, wrote "A Requiem for North American Overkill." They find meager and circumstantial evidence for human predation causing the extinction of 35 genera of mostly large animals. The timing of human arrival and the extinctions are not particularly close. Of the 35 genera that vanished from their Pleistocene ranges, only 15 persisted later than 12,000 years ago to even have the chance of a connection with human predation. Grayson and Meltzer argue that many were already gone. They also wonder where the evidence is for kills and make comparisons to other documented cases of human-caused extinction.[b]

So what did cause the extinctions? The answer remains unclear and is likely more complex as each organism is considered separately. Most alternate explanations appeal to environmental change, including recent evidence for a comet that exploded over Canada causing the onset of the Younger Dryas.

Equability between seasons decreased near the end of the Pleistocene, causing fluctuations in food supplies for large herbivores. This situation could have caused animals to migrate larger distances than before, leading to extra stress on their health. Studies of the growth rings and the chemistry of mammoth tusks show there were migrations across many degrees of latitude in the Late Pleistocene. Habitats may have broken up into more complex and contrasting components, making it difficult for large herbivores. There is some evidence that the sheer size of some plants diminished because of changes in seasonality, temperature, and moisture.

Climate change explanations have problems, too. Late Pleistocene extinctions around the world are scattered over tens of thousands of years, but some extinctions do not match times of climatic stress. Some paleoecologists see the period in North America after about 18,000 years ago as better for large herbivores, even though some were becoming extinct there. Mammoth tusk studies show in some cases that animals were not dying from food shortage, because their tusks indicate they were eating well. Instead, the tusk ring patterns are consistent with predation similar to that seen in modern African elephants under human hunting pressure. In a completely different vein is the suggestion that humans brought foreign viruses or microbes to the continent, and these spread among animal populations.[c]

Wildlife biologist Charles Kay thinks that some megafauna were like large animals living today in numbers well below what the habitat can theoretically support, because they are predator limited rather than food limited. Kay's proposal is controversial, but at a minimum he broadens the emphasis from a focus on herbivores to a consideration of the large and fierce predators of the Pleistocene, such as short faced bear, sabertooth cat, and dire wolf. In Kay's view, since these predators kept herbivore numbers low, the introduction of human hunting pressure could have a significant impact without leaving slaughtered animals littered across the continent. Humans were a "keystone species" in that they had disproportionate effects on the ecosystem, not because humans were abundant or vicious but because of the particular niche humans occupied in the ecosystem.[d]

Mammoth specialist Gary Haynes includes a role for humans in the extinctions of some animals in some places. Haynes points out that extinction amounts only to a difference in the rates of deaths and births and that animals "die off" because they are "killed off" by various agents including starvation, disease, and predation. He suggests that the polar positions of "overkill" versus "environment" are part of an "annoying confusion" that takes effort away from "focusing our efforts on describing the events and processes undergone by Late Glacial mammals," because we place too much emphasis on "trying to explain or find a cause for the end effects of those processes."[e]

Ironically, but fortunately, Haynes' call for the study of events and processes is essentially the same as the concluding statement of Grayson and Meltzer in their "requiem" against a human cause.[f] Perhaps there is hope that we can treat the megafaunal extinctions as an ecological problem and not simply impose a false dichotomy of "natural" versus "human" causes.

We know that enough humans were spreading across the continent 13,000 years ago to leave an unmistakable archaeological presence and that a few people had probably been here for thousands of years before that. We have evidence that the colonists were mobile and in pursuit of large game. Once ancient humans became a member of Pleistocene ecosystems in the Americas, they made an impact every time they fulfilled their subsistence needs. People transformed the land into a human wilderness, and the effects of human predation cannot be discounted.

between Logan in Cache County to Payson in Utah County. Mammoth bones are also common, known from 10 localities, including several in Logan and Salt Lake City.[29] The dating on most of these finds is poor, and unlike the Huntington mammoth, none of the Utah localities yields any association between megafauna and human activity. The last of the megafauna and the arrival of humans are so close in time that it is difficult to restrain an image of these strange animals exchanging stares with humans.

The onset of the Younger Dryas period at 12,700 B.P. (see Chapter 2) flung the region back into glacial conditions. Lake Bonneville resurged, and although it would never again approach its previous expanse, the lake still inundated the site of downtown Salt Lake City. For the next 1,000 years, Utah's first colonists endured rapid and dramatic swings in climate and habitat.

A significant characteristic of the late Pleistocene for humans is the equability between seasons. The large animals, especially the megafauna, had adjusted to long, cool growing seasons. Plant communities during the Pleistocene may have been larger in scale and more homogeneous than the vertically stacked microzones we see today. Increases in seasonality altered the available forage for large herbivores such as mammoth, affecting their numbers and the size of their territories. During the Younger Dryas, these changes were magnified, even as the overall climate plunged back into colder times. Some habitats resisted the rapid climatic change while others could not, creating a patchwork quilt of local animal populations trying to adjust. Large animals migrated in search of better places, their standard response to habitat stress. More and more of the Pleistocene megafauna went extinct, a process that had been underway for millennia prior to the arrival of significant numbers of people.[30]

Wetlands were probably abundant during the Younger Dryas, and most were in a state of flux. However, the abundance of water caused streams and springs to flow where only desert is found today. The Old River Bed on the Dugway Proving Ground discussed above is a prime example, as were the once dynamic lake basins of the now parched Mojave Desert. During expansions of Lake Bonneville and Lake Lahontan in western Nevada, there may have been fish in the lake, including sucker and perhaps lake trout. These were the physical circumstances across the expanse of the region at the ecological moment of human colonization.

DIET, TOOLSTONE, TECHNOLOGY, AND MOBILITY

The record of the first colonists remains sparse, and because the dating is imprecise, it is difficult to distinguish the earliest people to enter the region from the continuous occupation that filled in the spaces behind them. We have a few well-dated sites, and many that are early, but most have yet to give up houses, fire hearths, refuse areas, and other physical features.

There is only indirect and spotty evidence of what Paleoindians ate, but our understanding of the landscape shows there was a huge array of resources available to the colonists. The cut marks on the Huntington mammoth and the stemmed point in association with camel in eastern Nevada contribute to the suspicion that humans and extinct animals were present, but we do not know how often such animals were eaten.

Recall that the early occupation at Smith Creek Cave was associated with bighorn sheep. Dried human feces (coprolites) of Paleoindian age from Spirit Cave in western Nevada indicate the consumption of small fish. Slightly later in time, Danger Cave and Bonneville Estates near Wendover show that rabbit, sage grouse, and pronghorn were on the menu. In the few other cases with evidence of diet, many modern species were taken, ranging in size from bighorn sheep to rabbits and waterfowl. Other sites across the region yield bits and pieces of evidence that a wide variety of animals were on the grocery list, but we remain in the dark about the relative contribution of specific foods to early human diets.

Human skeletal material can provide evidence for the composition of a diet accumulated over a lifetime. Analysis of stable isotopes of carbon and nitrogen in bones allows us to estimate the amount of meat, fish, and different classes of plant foods consumed. The number of Paleoindian skeletal remains is small, making each find extremely valuable for all who wonder about ancient people. Stable isotope analysis on a bone biopsy from the Buhl burial in Idaho shows that the young adult female ate a great deal of meat and fish such as salmon during her life over 12,500 years ago.[31]

The evidence of plant consumption is even more scant, but the Basin-Plateau parallels the continent-wide pattern of less reliance on grinding stones, the essential plant processing tool. Rather than indicating that plants were ignored, this means that plant foods requiring a great deal of processing were not prepared in bulk as keystone dietary staples, as they were in later periods.

The richest sources of information for this early period are the many stone tools and the debris from their manufacture. At first glance, this information may seem inconsequential, but knowledge of prehistoric stone tools, the way they were produced, and the way raw materials were procured is akin to understanding how oil, plastic and metal, and the logistics of their procurement shape the modern industrial world. Paleoindian technology relied on stone to make specialized tools of wood and bone, which together enabled the key industries of fiber and clothing. There are now studies that identify the sources of toolstones, as well as technological analysis on whole collections of tools and the flaking debris that tells how they were made.

Paleoindians used both local and nonlocal toolstone. An extreme example of the long-distance movement of stone is the Clovis point found decades ago at the famous mammoth kill site of Blackwater Draw, New Mexico. In 1988 a flyer advertising a conference titled "Ice Age Hunters of the Rockies" appeared in David Madsen's mailbox. The flyer featured a photograph of an obsidian Clovis point from the collections of the Denver Museum of Natural History, and the caption claimed that the point was from the famous site of Blackwater Draw in New Mexico. It turned out that the obsidian used to make that point originated in the Mineral Mountains near Milford, Utah. This is a distance of over 600 linear miles and was surely a thousand-mile walk for the people who passed this material to New Mexico over 12,000 years ago.[32]

Along the Wasatch Front, in parts of Nevada, as well as most of southeastern Oregon and eastern California, obsidian and fine-grained volcanic rocks can be sourced. Studies show long-distance movement of toolstone and tools, but also the use of local stone.

Charlotte Beck and Tom Jones found a north-to-south trajectory in the movement of toolstone associated with stemmed point technology in central and eastern Nevada. They showed that this system encompassed as much as 280 miles.[33] This is wholly consistent with Stephen Bedwell's proposal in 1973 of north-south mobility. Paleoindian mobility that was perhaps accumulated over a lifetime surely embraced large differences in habitat and climate during the environmentally dynamic time of the Younger Dryas. Beck and Jones's work also found that the valley dwellers tended not to transport toolstone across mountain ranges. People either knew that there would be toolstone in adjacent valleys, hence there was no need to carry it over the mountains, or they knew that north-south movement was a better decision than crossing the less productive, subalpine monoculture of the mountains merely to exploit adjacent valleys of similar latitude.[34]

There are hints, however, that tool production was also expedient and aimed at short-term use of locally available material. This appears to be the case at the Hell' n Moriah site, where high-quality chalcedonies were common. The toolmakers used the local material, and although they built the same Paleoindian-style tools, they did not worry as much about conservation. The same may be going on at the Sevier Desert site of 42Md300, where a Folsom point was made of obsidian from the Mineral Mountains only 50 miles away, and a Clovis point was made of obsidian from Black Rock about 30 miles away.[35]

Brooke Arkush and Bonnie Pitblado's study of stemmed point assemblages from the Wildcat Mountain area suggests something similar, as does David Madsen's work on the Old River Bed.[36] The habitats of these places may have been stable enough, even during the Younger Dryas, that people were tethered to the wetlands, moving out to obtain toolstone and exploit other habitats. This would require less long-distance movement of toolstone and less interest in conserving it, because this form of mobility was redundant and cyclical, rather than transient over large areas.

Bonnie Pitblado completed a large study of 15 types of Late Paleoindian points, their technology, and raw material variability. She focused on the Southern Rocky Mountains in Colorado, but her work draws attention to the fact that early artifacts are also found in mountain settings, despite all the attention to lower environments. Many of her samples were from the Basin-Plateau region, including 41 points from the Great Basin proper (western Utah only), 52 from eastern Great Basin mountain ranges, and 24 points from the

FIGURE 3.8

This map depicts the movement of toolstone (curved black arrows) in Paleoindian times to the Sunshine Locality (Jones et al. 2003:24). The transport of toolstone covered as much as 280 miles. As an exercise in analogy, the map superimposes the movement of foragers during the course of their lives as documented among the Nunamiut Eskimo by Lewis Binford (1983:115). The Nunamiut adjust their foraging ranges over decades, and named places accumulate as reference points on the landscape. The legend shows the life history names employed by the Nunamiut and their spans of use in years. The intent is not to argue that Great Basin Paleoindians and the historic Eskimo are the same culture but to alert us to the fact that forager land use must be comprehended on temporal scales larger than a typical year, and over lifetimes of movement. Thus, toolstone distributions may very well result from these larger scales of activity instead of discreet "trips to the store" to obtain raw material.

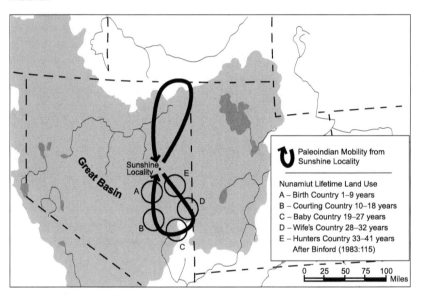

Colorado Plateau. By focusing on Late Paleoindian types, her study reveals patterns of the Paleoarchaic, the slightly later period when people were filling in the landscape "behind" the colonists. Pitblado found that obsidian and fine-grained volcanics were the most common material types in the Great Basin but that points from the mountains were more likely to be made of cherts. The points found in the mountains did not travel as far from their sources. This suggests that local toolstones were employed when people utilized mountain habitats and that at least some people were full-time mountain dwellers.

Raw material moves farther in the Great Basin valleys, and Pitblado found the movement to be on a northwest-southeast trajectory, a modest difference from Beck and Jones' north-south trajectory in eastern Nevada. I surmise that this difference is actually consistent in that both patterns follow the topography of their respective study areas. The valleys are narrow and aligned north to south in eastern Nevada, whereas the open terrain of Great Salt Lake, Sevier, and Escalante deserts of western Utah invite a northwest-southeast orientation of movement.[37] Pitblado's analysis of points from the Colorado Plateau suggests that fewer and less extensive wetlands there fostered a different settlement pattern. Mobility was still high, but the complex, dissected terrain of the Plateau negated the large-scale patterns of linear movement apparent in the Great Basin and constrained the option to tether to certain valley locations.

WHAT CAN WE SAY ABOUT PALEOINDIAN LIFE AND SOCIETY?

The first people in the Basin-Plateau were extensively mobile over the course of their lives, but they were not incessantly mobile. On the shorter temporal scales that anchor place, time was counted in residence of weeks and months and on redundant cycles of years at a time.

The Paleoindian food economy was driven by the availability of large-bodied animals that moved widely. People's decisions about movement were not impinged by neighbors—at least not at first. But these facts do not mean that people moved camp daily, nor does it mean that they ignored the other available foods. Nevertheless, the organization of Paleoindian life was fundamentally different from the wetland-lakeside adaptation documented for the historic period.

Paleoindian social organization was also different in some respects from the cultures of the historic period. People's knowledge of landscapes was not the same intimacy of place as the indigenous groups of history. Instead, it was an intimacy with new frontiers. The Paleoindian worldview reflected the wilderness circumstances that no people since have experienced.

The Paleoindian wilderness offered ecosystems untouched by humanity and a wide array of animal and plant resources. Bighorn sheep to mammoths, often found in sizable herds, would have been a strong attraction, because large game is in fact inexpensive to acquire relative to most other resources, once they are encountered. Their abundance in Paleoindian times would cause them to be sought

after whenever possible. Some comparisons of the Paleoindian's circumstances with the historic peoples of the region and foragers
elsewhere in the world can help us flesh out the Paleoindian diet and,
in turn, society.

Among historic peoples, when big game hunting failed, as it did
in an environment that had been under human impact for millennia,
smaller animals from rabbits to ducks and voles would be taken. An
insurance policy also existed in the "women's economy" (see Chapter 1:
Subsistence) providing plant nutrition that was expensive to produce
but in steady supply during the growing seasons. This pattern of subsistence is a strong one that occurs worldwide among historically
known foragers.[38]

Despite the attraction of large game, hunting produces variable
returns. Thus, although the label "Paleoindian big game hunters"
may indicate intent, it does not adequately describe the daily diet.
Some animals, such as mammoth, were probably so large that they
were difficult to hunt and process. Extinct bison, half again as large as
the dangerous modern bison, may have been too risky to hunt under
any but the most favorable circumstances. But the opportunities
to hunt large animals were greater than during the historic period.
Thus, decisions about big game hunting influenced other aspects of
life, including technology and material culture, mobility, decisions
about food storage and equipment caching, the size and composition
of camp groups, the gendered patterns of work, and the concept of
whether resources and material items were public goods or private
goods.

As the abundance of large game fluctuates, humans either change
their choice of foods or switch to a different territory. Modern foragers
will attempt to move when there is resource stress. Decisions to move
are facilitated by the widespread kin relations typical of desert foragers
(see Chapter 1) and by the memories of the elders whose life travels
serve as libraries of knowledge about landscapes. The collective, multi-
generational familiarity with regions that are larger than any single
person's experience is crucial to the success of movement among historically known foragers.[39] During the ecological moment of Paleoindian colonization, however, this collective knowledge and the kin
relationships with neighbors were less pervasively developed. There
were fewer relatives living in neighboring areas to facilitate such
moves, and among the colonists, few scouts or guides were available,
because most people had never seen large stretches of the new country.
However, there was no one to constrain movement, no indigenous

occupants to fear let alone obstruct a decision to move into new territory.

Given these circumstances, Paleoindian residential mobility was initially high, and people moved among base camps occupied perhaps weeks at a time. Over the span of a human life, mobility encompassed territorial ranges much larger than those documented for the historic period.

Colonial social groups were likely small, on the order of a few dozen people, but fluid in size and composition. Membership in these groups was strangely closed, because they were isolated. But within each group, most goods were likely seen as public—more so than among later peoples of the region. Among living foragers, resources that are acquired unpredictably, episodically, and in large packages are typically public and available to all. These are often "men's" resources and contrast with the private, in-family ownership of "women's" resources. Thus, meat from Paleoindian large-game hunts would have been distinctly public, but the women's resources, the small mammals and plant foods that sustained hunts during this period, may also have been public. If so, this pattern contrasts with most living foragers and with later Basin-Plateau foragers.

When Paleoindian groups encountered one another, their interactions took on a personality of openness and fluidity. Social encounters between groups were events of opportunity with some urgency, because they were temporary. These were not the structured interactions of familiar neighbors but moments of opportunity and risk. The public distribution of resources bonded the groups, but the private dealings between individuals and families brokered specific interactions and deals. Surely there were networks among people and recognition of band affiliation—these were not encounters among foreigners. But the intermittent nature of social interaction was consistent with a sense of place that was fluid. Kinship networks could be far flung, born during episodes of group encounter, and then flung apart by the inevitable movement of the group. Trade surely occurred, attested to so clearly by the movement of exotic toolstone. Some fluidity of membership among groups arose from gatherings that were a mix of public display and feasting, as well as private hoarding, exchange, and deal making. However, these events were not frequent, because population densities were low. The essence of the social organization is found in the day-to-day reality that Paleoindian groups were small and isolated with episodes of contact separated by isolation.

Paleoindian base camps were hubs for trips to obtain toolstone and other raw materials for manufacturing tools, equipment and clothing and to kill and butcher animals. Mobility during the colonization period was high enough that food storage was not worth the effort, nor could it contribute to suppressing risk if the tether to stored food kept people from exploiting the options made available through mobility.

It is possible that the division of labor by sex was strongly reflected in residence. Nicole Waguespack employs knowledge about women's work in contemporary foraging societies to argue that women were a central feature of Paleoindian societies in which decision making was driven by hunting. Robert Elston and David Zeanah use archaeological data and ecological theory to identify the distinct roles of men and women in food getting and in mobility and residence.[40] These studies show that men were absent for significant periods, drawn away by movements of animals and by trips to obtain raw materials. Women anchored base camps that moved when men had established a new hunting base elsewhere. This means that women's work was much more than the domestic stereotype during Paleoindian times. Among historically known foragers with meat-dominant diets, women's labor expands into a broader range of tool making, hauling goods, and all manner of construction, such as houses and roasting ovens. Women's foraging activities focused on local plant collection that likely revolved around roots and large species of seeds and berries, and on small animal hunting. A significant element of women's work in Paleoindian times was surely meat, bone, and hide processing.

Plant foods could be collected as the camps moved and provided a steady supply of food. Those plants requiring little processing were favored, such as roots, shoots, greens, and berries. Some plants that were staples in later periods, especially seeds or roots requiring extensive processing, were eaten only opportunistically. Paleoindians largely eschewed the labor required to make these into staples, because they were expensive and there were few incentives to store food.

Women were also likely important to animal processing. This begins with field butchering, especially after the initial field dressing. There is evidence that some fraction of the meat obtained was processed into pemmican and possibly jerky. The young woman known as the Buhl burial described above showed dental wear indicating that her diet of meat and salmon contained abundant fine grit. This sort of wear comes from the consumption of prepared meats, such as pemmican. Many variations exist on this theme, and in the Basin-Plateau, it is often referred to as "desert fruit cake." Pounded meat is held together by a paste of animal fat and often fatty nuts and seeds, juicy berries, and the starchy paste from roots to make a transportable form of food storage (see Chapter 1 Sidebar: Forager Cuisine).

The temporary nature of Paleoindian base camps and the extensiveness of the moves worked against investing a great deal of time to manufacture a ground stone tool kit. Surely foods were ground and pounded using flat stones, but unless there is an expectation to return, or a move is short enough that a heavy tool can be transported, the ground stone tools will not be carefully manufactured or receive a great deal of wear. Depending on the type of stone, a slab used even for a few weeks will often not develop enough wear to be evident to archaeologists, and there was little reason to invest the 100 or 200 hours to peck and grind a large *metate* such as those used by Native American farmers thousands of years later. Nor was there time for the debris of used grinding stones to accumulate on the landscape, because their production began for the very first time with these colonists. It would be several millennia before the landscape became a hardware store littered with manufactured ground stone implements that could be scavenged when a camp was established.[41] It is not unexpected that so few ground stone artifacts are found at Paleoindian sites and that when they are, they often show only faint evidence of grinding from a single use, or perhaps a few days. The people were eating plants, and they were using ground stone tools to process plant and animal products, but in a different way than later peoples.

Game reconnaissance and hunting were likely male activities, and base camps were moved when hunting events secured large animals. Kill sites and base camps were, however, not necessarily together but close enough to minimize the problem of transporting large amounts of food. Base camps had to be located for access to the hunt and where local plant and small animal foods could be obtained to support it. Thus, the much debated importance of plant and small mammal foods in Paleoindian times is less about quantity than it is about the role played in the decision-making system. The animals drove the mobility, but the plants and small mammals taken at base camps supplied the hunts. Paleoindians obtained fewer calories from plants and medium to small game than in later periods, but the role of these less heralded resources was absolutely central.

To put this system into effect, base camps were frequently placed in valley margin locations. These places mediated the need to provision the base camp and the need to monitor and hunt game and to obtain raw materials. Ariane Pinson explores the possibility that people chose the margins as a form of risk management. We often think of wetlands as endlessly productive, but they are not. In the Younger Dryas period, many wetlands may have been particularly unstable. Pinson thinks people lived in locations with access to several habitats that in combination created a niche with less variation. She finds that in this time period, minimizing risk was more important than gross productivity was.[42]

Paleoindian mobility was not relentless, incessant, or aimless. It was akin to the pulse of an erratic heartbeat timed to a scale of weeks and months. Once a new area was colonized, group size likely increased, and some stability ensued. These episodes may have been brief, on the order of a few weeks, until the next cycle: scout the game, plan a hunt, make the kill, and butcher the take. This was followed by a move to a base camp where the opportunistic pursuit of local plant and small mammal resources sustained the group during the hunt, and where the bounty of the hunt was consumed while the next hunt was organized and monitored. Life was cyclical and repetitive, but the tempo was erratic. The sense of place was not so much with the particular land being occupied, as it was an intimacy with the plant and animal inhabitants in a context of place that could be anywhere.

TRANSITION TO PALEOARCHAIC LIFE AND SOCIETY

As long as big game were plentiful and tracts in the landscape remained unoccupied by humans, the Paleoindian lifeway was advantageous. It led to population growth and the rapid colonization of the continent.[43] Yet, the large-scale environmental change closing the Pleistocene was well underway even before Clovis times. Species of Pleistocene megafauna had been going extinct for thousands of years.[44] Habitats were smaller and more partitioned, causing species diversity and abundance to decline. Add to this the effects of human predation, and a certain tyranny of evolutionary circumstance was inevitable.

Perhaps more significant than a decline in large game caused by habitat stress and hunting is the fact that settlers inevitably follow colonists. Virtually all societies we know from history result from the demands of people living around other people. The process of colonization became a process of settlement.

High mobility has its costs as well as its benefits. Mobility requires that people skip the opportunity to fully exploit a particular place. Instead, the Paleoindian colonists responded to resource stress by frequent movement to follow game populations. But this option evaporated as more neighbors moved in. Game populations declined, and the cost of hunting increased. People became tethered to smaller areas. This nascent form of "settling in" does not imply fixed villages occupied year round but means that people used places more fully and more intensively. They more regularly pursued a wider variety of foods. They took foods that required more processing. The investment in technology shifted from a tool kit geared for mobile hunting to one with greater emphasis on snares, traps, and nets for smaller animals, as well as ground stone and different types of basketry for plant processing. They placed greater emphasis on storage as the solution to short-term food shortages. In so doing they began to identify local sense of place, and a greater identity with territory became part of their worldview.

Risk-averse behavior continued to be favored, but for different reasons. Instead of isolated groups whose external social relations were shaped during episodic rendezvous with other mobile groups, social interaction became regularized and the connections more entwined. People had to deal with the same individuals and groups over and over again. Trade now occurred among distinct social entities and was structured more by social arrangements than by the opportunism of an occasional encounter. Local styles of projectile points, and probably many other things, began to develop as group identity took root. Ironically, this process of regionalization brought on an element of isolation, even as social networks structured more regular interaction. During the Paleoarchaic, we see the beginnings of social organization that continued to develop in many areas of the Basin-Plateau region for the next 10,000 years.

Exactly when this happened is not known. Since the archaeology is largely mixed together on the ground surface, we cannot easily tease apart the Paleoindian colonists from the Paleoarchaic settlers.

This is especially true for those locales without fluted points but with only the Great Basin stemmed point types. The latter could have been left by Paleoindian colonists or by Paleoarchaic settlers.

The southern Great Basin and Mojave Desert of California have perhaps the richest Paleoarchaic archaeology found in the Lake Mojave Complex discussed earlier. In that region, the small, mobile camps, diverse diets, and fluctuating group sizes and organization greatly blur the line between the categories of Paleoindian and Paleoarchaic. But then, such names are more conveniences than realities.

Areas near the Wasatch Front, including the landscape northwest of Great Salt Lake and the Old River Bed near Dugway, also yield early and later occupations with examples of the early fluted points, many stemmed points, and the "Late Paleoindian" leaf-shaped points such as the Scottsbluff and Jimmy Allen types. We have seen evidence that at the Old River Bed, Wildcat Mountain, and along the Utah-Nevada border people became tethered fairly early, broadening their diet and beginning to associate with place. The dating of these areas remains murky, so we do not know if the transition to the Paleoarchaic happened only a few centuries into the Younger Dryas, perhaps as early as 12,500 years ago, or later. Most archaeologists working in the region think that the Paleoarchaic is readily apparent after 11,500 years ago, or about 10,000 radiocarbon years ago.

Even the Paleoarchaic was only a beginning. Human numbers remained low. But the heyday of skimming the cream from a new land was over.

4

Eons of Foragers

In the wake of the Paleoindian explorers and colonists, settlers spread across the land, and over the next 8,000 years they would fully appropriate it. Archaeologists love labels and variously refer to this period as the Archaic, the Western Archaic, or the more colorful "Desert Culture."[1] There is danger in including such a long span of time under a single period, let alone a single people or tribe. It would be an error to homogenize what was a wealth of cultural diversity and change simply because we labeled it as one. Nevertheless, the Archaic period stands in contrast to the Paleoindian, because the time of exploration and initial settlement was over, and it would be thousands of years before the more populous agricultural cultures appeared.[2] The Paleoarchaic began about 11,500 years ago and spanned the next nine millennia until the arrival of agriculture 2,000 years ago in the eastern Great Basin and Colorado Plateau. Farming did not spread west across the Great Basin, and there the Archaic persisted until the arrival of Europeans.[3]

One of the difficulties of describing and ultimately comprehending the Archaic is the amount of time involved. If we again appeal
to the human scale of generations to gain purchase on an enormous
prehistoric past, we find that the Archaic encompasses 250 to 300
generations. It must be a rich history indeed.

A LONG TIME AND SOME BIG CHANGES

Archaic settlers developed local ways of life, regional styles, and
group identities linked to territories. These things did not come all
at once, and to see inside the Archaic period, it is useful to identify
some physical indicators of change, some major trends, and subdivide
the Archaic into Early, Middle, and Late. These categories and the
dates shown on the chart are mere guideposts, not cultural badges,
and they arise from patterns in the archaeological data.

Archaeology is adept at tracking culture with artifacts, and we
will find that seemingly minor technological shifts are mileposts for
changes in economies, social organization, and the ways people conceptualized and interacted with place. Two technologies marking
significant change appear in the first half of the Archaic. These are
milling stones (the *metate* and the *mano*) and coiled basketry. A
pioneer of the archaeology of the Desert West, Jesse D. Jennings, referred to these items as the "twin hallmarks of the Desert Culture."[4]
These seemingly mundane items signaled a change in the way people
chose and acquired food, and consequently where they settled and
for how long. They allow us to glimpse the societies who adopted
these technologies, and were in turn shaped by them.

FIGURE 4.1

Time line showing the major cultural periods of the Basin-Plateau.

Major Periods and Archaeological Cultures

Time B.P. (A.D./B.C.)
15,000 13,000 11,000 9,000 7,000 5,000 4,000 3,000 2,000 1,000 500 present
                                                                A.D. 0   A.D. 1300

? - - — Paleoindian —
                – Early Archaic – Middle Archaic –   Late Archaic   - -
                                                            (western Basin)
                                          – Late Archaic – Fremont – Late Prehistoric
                                          (eastern Basin - Plateau)

Of course, climate and habitats are always "underneath" cultural change, mediating and sometimes limiting choices. There are significant environmental changes during the Archaic. Wetlands were more common in the Early Archaic than today, but long periods in the Middle Archaic were the driest the region has ever seen. The vegetation patterns of the Basin-Plateau began to look "modern" during the Middle and Late Archaic. For instance, the pinyon pine spread to its modern limits. In some areas, the mere availability of this resource caused change, whereas in other parts of the region, the pine nut was used casually, becoming significant only much later. For centuries during the Late Archaic, Great Salt Lake expanded and reached from the Wasatch Range to the Nevada border. Pyramid Lake and Winnemucca Lake in western Nevada expanded, as did wetlands in many parts of the region (see Chapter 2).

The manner in which people used the land changed during the Archaic, and the distinction between the desert-mountain and the wetlands settlement patterns described for the historically known groups (Chapter 1) began no earlier than the Middle Archaic, becoming fully formed only during the Late Archaic.[5]

Sense of place changed again after 4,000 years ago, when there was a slow and spatially patchy acceleration in the intensity of the human presence. Populations grew significantly during the Late Archaic, and in some areas, villages sprang up that were occupied for much of the year. Economies became oriented around food processing and storage, not just food acquisition and consumption. This created intermittent surpluses, which hedged against food shortage but also led to inequalities of wealth. Nothing motivates opportunism and competition among people and spurs the organization of corporate groups with assigned status, role, and membership more than inequity.

The Late Archaic was a time when society, and the perceptions of the people who constituted it, reflected the evolutionary fact of an environment filled to capacity by foraging peoples. This image may not come quickly to mind when we think of foragers, whom we often envision as living in primitive equality and harmonizing with the land on which they lived lightly. They did not all live this way, the foraging spectrum was broad, and the Archaic exemplifies this.[6]

Significant changes in the Late Archaic came from outside of the region. The spread of the bow and arrow into the region after 2,000 years ago reminds us that the Basin-Plateau was part of a larger Native-American world that included the Pacific Northwest, California, and the Southwest.

The Southwest would be especially pertinent to the peoples of the Late Archaic when farming began in southern Arizona 3,500 years ago. Southwestern farming and the population growth it brought would shape the foraging peoples of the Desert West, from southern California and eventually north across the Great Basin for the next several thousand years. It was the source of colonists and immigrants bringing domesticated corn, beans, and squash to the indigenous people of Utah 2,000 years ago to form the Fremont culture.

As the Archaic unfolded, the indigenous peoples of the Basin-Plateau region were increasingly influenced by Native cultures elsewhere on the continent. The Archaic was the last time the region might be considered even moderately isolated, and by 2,000 years ago, the Basin-Plateau was clearly just one part of an interconnected, socially entwined landscape of Native-American peoples.

SETTLERS OF THE EARLY ARCHAIC
(9000 B.P.–7000 B.P.)

The "twin hallmarks of the Desert Culture," the milling stone and coiled basketry, made an early appearance in the west deserts of Utah. Grinding stones appear in the earliest levels of Danger Cave. Most are discarded fragments, illustrating an intense, redundant use of place that constantly exhausted these tools. The earliest baskets are twined styles, but between 9,000–7,500 years ago, the tighter, coiled types were increasingly made. Grinding stones and coiled basketry are present at other early sites, such as Hogup. A *mano* was found at Camels Back Cave at Dugway Proving Ground associated with a hearth dating to nearly 8,000 years ago.[7] No one occupied Camels Back Cave prior to this time, even though it is within view of the rich Paleoindian and Paleoarchaic landscape along the Old River Bed of western Utah. When Camels Back Cave was finally included in the repertoire of camps, grinding stones were used there, too. The significance of grinding stones and coiled baskets cannot be overestimated, not because they were elusive inventions but because of what they indicate about the choices people made and the cultural context shaping those choices.

Grinding stones show that foods, such as small hard seeds, that had been previously ignored because they required too much processing were now used. The milling stone pairs with the coiled basket, because tight, waterproof baskets, made by coiling split fibers

FIGURE 4.2

Archaic locations and sites referred to in Chapter 4.

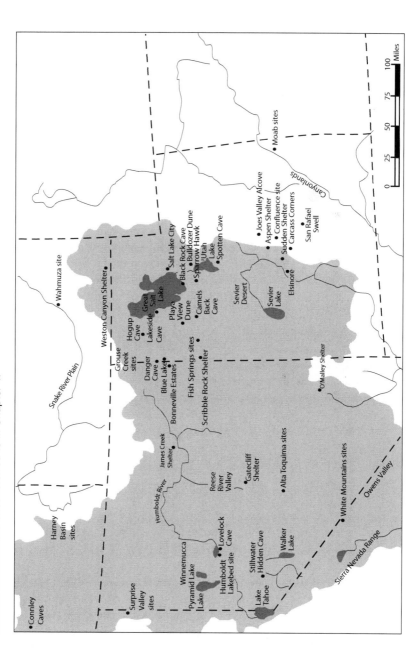

around a central rod or bundle and then stitching them together, were an enormous advancement for cooking seed foods over the twining techniques that had been used for millennia. Coiled baskets were used for cooking by immersing hot rocks into liquid foods such as stews and porridge that were based on seed flours.[8]

Like all technological improvements, milling stones and coiled basketry were expensive. The investment in such technology could pay only if it enabled access to previously ignored or lightly used resources that returned the investment as stored food that in turn reduced risk. Seed exploitation provided this opportunity, but the seeds had to be milled into flour to make a significant contribution to the diet, because humans are inefficient at digesting large quantities of whole seeds.[9]

Many events in human history are mistakenly treated as an unfolding of fate that "permits" people to move forward. Technology magically saves the people. Settled life is chalked up to "progress," as if there were some invisible force that makes people want to be settled. These are not explanations as much as they are reflections of our own culture's perception—"they" should want to be like us. New technologies surely arise from the human imagination, but the few ideas that actually spread do so in response to circumstances. The adoption of grinding stones and food storage are thus wrapped up with the decision to tether to locales more frequently. Instead of settling happening so people could use the "new" technology of grinding stones (of course it wasn't new at all), people settled a bit to exploit concentrations of foods. To employ storage means that you must retrieve the food, and perhaps remain close to protect it. In order to store, you need technology to process the seeds that were the basis for the storage in the first place. The staggered appearance of grinding stones and coiled basketry around the Basin-Plateau reflects people's decisions to adopt or not adopt options that are in front of them. People do not necessarily change at the drop of a cost-benefit evaluation, but neither do traditions resist all shifts in reality. The anthropologist Nicholas Blurton-Jones refers to this as the "tyranny of circumstance."[10]

The change signaled by the increased use of these simple but elegant tools is that the food economy of the Early Archaic encompassed the full array of possibilities. The diet was now "broad spectrum." Food storage increased over the Paleoindian period, although it would be millennia before storage became a central feature of the socioeconomic system.

Hunting continued to be part of the story, and jackrabbits are by far the most common food bone found in the earliest sites of the eastern Great Basin, such as Danger Cave, Hogup Cave, Bonneville Estates Rockshelter, and Camels Back Cave. Sage grouse were abundant in the lowest levels of Danger Cave, but pronghorn and mule deer were absent. The early levels of Hogup Cave yielded deer and pronghorn bone, although not in the abundance found a few thousand years later. Wetlands were nearby—Danger, Hogup, and Bonneville Estates all have waterfowl bone in the lower levels.[11]

The Dust Devil site exemplifies the concept of a broad spectrum economy. Beginning over 8,500 years ago, people came to this camp located in the open desert, but not far from marshlands along the Sevier River in western Utah. Food bone recovered from the site included small mammals, birds, and fish. The mammal and bird bones are so fragmented that it suggests they were intensively processed, even to the point of boiling the tiny bones for grease. Fish bones constitute 14% of the food bone at the site, even though fish bones are so fragile that most of them do not preserve. This suggests that fish were very important. Small camps at Dust Devil continued for a

FIGURE 4.3

Hogup Cave under excavation showing the stratigraphic layers revealing over 8,000 years of occupation of the cave. (Courtesy of the Archaeological Center, Department of Anthropology, University of Utah)

thousand years during the Early Archaic, proclaiming the tenacity of the broad-spectrum way of life.[12]

Marsh plants, such as bulrush seeds, are found in the early Archaic cave sites. The tiny seeds of the salt tolerant Pickleweed were used, and this plant indicates that the water table was perhaps only a half meter below the dry surface of the salt flats. Desert plants are also found, including familiar species such as Greasewood, Sagebrush, and Prickly Pear cactus. Useful plants were brought to the sites, including the water-loving Reed Grass favored for dart/spear shafts and the fibers of Dogbane and Milkweed necessary to make string and rope.

As we glance around the Basin-Plateau region, we find that increased use of milling stones and coiled basketry came at different times in different places but eventually encompassed the entire region. The earliest evidence of these cultural hallmarks is from the deserts of the eastern Great Basin and the northwestern Great Basin. The Colorado Plateau followed with milling stones in use by 8,500–9,000 years ago at places such as Joes Valley Alcove and Sudden Shelter in central Utah. The Mojave Desert of California clearly yields grinding stones by the Early Archaic. The deserts of eastern and central Nevada retained a relatively low use of grinding stones for the next several thousand years, appearing at places such as Gatecliff Shelter and other sites in Monitor Valley, and the Reese River Valley around 6,000 years ago, and even later in southern Nevada.[13] Yes, grinding stones were used earlier, even during Paleoindian times, but in the Early Archaic their use blossomed across the region.

Of course, there is more to life than grinding stones and coiled basketry. Where did people live, for how long, and what was the social fabric like? Most settlement remained tethered to the valleys in the Early Archaic. Great Basin stemmed points continued to be made, and a tally for the Wasatch Front in Utah shows that of 69 archaeological sites with stemmed points, 66 of them are from sites below 4,600 feet—essentially valleys and their edges.[14]

People directed their attention to the lowlands, as they did in the Paleoindian and Paleoarchaic periods—understandable given the continued presence of wetlands. But the uplands were not ignored; they were just not used in the same way as in later periods. For instance, Weston Canyon Rockshelter in southeast Idaho was a hunting camp beginning 8,000 years ago. Bighorn sheep were the most frequent prey, but a wide variety of large and medium mammals and

FIGURE 4.4

The "Twin Hallmarks" of the Desert Culture are coiled basketry and milling stones. They signify fundamental change in the economy, settlement pattern, and social organization during the Archaic period. These mundane technologies suggest a broader diet that increasingly included small seeds that were expensive to process, but storable. Grinding stones were used to process seeds and symbolize a stronger tether to stored foods. Coiled basketry was labor intensive to produce but was a necessary technology to handle large numbers of tiny seeds. These changes were not random but spread in a time and space-transgressive pattern across the region.

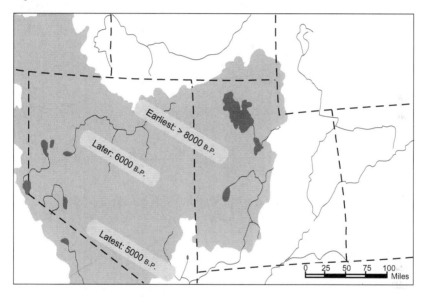

even a few fish were found. Many of the bighorn sheep bones were extensively processed, not only for marrow but for bone grease as well.[15]

Upland habitats were essential for other goods. Often overlooked is the need for medicinal plants to treat illness. It is not difficult to envision a shaman, alone or with a small group making trips to many different habitats to obtain medicines.[16] Forays into the uplands were made to seek toolstone, fibers, minerals for paints, and special woods such as Mountain Mahogany and Serviceberry.

The settling process of the Early Archaic led to a "built environment," a concept of place emphasizing the redundant use of a landscape through the construction of hunting facilities, caches of equipment, rock art, and a social organization for every habitat and every task. Even the lowly milling stone is part of the built environment

FIGURE 4.5

Sudden Shelter was excavated under the direction of Jesse Jennings and Alan Schroedl. It contained an 8,000-year record of occupation for the Colorado Plateau. (Courtesy of the Archaeological Center, Department of Anthropology, University of Utah)

of foragers, and these stones were often cached, or simply scavenged from earlier campsites. The use of the milling stone did not crescendo until the Late Archaic, but investment in a built environment grew from the redundancy of occupation in the Early Archaic.

Population sizes were low in the Early Archaic, but the social landscape was nevertheless identified, categorized, and allocated, regardless of whether it was directly inhabited at any given moment. The combination of a socially full place in a relatively empty land made for a very different social setting than what would occur later in the Archaic and thereafter.

Groups remained small, and even though people were more tethered than before, their stays were brief as they cycled among familiar valley locations. In some ways they appeared mobile, but the tethering made them appear settled. If this were the case, then scattered families knew one another and were routinely linked among kin. Group sizes probably varied and there was some fluidity in membership. Specialized tasks required groups to split into smaller segments for weeks or even months at a time. Large amounts of briefly available food, such as via rabbit drives or larvae blooms, could support larger groups, renewing far-flung group connections.

There was little in the way of territoriality. The use of storage tied people to places, but there was little fear of neighboring "tribes" raiding and killing for food. Stored food was likely hidden in underground pits, and caches of equipment were placed in any number of safe places in this enormous landscape. Instead of concern over enemy neighbors, territoriality revolved more around hoarding a stored cache of food or supplies from a close relative living nearby. Territoriality and competition were thus familial and local.[17]

Trade was also primarily local, with little evidence in the Early Archaic of the movement of exotics such as Pacific shells. The long-distance movement of some items must have occurred, but the low population densities and local character of life made it exceptional. One of the ironies of the settling and tethering process is that the development of local identities and connection to place actually seems to have decreased the amount of long-distance movement of goods from the more distantly mobile Paleoindian times. This pattern would reverse itself again by the Late Archaic.

Early Archaic life was nevertheless full, and a smattering of jewelry such as beads and pendants remind us that people adorned themselves, signaling status, availability, and identity. Nor did they go without music, as attested to by the bull roarer found in a 9,000-year-old layer at Hogup Cave.[18] A bull roarer is a wooden blade whirled around on a string to vibrate the air. Each bull roarer has a distinctive "voice," and this instrument is known on many continents.

The Early Archaic landscape was still a wilderness, people were few, and the land was not strained by their presence. Their worldview now centered on place instead of newness, and a social fabric blanketed the land. The fabric was light and open, however, creating a distinctive contrast between a socially enveloped land that would, in our minds, seem barren and empty.

HIGH-DESERT FORAGERS OF THE MIDDLE ARCHAIC
(7000–3000 B.P.)

The Middle Archaic was different. Foragers spread out even more, and although the overall population size was probably similar to the

SIDEBAR: THE BUILT ENVIRONMENT

The "built environment" of our modern world is so much a part of life that we hardly give it any thought. Imagine life without our homes, roads, churches, baseball fields, and schools. Where would we be without sewers, fiber optic cables, electrical generating plants, and factories? We rely on our infrastructure.

The prehistoric cultures of the Basin-Plateau also had built environments, and even though their technology was intelligent and exquisitely attuned to the needs at hand, the tally of tools was small, and the technology was relatively simple. But prehistoric foragers were not as materially poor as we might think, and they did not have to carry everything on their backs. On the contrary, they had a range of gear that could be cached, and even some specialized installations that were carefully arranged around their environment.

When it was time to hunt in the marshes, the travelers could swing by a "marsh cache." It might contain fishing line, hooks, and weights. There would be net bags, as well as snares to capture small mammals. There might be bone tubes for snorkels and duck decoys, such as those woven from cattail stalks 2,000 years ago and left in Lovelock Cave, Nevada.[a]

In the fall, the pine nut hooks (long poles used to pull branches down), large grinding stones, and hullers awaited the workers in the many pinyon groves. Even the houses were ready for refurbishment, as was the case at the Bustos wickiup site near Ely, Nevada. They were small huts but made with log superstructures that enabled them to quickly be placed into service for the several-week pine nut harvest. The nearby storage caches were also refurbished. A particular pinyon pine grove might have been used only every five years, but the structures and other equipment would have been in place.[b]

When it was time to hunt in the highlands, caches of arrow shafts made from the cane grass (*Pragmites communis*) that grows in valley wetlands might have been placed in the mountains in case more shafts were needed. A farmer in Willard, Utah, found a storage pit on his land that contained over 600 small arrow points ready for use. Snare bundles were surely kept in many places on the landscape, as were baskets, bags, woven mats, axes, and digging sticks; just about anything that allowed people to be prepared as soon as they arrived in a locale.[c]

Food-getting was not the only reason to cache. Rock art is very much a part of the built environment and brought meaning to places of everyday activity and, in some times and cultures, places of ritual. Shaman's bundles are known, too, such as the cache from Humboldt Cave near Lovelock, Nevada, that contained little pouches holding vegetal cakes, pitch, ocher, a stuffed weasel pelt with feathers in its mouth, and a host of other small objects. The Patterson Bundle, found in a pit near Thompson in eastern Utah, is a curing kit with pouches containing individual doses of herbs.[d]

As people used the landscape more and more fully, an inventory of *metates* and *manos* accumulated on the ground. These were sometimes stored in the crotches of juniper and pinyon trees, or leaned against their trunks so they could be easily spotted. When Isabel Kelly conducted field-work with the Southern Paiute near Kanab, Utah, in 1932, her informants told her that they would make a new grinding stone only if an old one could not be scavenged.[e]

Perhaps the most spectacular facilities of the built environment are pronghorn hunting enclosures. Most were made of brush, although a few subject to long use were made of stacked rocks. These are low fences or walls perhaps 3 feet high arranged in long arcing lines to form a keyhole pattern when viewed from above. A pronghorn enclosure near Montello, Nevada, is 600 meters in diameter. Pronghorn were driven from miles away over the course of days and expertly funneled into the corral-like enclosures. The traps were placed to exploit the natural predator avoidance behavior of the animals, enabling them to be driven with decoys of stacked brush and gentle maneuvering by experienced hunters. Once inside the enclosure, pronghorn turn with the fenceline rather than jump over it. Hunters kept the animals milling about in the enclosure until they were shot with darts or arrows, or until they faltered from exhaustion and were clubbed to death.

Dozens of pronghorn enclosures are known in northeastern Nevada alone. There are two near Park Valley, Utah, last used in the 19th century. One opened to the north to harvest during the fall when the pronghorn migrated to lower ground, and another one nearby opened to the south to exploit the spring migration.[f]

The built environment was not constant across prehistory. It was probably minimal in Paleoindian times, although the hoards of spectacular stone tools and raw materials such as the Fenn Cache epitomize the fundamentals of a built environment. By Middle Archaic times, when forager occupation spread more evenly across all elevations and habitats, opportunities for a built environment increased. People moved camps often, and the same habitat type might have been used every year, but the annual round did not necessarily return to the same places and camps. Population size and density remained low, and the built environment was scattered in caves, ledges, or crevices that could be easily described and located. As human use of the landscape increased during the Late Archaic, and distinctions among territories crystallized, the built environment became more pervasive and more subject to control, hiding, and defense. It is possible that the decline in the use of cave caches in the Carson-Stillwater area of western Nevada by 1,500 years ago was an example of changes in the social context of the built environment.

> Once again, we see that foragers are active participants in their human wilderness. They did not live hand to mouth, nor did they have to reinvent their world every day. As cultural perceptions and use of place evolved over the millennia, the built environment traced the increasing presence of foragers upon the land.

Early Archaic, people appropriated all of the landscape, not just by knowing of it and inhabiting it intermittently but also by directly weaving themselves into every nook and cranny.

The Middle Archaic is full of irony, because the footprint left across the Basin-Plateau is light, once provoking archaeologists to wonder if the region had been abandoned. Times were harsh, because many of the wetlands dried up, and there were two long periods as dry as any the region has ever seen. The Basin-Plateau began to look modern, not only with the arrival of the pinyon pine but because in some places the historically recognized patterns of native life can be glimpsed. People would never return to the footloose days of the Paleoindian colonists, nor did they live like the Paleoarchaic and Early Archaic settlers, with their loose tethers to the more numerous wetlands of those times.

Archaeologists no longer believe the region was abandoned. Foragers of the world occupy far more inhospitable deserts than ours. People scattered and developed an extensive use of place in response to an encroaching desert.[19]

The die was actually cast in the Early Archaic, when the economic system ensnared virtually all resources. Seeds are symbolic of this process, because they are the most expensive class of resource available to foragers anywhere.[20] Their processing costs are sky high, and many ethnographic and experimental studies show this. The high cost of seeds is outweighed by the benefit of larger quantities of storable food. This is a signal of the first tiny steps toward intensification, a process that continues in our world today—benefits are gained despite the high costs of channeling more and more energy and effort through the system. By the Middle Archaic, people were on a trail that our culture today recognizes as the mixed bag of "progress." It was a watershed.

The social fabric of the Middle Archaic also reflected the extensive use of place. The first hints of the historically known ethnographic patterns date to the Middle Archaic, when the desert-mountain settlement pattern identified by ethnographers many millennia later becomes evident (see Chapter 1: Mobility and Settlement).

The southern Great Basin and Mojave Desert exemplifies an extensive use of place. The Pinto Complex continues the Paleoarchaic and Early Archaic tradition of manufacturing stemmed projectile points of materials other than obsidian and cherts. But by Pinto times, the tool inventory featured the most grinding stones of any period in the Mojave. There was a boom in food processing. Large residential sites were founded in well-watered locations, but the entire landscape was used. There seem to be distinct local adaptations across the Mojave Desert and probably a variety of populations and cultures. The desert was drying out, but the lifeways begun in the early Archaic carried forward in the Middle Archaic as the Mojave Desert became fully enveloped by foraging peoples.[21]

The entire region did not turn into high desert. People living 5,500 years ago in Surprise Valley in northeastern California, settled in large, communal earth lodges up to 25 feet in diameter, with central fire hearths and entry ramps. The few wetlands anchored people to substantial settlements, and we might expect this for the Middle Archaic Wasatch Front. Southwestern Wyoming, although outside the Basin-Plateau, offers a rich archaeology yielding dozens of sites during the Middle Archaic (6000–4500 B.P.) with housepits and storage. The high, dry steppe of southwestern Wyoming offered combinations of desert roots and small to medium game that fostered brief but redundant camps and short-term storage. A diversity of lifeways marks the Middle Archaic, but it was the moment when we clearly see people wedded to all parts of the landscape.[22]

Several decades after Danger Cave was excavated, Jesse Jennings attempted to search for the places people went when they did not occupy the caves bordering the Great Salt Lake Desert. His field crews led by Gardiner Dalley found many sites in the sage-, juniper-, and pinyon-covered Grouse Creek Mountains. They found Swallow Shelter and Remnant Cave, but their earliest apparent use was no more than 6,000 years ago.[23] Swallow Shelter sits at 5,800 feet, just below the pinyon pine zone. It was repeatedly occupied as a hunting camp, especially for taking marmots but also bighorn sheep, mule deer, and cottontail rabbits. The occupants also gathered roots and seeds. The oldest radiocarbon date from Swallow Shelter is 5410 B.P. and this was midway up the lowest layer. The occupation at this time was very slight. Nearby Remnant Cave was also used for hunting, and even though it overlooked the Great Salt Lake Desert, it yields no evidence for the use of lowland desert plants typical of sites such as Danger and Hogup caves. Other upland cave sites near Grouse Creek were also used as hunting camps, and grinding stones indicate a broad use of resources in these places. Heavy occupation of the pinyon and juniper zone between 5,000 to over 7,000 feet in the Grouse Creek area is evident in the 65 upland, open sites found during the project, and, of the few dozen sites whose age can be estimated, 60% are Archaic.[24]

Higher elevations were also used, as attested by the Sparrow Hawk site at 7,840 feet in the Oquirrh Mountains near Salt Lake City. Located near a spring, it was first occupied 7,000 years ago. Sparrow Hawk was a hunting camp for deer and bighorn sheep, but grinding stone fragments were found in all levels.[25]

The use of the uplands cannot be explained as an exodus from lowland to upland settlement. The early, lowland sites such as Danger and Hogup caves continued to be used, and in some ways their use intensified. Furthermore, new lowland cave sites, surely visible to earlier peoples but ignored, were occupied for the first time. These include Lakeside Cave (5000 B.P.), Black Rock Cave (6100 B.P.), Sandwich Shelter (7000 B.P.), Scribble Rock Shelter (5000 B.P.), and Spotten Cave (5600 B.P.).

Sites such as Bulldozer Dune in Salt Lake City and Playa View Dune on the Dugway Proving Ground are Middle Archaic campsites located in sand dunes. Dunes were more widespread in the Middle Archaic as dry lake beds were scoured by the wind. Anything but useless, dunes store water deep within them, and if they are even partially stabilized by vegetation, they become biological magnets supporting seed plants, rabbits, mice, voles, and reptiles. When Playa View Dune was occupied 5,000 years ago, Indian Rice Grass stabilized the dunes, and the seeds attracted rabbits. The people exploited both and returned to the dunes again and again. The desertification of the lowlands across the Great Basin was thus creating new opportunities, even as the dying wetlands took others away.[26]

It is tempting to try to explain the addition of sites and their extension into the uplands by "finger-matching" cultural change with the levels of Great Salt Lake.[27] The lake nearly dried up between 7,000 and 6,000 years ago. It expanded just after 6,000 years ago, inundating wetlands and creating new ones, only to regress again about 5,300 years ago, very close to the earliest radiocarbon date at Swallow Shelter. Any number of changes in Great Salt Lake, its wetlands, or the surrounding environments might be matched with change in the archaeological record. On the one hand, the association is real, because the natural environment did in fact shape people's lives, as it does today if we really think about it. But matching lake levels with, say, the appearance of upland occupation explains nothing, even though it helps describe what happened.

An ecological evaluation of the changes in upland occupation during the Middle Archaic demands that we think in terms of process, not just correlations of individual causes, and that we think in terms of ecological relationships—trade-offs. The interplay of opportunities lost and found can be seen in the archaeology. Wetlands shrank and died, but sand dunes expanded and pinyon pines moved in. The tree lines continued their upward migration, and the sage and bunch grass shrublands that support grouse, mule deer, and bighorn sheep moved upward as well. The diminishment of wetlands is not all bad. Areas that were ponds and sloughs may have lost fish, mollusks, bulrush and cattail plants, and nesting areas for some types of waterfowl. But former ponds might be transformed into wet meadows of salt grass that supported other types of birds, as well as rodents, snakes, rabbits, pronghorn and, judging from the archaeology, bison. As with all change, the loss of the familiar is couched in the opportunities of the new.

The wetland at Danger Cave must have dwindled by the Middle Archaic—only a few waterfowl bones were found in those levels. The area was probably vegetated with shadscale and greasewood, and on the playa, pickleweed clung to a shallow water table under an otherwise barren surface. The marsh near Hogup Cave persisted, because duck and grebe bones were present in the Middle Archaic levels with only a minor depression in frequency from previous times.

Grassy shrublands and perhaps salt grass meadows covered the flats near Hogup Cave, because bison bone makes a marked debut in the Middle Archaic levels. Wetlands were certainly near Black Rock Cave, located on the south edge of Great Salt Lake, as attested by the bird bones and plant remains there.[28]

Wetlands just as surely persisted throughout the Middle Archaic at the foot of the Wasatch Front, where the lower reaches of the Jordan, Weber, and Bear rivers meandered across the dry bed of Great Salt Lake. Very few Archaic sites are known from the wetlands along the eastern shores of Great Salt Lake, but they are likely deeply buried in a geological environment where silts accumulate and obscure earlier sites. As we will see later, the wetlands east of Great Salt Lake yield hundreds of prehistoric sites, but the ones visible on the modern surface are much later.

A similar geological situation exists in Utah Valley, but sites such as Spotten Cave, on the slope overlooking Utah Lake above Santaquin, show that wetlands were nearby. It was first occupied around 5,500 years ago, just like so many others, and it yielded waterfowl and fish bones.[29]

A Middle Archaic burial was found eroding out of a beach near Mosida on the western shore of Utah Lake. The Mosida Burial was male, accompanied by a dog, some bone tools, a Northern Side-notched projectile point, and some basketry. The basketry is 4,700 years old. A stone fishing line sinker was also found at the site, although not in direct association with the burial. Sinkers were used with long "set" lines affixed with numerous hooks. A multitude of stone sinkers are documented at Pyramid Lake in western Nevada, and an increased investment in fishing technology may reflect another tiny step toward intensification in the Middle Archaic.[30]

FIGURE 4.6

Notched stones such as these were used as net and line sinkers for fishing. Typical fish hooks of bone and wood are also shown. (Sketch by Jennifer Hulse)

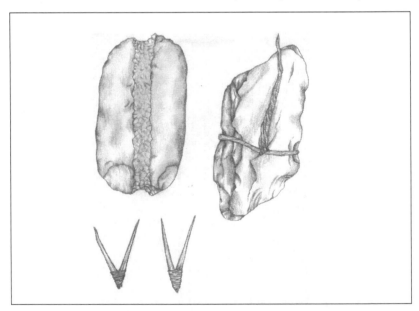

The once-enormous wetland on the Old River Bed at Dugway dried up in the Middle Archaic, explaining why most of the sites there are Paleoindian through Early Archaic in age. The vanishing of the

Old River Bed after millennia of abundance shows how much change can occur in some places, even as wetlands persisted in others. At Camels Back Cave, even the abundance of the drought-tolerant jackrabbit declined during the Middle Archaic.[31]

These changes were by no means limited to the eastern Great Basin—the drying out of the hard deserts of the Southern Great Basin suggest population densities so low in the Mojave Desert that the chain of cultural tradition seen in the Lake Mojave to Pinto complexes was broken during the Middle Archaic.[32]

Occupations were brief, people were mobile, and although most sites show a variety of activities, many stops were for specific tasks. The Middle Archaic stratum 5 at Hogup Cave contained a thin layer of pronghorn hair over the floor of the cave. Perhaps several pronghorn were taken nearby and people brought the hides to the cave to scrape the hair from them in preparation for tanning. Stratum 6 housed a "homogeneous band of pickleweed chaff," conjuring images of huge mounds of the plant brought to the cave to winnow the tiny seeds from the abundant chaff. There is a correlation between the number of rabbit bones at Hogup Cave and fragments of netting and cordage used to trap rabbits, showing the fit between individual occupations, the equipment used, and what the land had to offer.

The epitome of Middle Archaic opportunism and thoroughness is Lakeside Cave. Located in an embayment on the west side of the Lakeside Mountains, the beaches outside the cave occasionally became a spectacle of superabundance. When the winds and water on the playa were right, untold millions of drowned grasshoppers were washed into ankle deep windrows that could be 10 miles long. The naturally dried and salted grasshoppers were processed in the cave, and layers of the distinctive oolitic beach sands of Great Salt Lake attest to the transport of hoppers to the cave. People surely gorged on the windfall; the coprolites, the dried human feces found in the cave, bristle with grasshopper exoskeletons. Hoppers were also ground into a paste to make desert fruitcake, a product that could be transported and stored (see Chapter 1 Sidebar: Forager Cuisine). People knew the signals of wind and storms that made them travel to Lakeside for the event, and hoppers were harvested there from 5,000 to 1,000 years ago, with a three-century heyday beginning 4,700 years ago. People in all kinds of societies eat insects. Roasting and eating grasshoppers at Lakeside Cave with colleagues in the early 1980s, we found that the strip of white meat down their backs is reminiscent of shellfish. We dubbed them "desert lobster."[33]

FIGURE 4.7

This human coprolite (desiccated human feces) from Lakeside Cave bristles with fragments of grasshopper exoskeletons. (Courtesy of David Madsen and the Utah State Historical Society)

People moved across the landscape with fluidity and an intermittent presence in any particular place. Frequent layers of dust and sometimes layers of rock spall from the roof of cave sites attest to times when people were absent. For instance, a layer in Camels Back Cave identifies a 400-year span beginning about 5,600 years ago when the cave was completely ignored.

The connection of people to each place was finely tuned to an intimate knowledge of the entire landscape, and the people's annual movements habitually encompassed all habitats. Over the centuries, when climate change made new resources available, successive generations learned to live with the new. The spread of the pinyon pine during the Middle Archaic is an example of human response to shifting options and tradeoffs.

Pinyon pine spread in the eastern Great Basin during the Early Archaic and appears at Danger Cave over 8,000 years ago, but it took thousands of years to colonize all the places we find it today. A key feature of the desert-mountain settlement pattern of the historic period is the exploitation of pine nuts (see Chapter 1: Subsistence).

The Early Archaic use of the pinyon nut was, however, incidental because of the irregular nature of upland use. As time wore on, the pinyon pine increased in importance, and so did the number of archaeological sites located in the pinyon forests. The beginning of the desert-mountain settlement pattern seems rooted in the Middle Archaic.

The peoples of the Middle Archaic were of the same heritage as those who came before. This is attested by the basketry, a subtle art form that takes a long time to learn, and conveys a great deal of information about traditions and change. The earliest basketry was constructed by twining. The coiled baskets that make their appearance in the Early and especially the Middle Archaic grew out of this twining tradition. Together they show continuity of heritage in construction and style throughout the Archaic in the eastern Great Basin.

Eastern Great Basin basketry also shows connections with the peoples of southern Idaho, southwestern Wyoming, eastern Nevada, and the entire northern Colorado Plateau all the way south to the Colorado River. But it contrasts with the northern and western Great Basin. The use of coiled basketry is not as common or as early there, but then routine seed processing seems to come to those places later. The basketry reflects the huge geographic extent of human associations during the Archaic and is another symbol of an expansive sense of place.

James Adovasio of Mercyhurst College in Pennsylvania has examined more prehistoric basketry from our region than anyone. He observes that by 6,500–6,000 years ago, the Eastern Basin Basketry Tradition is so distinct that a "frontier" can be seen with other regions, especially the American Southwest. The differences within the various Basin-Plateau basketry traditions are less obvious and indicate common roots. Contrast between Adovasio's Western and Northern Great Basin Basketry Traditions and those of California is apparent after 4,000 years ago, but these differences are less than between the Basin-Plateau and the Southwest. Centers of isolation and appropriation of space, as well as interaction, were thus defined during the Middle Archaic.[34] In ethnographic cases of American Indian band societies, the manufacture of basketry is most often done by females. Could these broad patterns in the occurrence of basketry techniques be a window to women's movement over landscapes on scales of centuries and millennia?

Sidebar: Humans and the Pinyon Pine

Life among the historic period Native Americans across much of the Great Basin revolved around the abundant, nutritious, and storable pinyon pine nut. Pine nuts are inexpensive to collect, relative to many other storable wild resources. But the pinyon tree was once rare in the Great Basin, and Native American life without it was decidedly different.

Pioneering archaeological research in the early 1970s by David Thomas explored the relationship between native peoples and the pinyon pine. Thomas used the 1930s ethnographic work of Julian Steward to construct a model predicting the kinds and locations of archaeological remains expected if the pinyon-using pattern existed in the past. In the Reese River Valley in central Nevada where Thomas worked, pinyon nut exploitation similar to that of the historic period Shoshone began only about 5,000 years ago. A few years later, Thomas excavated Gatecliff Shelter in central Nevada and found evidence that pinyon arrived in the area only about 5,000 years ago.[a] Humans adopted the pine nut and adjusted their lives about the time it became available.

Twenty-five years ago, the presence of pinyon forests in the Great Basin was seen as the result of a mass migration of the tree from its Pleistocene range in southern Nevada, Arizona, and Mexico. The tree has a symbiotic relationship with the Pinyon Jay, Clark's Nutcracker, and other jaybirds. The birds harvest the nuts and fly away to their nests, sometimes beyond the grove of trees. A few of the seeds fall to the ground and sprout, giving birth to new forests. Estimates by botanists based on the growth rate of the trees and the habits of the birds show that the migration rate varies from one to two miles per year. Using these numbers, we can estimate that pinyon could have migrated from southern Nevada, where it lived 11,000 years ago, to its northern limits in only 2,000 to 3,000 years.

Research using the botanical treasures from wood rat middens and archaeological sites shows that the migration of the pinyon tree is not as straightforward as once thought. The trees don't arrive in the mountain east of Ely, Nevada, until 6,300 years ago, but farther north at Danger Cave near Wendover, the trees were nearby 7,900 years ago. Pinyon did not reach the Owens Valley in eastern California until after 2,000 years ago and even later in the Stillwater Mountains east of Reno, Nevada.

It turns out that climate and topography may be as important as the birds. In the eastern Great Basin, the pinyon pine may have been present during the Pleistocene in small groves along the edges of some valleys. As climate warmed, they spread and appeared early in some places. Warming during the Middle Archaic fostered the spread of pinyon forests toward their present range, where they now occupy a thermal belt along the lower mountain flanks. In the high valleys of the central Great Basin, pinyon probably did not survive the Pleistocene and thus had to migrate from southern sources. The western Great Basin may represent yet a third migration route. The path from the Pleistocene homelands of the trees in the southern Great Basin had to cross hot desert and low, dry mountain ranges. These impediments, along with the different climatic regime downwind of the Sierra Nevada Range, may have slowed pinyon migration until relatively late in antiquity.

People used pine nuts as soon as they became available, as they did at Danger Cave in the Early Archaic. David Madsen and David Rhode analyzed a column of the cave deposits that were not excavated by Jesse Jennings in 1950. Conducting a more intensive analysis, they found many pinyon nut hulls that had been overlooked but did not find the pine needles and cone parts that would be expected if the trees had grown nearby and had been introduced by animals or wind. It appears that people transported pine nuts to the cave 7,900 years ago.

As long as the trees remained limited in distribution, and as long as people were focusing their occupations in the valleys as they were in the Early Archaic, pine nut use would remain incidental. When the tree became widely available in the Middle Archaic, the stage was set for the nut to constitute a significant niche in the economy.

By the Middle Archaic in northwestern Utah, the number of sites located in the pinyon vegetation belt increased markedly. Sites such as Swallow Shelter yield the seeds of Great Basin Wild Rye and Indian Rice Grass, and experiments show that these resources are far more expensive to procure and prepare than pine nuts. Unfortunately, no one has gone back to Swallow Shelter to see if the elusive pinyon hulls were in fact present. The significance of increased pine nut use in the Middle Archaic is that the desert-mountain settlement pattern that we recognize in the historic period is rooted in these times.

In other parts of the Great Basin, the pinyon pine arrived much later, or the nuts were ignored for awhile even after they were available. The settlement pattern in the Owens Valley in eastern California was centered on villages in the valley. Pinyon nuts are cheap to collect, but studies show that they are very expensive to transport. Lowland dwellers would have literally eaten the nuts off of their backs before they could return significant supplies from the mountains to the village bases. For this reason, pine nut use remained opportunistic and local in some parts of the Great Basin.

By the historic period, the pine nut was the centerpiece of the economy across much of the Great Basin, and people located their winter villages to be near the cached nuts. This pattern may not have been as strong during the Middle Archaic, but it began during those ancient times.[b]

FIGURE 4.8

Map of basketry complexes of the Archaic period that reflect 6,000 years of heritage in the Basin-Plateau. Basketry is an intricate technology learned through long tutelage. It can reflect technological change, ethnic heritage, and connections among peoples. It may be one of the clearest indicators of female lineage to the extent basket weaving was gendered in the past as it is among historic-period Native Americans. The Eastern Basin-Plateau basketry complex is significant for understanding the post-Archaic Fremont culture. The Western Great Basin complex shows the role of Californian peoples in the Archaic western Basin. The Northern tradition symbolizes the connections of Archaic southeastern Oregon peoples with those on the Columbia Plateau.

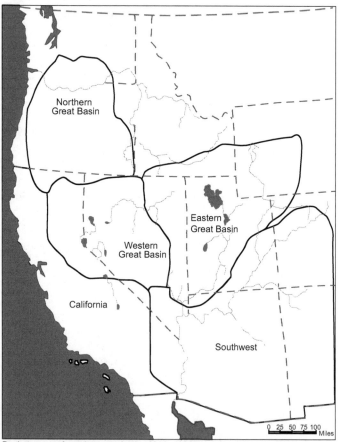

Basketry manufacturing complexes: 6000–4000 B.P. (after Adovasio 1974)

Northern Great Basin. Open and close, flexible and rigid twining. Coiling in minor quantities.

California. Twining or plaiting probably present in some form. Coiling may be present near end of this time.

Southwest. Open and close, flexible and rigid twining. Several varieties of coiling present. Ties with Great Basin, Mexican affinities in the south.

Eastern Great Basin. Twining present but relatively insignificant. Stacked coiling varieties dominate one-rod and bundled foundations present.

Western Great Basin. Open and close, flexible and rigid twining. Bunched foundation coiling introduced from Eastern Great Basin. Coiling begins to dominate by end of period.

Change was afoot in the Middle Archaic, and some new projectile point/knife styles made their appearance. Stone tool making was certainly not restricted to men, but again taking a cue from ethnographic cases of Native American band societies, the record of living peoples suggests that the manufacture of projectile points of defined styles was largely male. Are the far-flung patterns in Middle Archaic projectile point styles telling us something about the long-distance movement of men during their lives, and over generations of men?[35]

The Gypsum and Pinto point styles, and the slightly later Elko Corner-notched points, spread widely across the region. Elko and the Northern Side-notched types spread across the Rocky Mountains to the Columbia Plateau. It would be as risky to use point styles to identify specific "peoples" as using the type of automobile one drives to do the same, but, nevertheless, the similarity in point styles traces connections in some sense. These far-flung styles show that people interacted widely across the region.

But the character of mobility was changing. Camps were occupied briefly for particular tasks, but they were occupied again and again. Stone tool kits were prepared for repeated use of the same place, and this is why the Middle Archaic stone tool technology resembles that of more settled people. Mobility during the Middle Archaic was more redundant than in previous times, even as the total geographic range of mobility was higher than in the Early Archaic.[36]

Change in social arrangements was also afoot, and as with food ways and settlement patterns we gain our first glimpse of the desert-mountain social organization described ethnographically. Kinship, group identity, and the frequency of contacts among people were structured by the role of food storage in the historic period system. The Middle Archaic was only beginning to move in this direction, and since population numbers remained low, it is tempting to compare it with the ethnographic period when native populations were also low in the wake of Euroamerican contact. However, the ethnographic pattern, particularly the use of pine nuts, seems more intensive in some parts of the Great Basin, such as California's Owens Valley, during the historic period than it does in the Middle Archaic. Storage was probably less important in the Middle Archaic, and mobility was probably higher than in the historic Basin-Plateau. Thus, some distinction remains warranted between the cultural patterns of Middle Archaic peoples and those of the indigenous peoples of recent centuries.

Hints about sense of place are detectable in the record of obsidian toolstone found at Danger and Hogup caves. The sources of obsidian

FIGURE 4.9

Examples of Middle Archaic lifeways 6000 B.P.–2000 B.P. High desert foragers were widespread across the region, and the Wetlands Pattern was sprinkled in places where a logistic system paid off. These contrasting lifeways could have formed the basis of linguistic and ethnic difference, but clearly they were not hard boundaries. This seems especially true when we break from the tendency to characterize ancient life as moments in time rather than real people whose life histories could be subject to significant change.

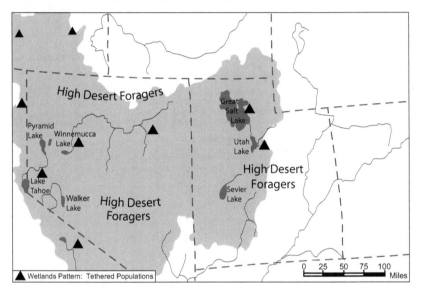

in tools and flakes discarded or lost at the caves suggest a two-part procurement system. Most of the obsidian at Hogup cave came from near Malad and Brown's Bench in southern Idaho. Yet at Danger Cave, only 45 miles across the salt flats to the south, the obsidian from Topaz and other Sevier Desert sources to the south were favored. Some obsidian crossed this boundary, and although this may indicate two distinct forager settlement systems, the mixing is consistent with some fluidity among group membership.[37]

Many years ago, Gary Fry and James Adovasio compared basketry, points, and other artifacts between Danger and Hogup caves and speculated that they were used by different groups of people. As with the obsidian sourcing, there is a hint of distinction across the Great Salt Lake Desert. But how can we conceive of different "groups" of real, living people when the patterns found in these comparisons span thousands of years—scores of human generations? We can't, but perhaps it is even more intriguing that the connections span eons, and transcend the lives of individuals, even as the demands of living made much of life decidedly local.[38]

THE LATE ARCHAIC AND A LAND FILLED WITH FORAGERS (3000–1000 B.P.)

If the Middle Archaic is a watershed, then across much of the Basin-Plateau the Late Archaic is a culmination of the foraging way of life. Once the entire landscape had become ensnared during the Middle Archaic, and every possible resource was fair game, shortfall could no longer be handled by simply adding a new resource or a new place. During the Late Archaic, the wilderness came under the brunt of the foraging presence, bringing fundamental change to the way most societies in the region were organized. This is the story on a large scale, but as we will see, the diversity of lifeways and probably ethnic groups, and the local variation that long characterized the Archaic, continued to play out on smaller scales across the region.

The historically known wetland settlement pattern was added to the nascent desert-mountain pattern. These were not the tethered wetland-valley settlements of the Paleoarchaic or Early Archaic, nor were they the few isolated cases of residence anchored to the sparse wetlands of the Middle Archaic. The wetlands pattern described for the historic period features villages for at least part of the year, with goods transported and stored at these central bases. People were concentrated in these places, increasing the overall population of the region.

Population growth was not restricted to the Basin-Plateau, nor was the region isolated. Indigenous populations in Mexico and the Southwest grew significantly after 4,000 years ago. The northward spread of farming, and especially farming immigrants, brought new cultures, new languages, and enormous change to the Basin-Plateau. The demographic effects of Southwestern farming likely extended well beyond the range of farming per se, pushing into the deserts of the southern Great Basin. Too, population growth on the Northwest coast and coastal California would also have been felt in the Great Basin. The spread of bow and arrow technology across the Basin-Plateau during the Late Archaic likely was wrapped up with demographic patterns elsewhere on the continent.

The archaeology of the Late Archaic contrasts with the scant record of the Middle Archaic. In the well-studied western Great Basin, the number of sites and villages dating between 4,000 and 1,500 years ago is truly remarkable in comparison to the previous millennia.[39]

The Stillwater region of western Nevada has long been known for yielding early "villages," such as the Humboldt Lakebed site. Archaeologists such as Robert Elston, Christopher Raven, Robert Kelly, and David Zeanah show that beginning about 3,000 years ago, the shifting wetland habitats of the Stillwater Marsh became hubs of population. Villages served as the anchor, and instead of moving a scattered people to the resources, more resources were being moved to larger groups of people.[40]

There was a large, relatively healthy population in the Stillwater area, as attested by hundreds of skeletal remains studied with the permission of the Northern Paiute tribes. The skeletons revealed a strong distinction in the mobility of males and females, a tale told by the growth patterns of limb bones. Engineering analyses of long bones can distinguish mountain hikers from flatland walkers, and can identify those who bent over to work with their arms. Stillwater males hiked frequently over steep terrain, moving in and out of the lowlands to obtain everything from game to nuts, toolstone, medicines, and special woods, to name just a few. Female skeletons show strenuous upper-body labor, but not as much long-distance walking over rugged terrain. Women anchored the villages, moved locally, and did the work. People suffered from episodes of nutritional stress, especially when they were children, reminding us that even with all their knowledge and techniques to hedge against risk, life remained a gamble, just as it does today.[41]

The famous equipment caches from Lovelock Cave and other caves in western Nevada offer a window to a changing sense of place. In one pit at Lovelock Cave there were exquisite duck decoys and snares, but they were hidden below a false bottom and covered with dried fish to make it look like an innocuous food cache. Caches such as this served as lifelines into remote areas (see earlier Sidebar: The Built Environment). The use of this particular kind of cache seems to decline by about 1,500 years ago. As people attached themselves more to the wetlands, they would be less interested in maintaining caches to access far-flung locations.[42]

Perhaps the Stillwater area simply filled up with people between 3,000 and 1,500 years ago and was used to the point where the Lovelock style of cave caching became obsolete. Equipment and goods were increasingly transported and cached at the villages. Indeed, more neighbors may have worked against maintaining the

FIGURE 4.10

Hidden Cave (*dead center, left of road*) was excavated by David H. Thomas and is an example of a caching site located at the gateway to the Stillwater Marsh. The entrance to the cave was a low, narrow passage, and it was not an ideal place of residence. It was, however, an excellent place to cache equipment, food, and perhaps medicines and raw materials; a warehouse in the built environment. The light-colored areas in the background and foreground were, at various times, ponds, marshes, and salt grass meadows harboring a diversity of plant and animal life important to foragers. (Photo by Richard Holmer and Steven Simms)

cave caches, because people could no longer control who knew about them and who would use them. Cave caches no longer served as a public good, because neighbors and kin reduced them to a tragedy of the commons. The increasingly human landscape caused people to place more emphasis on privately owned and controlled goods. We will see the significance of this change below.

Trends similar to those at Stillwater are evident elsewhere. In the Harney Basin of southeastern Oregon, semipermanent villages associated with wetlands and Malheur Lake are known from over 4,000 years ago and endured until about 1,000 years ago. The pattern resembles that recorded historically for the Klamath-Modoc groups of southwestern Oregon, who constructed substantial pithouses anchoring winter villages. Mobility increased in other seasons as summer camps supplied the villages. Late Archaic structures from Harney

Basin, such as at the Dunn, McCoy Creek, and Blitzen Marsh sites, are earth lodges located near wetlands. They contained substantial numbers of large, heavy ground stone tools, including net weights for fishing and the great diversity of tools we would expect to find at villages. Food remains included fish, waterfowl, aquatic mammals such as muskrat, and the usual deer, bighorn sheep, and rabbit. Many smaller, special use sites were found in both the wetlands and uplands. These verify that village life and concentrations of people demand the full exploitation of large amounts of terrain.[43]

Surprise Valley in northeastern California offers an important twist on Late Archaic use and, like the Stillwater area, reminds us that we are not talking about an arrow-like progression from desert nomads to wetland villages across the region. Recall that Surprise Valley was home to substantial earth lodges in the Middle Archaic, over 5,000 years ago. Later houses in Surprise Valley are smaller and lack the huge investment of the earlier houses. But they are still large (3–6 meters in diameter), and there were dozens of them, often stacked one on top of the other from centuries of rebuilding. Mobility seems to have increased, but the occupation of this narrow valley with many habitats available close by remained intense and regular. Even during the Middle to Late Archaic transition, local environments and cultural traditions continued to produce local ways of doing things.[44]

Population also grew in southern Idaho, but villages and intensive salmon fishing awaited the passage of more time. At the Wahmuza site on the Fort Hall Bottoms in southeastern Idaho, occupation over the last 3,000 years shows that large dwellings were used repeatedly, and, although changes came and went, the record is strikingly uninterrupted right up to historic times.[45]

The filling of the land with foragers is not as clear on the Colorado Plateau. Indeed, some years ago David Madsen and Michael Berry reevaluated the stratigraphy of cave sites to argue for a clean break between the Late Archaic and the subsequent Fremont farming populations. Certainly there were changes in the way places were used, and some places even fell out of use, but accumulating evidence suggests that the eastern Basin and Plateau did not experience regional depopulation during the Late Archaic.[46]

The Late Archaic across the Colorado Plateau was a prelude to major changes. The pattern of high-desert foraging continued, but there are hints that some people settled down a little more, in

FIGURE 4.11

Late Archaic Transformations: 2000–1000 B.P. Immigrant farmers from the Southwest play a role in founding the Fremont. Tethered Wetlands foraging populations are found in the Late Archaic, such as those well documented in western Nevada. In turn, those areas shaped the circumstances of the high desert foragers by forging more connection and tethering even for those rural dwellers. Every place did not proceed alike, and the example of greater mobility in Late Archaic Surprise Valley, California, is an example of variation among these patterns. Alpine villages were founded at astonishing elevations, but only in some places. The high-altitude villages of the Late Archaic and thereafter depart from the previous pattern of sporadic use of places over 10,000 feet. Together these patterns show the variety of ways that sense of place changed in the Late Archaic, a land filled with foragers.

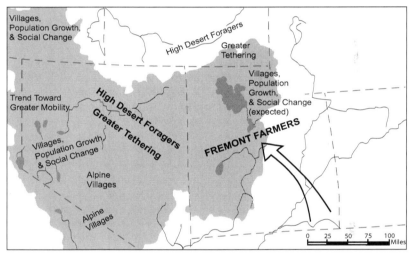

Late Archaic Transformation: 2000 B.P. - 1000 B.P.

larger groups, and with a more complicated social organization. The investment in housing increased during the Late Archaic on the Plateau; a light structure at the Carcass Corners site a short distance from the Fremont River near Teasdale was used 2,200 years ago; a pithouse at the Confluence Site along Muddy Creek on the San Rafael Swell, and found during construction of Interstate 70, was used 1,600 years ago; the Sandy Ridge pithouse south of Moab was used 1,800 years ago; and the Orchard pithouse in Moab was used 2,200 years ago. These were in well-watered places, but Late Archaic house structures found at Aspen Shelter at 8,200 feet on the Old Woman Plateau above Castle Valley and used between 4,000 and 1,000 years ago suggest that even the higher terrain was more densely settled.[47] As elsewhere, sites on the Plateau varied in how they were used, with some showing no Late Archaic occupation. As more and more dates are found in open sites, complementing what we know from cave sites, it is increasingly apparent that the Late Archaic on the Colorado Plateau was a busy time at least in some places.

The fascinating split-twig figurines of the Colorado Plateau may suggest changes in social organization during the Middle to Late Archaic. Known since the 1930s from isolated ledges and caves in the Grand Canyon, split-twig figurines are the images of deer and bighorn sheep fashioned of a single long strand of split willow. They are often about 5 cm high, and although they look like "toys" at first glance, they are symbolic objects with magical implications and were often cached in tiny crevices on cliff faces. Split-twig figurines have long inspired archaeologists and Native Americans and provide a window into the relationship between social organization and worldview.

There are now many examples of dated split-twig figurines, and we can recognize two traditions of manufacture, perhaps reflecting changing social contexts. The long known Grand Canyon figurine

FIGURE 4.12

Split-twig figurines are more than mere "ceremonial" objects; they are a window into past social systems and how they changed. Their use begins after 5000 B.P. when they are placed in remote locations, sometimes in association with shamans' bundles. After 3500 B.P., they also appear in less remote, even residential settings. Objects such as these play various roles in historically known band and tribal societies ranging from personal fetishes related to vision and power questing to clan totems signifying a connection between lineage and place. (Courtesy of Alan Schroedl)

complex employed the figurines as personal fetishes that were hidden in cliffs along the Grand Canyon. Figurines of similar age from Newberry Cave in the Mojave Desert in California may be associated with shaman's caches and activities. A later complex of split-twig figurines is typically found in the refuse of habitation sites in Canyonlands, the San Rafael Swell, and near Moab. Instead of isolated personal fetishes this complex, which spans perhaps 80 human generations, more likely represents clan totemism. First used as ritual items between 4900–3700 B.P., the figurines connected clans to place. After 3,500 years ago, they may represent the emblems of clans and corporate groups, showing an increase in the organizational complexity of Late Archaic foragers. Some sort of upheaval or discontinuity in social organization caused a decline in their use, although three of the figurines dating to only 2,100 years ago suggest some persistence to and perhaps continuity with the earliest period of agriculture in the Southwest called Basketmaker II.[48] Split-twig figurines are just one small line of evidence, but we will see below that they are a milepost for basic changes in social organization in the Late Archaic.

The unification of society and landscape, and the expression of the sacred and the secular as one, is perhaps no more apparent than in rock art. Rock art traditions are as old as human occupation of the region, and by the Late Archaic rock art dotted the landscape in important ways. Once thought of largely in terms of hunting magic, maps, and literal communication, rock art studies increasingly recognize that although rock art communicates, it is not something that can be translated per se; it is part of forager cognitive systems that are decidedly non-Western.

Rock art was created in a variety of social and gender contexts and served many purposes. Some was associated with the pragmatic and was created in important landscapes such as seed or root collecting areas. Some was created in places of power that may be linked to rituals, such as rites of passage, as well as journeys, oral history, and worldview. A burst of rock art production in the Late Archaic southwestern Great Basin may be related to the elevation of big game hunting to prestige seeking—an activity that heightens the social significance of an activity that had long been spiritual as well as economic. Rock art harmonizes the sacred, the secular, and place. Dating of rock art remains difficult, but its production over time grew, and by the Late Archaic there are many local variations and broad regional traditions.[49]

Even in the places without villages, there is evidence of increased human activity in the Great Basin. From southeastern Nevada at O'Malley Shelter to Connley Caves in southeastern Oregon, sites continued to be occupied for the first time after 4,500 years ago. The percentage and frequency of Elko projectile/knife points steadily increased in the eastern Great Basin during the last 3,000 years, and the trend is so pervasive that it suggests population growth, not merely change in fashion.[50]

James Creek Shelter near Elko, Nevada, offers a glimpse of life in the high desert. Excavation in 1984 by Robert Elston and Elizabeth Budy showed that the site was first occupied about 3,200 years ago. It is located in an isolated rock outcrop overlooking a sagebrush steppe. Infrequent stopovers by hunting parties identify the first centuries of use, but people were using toolstone from the Tosawihi quarries over 30 miles away. Later visits were related to large and medium mammal hunting, seed processing, fishing, and bison hunting. The use of more local toolstone increased then, too. By 2,000 years ago, occupations at the shelter lengthened, and even though visits were brief, it became a base camp. Occupations were frequent enough that the camp features, such as activity surfaces and hearths, served as templates for the next use of the camp. Over the next 1,000 years, the intensity of use greatly increased, and the occupation layers were closely packed. People not only used the tools they brought to James Creek Shelter but also manufactured stone tools, cordage, and basketry there. Small residential structures appeared in the shelter, housing families for stays of perhaps weeks. True village life did not come to the high deserts of the northeastern Great Basin in the Late Archaic, but even there sense of place reflected a move toward relentless utilization.[51]

The use of alpine environments also changed. Extremely high places over 10,000 feet in the White Mountains on the Nevada-California border and at Alta Toquima in central Nevada were used as hunting camps beginning about 4,500 years ago. After 1750 B.P., small, summertime villages appeared in these exceptionally alpine areas. There are house foundations of rock, grinding stones, and other tools. The archaeology suggests that whole families spent the summer near or above timberline, and some of the villages are over 12,000 feet in elevation! Not all Great Basin mountain ranges have these Late Archaic villages, and their use does not seem to have been driven by population pressure in the lowlands, at least not on a local scale. Nor is it explained by peculiar cultural characteristics. Like the case of

Surprise Valley, the patchy occurrence of this striking phenomenon reminds us that much of life was based on people meshing their broader cultural traditions with the local "tyranny of circumstance," even as the region as a whole was filling up, gearing up, and undergoing significant cultural change.[52]

The movement of nonperishable items such as toolstone helps trace trade patterns. The long-distance movement of stone by mobile Paleoindian colonists gave way to greater use of local stone in the Middle Archaic. The movement of marine shell used for jewelry further traces changing trade patterns. Olivella shell comes from the warm waters of the Pacific Ocean off the coast of southern California and appeared by the Middle Archaic at Danger, Hogup, and Camels Back caves. The volume of long-distance movement of stone, and especially shell, increased over time, and, significantly, the peak period of trade between California and the Great Basin occurred between 4,000 and 2,000 years ago—the transition from the Middle to Late Archaic.[53]

A fascinating example of intensification is the use of snares and traps. Snare manufacture is an investment in a technology that demands that the hunter know an area intimately and intends to use it repeatedly. It is a window into the mind of the hunter and signals a willingness to invest in the future. The equipment must be maintained, and the take is small and expensive compared to hunting larger game. But unlike with big game, the harvest is steady, it works while people do other things, and the investment in the equipment pays off in the reliability of provisioning for a family whose needs are renewed every few days.

Sites across the region, but particularly the caves of the eastern Great Basin, track changes in the use of snares and traps. The curious artifacts known as Promontory Pegs were triggers for snares and deadfall traps, and they are found by the hundreds. These are merely shaped sticks a few centimeters long with a point on one end. Promontory Pegs were used in the Middle Archaic (and probably earlier), but their frequency increases dramatically only in the last few thousand years.[54]

We find mixed signals in the archaeology of the Late Archaic on the Wasatch Front. On the one hand, human sprawl extends to new sites. At Fish Springs, on the southern edge of the Great Salt Lake Desert, occupation at Crab Cave began at 4400 B.P., Barn Owl Cave at 4000 B.P., and Fish Springs Cave at 2500 B.P. A little to the north at the wetlands surrounding Blue Lake south of Wendover, the

Mosquito Willie's site began at 4000 B.P. and intensified thereafter. Intriguing hints of occupation 2,500 years ago, and the possibility of fish exploitation, come from one part of the Goshen Island site on Utah Lake. The Hot Springs and Airport sites north of Salt Lake City also yield Late Archaic occupations.[55]

On the other hand, familiar lake-edge sites such as Hogup and Danger Caves experienced much lighter use from 3,000 to 2,000 years ago, and Black Rock Cave may have been abandoned. This pattern was not restricted to the lowlands and cannot be explained as a migration from lowlands to uplands. The Wasatch Plateau uplands located between the San Pete Valley and Price, Utah, were not used as intensively between 3,500 and 2,000 years ago.[56]

At one time, the evidence for a Late Archaic interruption of occupation at cave sites across the eastern Great Basin and northern Colorado Plateau was so graphic that some proposed that the region was abandoned. Reminiscent of the speculation of an Altithermal abandonment in the Middle Archaic, this Late Archaic "hiatus" suffered as sample sizes grew and the overall tally of dated sites increased.[57] Those who saw abandonment and hiatus were not dreaming; there are indeed particular places where the human landscape changed drastically during the Late Archaic. But, overall, more and more foragers were living here, not fewer. The distribution of foraging societies is more mosaic than monolithic.

Add to these mixed signals the near complete absence of information about the marshlands bordering Great Salt Lake and Utah Lake. If the Wasatch Front were anything like Stillwater Marsh, the Harney Basin, and Surprise Valley cases, we would expect substantial settlements in these areas. Two very different factors are at work here. One is the nature of the geology, and the other is the nature of the climate and habitats during the Late Archaic. The problem is that each of these factors confounds the other.

The surface geology of the Great Salt Lake wetlands causes Archaic-age sediments to be buried, often deeply. There is nothing unusual about this, because geology always conditions what we see on the surface. Although some desert surfaces can be very old, accumulating everything that people did for thousands of years, others are alternately hidden and exposed. But so far, the record of the Late Archaic is very weak on the Wasatch Front and in other similar situations such as Utah Valley and the Sevier Valley in central Utah. We know Late Archaic people were in these places, because projectile points of this age abound, not only in the uplands but in the lowlands, too. The Hot Springs and Airport sites are examples, and the Burch Creek site in South Ogden and Green Canyon Cave near Logan show an Archaic presence, as do the contents of numerous private artifact collections. As more sites are found from large projects such as the Kern River Expansion Project, we recognize that the Late Archaic was a time of dramatic change that provides rich archaeology.[58]

The upland habitats may have improved at the time in response to increasing moisture beginning about 3,000 years ago with the Neoglacial. Zooarchaeologists David Byers and Jack Broughton used data from Hogup Cave, Camels Back Cave, and Homestead Cave to show that during times of increased moisture, there were more deer, bighorn sheep, and rabbits. They also find that the Utah sucker returned when the waters of Great Salt Lake were less saline during high stands.[59]

The geology does not allow us to really know the full picture of settlement for the Late Archaic eastern Great Basin, but our knowledge of the climate and habitats suggests that much should have been happening. We should not be surprised to find substantial settlements associated with lowlands similar to the Late Archaic houses in Surprise Valley. The settlement pattern may have been similar to the Stillwater pattern of shifting small villages. We simply don't know, but it is premature to assume the Late Archaic was a time of fewer people, much less an abandonment of lowland use, along the Wasatch Front, and other valleys of the eastern Great Basin.

A CULTURAL SEA CHANGE: THE SHIFT IN VALUES FROM PUBLIC TO PRIVATE GOODS

The Late Archaic might be the first time we can say there were concentrations of people in lowland villages and surrounding, scattered populations of high desert foragers. This brought hints of inequality to Basin-Plateau societies that had been egalitarian up to this point. The inevitable consequence of filling the land was to nudge societies toward territoriality, magnified notions of private property, and kinship arrangements that emphasized group boundaries more than fluidity in group membership. Recall that in the ethnographic Great Basin, corporate groups were more often found in the wetlands settlement pattern than in the more fluid desert-mountain pattern (see Chapter 1: Social and Political Organization). To be sure, the

Basin-Plateau never saw strong social hierarchies or inherited chiefs, let alone kings, but the road toward social complexity was taken in the Late Archaic.

Robert Bettinger observes that after 4,000 years ago, and especially by 2,000 years ago, there is a change in how societies were organized. In addition to the larger populations and more frequent use of settlements, there is evidence of intensification of effort across a variety of measures. He cites increased food storage, changes in stone tool technology, and, after about 2,000 years ago, the spread of the bow and arrow and even pottery among Basin-Plateau foragers.[60]

Society and sense of place adjusted to these changing times. Up until now, goods, foods, and places were seen as public things. Everyone could use anything, and the rules of marriage, family, and the tracing of lineage all promoted these public values. Kinship rules fostered connections among places, lineages, and bands. Some connections surely spanned language groups and fostered multilingualism. Boundaries among groups were weak, because people were scattered and groups had to be fluid and responsive. At times, populations were too small, producing a shortage of marriage partners. A social system that was fluid in membership would, under these conditions, have been more successful than a closed, corporate system.[61]

In public systems, notions of private ownership and exclusion were unethical and dangerous values. The concept of territory referred to where people lived, not to perceptions of ownership. Stored food and caches of equipment in the built environment were scattered, and there was little risk in leaving things behind or going out of one's way to defend them.

As the Late Archaic wore on, there was a shift in some places to a different perception of appropriate behavior and ethics. Increasingly, goods, things, and places became private, not in the personal sense but in the sense that my kin and my people needed these things and saw them as important. Kinship systems evolved to place more emphasis on the maintenance of group identity and corporate membership. Larger population sizes and villages were often in places of intermittent, surplus production that required more storage capacity than before. These circumstances favored a trend toward a private goods system.

Territoriality accompanies such systems, and by the Late Archaic it was probably more common to find places and times of high production appropriated by defined kin groups. Obsidian sourcing in the Owens Valley and others of eastern California shows that during the

Late Archaic people obtained their obsidian closer to home than in previous times. Place was being carved up into territories. The greater use of food storage also contributed to boundaries among people and concern over turf. The accumulation of stored food, control over facilities such as hunting blinds and pronghorn enclosures, and control of events such as fishing drives all became more common. Success in these afforded power, not in terms of force but in terms of negotiation, the ability to recruit new members to the group via marriage, and creation of networks of obligation.[62]

It should be no surprise that prestige became more important during the Middle to Late Archaic. Prestige thrives when there are more people, territoriality, and inequality. Kelly McGuire and William Hildebrandt think they have found evidence for this in the archaeology. They document an increase in big game hunting after about 4,000 years ago that continues for the next 2,000 years. Part of the increase in game was caused by improving climate, but it comes at the same time that we see all the other things that are the stuff of major change in the social organization—population growth, reduced mobility, territoriality, inequality, and artistic elaboration. In some places, plant resources also seem to have been used more intensively, suggesting that the increased attention to big game hunting was added to an economic system already running at full tilt. They argue that the effort to hunt more and more big game in the face of declining numbers was prestige seeking.[63]

Studies of hunter-gatherers around the world show that meat from large animals can play a key social role in a community. Hunters travel long distances and expend great effort to return with a prize that can be shared widely. With the advent of more settled villages, hunters would have had to go farther and work harder to do this, and the payoff was prestige and its benefits. These circumstances may even have favored the spread of the bow and arrow, a technology more amenable to individual hunting than the atlatl and the dart. Prestige seeking, privatization of resources, and the bow and arrow may go hand in hand.

These significant social changes did not happen everywhere. In the Owens Valley and others east of the southern Sierra Nevada Range, extensive seed and pine nut use did not appear until after 2,000 years ago. But in many places, prestige hunting was one more hint of change in people's social milieu, their conception of place, and of one another.

The split-twig figurine complex described previously is yet another window into Middle to Late Archaic social change. Nancy Coulam and Alan Schroedl argue that split-twig figurines were used as totems. They appeal to the rich worldwide ethnography describing totemism and find that totems occur in societies that are divided into corporate groups. Totems pass from generation to generation to maintain those groups and the statuses of their members.[64] The split-twig figurine complex, both in its ritual form featuring hidden caches of figurines in caves such as those in the Grand Canyon and at Newberry Cave in the Mojave Desert and the later examples found in domestic, household contexts on the Colorado Plateau, suggests an increase in corporate clans and a private goods system beginning after 5,000 years ago and continuing to 3,200 years ago and perhaps even later.

Of course, a private goods system is recognizable to any modern American, with our sacrosanct private property laws and high degree of individuality. The most important aspect of this change, however, is not a judgment about whether it was good or bad, right or wrong, but that it set the stage for rapid change.

During the Late Archaic it was more culturally acceptable, even necessary in a land filled with foragers, to make gains on one's neighbors by working harder and manipulating the fruits of that labor. Among foragers, chiefs were always charismatic figures, but when such people also controlled resources, their influence only increased. Although this trend toward intensification was a far cry from values that we embrace today, even the spotty and weak form this took in the Late Archaic set in motion a very different set of social arrangements.

The Late Archaic is at once a culmination and a presage of even greater change. The first hints of agriculture sprang from the seeds of decisions made by people living in the Late Archaic, locally and continentally. As with all history, the choices of those who came before constrain and shape the options of those who follow.

FARMING COMES TO UTAH

The earliest known maize in Utah was found in a storage pit dating between 1950 and 2100 B.P. at the Elsinore site south of Richfield.[65] It signaled a spread of farming that would proceed in stops and starts over the next 10 centuries. This was no wave of advance of a mighty new world order. Farming was brought by small bands of explorers and colonists from the Southwest, and also adopted by some indigenous foragers. Regardless of who made the choices, the enormous consequences of farming far outstripped those halting, initial decisions.

The answer to the question "Why did farming come to prehistoric Utah?" might seem obvious to modern Americans who experience the benefits of farming every day. But the picture is not so simple. Maize was domesticated over 5,000 years ago in central Mexico, thus its "invention" preceded its arrival to Utah by 100 human generations! Beans were domesticated almost as early, and squash maybe even earlier. By 3,500 years ago, farming reached southern Arizona and only a few centuries later spread to northwestern New Mexico.[66] Indigenous foragers of the Basin-Plateau had wide-ranging mobility patterns, far-flung trading connections, and obvious patterns of cultural style that spanned broad regions. They were surely not so isolated as to be unaware of changes happening in the Southwest. The arrival of farming cannot be understood through the cliché of progress.

Ironically, the additional ingredients to understand this situation are also easily recognized by modern Americans. First, we need to take into account the cultural context of immigrant farmers as well as the variety of indigenous forager cultures in the Late Archaic. Modern retailers, industrialists, and educators certainly understand that cultural context shapes what consumers buy, whether there is a potential market, and how students learn. People are savvy and will judge whether something new is worthwhile to them. What matters in this cost-benefit "equation" varies among individuals, but, in the end, those who make some choices have a competitive advantage over those who make others. The implications of people's choices may not even be apparent to them at the time but will inevitably contribute to an outcome. This is the nature of cultural evolution, and the transition to farming is a stark example.

For those people in the Southwest already practicing some farming 2,500 years ago, the up-front labor investment in farming, the tethering to the fields, and especially the stored food were accepted ways of life. The social ramifications of an annual hoard of food that needed to be shared, carefully managed, and even defended were familiar and accepted. In contrast to the situation of many Late Archaic foragers making minimal use of storage and living a life of periodic moves across many habitats, the world of farming probably seemed strange, risky, and perhaps even foolish.

Studies of the cost of farming versus foraging show that pre-historic farming was not always better. My own research in the early 1980s identified the return rates in calories gained by collecting and processing various wild plants and animals. Most of the storable seed resources, primarily grasses, are among the most expensive foods. Recall that this is why small-seed use lagged behind the use of other resources from Paleoindian through Middle Archaic times.[67]

In recent years, researchers have documented the costs of pre-historic corn farming. Renee Barlow found that ancient maize farm-ing was better than gathering most wild seeds, far worse than hunting most large and medium mammals, and about the same as harvesting quite a few wild resources such as pinyon pine nuts. Farming was not always the best choice for the discerning forager.[68]

Why then would some foragers adopt farming while others were conservative and resisted the change—perhaps even seeing it as a threat to their traditional way of life? Recall that during the Late Archaic, some places harbored seasonally stable villages, increased storage, and logistic systems that brought food, tools, and raw ma-terial to the people. The Late Archaic also saw fundamental change in the social context of some foragers, a change to a system of private goods from the previous cultural ethic of public goods. For these for-agers, the circumstances of occasional surplus, kinship rules more attuned to the maintenance of corporate group identity, and stronger ties to territory made the adoption of farming less strange. In some cases, the addition of farming to the cultural repertoire enabled indi-viduals and families to achieve a surplus of produce. Like a fish or rabbit drive, or a grasshopper or bulrush-root harvest, farming pro-vided another avenue to temporary riches. In a social system based on private goods, this was simply another advantage in a world of com-plicated networks of obligation, reciprocity, and competition among neighboring foragers.

Like all cultural change, tension is created when some people adopt new things and others resist. Immigrating Southwestern farm-ers attempting to colonize Utah added population to the land and pressured the animal and plant populations on which indigenous foragers relied. The farmers had to develop ways to live with the indigenous foragers, but because the farmer lived in small villages, they had the advantage of defense and stored food. To the native foraging populations, the immigrant farmers were disruptive, and the appropriation of territory and resources was disastrous to some.

In many places during the Late Archaic, the life of the "high-desert forager" remained much the same. There simply was no perception that an investment in agriculture would convey an advantage over anyone else, because advantage over others was seen as irrelevant. Indeed, such behavior was likely seen as improper. For these people, farming would come only if they were pushed so far into marginal lands and an impoverished life that they were forced to attach themselves to a farming group, often "in positions of greatly reduced status."[69]

Farming thus came to Utah in three ways: colonists with a farming culture, adoption by foragers who perceived farming as advantageous, and through the acquiescence of foragers who became impoverished by the changes swirling around them. The sprinkling of farming communities across the northern Colorado Plateau and eastern Great Basin brought change to all and would play out over the next 1,000 years as the Fremont culture.

5

The Fremont

Farming in Utah has always been a risky proposition. Even today, those who attempt to grow crops without ditch or sprinkler irrigation are best considered gamblers. When the Mormon pioneers founded Salt Lake City in 1847, one of the first things they did was to bring water from the mountains to the fields via hand dug ditches. Even then the crop might fail. The climate of the high deserts of the northern Colorado Plateau and the eastern Great Basin promises erratic rainfall and a growing season often abbreviated by late freezes in June and early freezes in August. The seduction of water harbored in the mountain snow pack can lead to disappointment as it varies wildly from year to year. Then there are the usual plagues to farmers of bug infestations, rabbits, deer, birds, hail, and wind. Modern humans attempt to control the vagary with expensive dams, pumps, sprinklers, fertilizer, and pesticides. The costs of being a farmer—a food producer rather than a food collector—are inevitably extorted from the economy.

Prehistoric farmers in Utah generally went without irrigation except in perhaps a few dozen places. But they, too, had an investment in their cleared fields and granaries and in competing claims for the limited supply of prime land where water seeped near the surface. They had to stay around to keep birds, rabbits, and deer from damaging the crops and to weed and till. Important to all this were their networks of kin and place, which enabled them to navigate the climatic variability of the Basin-Plateau even as they pushed the

FIGURE 5.1

Map of important Fremont sites. Most shown here have been subject to some excavation.

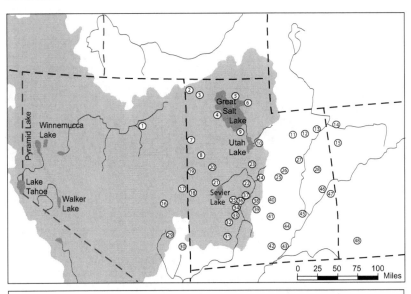

1 Scorpion Ridge	15 Douglas/Piceance creeks sites, Texas Overlook, Sky Aerie	33 Marysvale
2 Swallow Shelter	16 Steptoe Valley	34 Clear Creek Canyon, Five Finger Ridge, Icicle Bench
3 Remnant Cave	17 Amy's Shelter	35 Backhoe Village
4 Hogup Cave	18 Baker Village, Garrison	36 Elsinore Burial
5 Promontory caves	19 Scribble Rock Shelter	37 Kanosh
6 Bear River sites, Great Salt Lake sites, and burials	20 Fish Springs sites	38 Nawthis Village, Lost Creek, Round Spring
7 Danger Cave	21 Topaz Slough	39 Sudden Shelter, Aspen Shelter, Snake Rock, Poplar Knob, Old Woman, I-70 sites
8 Buzz-Cut Dune	22 Pharo Village	
9 Grantsville, Tooele, and Jordan River area sites	23 Nephi	
	24 Ephriam	40 Innocents Ridge, Clyde's Cavern, Pint-Size Shelter
10 Utah Lake area sites	25 Windy Ridge, Power Pole Knoll, Crescent Ridge	41 Fremont River area sites, Noel Morss
11 Felter Hill, Flat Top Butte	26 Cedar Siding Shelter	42 Alvey, Triangle Cave
12 Whiterock Village, Caldwell Village, Steinaker Gap	27 Nine Mile Canyon sites and Range Creek	43 Sunny Beaches
13 Dinosaur National Monument sites, Boundary Village, Wholeplace, Wagon Run, Burnt House, Cub Creek sites, Deluge Shelter	28 Hill Creek area sites, Long Mesa	44 Bull Creek area sites
	29 Pahranagat Valley	45 Cowboy Cave
	30 O'Malley Shelter	46 Turner-Look
	31 Median Village, Evans Mound, Paragonah	47 Coombs Cave
14 Yampa River area sites, Brown's park, Mantle's Cave	32 Beaver	48 Tamarron

farming of maize, beans, and squash to its limits in the high desert. Ancient farmers shaped a sense of place in marked contrast to the foragers of the preceding millennia. Farmers have an extractive relationship with the land. They invest labor with the hope of managing a surplus and hedging against risk. Place became more local, because people were tied to the fields, granaries, and villages. In that sense, the landscape shrank during the centuries of prehistoric farming. It was a successful enterprise lasting over 500 years.

Archaeologists refer to this period as the Fremont, named after the Fremont River near Torrey, Utah, where the ancient farmers were first identified during fieldwork in 1928.[1]

FREMONT PLACES, FREMONT LIFE, FREMONT PLACE

The Fremont period was a sea change. The ancient heritage of the Archaic forager societies became enmeshed in continental upheaval that brought immigrant farmers and a new way of life to the West. The Fremont was a culture—there were some broad, unifying themes in the rock art, ceramic design, basketry, architecture, and the use of space. But the landscape was large, and there was surely a mosaic of ethnic groups, tribal enclaves, linguistic variation, and shades of difference in lifestyle.

The earliest Fremont landscape, perhaps 200 B.C., was a frontier inhabited by Late Archaic foragers and a few explorers from the Southwest. Others followed, and by A.D. 500 there was a smattering of farming outposts in a wilderness of foragers. After A.D. 900, the landscape became a sea of farmers. People gathered into villages, hamlets, and farmsteads as they had never done before. In the best watered areas there were true villages of a dozen to several dozen homes. But most Fremont villages were small affairs. Archaeologists call the small Fremont farmsteads "rancherias"; often they consisted only of a single residential structure, but more often there were a few homes clustered together. Among the homes were outdoor activity areas, and probably ramadas for shade. There were racks for hanging things, caches of gear, piles of raw materials, and the refuse dumps that humans everywhere create. Embedded in some of the villages were communal storage structures made of adobe. In other cases, storage was kept inside the houses and was hence less public. In still other intriguing instances, storage was remote from the residences and evidently hidden in cliffs for defense.

The primary Fremont dwelling was the pithouse. Basement-like structures, pithouses were capacious, functional, warm in the winter, and cool in the summer. Pithouses were excavated into the ground from a few centimeters to over a meter deep. A log and pole roof supported by vertical posts (a four-square pattern is common) extended the structure well above the ground. When finished with various arrangements of smaller wooden roofing material and finally an earthen seal, pithouses looked like low mounds, or truncated pyramids, with a flat roof that provided a convenient and elevated outdoor living space. Pithouses had central heating, places for storage, and a ventilation system. Shallow, cheap-to-build pithouses had been employed in some parts of the Basin-Plateau for the last 2,000 years, but the extra settling that came with farming brought them into widespread use and escalated the investment made in pithouses during Fremont times.[2]

Examples of Fremont rancherias, hamlets, and villages are many. Well over 100 have been excavated, and we know enough about them to have a pretty good idea of what to expect when we visit the thousands more that have not been excavated. If we pick one, like a number out of a hat, it might be Caldwell Village near Vernal, Utah.[3] Caldwell has 22 pithouses ranging from 4 to 9 meters in diameter. Most had a central fire hearth and an entryway descending slightly from ground level. Entry to most pithouses was by a ladder through the smokehole in the roof, but some might have employed a ground-level crawlway that doubled as a ventilator duct.

At Caldwell, the storage pits inside the houses indicate that when the village was occupied in the 11th century, storage there was more private than public. By that time, pottery was the primary technology for storage and cooking. Grinding corn was a major activity, and *metates* were large, deeply troughed, and often had a shelf at one end—the characteristic "Utah *metate*." The human trappings of life are readily apparent at many Fremont sites. At Caldwell there were awls, whistles, beads, and gaming pieces. These things were present in earlier periods, but larger accumulations of material wealth became part of the culture with the advent of village life.

Despite the number of pithouses often found at Fremont sites, only a few were used at one time. This is true of virtually all Fremont village sites, and we should reject the temptation to see these villages as large just because the count of pithouses runs into the dozens or even hundreds. There were indeed large villages that were home to hundreds of people, but the images conjured by the terms "hamlet" or "rancheria" are a far more accurate description of life for the vast number of Fremont people scattered across the region.

Caldwell was occupied for perhaps a century, and as new houses were built, midden deposits of refuse from daily life and the ever-burning fire hearths accumulated. At some Fremont sites, these midden layers are thin, representing occupations of well less than a decade. Others are thick, indicating more disposal and of course more people. Most middens were built in stops and starts, signaling periods when places were abandoned and then used again. The Fremont were settled, but they were also on the move. A cycle of habitation, abandonment, and relocation structured life and place. This was a repetition that played out over the lives of individuals, as well as a pattern expressed over centuries and hence generations of people.

Other Fremont sites have above-ground adobe granaries used for maize and other products. These granaries are typically freestanding structures often over 5 meters long. They are protected from rodents with adobe foundations installed into footer trenches and thick, puddled adobe floors. Granaries are often found at true village sites where storage had a public face. At Grantsville, west of Salt Lake City, there are 200 pithouses and other structures that are probably granaries. At the Evans site north of Cedar City, dozens of pit houses and adobe granaries were constructed sequentially on one another. During the three-century occupation, the structures and trash accumulated into a readily visible mound, attesting to the anchor of place. Despite this tether, the lifespan of an individual pithouse was only a few years, and structures that survived more than a decade were rare. People returned and place was a magnet across generations even as particular places went unused for a time.

The Paragonah site only a few miles away from Evans was a large village. Excavation there in the early 20th century and then again in mid-century revealed an intentional organization of space. Adobe granaries were arranged around a courtyard in a rough square with pithouses scattered about. Community storehouses were literally on public display, indicating some form of central control and a deeply woven social, political, and religious web. The influential people in Fremont society were not isolated behind gates and walls but had to continuously reinvent their power through combinations of kin heritage, charisma, and public display. Paragonah exemplifies a fundamental shift in the sociality of space and the flow of power during Fremont times.[4]

The heartland of Fremont village life is strung along the mountains, forming the eastern rim of the Great Basin. Virtually every town traversed today by Interstate 15 from Cedar City to Brigham City has Fremont village sites. The locations chosen for farming by the Utah pioneers were the same places chosen by the Fremont—where mountain streams debauch onto the alluvial fans and spread their way to the valley floors, and where streams meandered along broad floodplains.

It may well be that the most populous part of this corridor during Fremont times was the Wasatch Front, just as it is the most populous part of the region today. Urbanization obscures and destroys a great deal of the archaeology, but Fremont village sites are known along all the streams entering Utah Lake and Great Salt Lake. Thousands of "Indian mounds" identify the location of prehistoric rancherias and villages. The filled-in pithouses and their collapsed adobe roofs and the melted adobe walls of granaries often leave barren circles in the fields, where they impede the growth of modern crops. A 19th-century farmer in Utah Valley had a business that offered horse-drawn earth-moving equipment to remove the mounds.

Northwest of Ogden near Willard Bay, the archaeology is so rich that places cannot be broken down into discrete sites but instead are a near continuous archaeological landscape of large villages, hamlets, camps, and resource processing sites littered with thousands of tools. Only a few decades ago, before vandals stripped the sites of many of their artifacts, single encampments the size of a baseball diamond could yield 1,000 Fremont-age projectile points. The abundance of arrow tips does not mark prehistoric battlefields; it results from people living near wetlands. The favored hunting grounds of dense rushes and masses of vegetation consumed arrows only to disgorge them centuries later on exposed mudflats. The wetlands attracted the Fremont as they had all the previous peoples of the region.

But the Wasatch Front had more than wetlands with abundant wild resources. It stands out from other Fremont places by the presence of Great Salt Lake and Utah Lake. These large bodies of water moderate the climate on their eastern shores producing a longer growing season for farming. This "lake effect" enables orchards and fruit stands to thrive today. Farmers can show you extensive Fremont village sites on their lands, barns full of *metates* and cylindrical grinders, and thousands of arrowheads. One of the best known of these big Wasatch Front sites, even though it is now gone, is the "Big Village" at Willard Bay State Park.

SIDEBAR: THE BIG VILLAGE AT WILLARD (BY MARK E. STUART)

When the Mormon pioneers settled on Willard Creek in 1853, they saw low mounds covered with pottery and flint chips as they cleared brush and plowed their fields. A few of the mounds were scattered along the creek banks, but most were on a large knoll of high ground overlooking the barrens—an expanse of grasslands, marshes, and meandering stream channels periodically flooded by Great Salt Lake. The concentration of mounds became known as "Big Village," and it gained a reputation as a good place to look for arrowheads and other relics.

The Big Village at Willard came to the attention of Don Maguire in 1873. Maguire lived in Ogden, Utah, and had worked for Major John W. Powell of the fledgling U.S. Bureau of American Ethnology. Maguire said of his first encounter with the Big Village: "Going there I soon found evidence proving this was a major prehistoric town site. Around the town was an earthen wall ca. 2 miles in circumference. Mounds that marked the foundation of buildings . . . Going carefully over the area of this old city, I estimated the site to have covered 20 to 25 acres more or less."[a]

Maguire hired two local men, a team of horses, and a scraper and began to excavate the biggest of the mounds, measuring about 6 feet high and 70 feet long. Over the next 15 years, he made numerous excavations into the Willard mounds. Like many others of his time, he considered the ruins to be of Mesoamerican origin and the northernmost outpost of the Aztec Empire. At the time of his excavations, 43 mounds remained of the estimated 70 present when the pioneers first began cultivation. The rest had been leveled by the plow. Of the seven mounds Maguire excavated he reported: "I unearthed 15 skeletons and a considerable number of broken Pottery; also lance heads, arrowheads, steatite slickers used in polishing and straightening arrows. There were also a number of Indian hand mills of superior make and size made from granite and hand stones of the same. On the floors of these rooms opened in the above mounds we found in a charred condition quantities of corn, beans, corn cobs and also cloth fiber in charred condition." Many of the finer Willard artifacts were exhibited at the Columbian Exposition in Chicago in 1898 and later illustrated by Julian Steward.[b]

Neil Judd of the Smithsonian Institution spent a week in 1915 examining the Big Village, but only 25 mounds remained. Judd excavated a mound 40 feet in diameter that rose about 3 feet above the surrounding field. He discovered the earthen floor of a pithouse with a clay-rimmed fireplace surrounded by four large post holes. He found evidence that the roof was constructed of poles 1 to 4 inches in diameter with bulrush and cane grass reeds laid across the poles. This lattice was stuffed with bunches of salt grass and daubed with mud that upon drying formed an adobe shell 2 to 6 inches thick.

FIGURE 5.2

The Big Mound at Willard looking west. The photo was taken by Andrew Kerr sometime between 1920 and 1930. (Courtesy of the Utah State Historical Society)

Julian Steward excavated four mounds in 1932 as part of an archaeology class at the University of Utah. Three of the four mounds contained large storage pits from 3 to 7 feet in diameter and 3 to 5 feet deep. All contained refuse except one that contained a cache of five slate chisels. Later, a burial was interred in a small pit dug into the southern wall of the former cache pit. The body was in a sitting position tilted to the left with the arms and legs flexed. Near the feet was a bone awl, a chipped stone point, two *manos*, and a large loaf-shaped lump of red pigment. An inverted Utah-type *metate* rested across the legs.

Steward's mound four contained two pithouses, one superimposed on the other. The earlier structure was like the pithouse excavated by Judd, except it was square instead of round and resembled those he would later excavate at Grantsville, west of Salt Lake City. Another, larger square pithouse was superimposed on this one. There was a shift from round to square houses sometime in the 12th century, and the presence of both at the Big Village indicates long occupation of the village.[c]

After this flurry of archaeological work, the Big Village was left to the relic hunters. J. T. Edwards was one of the land owners, and he made two remarkable discoveries. He found a 6-inch-high sandstone figurine with a tapered body painted with longitudinal red stripes and a cache pit 3 feet deep containing 600 Rosegate Corner-notched arrow points of obsidian. None of the points showed any signs of wear, and it appeared that at one time they were in a bag that had disintegrated over the centuries.[d]

Construction of Willard Bay Reservoir brought the final demise of the Big Village in the late 1950s, because the high ground on which the site stood would furnish fill material for the reservoir dikes. Francis K. Hassel of Ogden was a member of the Utah Statewide Archaeological Society and conducted a survey of the Big Village before it was too late. Willard Bay construction workers told Hassel that at least 20 human burials were disturbed, and one can only wonder how many burials found their final resting place within the dikes.

The former site of the Big Village now lies under the north marina of Willard Bay State Park. Renovation of the park in 2002 required extensive earth removal, but no trace of the former archaeological site was found. The Big Village at Willard is an example of the dozens if not hundreds of such Fremont villages that lined the Wasatch Front and other valleys along the eastern rim of the Great Basin.

The Fremont did not limit themselves to the most favorable climates and places. They pushed north into the Cache Valley and southern Idaho and west into Nevada, almost to Ely. The Baker site, located near Great Basin National Park on the Utah-Nevada border, was a full-blown farming village. Baker had pithouses, a central structure with smaller adobe surface structures around it, and an array of material culture from everyday items to exotics. Much of the pottery used at Baker Village was made elsewhere, somehow transported across the deserts of western Utah from the Parowan Valley to the southeast. Even these seemingly remote outposts were entwined in a trade network that reached across the western portion of the continent.

The Fremont were unable to take their lifeway across Nevada, because the rain shadow in the lee of the Sierra Nevada Range in California denies the Great Basin of the summer monsoon so crucial to maize farming. Nevertheless, Fremont foraging peoples near Elko, Nevada, were making pottery in the Fremont style and even importing some Fremont pottery from central Utah in the 11th century A.D.[5]

The intriguing locations of some Fremont villages imply an opportunistic sense of place. The Sevier Valley near Richfield was rich in villages, just as it is rich in productive farmland today. But along Gooseberry Creek perched 1,000 feet above the valley floor was Nawthis Village. At Nawthis, over 30 mounds contained adobe structures, pithouses, and ditch irrigation.[6] Despite the altitude, the site occupies a microclimate with a long growing season. It is above the cold air of the Sevier Valley floor, but not too high to prohibit farming.

The Fremont found and used the only flat, mile-long stretch of creek bottom that could be farmed. Over several centuries, they built hamlet after hamlet, and even a few villages, each in a different location along the creek as it changed course and altered the location of the best farmland. This was not unique. Just over a ridge to the west of Nawthis Village virtually the same thing happened in Lost Creek. The people knew of every nook and cranny. The Fremont were settled, but they were also opportunists.

Fremont rock art reflects the extensiveness of their presence across the region. A distinctive ensemble of anthropomorphic figures, wavy lines, spirals, dots, as well as naturalistic and stylized animals seems to occur in every canyon in the region. The amount of Fremont rock art dwarfs anything from the eons of the Archaic. Fremont rock art exhibits regional styles, but there are common motifs and a unifying manner of execution. Fremont rock art exemplifies the notion that a land once filled with foragers now bristled with enclaves of farmers.[7]

Fremont village sites on the Colorado Plateau were smaller, with relatively greater use of masonry architecture. Here, too, it seems that every possible agricultural niche was exploited. The Fremont fully utilized Castle Valley south of Price and along the San Rafael River. Streams coming from any available reservoir of snowpack were occupied, whether it be Ivie, Quitchupah, Muddy, Ferron, or half a dozen others flowing east across Castle Valley. Bull Creek flowing north from the Henry Mountains toward Hanksville was occupied. Thompson and Sego canyons incised into the Book Cliffs were occupied. Remote drainages in northwestern Colorado such as Douglas Creek and those near Rangely and Brown's Park on the Green River were farmed. Even rugged places such as Nine Mile Canyon and Range Creek north of Price were occupied, and, as we will see, used in some strange ways. Any locale able to provide opportunities for agriculture was at one time or another thrown under the social and economic net. Fremont sense of place was appropriative.

Clear Creek Canyon south of Richfield provides a glimpse of community size and organization. The construction of Interstate 70 led to large-scale investigation of a Fremont landscape led by Richard Talbot, Lane Richens, and Joel Janetski. The canyon contained at least three villages occupied from A.D. 1100 into the 1300s. The largest is Five Finger Ridge and consists of several clusters of pithouses. Perhaps a dozen pithouses were occupied at any one time, with double that during a zenith in the last decades of the 13th century. Other villages such as Icicle Bench and Radford's Roost were smaller but appear to be contemporaneous with Five Finger Ridge. Farmsteads and rancherias were scattered among the larger villages. There were also storage sites and rock art, and all kinds of specialized processing and resource extraction locations. Taken as a whole and at its height, Clear Creek Canyon, and the surrounding uplands, was a thoroughly human place.

The archaeology hints at this intensified, exploitive sense of place. Five Finger Ridge overlooks the canyon floodplain, and the village occupied a lobed ridge joined by a flattened saddle. Clusters of homes dotted the ridge and most likely represented different lineages of extended kin. The saddle between the clusters featured a plaza and perhaps public buildings that linked the clusters of homes on the ridge lobes. There is evidence for differences in status among people both in house sizes and arrangements, as well as in burial goods and other exotic items of material culture.

The people, or perhaps just the leaders at Five Finger Ridge, were well connected to other regions. They had exotic stones and seashells, and they imported Anasazi ceramics and turquoise from Nevada and Southwestern sources. Trade increased in Clear Creek Canyon after about A.D. 1100, aligning Fremont connections to the Southwest with the waning days of the major center of political and religious power at Chaco Canyon, New Mexico. Indeed, trade with the Fremont seems to have increased during a period of political and economic upheaval in the Southwest, when the Chacoan center of power shifted north to the San Juan Basin.

Clear Creek Canyon is a window into Fremont place that was appropriative, opportunistic, and in some cases, competitive. Fremont place was mostly local, but in some sense it was also continental, because the Fremont were part of an intensely occupied America during the 10th through 13th centuries.[8]

KEYS TO FREMONT ORIGINS

The earliest traces of maize known in Utah date to 2,100 years ago (see Chapter 4: Farming Comes to Utah) in the Sevier Valley. Over the next few centuries, maize appeared across the region in locations as scattered as Steinaker Gap in the Uinta Basin, Brown's Park on the Green River, the Confluence site and Clydes Cavern on the San Rafael Swell, Nine Mile Canyon and Cedar Siding Shelter near Price, the Alvey site and Triangle Cave in the Escalante River area,

FIGURE 5.3

Five Finger Ridge was a large village, at times home to several hundred people. Residential and storage structures, as well as open areas and a plaza, were situated on the ridge. Smaller villages, hamlets, and, of course, agricultural fields were strung up and down the floodplain below. Clear Creek Canyon is the most thoroughly studied Fremont village complex but is one of dozens of similar situations along the eastern rim of the Great Basin. (Courtesy of Fremont Indian State Park)

and Cowboy Cave in Canyonlands. Farming seems to have made its way north to the Wasatch Front a little later, although there are hints that it may have played a role before A.D. 500. Its early presence in the Sevier Valley suggests that the mountains between the Colorado Plateau and the Great Basin were no barrier to the spread of knowledge, agriculture, and people. Indeed, foragers living far north of the Colorado River probably knew of maize, of the ways of farming, and of farming people. They probably knew this for decades or even generations before they ever saw an agricultural field first-hand.[9]

The appearance of maize corresponds to a jump in the number of pithouses dating between A.D. 250 and 600, including the Sandy Ridge pithouse in Moab, Cocklebur Wash in the Uinta Basin, Carcass Corners near Teasdale, Icicle Bench in Clear Creek Canyon, Steinaker Gap, and the Confluence site. Other pithouses are more clearly Late Archaic, such as a pithouse at the Pavant Park site north of Richfield, the Orchard pithouse near Moab, and Hog Canyon Dune near Kanab.[10] Did some of these belong to Late Archaic foragers becoming more tethered and making greater use of pithouses even before farming arrived? Some of the Late Archaic houses are in locations similar to where the later Fremont built their houses, suggesting that a few foragers were already making the move toward farming. Or, could it be that farming, pithouses, and settling were imposed on the region by immigrants?

For nearly a century, archaeologists identified similarities between the Fremont and Southwestern cultures. They also identify clear links between the Fremont and the preceding Archaic cultures. Debate persistently casts the issue as a choice between whether the Fremont were indigenous people who adopted farming or immigrants who replaced the indigenous people.[11] Perhaps we are missing something by framing the problem as a choice between indigenous development versus a replacement involving two immutable cultural entities. The more powerful questions are about the nature of interaction between indigenes and immigrants during a time when a new culture was formed out of the interaction itself. There are several keys to the origins of the Fremont.

First, origins are not found in a single event but in processes that unfold over human generations. The origin of the Fremont is not the spread of farming or farming peoples into a wilderness but rather a frontier creating a new cultural milieu that changed both indigenes and immigrants. The Fremont did not spring full blown from some sort of cultural womb. The frontier that began the molding process was a place different from the Fremont we know at its zenith, much in the same way that America in 1776 contrasts with our America only two centuries later.

Second, forager populations during the Archaic experienced booms and busts. They were not all of a cloth but were diverse in lifeways, culture, and sense of place. Sometimes large portions of the landscape were thinly populated by "high desert foragers," whereas other times people were tethered in substantial numbers to villages (Chapter 4). Foragers already living in larger, more stable, albeit seasonal villages could add farming with some adjustments in their other activities.[12] However, foragers living the life of the high desert, moving in patterned stops and starts over large landscapes, had little reason to adopt farming. Any attempt to answer questions about why and how farming came to Utah and founded the Fremont culture must take forager diversity into account.

A third key to the origins of the Fremont lies in the Basketmaker II cultures of the Southwest. This is the label given to the first farmers of the high mesas and canyons south of the Colorado River. Basketmaker II peoples are identified by the characteristics of their homes, storage pits, sandals, burial customs, rock art, their use of the atlatl and dart, basketry, and an absence of pottery. They are also known through a substantial number of human remains indicating physical and genetic characteristics.[13] The Basketmakers were not all of a cloth and had local peculiarities of lifeway. They varied in ethnic and probably linguistic identities that developed for centuries before there were any traces of farming north of the Colorado River. Basketmaker II peoples initiated processes that would shape the region north of the Colorado River and far beyond for many centuries to come.

The final key to understanding the formation of the Fremont is the dynamic of "The Desert and the Sown"—a contrast between foragers of the desert and people who farmed.[14] This contrast is crucial to understanding Fremont origins and culture because during the Fremont period, the social landscape was transformed by the "Other"—people whose values, beliefs, languages, symbolism in and use of rock art, adornment, and physical appearance were different and hence subject to suspicion. A landscape that had been occupied for millennia by foragers became "shared" because of the presence of immigrant farmers. Some of these immigrants held elements of common heritage with the indigenous foragers while others were very foreign. The landscape was further shared with indigenous people who broke from their forager legacy when they took up farming. This was a milieu of Others, a situation very different from a mere blending or replacement of two monolithic cultures.

INDIGENES, EXPLORERS, AND COLONISTS: THE FREMONT FRONTIER

Farming is a seduction, because the more labor one puts into it the greater the reward and the greater the risk. Increased production creates increased needs, causing shortfall to flirt with catastrophe. The only way out of this predicament, so familiar to us in the modern world, is to keep investing more labor into the system—a spiraling process of intensification. Early farmers went to the trouble to prepare a field, sow seed, weed, and harvest. They did all this to produce an annual spasm of abundance that required a social fabric to organize the storage, defense, and distribution of food among hungry people. They took the gamble to produce food rather than just to collect it, and the nature of life and place inevitably changed to one of commitment and extraction. It also fostered rapid population growth.

The possibility of farming in the Americas originated in Mexico only a few thousand years before it arrived in Utah. The spread north from Mexico was fueled by the immigration of people with a farming way of life presumably looking for new land. Farming was established in the hot deserts of southern Arizona perhaps as early as 3,500 years ago. A pause in the northward spread of farming was mandated by the need to adapt maize to the high plateaus, but by 2,500 years ago (500 B.C.), a Basketmaker II culture committed to farming was fully ensconced in the Four Corners area of the Southwest.[15] Over the next few centuries the lands to the north destined to become the Fremont became a frontier.

The Basketmaker II peoples of the Southwest faced the consequences of farming. The reduced mobility of living near fields and the tethers to stored food reduced birth spacing and caused fertility rates to eke upward. The stark fact that some people had more maize than others bred competition. Increases in longevity brought by the advent of porridges that could sustain those without teeth pushed society a bit more toward a gerontocracy. A "tyranny of the elders" ensued as old people held on to positions of high status and influence and hindered the ascendancy of the young. New leaders, their young

SIDEBAR: FARMING, LANGUAGE, AND IMMIGRANTS

Archaeologists once thought that maize was domesticated in central Mexico 7,000 years ago and that this knowledge slowly spread north from group to group and into the Southwestern United States less than 3,000 years ago. More accurate dating on the Mexican maize shows that domestication began there only 5,500 years ago, and new discoveries in the Southwest show that maize was present well before 3,000 years ago.[a] These discoveries change our understanding of how farming arrived to the Southwest and to Utah.

The Uto-Aztecan language family is an enormous group of Native American languages across the western United States and central Mexico. Uto-Aztecan languages include Hopi and Tohono O'odham (Papago) of the Southwest, and the Tarahumara, Tepeman, and Nahuatl (Aztec) languages of Mexico. It also includes the Paiute, Shoshone, and Ute languages spoken by historic period foragers in the Basin-Plateau. Uto-Aztecan speakers blanketed the Desert West during the historic period and it turns out, their ancestors are important to understanding the spread of farming.

For decades, linguists thought that Uto-Aztecan languages spread from the deserts of North America southward into Mesoamerica. A northern origin for Uto-Aztecan was consistent with the linguistic evidence and since it was thought that maize was late in the Southwest, there seemed to be no relationship between the languages and farming. Now that we know that maize spread to the Southwest earlier, there may in fact be a relationship. More importantly, this relationship supplies some explanations for how Uto-Aztecan speakers could spread into a region already populated by foragers, and why there is so much diversity in the cultures of Uto-Aztecan speakers.

A new linguistic study shows that a southern origin better explains some relationships among Uto-Aztecan languages. A southern origin also fits better with the archaeological evidence, and with emerging biological evidence about the evolution of domesticated maize. It is also consistent with other cases in the world where farming fosters the spread of languages.[b]

Studies of the biological characteristics of prehistoric maize show that the most rapid change in the plant occurred between 5,500–5,000 years ago.[c] After initial domestication, maize spread through the deserts of northern Mexico and southern Arizona through immigration. Farming's productivity acted as a centrifugal force that ensured the relentless spread of people. When people left home to find new places to farm they took with them their native languages, and a farming way of life. This was the mechanism by which the Uto-Aztecan speakers spread northward into the Southwest.

FIGURE 5.4

Map showing processes important to Fremont origins. Utah was occupied by indigenous Archaic foragers, and the first immigrants into the Utah frontier were likely Eastern Basketmaker II. The Eastern Basketmaker II may themselves be a mix of indigenes and immigrants arising out of a several-century pause in the spread of maize from the low deserts of Arizona onto the high mesas of the Four Corners area. Indigenous peoples there may have begun adopting maize at that time. Thus, the Eastern Basketmaker II may be ancestral to the Kiowa-Tanoan speakers who became Anasazi and eventually the Rio Grande Pueblos of the historic period. Western Basketmaker II was possibly Uto-Aztecan and supplied later immigration into the Fremont region through the A.D. 1000s. Western Basketmaker II also became Anasazi and eventually the Uto-Aztecan Puebloan peoples of the historic period, such as the Hopi. These complex heritages suggest that it is possible that both the upper Rio Grande peoples of New Mexico and the Hopi of northern Arizona have ancestral ties to the Fremont.

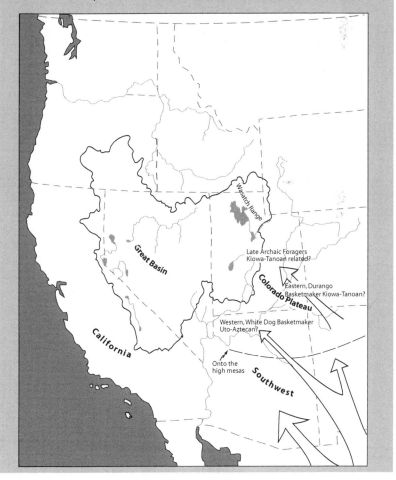

Between 5,000 and 2,000 years ago the rate of change in the maize plant slowed down. This shows that hundreds of small populations in Mexico and the Southwest now farmed maize, and had become isolated as they became tethered to their fields and communities. As the colonizing farmers were isolated from their parent populations, and pushed farther into new territory, languages diverged from their native roots. The Hopi language split off about 3,000 years ago. This process of isolation led to the great diversity of the Uto-Aztecan languages we see in the historic period.

What were the languages of the indigenous Archaic people who encountered these immigrant farmers? One candidate for an Archaic language family in the Southwest is Kiowa-Tanoan. This is another sizable linguistic family and includes the eastern Pueblo tribes of the upper Rio Grande River area in New Mexico. The Eastern Basketmaker II populations of the Four Corners area between 500 B.C. and A.D. 0 may have been Kiowa-Tanoan speakers.[d] The spread of maize occurred in stops and starts. One pause was when maize had to be adapted for the high plateaus of the Four Corners area. Another occurred before farming spread north into Utah. These pauses gave time for indigenous Archaic, perhaps Kiowa-Tanoan speakers to adopt farming, thus providing an indigenous element to what would become the first Basketmaker II farmers and eventually the Fremont. If so, the earliest Fremont languages might be Kiowa-Tanoan, later diversifying as Uto-Aztecan immigration changed everything.

families, and especially single males were flung away from their homes and toward new ones, if for no other reason than the quest for opportunity.[16]

The pressures for new land kept men on the move but at the same time fostered a connection to the land. Archaeologists now realize that Basketmaker II peoples were far more reliant on maize agriculture than once thought. The northward push of farming and the incessant population growth created a dual tension to move on and at the same time hold on to the land one had, even if it meant conflict. The Basketmaker II was a time of colonization and conflict. Under such circumstances, elder brothers are more likely to take the positions of status at home, leaving fewer opportunities for their younger, and perhaps equally capable, siblings. Women remained at the farms and anchored place.

Eventually these pressures led to the matrilineal kinship pattern found in the historically known Hopi and Zuni cultures, where descent is traced through the female lineage. In these systems, the female lineage anchors the people to the land. Marriage takes the men across boundaries of kinship and across landscapes as they go to live with the maternal clans of their wives. A full-blown matrilineal kinship pattern was probably not in place by Basketmaker times, but the selection pressures that caused it to become widespread in the Southwest were beginning to be felt.[17]

All the pressures in these early farming cultures gave young men a good reason to leave home. The process repeated itself across Mexico and ran northward to the climatologic limits of farming. Under these circumstances it was men who flowed across the landscape and perhaps across ethnic and linguistic boundaries. The first exploratory parties pushing into what would become Fremont country were probably mostly males, and probably often brothers; in these kinship systems brothers include those we consider to be cousins. The northward movement of predominantly male groups explains why the Fremont look like immigrants in some ways, and indigenes in others.

There are clear connections between the Fremont and the Southwest in many traits, including house form, art, and the use of ceramics. Fremont mitochondrial DNA inherited through the maternal lineage is in some respects similar to ancient Anasazi and modern Puebloan samples. Patterns in DNA from across the Southwest follow the archaeological categories more closely than the historically known languages, but groups of speakers can include recruits from diverse genetic legacies. Importantly, the DNA suggests that northward migration through the Southwest comprised more males than females.[18]

Like most stories of contact between cultures, there is more to it than a general reference to the arrival of immigrants. The Rasmussen burial from Nine Mile Canyon in north-central Utah, first mentioned by Noel Morss in 1931, is a tantalizing symbol. The artifacts interred with the adult male "closely resemble what could be expected in a Basketmaker II burial, except for the hide moccasins and leggings." The moccasins are similar to what would become the classic Fremont hock-moccasin, suggesting indigenous roots.[19]

Elements of Fremont heritage are deeply indigenous to the Archaic period. Fremont basketry is by itself a compelling demonstration of this legacy. The bases of Fremont basketry technology are the one-rod and bundle, and the half-rod and bundle foundations. These and an associated constellation of traits distinguish the industry. Not only is Fremont basketry fundamentally different from that of the Anasazi, it shows a clear continuation of the Archaic basketry tradition that unified vast portions of the eastern Great Basin and the northern

Colorado Plateau for the past 6,000 years.[20] The absence of full-blown female immigration in the founding of the Fremont is glimpsed in the stark distinctions between Fremont and Anasazi basketry. It was thus the indigenous women who gave birth to the Fremont and carried forth their Archaic heritage. Immigrant women must have been so few at first that their ways became enmeshed with the indigenous people they encountered. This is occasionally seen in basketry, such as a fragment of a basket from Coombs Cave in the LaSal Mountains above Moab with both Fremont and Anasazi stylistic elements.

The Fremont began as a frontier of Late Archaic indigenes and Southwestern explorers and entrepreneurs over 2,000 years ago. This ancient frontier may have been something akin to the English,

FIGURE 5.5

Chart that employs evidence from basketry to illustrate the relationships between indigenous Archaic cultures and immigrant Eastern and Western Basketmaker II traditions important to Fremont origins. Key events in Fremont history are shown at the left.

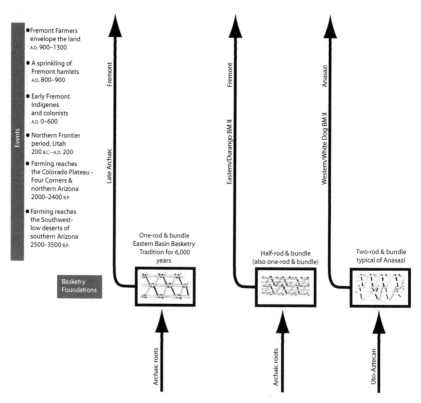

French, and American fur trappers and traders pushing west ahead of
the settlers. It was a cultural milieu of both resistance and change.

During the Archaic-Basketmaker-Fremont frontier period,
fortunes changed and some lifeways died out. Southwestern explorers
took home stories of new lands and peoples. The consequences were
surely felt in both directions. Indigenous hunters could trade meat
and resources such as toolstone, minerals, and medicines obtainable
only through intimate knowledge of the land to the newcomers who
knew little but who were worldly and who had networks to the south.
Marriage between native women and the arriving Basketmaker
frontiersmen is suggested by the presence of Late Archaic basketry
styles in Colorado Basketmaker II sites. The presence of new peoples,
"Others," spurred some foragers to intensify their efforts and unwittingly urged them toward farming.[21]

High desert foragers were pushed to the fringes of the landscape
and became the "people without history," essentially the same thing
that happened to the remaining foragers in the world of the 19th and
20th centuries. Some people, especially women and children, likely
had no other option but to attach themselves to a farming community
"under conditions of greatly reduced status."[22] As exciting as it was,
frontiers are transient places, and this period did not last long.

LANGUAGE, ETHNICITY, AND A SPRINKLING OF
NEOLITHIC COMMUNITIES

Farming spread via immigrant populations and through economic
intensification by indigenes. It did so because farming promotes growth,
instability, and more growth—inevitable cycles of expansion. These
massive changes did not spring upon a wilderness but upon a frontier
of cultural diversity, and they constructed a new cultural form.[23]

The young farmers who left their Southwest homes leapfrogged
across landscapes in search of places familiar to them—the good
places to farm. In this way, the Fremont region became "sprinkled with
neolithic communities."[24] Who were these people? The archaeology
of the Basketmakers and new research in linguistics provide some
hints.

Basketmaker II culture occupied the Four Corners region centuries before the earliest hints of the Fremont. Archaeologists have
long suspected an east-west distinction among the Basketmaker II

cultures. Each of these immigrant cultures had very different interactions with the indigenous peoples.

The Eastern Basketmaker people of the Four Corners area were
farmers bringing agriculture to indigenous Archaic populations. As
they moved north, the high plateaus of the Four Corners stalled the
movement of maize, because it took time for people to adapt the plant
to the altitude and shorter growing season. This fostered the development of local adaptations and the participation of indigenes as well
as immigrants. Hints of the indigenous, Archaic roots are found in
projectile points, rock art, and especially textiles, including basketry,
sandals, and cradleboards. Indeed the occasional similarity between
Late Archaic and Basketmaker II coiled basketry foundation types
is the only example of similarity in basketry between the cultures of
the Southwest and the Fremont.[25]

The archaeologist R. G. Matson explores the mechanics that
produced Basketmaker history by bridging the fields of archaeology,
cultural anthropology, and linguistics. He proposes that the Eastern
Basketmaker were Kiowa-Tanoan speakers. These are the languages
spoken by the Rio Grande Pueblos of the historic period, arisen from
Archaic peoples. They stand in contrast to the Mexican origins of the
Uto-Aztecan speakers, including Hopi and many other Native
American groups of the Desert West. Thus, some of the Eastern Basketmaker II may be remnants of the Late Archaic who adapted maize to
the difficult climate of the high plateaus.

The Western Basketmaker II of northern Arizona, sometimes referred to as the White Dog Basketmaker, are distinct from the Eastern
Basketmaker in archaeological traits, including the powerful indicator
of heritage found in rock art. A growing sample and better study of
the human skeletal evidence supports a long-held suspicion that the
Eastern and the Western Basketmaker are also physically distinct,
making the differences more than a matter of ethnic identity. Indeed,
Matson proposes that the Western Basketmaker may be immigrant
Uto-Aztecan speakers pushing their farming way of life into northern
Arizona.[26]

Encounters between the Uto-Aztecan-speaking Western Basketmaker and the indigenous foragers to the north were conditioned by
geography and cultural difference. A labyrinth of canyons and seemingly endless red rock country stretched north from the Colorado River
into Utah to create a geographic obstacle. The cultural, linguistic, and
geographic chasm between immigrants and indigenes led to violence.
Western Basketmaker sites tend to be in defensive locations, and

there is human skeletal and rock art evidence suggesting mutilation, trophy-taking, and scalping. Basketry scalp stretchers are similar among both immigrants and indigenes, suggesting that conflict was a standardized ritual along the western frontier.[27]

It would be the Eastern Basketmaker who would make direct inroads across Utah. Common Archaic heritage between the foragers of Utah and at least some of the Eastern Basketmaker was enough to promote an entrepreneurial frontier with the exchange of goods, mates, language, and culture. Geography fostered the movement of people north along the western slopes of the Rocky Mountains in Colorado and across the broad plateaus of eastern Utah.

One candidate for an Eastern Basketmaker immigrant outpost is the Steinaker Gap site near Vernal, Utah, excavated by Richard Talbot and Lane Richens. By A.D. 250, Steinaker was a hamlet of light residential structures and bell-shaped storage pits for maize. Stable carbon isotope study on biopsies of human bone shows that at that time nearly half the calories consumed were from maize. The strength of the farming tether is attested by the earliest irrigation ditches ever found at a Fremont site—A.D. 250–400.[28] The inhabitants of Steinaker farmed small plots of land and fleshed out the economy with foraged products from the surrounding area. The bell-shaped pits used to store food were then used as burial chambers in the Basketmaker style. Other sites in the Uinta Basin, as well as places such as Douglas Creek south of Rangely, Colorado, may also be immigrant Basketmaker outposts, but it will always be difficult to tell archaeologically—what is needed are human remains and biopsies for DNA studies.

Indigenous foragers surely saw these invasions as a change for the worse. The quality of hunting declined near the new farming villages. Prime foraging grounds for seeds, roots, and nuts were appropriated by the immigrants. These settlements were different from the previous forays of Basketmaker frontiersmen who came from farming communities to the south but who did not attempt to farm. Each people had its advantage and disadvantage. For the foragers, place was expansively intimate and passive. For farmers, place was extractive and defined by their tethers to field, stores, and home.

The indigenes were not all the same. Where foragers were tethered to concentrated resources and practiced more food storage, the nature of place was already changing. Late Archaic pithouse hamlets appear in Utah well before agriculture. When James Wilde and Deborah Newman reported the earliest maize in Utah from the

FIGURE 5.6

The Steinaker Gap site may be an example of Basketmaker II immigrants who settled in northeastern Utah as early as A.D. 250. Bell-shaped underground storage cists typical of Basketmaker II occupations in the Four Corners area were found at the hamlet. Irrigation ditches served the fields sometime before A.D. 400, and the local farms provided enough maize to supply half of the people's needs. (Courtesy of the Museum of Peoples and Cultures, Brigham Young University)

Elsinore site only a few miles south of Richfield, they suggested an indigenous role when they observed "a Basketmaker II-like adaptation was becoming established around 200 B.C. on the eastern edge of the Great Basin."[29]

This period of reorganization among the foragers is not well understood. There are changes in the projectile point styles, such as the appearance of Gypsum points, but it is shaky to trace ethnicity with a single dart-point style. Unlike the complex craft of basketry that requires long tutelage, point styles can flow freely across groups. The split-twig figurine complex that represents some social complexity may have disappeared by 3000 B.P., but there are hints that it persisted to more recent times.

Most archaeologists see significant change at the end of the Archaic on the Colorado Plateau portion of Utah, but the sample of well-dated sites is small enough that it is not clear if the changes reflect land use patterns, perhaps related to social organization, or if some greater upheaval was occurring. The massive evidence for continuity between the Late Archaic foragers and the Fremont farmers suggests that people lived in the region all along.

The well-watered valleys of central and northwestern Utah are the most likely candidates for concentrated settlements of Late Archaic foragers, and the wetlands of the Wasatch Front preserved a foraging lifeway throughout the Fremont period. The Late Archaic settled forager societies in these locales were important to the formation of the Fremont. They would be spurred toward the spiral of farming and the extractive life only by the pressures of displaced indigenes, immigrants, and the seduction of cultigens.[30]

THE BOW AND ARROW, CERAMICS, AND MAIZE

The bow and arrow, ceramics, and the evolution of maize enable a glimpse of the processes forming the Fremont. They did not arrive as a package, and each helps us perceive how the Fremont was a new culture borne from the interaction of the indigenous and the immigrant.

When we think of Fremont farmers our attention is necessarily directed toward the Southwest, but the bow and arrow seems to spread from the northwest, across the Great Basin and toward the Colorado Plateau. Sometime after 2,500 years ago, the bow and arrow was used at Dirty Shame Rockshelter in southeastern Oregon. It is found after 2000 B.P. in western Idaho and was probably in northwestern Utah by then, too.[31]

The spread of the bow and arrow in prehistoric America is somewhat of a mystery, in part because when it appears, it happens so fast that it exceeds the precision of archaeological dating. Moreover, the bow and arrow leapfrogged its way across the landscape so rapidly that it does not show up everywhere simply because some sites may not have been occupied at the precise moment of its transit. For instance, the bow and arrow does not make it to James Creek Shelter near Elko, Nevada, until after A.D. 600—centuries after its first appearance in some Utah sites. But then James Creek, like so many forager encampments, probably stood unused for years at a time in between occupations. James Creek is not exceptional—most forager sites were probably like that.[32]

The bow and arrow is superior to the atlatl and dart for some types of hunting, especially medium and small game. It may also be better for shooting other humans, and conflict is sometimes offered as important to its spread. Despite the advantages of the bow and arrow, technology alone does not seem to explain its patchy appearance across the continent. Its adoption by any particular group of people is likely a function of the frequency of social contact.

The bow and arrow improves the solitary hunting of large game such as mule deer because one can shoot from a crouch. Thus, its adoption may be linked to the transition from public to private control of resources that occurred with the rise of corporate social organization in the Late Archaic and early Fremont. Once adopted and used deftly by some, others will soon want to acquire it and develop the same skills. Indeed, failure to do would be a disadvantage. If the bow and arrow, for instance, improved the hunting success of individuals who could exert more personal, "private" control of big game meat, that may have conveyed prestige in addition to calories; then others might have been stimulated to follow suit.

Violence, too, may have been relevant to the spread of the bow and arrow. If contact among neighbors was episodic, the bow and arrow would not have spread as fast as when there was conflict. The early Fremont of southern Utah provides an example.

The Western Basketmaker II populations south of the Colorado River did not commonly have the bow and arrow until at least A.D. 600, although there are hints that some may have had it earlier.[33] In contrast, the indigenous Fremont populations in the canyons north of the Colorado River had the bow and arrow by A.D. 100 to 200. As we have seen, these two groups were culturally distinct. The early Fremont had Archaic/Eastern Basketmaker II roots and possibly spoke a now lost Kiowa-Tanoan language. In contrast, the Western Basketmaker II were Uto-Aztecan immigrants. The two were isolated by this cultural gulf and by the dissected terrain of southern Utah's Canyonlands. However, we have seen that when they made contact it was violent. The spread of the bow and arrow was impeded by isolation but fostered on a local, case by case basis by conflict. Thus we find a regional boundary of bow and arrow versus no bow and arrow, but we also find pockets of bow and arrow use within that general pattern.

The Eastern Basketmaker II and Fremont are a different situation. Linked by some common Archaic roots, a geography that favored movement, and a frontier period that lasted several centuries, the bow and arrow moved more readily into Basketmaker II life in the Four Corners area. There are hints of its presence in Basketmaker II

sites, perhaps by A.D. 150–450.[34] When early arrow points are found
in Basketmaker II sites, east or west, they show some differences
from those found north of the Colorado River; another sign of
Fremont distinctiveness.

Yet another face of the Fremont frontier is seen at the Steinaker
Gap site in northeastern Utah. The use of the atlatl and dart by
Basketmaker II immigrants persisted there for several centuries
after the bow and arrow arrived at sites to the south. Perhaps the
immigrants at Steinaker became isolated on the frontier, until the
bow and arrow spread to them from the indigenous locals.

Ceramic technology is part of the identity of Southwestern
farmers, and when early 20th-century archaeologists such as Neil
Judd began finding broken pottery in Utah, the connection to the
better known Anasazi farmers of the Southwest was a natural one.
We now know that pottery arrived several human generations after
the initial formation of the Fremont. This is because the decision to
adopt pottery is associated with mobility. It is one thing to use a pot
if given one, but to invest in its manufacture is not to be taken lightly.
A well-made pot is better for a lot of things than a basket and cheaper
to make, but pots don't move well. The development of a ceramics
industry, often after centuries of exposure to the technology and
even trade that brings a few pots into use, is a milepost of the settling
process and all the trappings of a stronger leash to place. Ceramics
mark not only village life but also an intention to return when several
residences are used in the course of a year.

Plain, gray, everyday-ware ceramics are apparent in Fremont sites
during the 4th century A.D., although they were not common until a
few centuries later. All the early pottery was undecorated and made
of local materials. This shows that Fremont ceramics arose from a
connection of ideas with the Southwest, rather than the importation
of pottery. The boundary between the Fremont and the Anasazi
solidified by A.D. 500, and after that few vessels moved between
Anasazi and Fremont villages. Among the Fremont, large numbers of
pots were traded from manufacturing centers such as the Parowan
Valley to other places in southwestern Utah. Ceramics became a
specialty for some villages and locales after A.D. 1000 as population
centers were established. But, for the most part, Fremont pottery was
locally made, even when designs were copied.[35]

Maize spread to its limits during the Fremont period, reaching
southeastern Idaho, eastern Nevada, northwestern Colorado and

perhaps even along the Utah-Wyoming climatic frontier as people adapted maize to local conditions.

Maize is undeniably an import from the south and another example of connection and isolation. The earliest maizes in Utah were Basketmaker II forms that were already hybrids from centuries of experimentation in the Southwest. Maize appeared at various sites in southern and central Utah in the first few centuries A.D., and Clyde's Cavern, located where the San Rafael Swell meets Castle Valley, provides a glimpse. The earliest maize at Clyde's Cavern is of the Chapalote series found widely in the early Southwest. The cobs were small and relatively unproductive even during the A.D. 600s. Another early maize was the 8-rowed "Maiz de Ocho," a hallmark of the Basketmaker cultures. Once these Southwestern maizes were carried north of the Colorado River, they became isolated, and they adapted to the high plateaus and latitude of the Fremont area. "Dent" maize was distinctively Fremont and was drought and cold tolerant. The maize had a dimple or dent in the top of each kernel, an old trait seen in Mexico and in the Southwest that has been somewhat lost. Fremont Dent maize is evident at Clyde's Cavern by A.D. 600, and this 12- to 14-rowed maize went on to become the typical maize across the Fremont region.

In subsequent centuries, Fremont Dent developed into regional varieties such as those of the Uinta Basin and the Wasatch Front. Connections to the Southwest were not severed—a fragment of the standard, Anasazi two-rod and bundle basketry was found in Clyde's Cavern in a level probably dating after A.D. 500 and containing maize. Over the next five centuries, as the Fremont reached its peak and extended its networks, the connections with the Southwest seem to resurge as more 8-rowed varieties of maize appear at Fremont sites along the southern tier of the state, such as the Parowan Valley near Cedar City.[36]

THE DESERT AND THE SOWN

The centuries between A.D. 800 and 1300 saw a dramatic rise in population size, with the precise timing depending on location. Many now rural areas such as Castle Valley, the Sevier Valley, and Parowan Valley were more widely populated than the same areas are today. The Wasatch Front may well have been the most populous part of

FIGURE 5.7

The distinctive Fremont "Dent" maize characterized by a dimple on most of the kernals. Dent maize is found elsewhere in North America, but through isolation from the Southwest and because it became adapted to the high, cold valleys and mesas of Utah, it was the typical maize of the Fremont. (Sketch by Jennifer Hulse)

Utah, just as it is today. Archaeologists have a dual personality when it comes to the Fremont. On the one hand, we have long known they were farmers. When Noel Morss prospected along the Fremont River near the towns of Loa and Torrey in the 1920s, local farmers showed him the ancient Indian irrigation ditches. Nearly every Utah town founded by Mormon settlers between Brigham City and Cedar City is built on top of Fremont homes and fields, because both peoples chose the best places to farm with the least effort.

On the other hand, archaeologists realized the Fremont were not as married to farming as were the Anasazi of the Southwest. The Fremont was seen as a "northern periphery" relegated to part-time hunting and gathering by the harsh environment of the high plateaus. This became the stereotype of the Fremont.

We now know that many Fremont people ate as much maize as many Anasazi. This story is told by the stable carbon isotopes housed in human bone that estimates the amount of maize consumed during a person's life. Maize and similar plants contributed between 73% and 85% of the diet of Fremont people living at Nawthis Village above Salina, Caldwell Village near Vernal, the Evans Mound near Cedar City, and Backhoe Village at Richfield. The isotope technique is not perfect, because some wild plants eaten by humans mimic the signature of maize, but when we find the same percentages in skeletons from Anasazi sites, we realize that the amounts of maize in their diets were similar.[37]

It may be tempting to replace the stereotype of mixed farmer-foragers with the stereotype that the Fremont were every bit the farmers that the Anasazi were, but further research suggests both labels miss the mark. Flooding of Great Salt Lake in the late 1980s exposed the largest collection of Fremont human skeletal remains ever found. At least 85 people were studied with the permission of the Northwestern Band of the Shoshone nation, the modern tribe living nearby. This was not only a large sample but also a more representative sample. Up to this time, most Fremont skeletons came from Fremont farming sites, because archaeologists chose those to excavate. Most burials came from pithouses within villages, further selecting for only a fraction of the population, because not everyone was buried inside a village. In contrast, when the waters of Great Salt Lake receded from an area covering nearly 30 square miles, the skeletal sample exposed by Mother Nature did not discriminate. For the first time, we could glimpse everyone who was buried there.

Over 50 individuals were tested, much as if they had gone to the doctor for a biopsy. A tiny sample of bone enabled each person to be dated and provided tissue for DNA testing and stable carbon isotopes to identify how much maize they ate over significant spans of their lives. The results both fit and did not fit what archaeologists had found before, but most of all it elevated our understanding past a simple dichotomy between nomadic foragers and settled farmers.

Even the most devoted farmers in the Great Salt Lake sites ate a little less maize than did Fremont people in other places, but the skeletons also revealed a high degree of variation. Maize and related plants constituted only 35% of the diet for some, 50% for others, and nearly 70% for the tenacious farmers. It did not matter if the person ended life with a funeral in a large farming village such as the Big

Village at Willard or was buried in a simple ceremony at a campsite in the marshes bordering Great Salt Lake.[38]

For a while it looked as though this finding was just more of what archaeologists already thought about the Fremont—that they were a "mixture" of farming and foraging. A natural conclusion from these results is that there were different peoples living in the same area—a farming people and a foraging people.

Perhaps these were not categorical distinctions but changes in lifestyle from birth to adolescence, adulthood, and old age. Perhaps Fremont life was more dynamic than we thought. Is it possible that someone might be born in the desert as a forager, grow up there, and as a young adult find himself marrying into a village and eating maize for the rest of his life? Or perhaps after a few poor years of farming a village might break up, with some families being sent to live with relatives where people relied on a mix of farmed and wild foods. Archaeologists have long wondered about these things, and it began to look as though the scale were tipping toward a dynamic between the desert and the sown.[39]

Further analyses of the Great Salt Lake skeletons shed light on this question. Mitochondrial DNA traces maternal inheritance and shows that the Great Salt Lake Fremont sample was relatively homogeneous even though it spanned three centuries. The full-time maize eaters were of the same genetic legacy as the full-time foragers, as were all those with diets in between. Whatever variations there were in identity, ethnicity, and perhaps ways of speaking, the flow of genes effectively unified this diversity.

The Great Salt Lake skeletons were also studied for lifetime activity patterns revealed by a biomechanical analysis of CAT scans of limb bones. This analysis identifies the intensity of upper body work and detects differences in lower body exercise between people who hiked steep terrain versus smooth terrain, and those who were settled and did not range far. The CAT scans showed that males traveled widely over rough ground, and the females did not. The women exhibited hard lives of upper body work, and they and their children probably anchored villages and camps located in the marshes along the Wasatch Front. The men hiked the mountains to obtain raw materials and hunt animals not available in the lowlands. The biggest finding was that this activity pattern held regardless of how much maize a person consumed in a lifetime. Again, the farmers and the foragers looked the same.

The DNA and activity patterns show that some of the differences archaeologists saw were reflections of the life history of individuals, rather than categorical differences between people who lived one way or another all their lives. It is the same story of unity as told by the distinctive tradition of Fremont basketry—they were all of a cloth. The Fremont cultural tradition was a tapestry of local ethnicity and variations in ways of life woven together by the social connections that came from the flow of people across the landscape.[40]

Archaeologists see much more than a simple story of foragers settling down to become farmers. The farming life indeed reduced residential mobility as long as people kept farming in a particular place. But excavations of Fremont sites show that most were not occupied long before being abandoned. Absences were sometimes brief, perhaps only a few years, before people returned. In some places, a striking consistency in architectural style and in the building sequences leaves the impression that it was the same people returning and picking up where they left off. Over time, some Fremont villages accumulated into huge expanses of homes and other buildings superimposed on earlier buildings, including all kinds of remodeling. The Evans Mound near Cedar City grew in stops and starts over three centuries, growing into a low hill the size of a football field. There are similar examples in the towns of Beaver, Richfield, Nephi, Kanosh, and, of course, Utah and Salt Lake valleys. Like the Anasazi, the Fremont abandoned frequently, and this was part of life and place.

To modern ears, the term "abandonment" sounds like a failure to progress, but perhaps this is the wrong perspective. Abandonment was part of their success. It was part of a sense of place characterized by rhythmic tempo anchored to the land. Fremont farmers flowed over places as the patchwork quilt of arable land changed year to year in response to myriad cues. It might have been the depth of mountain snowpack and consequently the spring and summer runoff. Or it might have been minor differences in elevation, where only 100 meters mattered. A plot might fail or succeed, depending on whether the first frost arrived in August or September. Even the annual exposure of land to sun and shade changed. In some years, a sunny southern exposure might have fried the fields while a nearby northern aspect at the base of a slope leaking moisture might have saved it. In other years it could have been the reverse.

Where did people go when they abandoned places? The first choice was to move to other plots controlled by their family, lineage, and alliances among communities. A portfolio of fields in a variety of small settings hedged risk. Over decades, the plots of arable land might move up and down slope as the climate changed. During drought, only the best places might produce, and as population grew, previously unexploited plots could be added. But this approach worked only until the 11th and 12th centuries, when all the arable land was used. The social fabric mediated a dynamic between the desert and the sown, the inhabited and the abandoned, and the tempo of life and place.[41]

BIG VILLAGES, INEQUALITY, AND HIERARCHY

The dynamic between the desert and the sown is a window into a Fremont social life that grew from a culture of mixed heritage on a landscape that had never seen so many people. Neighbors were everywhere, and in many places all the farmland had been appropriated. The circumstances of Fremont life produced social complexity—social status, roles, and rules to manage inequality—and the spiraling extraction of energy from the land to support more people.

Scholars of the Fremont have long resisted the temptation to infer too many trappings of civilization to the Fremont, and not without reason. Even the biggest Fremont "villages" with hundreds of pithouses mostly resulted from the accumulations of smaller occupations over centuries. Nor is there a lot of variation in the size of the houses that would suggest large differences in wealth. We don't see large food storehouses like those at Chaco Canyon, New Mexico, and there are no massive public works projects.

Archaeologists often rely on the degree of adornment in burials to identify inequality and social complexity. A burial excavated at the Evans Mound near Cedar City was an adult male placed on a woven mat and interred in the floor of a pithouse. He was accompanied by a finely made knife, quartz crystals, a whistle, a belt that employed the skulls of nine magpies, and a headdress using the skull of a great horned owl. But only a handful of Fremont burials stand out like this, and for the most part Fremont funeral arrangements do not suggest much showing off, or much inequality.[42] Add to this the fact that small Fremont sites far outnumber the larger villages, and images of the Fremont as simple egalitarian farmers become a romantic temptation. But it is becoming clear that such stereotypes are misleading.

The studies at Five Finger Ridge by Brigham Young University archaeologists under the direction of Richard Talbot and Lane

Richens show that true villages did in fact exist. The population estimates for Five Finger Ridge at its peak during the A.D. 1200s are conservatively placed at around 100 people. This is based on the minimum number of houses in the same stratigraphic levels that could be used at one time. A minimum estimate is just that, and it is an artifact of archaeological conservatism. Five Finger Ridge was clearly a village and at times may have been home to hundreds of people. There were differences in the sizes of homes and a public plaza. The excavations at Five Finger Ridge captured the attention of archaeologists lulled by decades of perceiving the Fremont as rural hunter-gatherers who also did a little farming. It turns out that Five Finger Ridge is not an exceptional case.[43]

Amid the backdrop of farmsteads and hamlets that so color our understanding of the Fremont are dozens of larger sites, and there is reason to believe that they represent the tip of an iceberg. Neil Judd was eager to excavate at Paragonah, because the number of mounds was rapidly dwindling even in 1915. Only a few decades earlier there were reports of up to 400 mounds in the area. By the early 20th century less than half remained, most of them removed to prepare agricultural fields.[44] Name the Utah cities and under them are Fremont villages. The few remaining places where archaeological excavation might encounter large villages are in urbanized settings or on private farmland being gobbled up by urban sprawl. There are probably some sizable villages in remote places such as Range Creek, but that environment would not produce the biggest ones. Even in the few cases where some archaeology is allowed and funded, excavation only nibbles at these huge sites. In the largely rural Parowan Valley, once home to hundreds of mounds, we have relatively modern archaeological knowledge of only two—the Evans Mound and Median Village. If we ignore the evidence for villages just because we have not excavated them, we risk casting the Fremont as something they were not.

The Paragonah site offers a glimpse of the social power of villages with their courtyards and adobe granaries built where everyone could see them. Neil Judd and some archaeologists to follow recognized that the use of space at Paragonah and other villages placed the Fremont within the Ancestral Puebloan world order of the Southwest. The Fremont were not Anasazi, but as they knitted social fabrics in response to peak populations after A.D. 1000, their Southwestern roots are evident even across what may have been

FIGURE 5.8

Median Village was excavated by John Marwitt and Jesse Jennings and is an example of the many large villages of the Parowan Valley, southwestern Utah. Circular pithouses are often superimposed on one another, and rectangular structures of adobe were used as maize cribs. The wavy trench at the lower left may be an irrigation canal. The excavation uncovered only part of the village, and the Parowan Valley was once dotted with many hundreds of such places. Median Village now lies under Interstate 15. (Courtesy of the Archaeological Center, Department of Anthropology, University of Utah)

considerable linguistic and ethnic diversity within what we now call the Fremont.[45]

During the most populous period from the late A.D. 900s through the A.D. 1200s, villages anchored the backdrop of scattered farmsteads and hamlets. But this is not a debate as to whether the Fremont were centralized or dispersed. They were clearly both. Instead, the nature of Fremont social fabrics is found in the connections between the centralized and the dispersed. Like the desert and the sown, there is a dynamic between larger and smaller segments of the system, and this dynamic created a degree of social hierarchy not seen before in the prehistory of the Basin-Plateau.

The big village at Five Finger Ridge sits above and anchors smaller villages, hamlets, and farmsteads up and down Clear Creek Canyon. Perhaps Icicle Bench, Radford's Roost, and Lott's Farm are a few

FIGURE 5.9

Fremont radiocarbon dates show the initial forays into farming in the early centuries A.D. and the dramatic rise in activity and population during the Medieval Warm Period of the A.D. 900–1000s. The "punctuations" between A.D. 900–1200 result from the interplay of a populous, and perhaps overpopulated, farming culture facing the vicissitudes of Basin-Plateau climate. The rapid decline after A.D. 1200 marks the onset of the Little Ice Age, beginning a several-century period when farming would have been impossible in many years, or perhaps restricted to only a few favorable microclimates in the region.

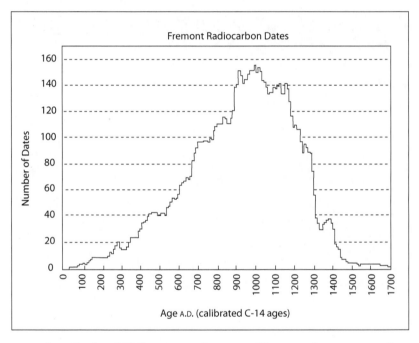

examples. Richard Talbot uses the term "dispersed community" to signal the social connections among the segments of a system linking people of varying means, power, and prestige through kinship and common perceptions of the world order. Each segment of the society was egalitarian, but inevitable differences arose from the usual channels of achievement and luck. There were connections through marriage, lineages of living kin, and even connections with dead ancestors who could mediate the spirit world and the temporal world. The symbolism found in rock art and the distinctive Fremont figurines perhaps played a role in this mediation. A nested set of hierarchies structured what people did whenever they interacted beyond their own farmstead, and a common ideology facilitated interaction both collaborative and hostile.[46]

Sequential hierarchies, or heterarchies as they are sometimes known, are difficult to imagine, because we don't find this sort of arrangement in modern America. They are an unfamiliar mix of egalitarianism, inequality, and communal processes. We tend to think of power mostly as wealth—especially its display. We expect large buildings, lavish burials, huge homes for the rich, and storehouses owned by the "chief." These understandings of what constitutes social complexity conflict with what we know about societies such as the Fremont and others of the ancient Southwest. There was inequality and there were leaders, but the trappings of hierarchy as we conceive of it did not exist.

A similar struggle to explain complexity is found in the American Southwest. A great deal of ethnographic and archaeological study leads to the realization that cases such as Chaco Canyon, New Mexico, were centers of large-scale regional connections that ranged from direct and coercive to indirect and ideological. We know that there were places and times of significant complexity, but like the Fremont, most Anasazi archaeology consists of small scattered farmsteads, each having lasted only a few years or decades before another was built. Archaeologists realized there were larger political organizations at work, but they were unsure what form these took. We were trapped by our own metaphors—complexity must look like our society, in which inequality in power and prestige is expressed in terms of material wealth and its display. We now realize that there are many paths to complexity.[47]

The kinds of complexity found in the ancient Southwest and among the Fremont were corporate, with assigned status and role and clear rules of membership. But they were also decentralized, with each semi-autonomous segment nested within a loose hierarchy. Michelle Hegmon describes leadership in the ancient Southwest as "faceless." Leadership and power are ritualized and cannot live outside a symbolic context. The pathways to leadership tended to be closed, because the connection to symbolic power was more important than merely having wealth.[48] Power came from the movement of wealth, not from its possession or display.

Hegmon also observes the wealth of anthropological evidence showing that burial goods were not necessarily an indicator of wealth in life. In corporate systems, burial adornment may reflect the manner in which a person died, rather than his power and status while he lived. The lack of burial adornment among the Fremont seems at first glance to indicate that there was little social complexity compared to the Anasazi, who seem richer given their spectacular pueblos and cliff dwellings. There is a difference in degree, but the vast majority of Anasazi were buried with little material display of wealth. Fremont burials were even less adorned as a group, but when a broad sample is considered, Anasazi people buried away from the large Pueblos also tended to pass on with little.[49]

None of this means that the peoples of the Southwest and their Fremont neighbors practiced some sort of primitive communism. Inequality was real and consequential to people's lives. Leaders in corporate systems exercise their power for the good of themselves and for segments of the hierarchy to which they are most connected, not for the entire group. People could be made poor, coerced, enslaved, tortured, and killed. Segments in such hierarchical systems can be recruited to collective action, because each segment is nested within larger, more powerful, and coercive social realities bound together by a common perception of the way the world is supposed to be.

FAMILY, LINEAGE, CONNECTIONS, AND CONFLICT

We can think about Fremont kinship using the analogy of their descendent cultures of the historic Southwest—the Rio Grande Pueblos and possibly the Hopi. Those societies were matrilineal, tracing lineage through the female line. Matrilineages are mostly found in societies with small-scale horticultural production that requires local labor and solutions rather than large-scale production and waterworks. Women were anchored to the land, and men moved among lineages and across places upon marriage—taking residence in the family of their wives.

Women held significant decision-making roles within the household, in local craft production and resource procurement, and in matters of farming. Men's influence resided in matters requiring lineage and place to be crossed, such as the management of food storage and the structure of labor between farms and villages. The broader connections of men fostered the assembly of men's groups for hunting parties, for securing natural resources, and for long-distance political encounters for alliance, trade, marriage, and conflict. Men's connections, perhaps ritualized, formed the pliable elements of a social fabric that was anchored by female lineage, work groups, and place.

Matrilineal kinship is a social fact in the historic Southwest and is strongly suspected in the ancient centers such as Chaco Canyon. We also know that by Basketmaker II times, Southwestern peoples were moving more strongly toward maize horticulture than previously thought. The forces for matrilineal society were laid early, and it was probably a characteristic of the Fremont to varying degrees.

The lowest rungs in the Fremont hierarchy are the family and farmstead. Next was the village that anchored the dispersed community. Village leadership orchestrated seasonal ritual events and trading festivals, made political negotiations, and resolved disagreements and feuds. Bridges to other dispersed communities were built through known kin relations, arranged alliances, the exchange of goods, and the symbolically validated beliefs in shared ancestors. Religion in such societies assumes the perception of common ancestry.

Fremont matrilineal society was most developed where large villages anchored dispersed communities. In the wilderness, where farming was more episodic and mobile and where full-time foraging remained a part of life, there was a higher frequency of people who set up their own households when they married and traced lineage through male or female lineages depending on their circumstances—much like the Archaic foragers had done for millennia. The fabric of Fremont kinship was thus pliable, not monolithic.[50]

Larger scales of nested connections were also sustained. Pottery used in the Clear Creek Canyon community was routinely imported from the Parowan Valley, a distance of over 40 miles. These were not exotic goods. Corrugated cooking vessels were used every day, and although they could easily have been made locally, between 87% and 95% of the corrugated pottery fragments and half the painted vessels at Five Finger Ridge were imported. This holds at other Clear Creek Canyon sites, too. The movement of exotic items to Clear Creek, such as carnotite from the Uinta Basin, jet from the San Rafael Swell, turquoise from Nevada, and sulfur and gypsum from Utah's West Deserts, is not just the movement of goods but symbolizes the social fabric stretching across the landscape. It is this fabric that makes Fremont basketry, and the themes in the rock art and figurines, similar across large areas. It is also the source of similarity in the cultural logic of the Fremont and the Southwest.[51]

Rock art is an expression of Fremont cultural logic in relation to place. Rock art specialists such as Polly Schaafsma and Sally Cole describe the underlying unity that distinguishes Fremont rock art from neighboring regions and from the cultures that preceded and followed. There are hints of connection to the Archaic, such as elements of the Great Basin curvilinear style and elements of the Barrier Canyon style of the upper Colorado River. Sally Cole argues for stronger connections with the Eastern Basketmaker but also some elements of later Anasazi styles. Fremont rock art thus traces the mixed heritage of the Fremont, as well as its distinctiveness and unity. Rock art also reveals the localness of Fremont societies and suggests that boundaries did exist. Regional Fremont rock art styles include the Classic Vernal style of the Uinta Basin and the San Rafael, Sevier, and Western Utah Painted styles.[52]

Cultural boundaries are also apparent in the movement of goods. Trade of ceramics between the Fremont and the Anasazi was limited compared to the ceramic trade among the Fremont. Recent archaeological studies along the Fremont-Anasazi frontier in Capitol Reef National Park and near the town of Escalante suggest a dynamic frontier with distinct ethnic and perhaps linguistic boundaries that ebbed and flowed over decades. Some places were used by each group, but at different times. There were probably ethnic and linguistic distinctions across Fremont land. Rock art traditions vary between the eastern Great Basin and those on the Colorado Plateau. Architecture varies a bit, and the projectile points vary a lot. Nascent and largely unpublished measurements of cranial features from a growing sample of skeletal remains also suggest that there were different Fremont populations.[53]

The reach of Fremont social fabrics was not limited by the desert. Baker Village, located on the Utah-Nevada border, was a small village in the 13th century with pithouses arranged around a large adobe structure and public storage. It is an example of Fremont village planning—the structures are aligned to within 3 degrees of one another, and their positions mark the winter and the summer solstices. Bryan Hockett found large numbers of bone from bighorn sheep, mule deer, and rabbits. A few other Fremont villages show the same thing.[54]

The people at Baker Village routinely traversed the Escalante Desert to the Parowan Valley and probably Clear Creek Canyon— well over a third of the ceramics at Baker Village appear to be imported. Baker itself was probably the centerpiece of a dispersed community with significant differences in power and prestige among its components and with relationships with other communities in western Utah and eastern Nevada.[55]

PLATE 1

A curing ceremony using a sucking tube is hosted inside a tule mat home in the Great Salt Lake wetlands of northern Utah. Female shamans were known in the Great Basin but were apparently not as common as male curers. Shamans could be specialists or generalists, and if their work did not go well, they could be seen as sorcerers. Their skills were thus a blend of social and spiritual power, and knowledge of illness and curing. This shaman holds a rattle while she bobs forward and back using the sucking tube to draw illness out of the patient. She combines this with a poultice using medicinal herbs ground into a paste using small mortars and pestles. She is dressed in fiber clothing, by far the most common fabric in prehistory. Textiles were the technological foundation of ancient foraging societies. (Artwork by Noel Carmack)

PLATE 2

Fish taken during spawning season were a resource that could strongly tether people to place. The most common fishes taken in antiquity were suckers. Trout were also caught but constitute a small but constant fraction of archaeological fish-bone assemblages. Fish could be taken in many ways, including nets, bow and arrow, spears, hooks, or by hand. They could also be driven by rolling a mass of brush along the stream to herd spawning fish into a swarm lifted onto the banks with nets or by hand. Boats made of cattail stalks were used to transport equipment and the harvest of fish. In this scene nets, anchored by stone net weights are used to capture fish that will be dried and stored for future use. Although the potential for a large harvest is an obvious tether to place, it is the storage of the food that makes the tether tenacious. (Artwork by Eric Carlson)

PLATE 3

Roots are an important food in many foraging societies, because they are typically starchy, supply a range of nutrients, and can be stored. Roots often occur in great number in patches that persist for centuries. Roots were dug with digging sticks often made of hardwoods such as mountain mahogany. Chipped stone tools known as crescents may have served to scrape the skin from roots. Here is a party in the northern Great Basin harvesting bitterroot in the early summer. The roots could be baked, or simply roasted over hot coals, and many were dried for ease of transport in burden baskets or for storage in underground pits and bags. A root-collecting episode such as this one could involve dozens of people and last for weeks before the camp group was adjusted in size and composition to pursue the next bounty. (Artwork by Eric Carlson)

PLATE 4

Atlatl thrower. The primary large-game hunting weapon since Paleoindian times is a cane dart tipped with a hardwood foreshaft affixed to a stone point. The atlatl leveraged the dart to a high velocity. This atlatl incorporates a weight, but many did not. They can be thrown using a variety of postures, except kneeling or crouching. The learning curve to become expert is steep, but in skilled hands the dart can be directed with astonishing accuracy, consistently hitting the center of archery targets at 30 meters or more. Experiments show that atlatl-propelled darts can penetrate the hide of African elephants. The clothing in this depiction indicates one possibility for Late Pleistocene–Early Holocene attire comprising a mix of skin and fiber clothing, and substantial footwear. (Artwork by Eric Carlson)

PLATE 5

Butchering the Huntington mammoth 13,000 years ago. The connection between this mammoth and humans is not clear, but cutmarks on the bone suggest butchering with stone tools. The mammoth is on display at the Prehistoric Museum in Price, Utah. It was found on the Sevier Plateau at 9,000 feet in what was an alpine forest ecosystem with marshes and bogs in the Late Pleistocene. It died in one of these bogs and was so well preserved that feces revealed it dined on spruce needles and other alpine plants. A kill of this size could involve a sizable work force of men, women, and children, because there would have been many tasks to harvest and prepare the wide range of resources from this animal, including tusk, sinew, hide, and brains, to name just a few, in addition to the meat. This depiction shows the facial characteristics often found among Paleoindians indicating the connections of the earliest Americans to various east Asian and Pacific Rim populations. The facial characteristics of most Paleoindian Native Americans differ markedly from their more recent Native American descendants. (Artwork by Noel Carmack)

PLATE 6

Images of Paleoindians wandering tundra environments in small groups looking for "big game" underestimates the organization required for a viable economy in Pleistocene environments. Group sizes may have been substantial, at least episodically. Settlements were surely not permanent but probably lasted for weeks or a few months at a time even as the resident composition fluctuated with the tasks at hand. The mammoth skull attests that big game were driving economic decisions, but the burden baskets are filled with waterfowl at this camp in a marshy Great Basin valley. A wide range of plant and animal foods were eaten. There are no examples of Paleoindian housing in the Basin-Plateau, but elsewhere on the continent and among Arctic foragers today, housing may have been above-ground structures of stone, wood, hides, or bark. Racks for hanging meat were routine. A camp such as this anchored the activities of a locale, but over the life histories of individuals, mobility was probably higher in Paleoindian times than in later periods. (Artwork by Eric Carlson)

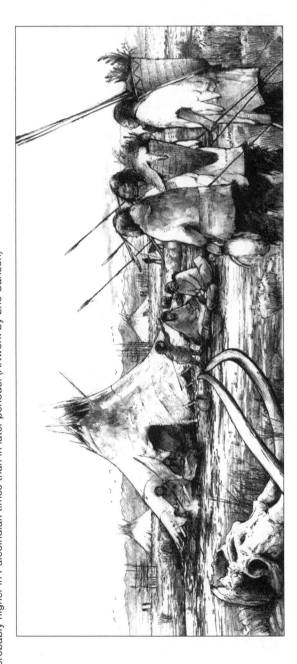

PLATE 7

Far from being cast into a wilderness with only the food and tools on their backs, ancient people lived in a highly managed, "built" environment. This man is retrieving a cache of 88 stone tool blanks. Each blank is flaked on both sides and prepared for final manufacture into knives, scrapers, arrowheads, drills, and gravers. This cache was found by amateur archaeologists in 1990 in the marshes northwest of Ogden, Utah. The obsidian is geochemically sourced to a location 60 miles away, northwest of Malad, Idaho. Such pits were common and enabled people to work without having to carry everything they need wherever they went. The flakes were carefully placed in a shallow hole along with a small, round quartzite pebble. Perhaps the pebble conveyed power to the cache or signified the man's intention to return. We will never know the reason why the man who created this cache never retrieved it, but through his misfortune we can glimpse his life (Cornell, Stuart, and Simms 1992:159).

PLATE 8

High desert foragers of the Archaic used a variety of techniques to acquire game. Here a hunter retrieves his trap line of scissors snares and his take of Cottontail rabbits. The most common food bones found in Basin-Plateau archaeological sites of any period are Cottontail rabbit and Jackrabbit. (Artwork by Noel Carmack)

PLATE 9

Hunting is not restricted to men, and this especially applies to small-game hunting. Women in groups hunted small mammals where their burrows were concentrated using mass techniques such as diverting a creek into a field of burrows to flush animals out. They participated in rabbit drives with men and children where hundreds of rabbits were driven into nets and clubbed. Women could also run trap lines, a type of hunting that could be embedded in other activities from child care, to basketry, to root and seed gathering. Here a woman uses large scissors snares to take squirrels. The illustration shows how the animal is attracted to the bait and how the snare seizes the animal once it is tripped. Note the woman's fiber clothing, by far the most common fabric in the history of humanity. (Artwork by Eric Carlson)

PLATE 10

This is a Fremont rancheria occupied by about two dozen people. That roofs of pithouses were commonly used for daily activities is shown by the number of artifacts found on top of the roof fall when pithouses are excavated. Most activities were carried on outside; hence, ramadas were probably common, as were outdoor hearths, and racks for drying meat, roots, and even maize. This area may have been wooded at one time, but most of the trees around Fremont residences would have been quickly used up for building and especially for fuel wood. Waffle-shaped agricultural plots cover the slope in the background but would have been located on such slopes only when the groundwater situation was favorable. Other fields were placed along the floodplain of the stream. The people at this rancheria were likely part of a dispersed community anchored by a village, and managed through a network of social connections and hierarchy.

PLATE 11

Typical Fremont pithouse with a four-post support pattern, leaner poles overlayed with a lattice, and a shell of mud and dirt. Many pithouses were not as deep or as substantially roofed as this one. The central fire hearth is typical as are sand-filled basins in the floor used to support curved bottomed pots. Pithouses are used around the world and tend to correspond with societies that are semisedentary and that move among several homes each year or every few years. Round pithouses indicate more mobility; the square pattern indicates more settling. The average life of a pithouse was about a decade, and many pithouses ended with accidental, or in some cases, intentional burning. This pithouse is a hub of activity, as demonstrated by the large "Utah type" *metate* (with a shelf on one end), pots, basketry, gear hanging from the rafters, and debris on the floor from the work that had to be done every day. Fiber mats may have been used as carpeting.

PLATE 12

The site at Paragonah was excavated by Neil Judd in 1916–1917 and again by Clement Meighan in the 1950s. They found an arrangement of large adobe granaries around a courtyard with a large semisubterranean structure in the center. To the extent the Fremont parallel the cultures of the Southwest, this large structure may have been a community building of ritual and clan significance. Smaller, residential pithouses were scattered about. No one knows the exact look of the Paragonah site, but this reconstruction serves as a reminder that large Fremont villages existed. Since archaeologists tend to excavate small sites, or only tiny portions of large sites, it has taken a long time to recognize that villages were not the exception but a common part of Fremont society. Villages of dozens and possibly several hundred people were scattered in central locations around the region, but especially along the eastern rim of the Great Basin from Cedar City, Utah, to Preston, Idaho. Most of these were either buried or destroyed by modern towns and cities, because the big villages occupied the same places chosen later by Euroamerican pioneers for farms and towns.

PLATE 13

A funeral for this Fremont woman was held in the marshes bordering Great Salt Lake in the 11th century A.D. She died between the ages of 30 and 35 from severe metastatic carcinoma. The cancer metastasized from the breast, the thyroid, or, most likely in this case, from the nasopharynx. The pattern of anatomic change and lesions seen in radiographs are most consistent with the last possibility (Loveland and Gregg 1994). This form of cancer spreads rapidly, and although she was clearly cared for, she must have been in severe pain, because by the time of her death there were lesions on nearly every bone in her body. Her flexed position was achieved with bindings, a common burial practice in many cultures. She was interred simply, with only a grinding stone and a freshwater clam shell.

PLATE 14

This man died in the Great Salt Lake wetlands A.D. 775–979 and was buried in a small cemetery in the marshes where at least 11 people were interred over a century or more. Several of the burials contained grave goods, such as a Utah-type *metate*, sewing awls, gaming counters, a duck's head effigy, and a horn from a juvenile bison—all rubbed with red ochre. This man died between the ages of 35 and 40 years of age, but at some point in his adult life his hip fused with his thigh, and he lived with his left leg elevated. All his lower limb bones on the left side are smaller than the bones on his right. His left arm was more robust than his right, perhaps from supporting himself for years after his hip fused. His vertebrae were also affected. The condition does not appear to result from a birth defect or trauma but may be secondary to tuberculosis. His condition, ankylosis, was occasionally known to doctors practicing in the 19th and early 20th centuries (Loveland, Furlong, and Gregg 1992). Stable carbon isotope analysis shows that his diet was mostly wild food, even though he lived among and was buried with people who farmed. His daily habits surely changed with the onset of his condition, but the fact that he went on with his life shows the support of the social fabric.

PLATE 15

The Orbit Inn site located at Brigham City, Utah, on the edge of the Great Salt Lake wetlands is an example of life during the Promontory period. This camp was used repeatedly between A.D. 1425 and 1450 for taking Utah chub and other suckers during the spring spawn, and again in the late summer for hunting waterfowl during their molt. Seed resources and small mammals, especially muskrats, were also taken. Each time the camp was occupied for perhaps a month; it was one of several points of anchor as people cycled among the wetlands during the year. Specialized task parties went to the mountains for resources ranging from toolstone to mule deer. A brown chert commonly used at the Orbit Inn came from a mountain pass about 12 miles to the east. Even though, in contrast to the preceding Fremont farmers, the Promontory economy was based on foraging, a tradition of pottery making continued. Despite the degree of continuity in heritage, the demise of farming fundamentally altered the notion of place and life itself.

The dispersed community anchored by Baker Village reminds us
that to some extent communities also included the foraging peoples in
the rural hinterlands—the desert and the sown. At places such as Buzz
Cut Dune on the western edge of the Great Salt Lake Desert near
the modern outpost of Callao, Fremont people foraged locally over a
15-mile radius. More distant connections are evident in the Tosawihi
chert from northwest of Elko, Nevada, and the obsidian from Malad,
Idaho, that ended up at Buzz Cut Dune. Ceramics were styled like
those of the Wasatch Front, but some were made of local materials,
whereas other vessels were imported from distant villages, perhaps
via camps such as Camelsback Cave on the Dugway Proving Ground.
Camelsback Cave was a brief stopover between the big villages along
the Wasatch Front and the people of the desert. Ceramics found in
Camelsback Cave are both local and imported.[56]

The dynamic between the desert and the sown suggests that over
the life of individuals there were some who fell away from farming
to become forager refugees in the mountains and deserts. Organized
parties of hunters who spent weeks or months hunting big game
surely encountered, or temporarily became, this Fremont "Other"
in the wilderness. Perhaps an injustice of the time was a wilderness
increasingly used up as the Fremont period wore on. People born
as foragers were the indigenous natives, but they watched their lifeway dissolve as farming and population growth appropriated the
landscape. Many foragers would have slipped into poverty, and some
might have sought refuge as squatters on the outskirts of villages.
Some might have gained a foothold through marriage and servitude,
but their lifeway and old culture steadily died.

A fully humanized understanding of the vibrant Fremont social
landscape also requires us to confront social tension, conflict, and
violence. Rather than mutually exclusive, cooperation and conflict are
two sides of the same coin. The most incessant violence in any society
comes from within and is usually played out among families, lineages,
and communities. Furthermore, most Fremont social tension was
local, because there was little opportunity for, and few means to support, large-scale conflict among regions.

Perhaps the most compelling images of Fremont social tension,
and even conflict, come from the West Tavaputs Plateau north of
Price, Utah. Nine Mile Canyon and the now famous Range Creek
Canyon cut through the plateau. Spectacular archaeological finds
encompass the full range of Fremont life and, in their own oddly
extreme way, help us glimpse strife among the Fremont in general.

The Fremont occupations in Nine Mile and Range Creek canyons grew substantially after A.D. 1000. Both canyons harbored the typical hamlets situated near the best floodplain farmland, and Range Creek seems to have some substantial villages, too. Arable plots in both canyons were for the most part small, numerous, and tenuous. Like other Fremont but to a greater degree, people cycled across the landscape producing abandonment, the founding of new places, and the reoccupation of the old. The trash heaps found in Fremont sites in Nine Mile Canyon are particularly thin and have the feel of short occupations. Storage of maize and other products was in small cists dug into the ground, sometimes under rock shelters, and in stone granaries on the ubiquitous ledges along the narrow canyon walls. Like the fields, storage facilities were small and contrasted with the big adobe granaries of the Parowan Valley or even Baker Village. There were connections to the south toward the San Rafael Swell, and some of the pottery in Nine Mile Canyon may have been imported from those places. The other logical connection is to the Uinta Basin to the north, and there was surely interaction with people there, too. Daily life in the canyons of the West Tavaputs Plateau was simultaneously on its own, yet nested within the larger world.[57]

Nine Mile Canyon and Range Creek were caught up in the same cycle as other Fremont and the larger world of the Southwest. Populations grew, all the available farmland was used, and the colonization of new frontiers was no longer possible. Each episode of abandonment or even seasonal movement placed strains on the social system, like people jostling on a crowded bus. The limited canyon environments of the West Tavaputs country yielded fewer options, and the response to fickle agricultural production in the 11th and 12th centuries was as extreme as we see anywhere in Fremont land. Storage structures were perched in sandstone cracks hundreds of feet above the canyon floor. Some of these can be reached today only with technical climbing gear, and the Fremont probably had clever and skilled ways to gain access to these. Storage in the cliffs was frequent enough to make the casual visitor fantasize that the Fremont were just acting on impulse—"maybe they just liked to store their corn up high to be near the sky." At the same time, masonry enclosures were positioned on eminences overlooking the floodplain below. Difficult to access and useless for farming, these structures are variously dubbed defensive "forts" or places of ceremony. But these may be one and the same; conflict is ideological, and religion is economic.

The cliff granaries and parched outposts above the canyon floors in Nine Mile Canyon, Range Creek, and others were perhaps no more part of Fremont daily life than Napoleon's army was to a French farmer—until the moment they sprang into use in dire situations. They represent episodes of strife and almost certainly conflict. Some granaries probably stood unused for years at a time, serving only as reminders of the past and of alliances, tensions, and old scores. These, too, were part of the social fabric and surely came into play whenever circumstances drove people to hoard, hide, and guard their food supplies. They likely date to the 12th and 13th centuries. They were probably used when drought was widespread and affected everyone equally, in contrast to the usual pattern whereby some fields produced well and others did not. The social fabric could handle the latter by moving people and food, but it tore badly at the prospect of universal shortage, especially in constrained areas such as Nine Mile and Range Creek canyons. They may be analogous to food hiding among the Bedul Bedouin near Petra, Jordan, who build strikingly similar structures to hide food. Some are intentionally hidden from view, most require intricate routes of access, and some cannot be reached without risking full public view from the canyon below. They are all about power, authority, and the control of food storage within extended families. The Bedul used the facilities only a few times each century during severe droughts. Our informant accounts of their use match the rainfall records of drought for the area.[58]

The case of Nine Mile Canyon and Range Creek may be extreme, but what happened there mirrors stresses that all Fremont had to face at one time or another.

An eerie reminder of the violent side of Fremont life is the presence of human bone that is burned and fragmented and that shows signs of butchering. Sometimes they are found scattered across living areas, or in structures that were destroyed. Sometimes they are mixed with other refuse in the dumps. These are not burials but violent deaths, and perhaps even remnants of cannibalism associated with ritual and witchcraft. Such finds probably represent spasms of violence in particularly difficult times and places. Unsavory to ponder, violence was also an occasional part of Fremont life.[59]

There was greater inequality, more direct use of power, and more conflict during the last few centuries of the Fremont than at any other time in the past. It was not a peculiar Fremont ethnic or psychological characteristic, only the tyranny of circumstance. Fremont land was full. Labor was invested in irrigation ditches and granaries, and the social costs of defending, managing, and distributing the limited supply were high. The hinterlands were hunted and foraged, and the human predator was king.

The Fremont did not act alone. They were caught up in a larger world that included the Southwest. The 11th century saw the rise of Chaco Canyon, New Mexico, and its regional network of roads and outliers. The 12th century saw drought and chaos, including a 50-year period of attacks, death squads, sacrifice, ritual cannibalism, and terrorism in the Four Corners region at the edge of the Fremont world. As Chaco declined, the power moved north to Salmon and Aztec ruins, even closer to Utah. During the 13th century, the power shifted toward Mesa Verde and even west into southeastern Utah. These same centuries brought pulses of Anasazi populations north from western Arizona into the Grand Staircase and past the Kapairowits Plateau as far north as Escalante and Boulder, Utah.

The larger world also extended to California. It grew apace with the Southwest, and by the 12th and 13th centuries there were large populations along the southern California coast. Maritime resources were beginning to be stressed, and the inland resources were so allocated that there was a striking degree of linguistic isolation, producing the tribelets and partitioning known to historic California. Subtle changes in ocean temperature and currents altered maritime productivity, and a combination of factors led to considerable violence and competition there. By the 12th and 13th centuries, the California coast was likely exporting immigrants, too. The continent had grown up, and it did so centuries before any significant contact with Europeans. The last millennium of Pre-Columbian America is bound up with the fact of this maturation.

Like any rural people, the Fremont and other peoples of the Desert West were shielded by distance and by cultural boundaries, but not completely. Oddly, the ultimate fate of the Fremont is, like its origin, wrapped up with happenings elsewhere. It was a beginning not an end.

6

The Late Prehistoric Millennium

It is tempting to assume that the most recent centuries provide the clearest picture of the past, but the Late Prehistoric period is in fact poorly known, and the number of excavated Late Prehistoric sites is small relative to the earlier periods. It remains as murky as the Paleoindian, the earliest period of human occupation. Perhaps this is because archaeologists do not rush to study sites only a few hundred years old when they can study ones that are 10,000 years old. A more likely culprit is the unconscious tendency to know the recent past by simply extending history backward. After all, we have the historically known peoples, including the Northern Paiute, the Shoshone, the Ute, and the Southern Paiute. The temptation is strong to project the richness of contemporary lived experience to know an otherwise still-born antiquity. Diaries, photographs, paintings, eyewitness accounts,

229

and folklore are palpably human and seduce us into believing that they suffice to represent the ancients.

Succumbing to this temptation would be an injustice to the richness and distinctiveness of the ancestors of the modern tribes. Those ancestors did not grow from the living peoples of the last two centuries, but from those who went before. Thus, it is the ancients to whom we must look. As usual, time looms large, and even this most recent period of antiquity spanned a Late Prehistoric Millennium— more than 33 human generations.

We will find there was tremendous upheaval and change during the Late Prehistoric, long before any contacts with Europeans. The cultural fabric of the Late Prehistoric Millennium comprises diverse peoples bearing the weight of different historical trajectories.

First, there is the question of what happened to the Fremont and Anasazi farmers. After more than a thousand years, this successful way of life changed fundamentally in the 12th through 14th centuries. The fates of these peoples shaped much of what would follow.

Second, is a parallel historical thread in the western Great Basin. Agriculture never reached those places, but while Fremont farming overtook the forager lifeways in the east, the peoples of the Stillwater Marsh in western Nevada, the Owens Valley in eastern California, and the marshy basins in southeastern Oregon also grew in number, built substantial villages, and lived in much more structured social systems than those who preceded them. Meanwhile, the desert and mountain hinterlands of central Nevada continued to support the more mobile "high desert" foragers living in their less structured and more fluid social systems.

Third, the Southwest and California reached their peak populations by the beginning of the Late Prehistoric Millennium, and they would shape the world around them. A scale larger than the Great Basin and Colorado Plateau is essential to understanding the last millennium of the region.

Climate, too, dealt a new hand to the peoples of the West. The several-century span of warmer winters and late summer rainfall (in the eastern Basin and Plateau) of the Medieval Warm Period gave way to the Little Ice Age characterized by lower temperatures and spates of storminess beginning in the 14th century. Across the western and southern Great Basin the Medieval Warm Period intensified the heat of the deserts.

Finally, the most catastrophic event in the last millennium was not climate, or the influence of indigenous neighbors, but the diseases brought by the European invasion of the Americas, which would cause massive depopulation of native peoples. Once again, what happened in the Basin-Plateau cannot be fully understood without knowing its place in the larger scheme of things.

THE END OF FREMONT PLACE

The archaeology shows a clear break between the Fremont and Anasazi and the people who came later. Julian Steward saw it in the layers of sediments in the Promontory Caves in northwestern Utah in the 1930s. He found a change of the guard in everything from stylistically unique moccasins, to the ethnic distinctions revealed by basketry, to different techniques of pottery manufacture. He recognized that these items signified people with different historical traditions. There was no radiocarbon dating at the time, but tree ring chronologies for the Anasazi in the Southwest and Steward's experience in cave excavation led him to estimate that this historical break occurred about A.D. 1200.

Mark Harrington and Irwin Hayden excavated Anasazi caves and villages in the Moapa Valley near Las Vegas in the 1920s. They remarked: "The record of the laminae is legible in the deposit, dividing the Paiute from the Pueblo layer. . . ."; "It would appear reasonable to assume . . . a progressive thinning out of the Pueblo population as village after village was abandoned and the people evacuated the valley. Meanwhile, those who held on and retreated to the mesas would be able to oppose the nomads with less and less effectiveness and would eventually have to seek other territory."[1]

After 12 centuries of farming, the Fremont culture dissolved. Ironically, the roots of this change are found in their successes. To understand why and how the Fremont ended, we must trace the consequences of their success and the characteristics of their culture that arose from farming in a wildly variable land and climate.

The rise of the Fremont and Anasazi after A.D. 0 was aided by a climate favorable to farming maize, beans, and squash, although the centuries before A.D. 700 were variable with spates of good or bad climate lasting for several decades. Between A.D. 700 and 1000, the variations in climate shortened to only a few years each, short enough for people to recognize, remember the change, and adjust.[2] As long as populations were small and there was plenty of room to select the best locations, all was well, and the Fremont grew.

By the A.D. 1000s, good fortune kept the ball rolling when the Medieval Warm Period brought a couple of centuries that were warm enough to grow maize requiring over 100 frost-free days to mature, but not so warm that the mountain snowpacks melted too soon. A northward shift of the monsoons brought rain at planting time and again just before fruit. This pattern of rainfall even helped the canyon and the valley floodplains to fill with sediment into broad fields ready to plant—a striking contrast to the same canyons today, where streams are entrenched several meters below the surrounding floodplain. The Medieval Warm Period was a godsend to the Fremont, just as it was to the people of Europe. Wine grapes were planted in England and Switzerland, wheat fields started in Norway and Scotland, and the North Atlantic opened up Greenland and New-foundland to the Norse. As might be expected, European populations grew at unprecedented rates.[3]

The Medieval Warm Period in Fremont-land was, however, a climatic balancing act. Farm production was different every year, with bunches of five to ten good years punctuated by an equal number of poor years, and sometimes longer spans of good and bad times. Each time people survived a drought or a cold stretch, population sizes lunged forward, and people invested a bit more in their fields. This seemed to work, and the Fremont culture grew. If the Fremont were so good at managing a fluctuating climate and a diverse, dynamic people and land, why did their success ever end?

A glimpse into this puzzle is provided by the Fremont response to a long drought in the late 12th century. Bristlecone pine records indicate 25 years of drought after A.D. 1150. Pollen records from south-western Colorado show a decrease in the amount of crucial late summer rainfall from A.D. 1146 to 1193. Furthermore, this drought was felt uniformly over the region, in contrast to previous droughts that had expressed themselves as a patchwork, enabling some places to escape drought and providing refuge for those in trouble. This was a great drought lasting several decades, and it affected everyone.[4]

Farming was replaced by foraging in the Uinta Basin by the time of this drought, showing that agriculture was already tenuous in some places. Defensive food storage had already come to Nine Mile Canyon and Range Creek during previous droughts and would only fluoresce during such a stressful time. Stable carbon isotope analysis of human bone indicates that after A.D. 1150 the Fremont along the Wasatch Front spent less time farming and switched to the abundant wild foods available in the wetlands. The Sevier Valley may have fallen on hard times, judging from the few radiocarbon dates there after A.D. 1150. The Evans Mound village ended its three-century run during this persistent drought, illustrating that social upheaval was possible even at the highly favored locations in the Parowan Valley. Nawthis Village occupied a prime microenvironment perched above the Sevier Valley, but the accumulation of 75 mounds ended its two-century run in the late A.D. 1100s.[5]

Not everyone weathered the great drought through warfare, hoarding, abandonment of their homes, or drastic shifts in their economy. From Glen Canyon to the San Rafael Swell near Hanksville, and west to places such as Snake Rock Village at the southern end of Castle Valley, there seems to be a greater degree of blending between the Fremont and the Anasazi from the late A.D. 1000s and on through the 1100s.[6] Perhaps this resulted from a multicultural perception of place where people moved among one another and blurred the ethnic lines. Whether the challenge was population growth and economic success or drought and social stress, some people bridged cultural differences to make their way, while others built walls and clung to conflict to resolve their problems. The Fremont did not respond in unison.

The ironic lesson of the great drought of the late A.D. 1100s is that it did not end the Fremont but only spurred it on. The huge communities in Clear Creek Canyon experienced their greatest growth in the A.D. 1200s, as did Baker Village out on the Nevada border. Thus, it is incorrect to attribute the fall of the Fremont to drought—or any particular event or person in history. The answer lies in the cumulative decisions of generations that compounded mistakes and successes into an inexorable evolutionary change. The Fremont is no different from any other culture, and its fundamental transformation was inevitable.

The world's climate began a prolonged cooling trend and an erratic rainfall pattern in the 13th century. We see the effects of this period most clearly in Europe. After centuries of smooth sailing, the Norse experienced more extensive ice packs and gales in the North Atlantic, and by A.D. 1250 far fewer ships were crossing from Iceland to the Greenland colonies. Northwestern Europe experienced more frequent cold, stormy years. These came on the heels of the preceding warm period, and the higher sea levels meant that the storms caused massive ocean surges to devour the coasts of Holland and Germany

in the A.D. 1200–1300s. In Scotland, more than 100,000 people died
in the great storms of A.D. 1421 and 1446. The Norse began to give
up on their Greenland settlements by the mid A.D. 1300s.[7]

Climate only changed the script. The stage was already set by a
millennium of Fremont success and growth—progress. In fact, most
of the climate changes played out over spans of time that were too
long for Fremont people to agree on what was happening and to
respond. Like all cultures whose end is near, the Fremont mostly
reacted by doing the same things, and probably even by clinging to
what they perceived to be a sacred past.

Utah pollen records show more winter rainfall by the late A.D.
1200s and less falling when farmers needed it. Winter rains caused
the streams that once meandered across broad silt-filled floodplains to
cut downward and entrench themselves into the earth. This lowered
the water table, and the once fertile fields dried out. The cooling
trend meant more late frosts to kill young maize, bean, and squash
plants and more early frosts to kill them before the harvest was fully
in. Episodes of stormy winters and massive rainfall might be followed
by years when all seemed normal, further convincing people that
their problems were only temporary and that soon all would be well
again.[8]

These things took a toll on a landscape filled with people, where
the arable land was used, where place was socially allocated, where
some people had more than others. In some years, the old techniques
of storage, sharing, and communal risk management could work. In
others, the equally old practice of hoarding and raiding sufficed. But
as the decades wore on and the trend toward cooling worsened, the
social fabric increasingly frayed. Local abandonments that were once
a routine part of Fremont place became final emigrations. A few
people could fade into the wilderness and become foragers as they
had on other occasions. But there simply wasn't enough wild food to
support everyone.

Research among the Anasazi of the Southwest indicates that
much of the abandonment of Mesa Verde, Colorado, in the late
A.D. 1200s and 1300s was by groups of people moving together and
founding new villages. This time the abandoning way of life involved
longer moves and much greater risk.[9]

The Fremont likely emigrated in the same social cliques, ethnic
boundaries, and among the friends and enemies who made up their
settled existence. Their sequential hierarchies of hamlets, villages, and
dispersed communities at once enabled coordinated efforts by large

groups of people, while others broke into fractious segments. Some groups might find places to hedge their bets, leading to a resurgence of population in a few harbors of refuge. Five Finger Ridge and the Baker site are two examples used here, but the number of such places is surely higher.

Other people moved farther and founded new places. The wilds of northeastern Utah and northwestern Colorado host some of the latest known occupations for things recognizably Fremont. Sites such as Texas Overlook near Rangely, Colorado, and Allen Village north of Vernal, Utah, may have been occupied as late as A.D. 1500.

By A.D. 1350, most Fremont villages, hamlets, and rancherias were empty for the last time. The moccasins, figurines, and the rock art were no longer produced, but the most telling loss is the complete disappearance of the distinctive Fremont basketry tradition rooted in grandmothers, mothers, and daughters for 6,000 years.[10]

It took a century or two for Fremont farming to fade into impossibility. Climate change was part of the story, but the Fremont culture declined in part because they had adapted to the climatic changes of preceding centuries. When climate took a different direction, as it always will, the traditional gave way to change so great that the Fremont culture became unrecognizable from its previous forms. What about the people? Where did they go? Who replaced them? For this we need to take a broader view and turn our attention to a geography that includes the western Great Basin, desert and coastal California, and of course the Southwest.

FORAGERS TO THE WEST, PEOPLE FROM THE WEST

Farming never pushed into the central, western, and northern Great Basin, but the foraging cultures there changed personalities during the Late Prehistoric Millennium. A historical trajectory of change was already in motion, and it would set the stage for the arrival of new peoples.

Populations of the Archaic before 4,000 years ago were small and scattered widely across the landscape. Only a few places harbored the higher densities of village life, and these were tethered to the few wetlands of the period.

Populations increased in the western Great Basin, especially around 2,000 years ago—the same time maize and immigration lead to the formation of the Fremont. By that time, the Neoglacial climatic regime created more wetlands, and these anchored population. Social change in those places altered the conception of place and how people interacted with one another. There were more social hierarchy, prestige seeking, and stronger notions that some resources were private instead of public. Toolstones such as obsidian tended to be obtained from sources closer to home, indicating contraction in the size of territories. These changes were not just the result of local history but were tied to the growth of populations and society in the Southwest, Oregon, and California.

We know the foragers of eastern and southern Nevada were aware of the Fremont and Anasazi farmers. David Rhode used thermoluminescence dating on pottery to show that the foragers made their own styles of pottery to fit their needs once the cultures of the Southwest did so. In a few cases, the copying began early, but most of it dated to A.D. 1000s and after. The Scorpion Ridge site near Elko, Nevada, is well above and west of the range of farming but shows connection rather than isolation between the foragers there and the Fremont farmers of Utah. Bryan Hockett and Maury Morgenstein found that the people at Scorpion Ridge manufactured their own Fremont-like pottery using local materials prior to A.D. 1000 and even imported a small amount of genuine Fremont ceramics, possibly from as far away as Clear Creek Canyon in central Utah.[11]

Despite their different cultures, the Fremont farmers and the foragers of eastern Nevada shared a common heritage. These roots push deeply into the Archaic period, as is apparent in the Eastern Great Basin basketry tradition. But after 6,000 years of continuity, something happened during the Late Prehistoric Millennium. Fremont basketry and with it the Eastern Great Basin basketry tradition disappeared, and the subsequent basketry traditions were strikingly different. New peoples were involved.

Connections between Great Basin peoples with those of northern California and Oregon are also evident. For thousands of years, obsidian from the interior was traded for Pacific shell such as abalone and Dentalium. The Northern Great Basin basketry tradition, like its eastern Basin counterpart, shows roots deep in Archaic times. Unlike the Fremont, the earlier basketry traditions in the west did not become extinct but moved to new places. The ancient basketry of southeastern Oregon is evident in the historic basketry traditions of the Klamath-Modoc peoples of southwestern Oregon nearer to the coast. But the Late Prehistoric and historic period basketry of southeastern Oregon and northwestern Nevada is fundamentally different from what came before. Once again, new peoples were involved.[12]

FIGURE 6.1

Map of basketry complexes of the Archaic to the Late Prehistoric period showing the relationships between historic peoples of the Western Great Basin and those of California and peoples of the Northern Great Basin in Oregon. Basketry is just one measure of heritage, but the diversity of Archaic basketry traditions across the historic range of the later Uto-Aztecan, Numic speakers suggests that the historic peoples of the Basin Plateau hold a diversity of heritages deeply rooted in the past.

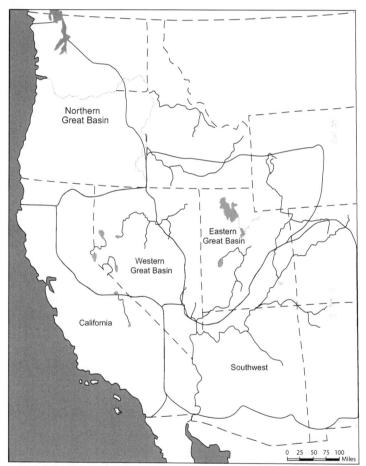

Northern Great Basin. Open and close, flexible and rigid twining dominate. Coiling present but insignificant. Ties to Western Great Basin and California.

California. Open and close, flexible and rigid twining. Coiling present, after 2000 B.P. and basic affinities north and east.

Southwest. Anasazi, Hohokam, and Mogollon are clearcut entities. Well defined boundaries between Southwest and Great Basin. Mexican techniques are evident.

Eastern Great Basin. One-rod and bundle stacked foundation coiling dominates. Twining insignificant. Complex gives way to Numic basketry.

Western Great Basin. Bunched foundation coiling continues, while twining declines. Lovelock wickerware appears. Complex gives way to Numic basketry.

In the western Great Basin, people inhabiting the village sites of the wetlands and surrounding areas were of the Western Great Basin basketry tradition. Their "Lovelock Wickerware" is distinguished from the eastern and northern traditions in that it was a largely twined basketry tradition. As in the other places, the basketry that would follow was starkly different.

Fundamental change was underway across the region, and since the early 20th century archaeologists and linguists have speculated that one people replaced another. But there was no consensus, and occasionally scholars saw continuity between native peoples of the historic period and the cultures of many millennia ago. Perhaps this is not an either/or issue. If we look at what happened to people's lives during the Late Prehistoric Millennium, we can glimpse a process spanning dozens of human generations that cannot be done justice by terms such as "population replacement." Again, the western Great Basin offers a glimpse of these things.

Despite the significant social change in the Late Archaic western Great Basin, some things came later than in the eastern Basin and Plateau, including a major role for pine nuts and small seed resources in the economy, and pottery. Experimentation with pottery began as early as A.D. 600, as the influence of the Southwest was felt even in the shadow of the Sierra Nevada Range. But the regular use of pottery in the Owens Valley and other valleys of eastern California did not occur until after A.D. 1400. Jelmer Eerkens builds on decades of study by western Basin scholars at hundreds of Late Prehistoric sites, which suggests an increase in the importance of small seeds only in the last millennia and a fundamental change in the way many people organized their economies. His study of pottery takes the next step and links the expansion of seed use to a shift toward the privatization of seed resources. Seeds assume this role by A.D. 1400, and pottery was widely adopted, because it improved seed storability and hoarding. Seeds gave women and the household more power, and added one more building block to these increasingly structured, hierarchical, and competitive social arrangements.[13]

Seemingly insignificant at first glance, small seed use tells us a great deal about the forces in people's lives and the ways they co-operated and competed. Seeds are expensive to harvest and process, and that is why they are used either in the harshest environments or where population growth and the overexploitation of cheaper resources forces them into a larger role in the economy (see Chapter 4).

With the addition of seeds to the economy toward the end of the Archaic period, every resource Mother Nature had to offer was brought under the economic umbrella. The most prized resource of all, big game, was showing signs of becoming luxury food, playing a role in the acquisition of prestige and aiding the manipulation of some people by others.

Seeds were already important in some parts of the region where options were few. Seeds were the lynchpin of Fremont economies. After all, maize is a seed—an annual grass that is expensive to grow. In the western Great Basin, the growth of society paralleled that of the farmers in the east as highly storable small seeds became the maize of the west and a source of power. The shift from public to private goods happened among the Fremont farmers of the Colorado Plateau and among the foraging cultures of the western Great Basin.

The population growth, the social hierarchies, the economic intensification, and the shifts from public to private goods brought an important change to Great Basin foraging societies: more and more unrelated people were living together. Many indigenous traditions rooted in the Archaic were shaken, and the birth of the Fremont out of a milieu of immigrants and indigenes is the most graphic example of this.

The same thing was happening just a little later in the western and northern Great Basin. Indigenous Native Americans faced change brought by immigrant Native Americans living in societies increasingly geared to managing diversity and strangeness. The historically known peoples of the Basin-Plateau, including the Northern Paiute, the Shoshone, and the Ute-Southern Paiute language groups arose from this time of connection and disconnection from their pasts.

The social fabric of the Late Prehistoric millennium is at once rooted in the past and with us in the present. But it was rent, torn, and rewoven by forces inside and outside the Basin-Plateau. So far, we have traced some of the reasons for this by drawing comparisons to large-scale trends in the nature of economy and society among the Fremont farmers and western Great Basin foragers. They are historical soul mates. The Fremont were part and parcel of change and immigration from the Southwest. It would be the Southwest in tandem with already populous California that motivated change in the southern and western Great Basin—change that would eventually encompass the entire region.

LANGUAGES OLD AND NEW

Euroamerican settlement brought catastrophe to the peoples of the Basin-Plateau. Not only were lives ruined, but heritage, too. Native languages were threatened with extinction, yet in these societies, the historical legacy of a people, the libraries if you will, are housed in speech. Scholars recognized this, and in the late 19th and early 20th centuries anthropologists and linguists rushed to record the languages of the native peoples of the American West. Their resulting

FIGURE 6.2

Map of the Basin-Plateau region showing historical tribal-linguistic boundaries.

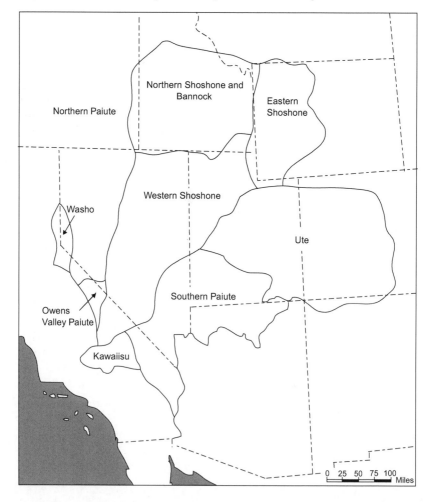

classifications of Basin-Plateau languages enabled them to glimpse the movement of peoples during the most recent spans of antiquity by comparing similarities and differences among vocabularies and the structure of speech. Greater differences meant more geographic isolation and/or more distant historical connections. Linguists used their evidence to interpret, even to speculate on, the degree of relatedness between the ancients and the living indigenous peoples of the region.

John Wesley Powell's linguistic studies among the Southern Paiute on his trips down the Colorado River, and Alfred Kroeber's work with informants in California and Nevada, showed that the languages of the region are similar across this enormous landscape. Early on, Kroeber did more than anyone to compile the many recordings of Native American languages of California and the Great Basin. He classified three related pairs of languages, including Shoshone/ Panamint, Northern Paiute/Mono, and Ute-Southern Paiute/Kawaiisu as dialects of a common heritage that he termed Numic (pronounce the "u" as in "nut"). When the variations among these languages are plotted geographically, an unmistakable fan-shaped pattern anchored in southeastern California is apparent to virtually every linguist since Kroeber.

Linguists also found that the Numic languages are part of the vast linguistic family termed Uto-Aztecan, a suite of several dozen languages stretching from the western United States to central Mexico. The Uto-Aztecan languages contrast with the also massive Penutian and the Hokan language families occupying much of central California north into the Pacific Northwest. The differences among these language families are greater than those distinguishing the Romance languages of Europe such as Spanish, French, and Italian from the Germanic and Anglo Saxon languages to the north.

Curiosity about the American past is insatiable, and the variations among the historical Native American languages quickly led to speculation about ancient peoples. Emigration and immigration are the basic stuff of human behavior, and languages move with people. The devil is, of course, in the details. Kroeber wrestled with the historical significance of the Great Basin languages. At first glance, the fan-shaped pattern seems anchored by Mono, Panamint, and Kawaiisu, like a root from which the fan spread. But as Kroeber observed: "It is highly improbable that they have actually spread out thus. We must rather look upon the focus as the region where the condensation has been greatest, the tract where newcomers gradually agglomerated, not

FIGURE 6.3

Map showing the distribution of the Hokan and the Penutian language families during the historic period. These are the indigenous speakers of the Archaic who encountered the immigrant Uto-Aztecan speakers. Together, over a period of 2,000 years, these peoples forged the historically known cultures of the Great Basin now represented linguistically by the Numic, Uto-Aztecan languages.

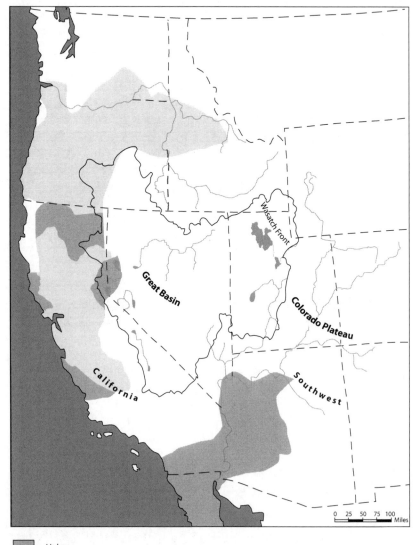

the hive from which the whole body swarmed." Kroeber was speaking
not only of the Great Basin Numic languages but also of their sister
Uto-Aztecan languages scattered across the Desert West. He realized
that the patterns in the distribution of the languages, such as the
fan-shaped pattern, may indicate less about where people came from
than about where they ended up. At the same time, he suspected
that the differences among the Numic languages were recent, but he
kept this separate from an assumption that they were unrelated to
the ancients before them. Let's examine these two things: the time
expired since the Numic languages became distinct, and the matter
of where they came from. Only then can we turn our attention to the
archaeology and an explanation of why.[14]

In 1958, Sydney Lamb used a linguistic method called glottochronology to estimate how long it took for the differences among
the Numic languages to form. Lamb proposed that the base of the
fan was a provisional "homeland" from which the Northern Paiute,
Shoshone, and Ute-Southern Paiute languages separated as much as
1,000 years ago, but most likely between 500 and 700 years ago (A.D.
1300–1500).[15]

Glottochronology compares a list of cognate words for subtle differences in sound and meaning. Sometimes the differences are based
on basic vocabulary, whereas other times the evaluation is intuitive,
based on the linguist's impression of word and sentence structure
and sounds. Glottochronology estimates the differences and the similarities among languages as they change over time through isolation.
The rate of change necessary to estimate a calendar date for a split
between languages comes from the historically dated divergences in
European languages. With this rate of divergence in hand, a linguistic
"clock" could be applied to other languages around the world.

The work of Sydney Lamb continues to be embraced by archaeologists, because the estimate of 1,000 years matches changes that
archaeologists have long seen in the dirt. In Lamb they found their
corroborative evidence.[16]

Meanwhile, both linguists and archaeologists debate the value of
glottochronology. Linguist David Shaul used studies of Australian
aborigines to suggest that linguistic change among foraging societies is slower than in the European cases used to derive the rates of
change. Foragers are more mobile and have large territories. This
would push the split between the Numic languages farther back in
time. But farther back from which estimated date? If the split was

farther back from Lamb's "statistical estimates" of 500–700 years, perhaps his figure of 1,000 years is accurate. The matter becomes more
intriguing when we find out that Lamb's figure of 1,000 years was not
a maximum but a concept linguists call a "minimum century"—the
minimum time necessary to account for the linguistic differences if
the split was sharp and there was substantial isolation among peoples
after the split. Neither of these prerequisites is likely with societies as
fluid as Great Basin foragers.

Even Sydney Lamb seems to have become doubtful; he told
archaeologist David Thomas in 1993 that, in retrospect, he thought
that the differences in the Numic languages could have been so
gradual that they began 2,000 or even 3,000 years ago. Obviously,
the linguistic studies provide estimates that require additional information to evaluate. How much isolation was there? Was there immigration, or did the language change happen in place? How much
mobility was there among people's settlements? What was the nature
of hierarchy, territoriality, cooperation, and conflict? Did the social
organization and sense of place bring different ethnic groups and different peoples under the social umbrella? All these things can help
shake out the time of divergence in Numic languages.

Most seem to agree that the Numic languages moved from southwest to northeast and that there were great changes in the region
during the past three millennia. There is less agreement when the
issues are framed more narrowly. The linguist Wick Miller points out
that each boundary between the Numic languages is a "dialect continuum," giving reason to blur the fan-shaped pattern and the strict
boundaries that gain reality, because they are drawn on a map.
Perhaps the problem is that we have framed the Numic Spread too
narrowly and in terms of either/or, rather than in terms of process
and time. Most matters of culture are not black and white even when
they are cast that way in historical retrospect.[17]

THE ROLE OF CALIFORNIA

California is the agricultural breadbasket of the United States, yet
farming was not a significant part of ancient life there. Unlike the
Southwest where agriculture was the economic engine behind the development of places such as Mesa Verde and Chaco Canyon, ancient
California was populated by foragers. Once again, our perception of
foragers as mere hunters and gatherers tilts us toward images of a

scattered few living lightly upon the land. Nothing could be further from the truth during the last 3,000 years along coastal and inland California. When early anthropologists began documenting the indigenous peoples of California, they found myriad peoples, ethnic groups, languages, and dialects anchored in often tiny geographic and social compartments across the interior valleys and along the Pacific coast. The term "tribelet" was employed to describe these discreet entities as anthropologists struggled to accommodate a degree of social partitioning rarely seen among the world's foragers. In some cases, individual river drainage systems bound by rugged, shrub-covered ridges housed a distinct dialect or even language. Population densities were high, and the many villages were often home to 100 people and sometimes many more. Paralleling the unprecedented population growth of the Southwest, California's population rose during the 11th and 12th centuries to some of the highest densities ever found in foraging societies anywhere in the world.[18]

The trend began about 3,000 years ago, when there were the first inklings that people were placing pressure on their environment. Zooarchaeologist Jack Broughton joined an increasing number of scholars who were skeptical of claims by early explorers and pioneers that California was a Garden of Eden basking in superabundance. The archaeology suggested otherwise, and Broughton set out to devise a test of the proposition that growing forager populations shaped animal populations over the last several thousand years. The archaeology of large villages such as the Emeryville Shell Mound on the eastern shores of San Francisco Bay, as well as other sites to the east near Sacramento, provide a rich record of fish, elk, small mammals, and birds. Broughton's painstaking work of identifying often fragmentary bone, counting it by level, and assembling data from site after site, shows declines in the populations of tule elk during the past several thousand years. His findings contrast with descriptions of endless herds of deer and elk by explorers from Sir Francis Drake in A.D. 1579 to the pioneers of the Great Valley north of Sacramento in the 1850s.

When Broughton turned his attention to fish, he found that increases in native fishing technology and effort caused declines in populations and sizes of sturgeon during the same period. These were not minor episodes, nor were they the actions of a few errant people, but a fundamental change in the nature of place that unfolded over many human generations. Rather than leading to catastrophe, the effects of population growth actually directed people's attention to new resources.[19]

One such resource is acorns. Archaeologists Mark Basgall and Paul Bouey found that the acorn, so important to Native Californians during the early historic period, played only a niche role in the economy until the last few thousand years. The mortars and the pestles needed to pound acorns into meal proliferated in the San Francisco Bay region 3,000 years ago, and by 2,000 years ago the acorn was the cornerstone of an economy spanning the foothills of the Sierra Nevada to the Coast Ranges, and some places in between. The increased desire for acorns is not a matter of random preference but results from larger historical trends. As more easily acquired foods such as sturgeon and elk declined from predation by growing numbers of humans, California foragers did exactly what the farmers of the Southwest did, and for that matter what people everywhere do—they turned to new resources and invested more time and energy to get them.[20]

Acorns are nutritious and were stored in huge caches that housed up to a ton of nuts. Their importance was suppressed for thousands of years by the high cost of processing them. Acorns contain tannin that must be laboriously leached to make them edible. They also need to be ground into meal. Like the seeds of the Great Basin and the maize of the Southwest and Fremont land, acorns could take the population to new levels and brought fundamental change to life and place. But the price was a more intensive economy, and a more structured and hierarchical social system to make it run. There were other effects, too. Acorns are a major food for deer and elk, and as the humans harvested more acorns, it put even greater pressure on the dwindling herds. In some times and places, and for those hunters who could control other people's labor, big game became a luxury good whose acquisition was value added in the form of prestige and social power.[21]

A similar process unfolded along the Pacific coast, where substantial villages grew on the rich marine resources of the estuaries and the open sea. Over the past 3,000 years there was a shift from the more easily acquired resources that lived on the shore, and on the rocky islands hugging the coast. The species of seals, sea lions, and otters preferring the coast showed the first declines, and with the approach of the Late Prehistoric Millennium, these were followed by declines in those species preferring points, rocks, islets, and islands of more difficult access in deeper waters. By then, the coastal foragers were working harder and investing in technology such as larger boats more capable of deep-water navigation. By A.D. 800–1000, this culminated in a flourishing of tomols, the fabulous plank canoes still used by a few tribes in historic times and revered today as a monumental connection to the past. Like the grinding stones, coiled basketry, and tiny seeds of the Great Basin—and the pithouses, irrigation ditches, and maize of the Fremont and the Southwest—the tomol, acorn hullers, and fish bones are bellwethers of change in society, place, and the manner of people's lives.[22]

By A.D. 1000, much of interior and coastal California was a fully occupied landscape with an intricate but delicate relationship among people, land, and the production of nature. Fluctuations in wild food production and human populations were inevitable, and as each change was negotiated through either cooperation or conflict, the system responded with even more effort to maintain the expensive social system that got them through these crises in the first place. Like the Fremont who weathered the great drought of the 12th century only to stick to their cultural guns as they faced inevitable change, California foragers pressed on through fluctuations in population and climate.

The Chumash people are an example. They occupied the coast along California's Santa Barbara Channel, and modern urban development ensured disturbance of their sizable cemeteries. Human skeletons represent the past through spiritual connection with the living tribes and through the secrets they reveal about life. Anthropologists realize the significance of both. They examined the skeletons to learn their forensic secrets, and the Chumash now ensure that the remains of the ancients will not be ignored.

Chumash skeletons reveal changes in people's workload as they intensified fishing and sea mammal hunting—incidents of arthritis increased in the centuries before A.D. 1100. Women's upper-body stresses decreased, perhaps because there was less emphasis on root digging and plant processing as these resources played a smaller role in the economy of a managed landscape. Infectious disease increased in response to more densely populated villages and nutritional stress. Iron deficiency increased among the children, typically the first to feel the effects of an economic downturn.

Most graphic of all, however, is the violence. Patricia Lambert and Phillip Walker found an increase in violence among the Chumash from A.D. 300 to 1150. The bow and arrow arrived in coastal and inland California between A.D. 500 and 800 and spread just as it did across Utah at the birth of the Fremont—in response to contact, isolation, changes in social interactions, and conflict. It is a useful tool for killing people. Wounds from arrows, dart points, clubbing, and stabbing are some of the most stark and disturbing indicators of social upheaval. Violence is a window into the society, not because the people were inherently violent but because, at times, their circumstances led to violence.[23]

The Chumash and many other Native Californians found themselves entwined in a delicate social net that at once knitted different peoples together even as California had become a highly compartmentalized suite of microsocieties. People managed change through a combination of ethnic identity, linguistic compartmentalization, territoriality, and near constant but socially regulated interaction via the movement of goods. This was more than mere "trade" among natives. It was a patchwork quilt of distinct peoples who could not live apart from the whole cloth they had created. Between A.D. 500 and 1300, California was one of the most intensive, cosmopolitan puzzles of forager societies and landscapes the world has ever seen.[24]

California paralleled the Southwest, and both reached a culmination in the 12th century. Both places presented different forces, and both sent ripples across the Basin-Plateau. The story of the Numic peoples cannot be told without them.

THE SPREAD OF THE NUMIC LANGUAGES AND THE MAKING OF THE NUMIC CULTURES

When farmers entered the Southwest over 3,500 years ago, indigenous foragers of many ethnic and linguistic backgrounds were displaced, absorbed, or simply overwhelmed. The process took several millennia and by the historical period left a plethora of Uto-Aztecan tongues from central Mexico to the Southwest, into the southern third of California, and across the Basin-Plateau.

Many places in the vast deserts of Mexico and the Southwest could not be farmed, yet Uto-Aztecan languages spread there, too. Farming was a centrifuge, flinging the excess population produced by the intensification of place into the hinterlands. Where new farms could be founded, farmers displaced foragers. But beyond the places where farming was possible, the nature of foraging society also changed. Some foragers simply moved farther into the wilderness, while others gave up and joined the farmers as squatters, laborers, and de facto slaves. We saw these processes with the origins of the Fremont, and it occurred historically among the Pueblos of the Southwest.

Still other foragers resisted and worked harder to invest more and more with the hope of survival. Donald Holly describes a case of hunter-gatherers in eastern Canada who responded to the occasional overlap of territories with other foragers by intensifying their own exploitation of the land. Those foragers who raised the stakes this way spawned a new kind of foraging society adept at invading lands occupied by other foragers.[25]

As Uto-Aztecan peoples moved north they encountered more and more regions where farming was impossible no matter how ingenious the people were. The Mojave Desert of southern California, the high deserts of the Great Basin, and the mountainous northern edges of the Colorado Plateau were too hot, too dry, too cold, too high, or too much of a combination of these things to farm without technology at least a millennium away. Yet, we find Uto-Aztecan languages in those places—the Numic languages.

Thus, one key to the spread of the Numic languages is the spread of farming from Mexico across the Southwest. It began the process. The Uto-Aztecan, Western Basketmaker tradition would found the Hopi, a language that linguists estimate split off from neighboring Uto-Aztecan languages about 3,000 years ago. They contributed population to the nascent Fremont and also pushed west across northwestern Arizona and southern Nevada.[26]

Other Uto-Aztecan speakers spread across southern Arizona into the deserts of California perhaps more than 2,000 years ago. They encountered natives along the southern California coast. Mitochondrial DNA studies suggest a mix of the Uto-Aztecan Luiseno speakers north of San Diego and the indigenous Hokan speakers just to their south. The parched Los Angeles basin would give way to Uto-Aztecan speakers and become Gabrielino. Uto-Aztecans pushed across the Tehachapi Mountains and into the southern fringes of the San Joaquin Valley near Bakersfield to become the Numic languages of Kawaiisu and Tubatulabal. Again, DNA studies suggest mixing with indigenous foragers in the southern San Joaquin Valley.[27]

Another key to the spread of the Numic languages is the fact that California experienced its own population explosion beginning 3,000 years ago. By A.D. 500, when the farming centrifuge flung people across the deserts of California, coastal peoples lived in societies with strong political hierarchy, the land was socially and economically partitioned, and violence and warfare were on the increase. The Uto-Aztecans hit a wall, and this wall is best seen in the stark linguistic and DNA distinctions between the Chumash peoples of the Santa

FIGURE 6.4

Map of the spread of Uto-Aztecan languages into the west. The initial thrust of
the spread into Arizona and New Mexico, and eventually into the Fremont region,
is rooted in the population growth consequent to agriculture. The Takic and
the Numic prongs of this spread also result from those demographic pressures
but are instances of foraging societies moving into regions where farming was
impossible. As Uto-Aztecan speakers encountered the large populations of Hokan
and Penutian speakers in coastal California, they turned north into the Great Basin.
The dashed lines along the Arizona-Utah border signify possible influxes of Uto-
Aztecan speakers after the founding of the Fremont to suggest additional streams
of immigration.

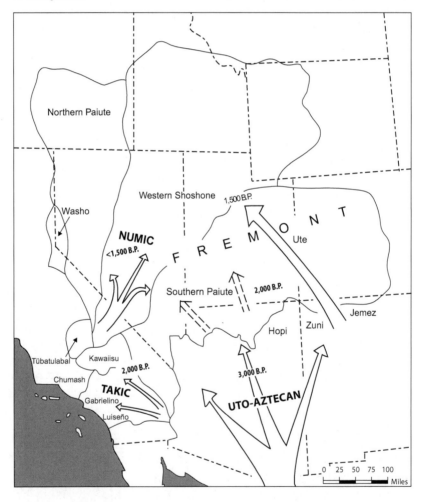

Barbara channel and the Uto-Aztecan newcomers. Other successful California tribes blocked Uto-Aztecan movement north into the San Joaquin Valley.[28]

Yet another key to the Numic Spread is the influence that the Southwest and California had on the relationship between immigrating and indigenous foragers in the desert regions between these continental population centers. The mere presence of large populations of socially and economically complex foragers in California and the abundant Pueblo farms of the Southwest created a new kind of forager and a different kind of place along the fringes of both regions. This would have a distinctive influence on the movement of the Numic speakers into the Great Basin.

The Uto-Aztecan speaking foragers migrating from the Southwest and from California took a more appropriative sense of place with them into the wilderness. They put more labor into pulling as much out of the desert as possible. They made the tiny seeds an even more important part of the economy than did the indigenous foragers, who had used seeds for millennia. They brought new tools such as seed beaters to knock larger amounts of seeds from the shrubs and grasses. Most important of all, they brought a social organization and a worldview that was geared to immigration.

Anthropologists Robert Bettinger and Martin Baumhoff called these people "processors" and contrasted them with the indigenous peoples of the Late Prehistoric western Great Basin, whom they referred to as "travelers." Processors settled into camps and villages anchored by their supplies of seeds and laboriously procured pine nuts still in their green cones so they could extract just a bit more from the groves before the birds and squirrels ate the nuts. Indeed, they emphasized green cone procurement even though it was more expensive than the brown cone procurement that had been practiced for millennia. Processors lived in larger groups, and their labor sustained them through the inevitable swings in production of Great Basin resources. The indigenous travelers moved more often and tended to place greater stock in hunting large and medium-sized game. They were the classic high desert foragers of the Archaic period, but they ended up being in the wrong place at the wrong time. Bettinger and Baumhoff employed the term "adaptive peak" from the language of evolutionary theory to describe this circumstance. The peculiar heritage of the immigrating Uto-Aztecan foragers that gave them their appropriative sense of place situated them at an adaptive peak relative to the less fortunate indigenous travelers.[29]

Processors are the kind of foragers archaeologists see in the western Great Basin when they find the widespread use of pottery, the privatization of seeds as an economic keystone, and the increasingly structured, hierarchical, and competitive social arrangements in the Late Prehistoric Millennium. Even the Mojave Desert was relatively full of people by A.D. 1000. Processors arose from the mixing of peoples and heritages, and they handled diversity better than the conservative, indigenous foragers did. These were surely exciting times, but probably hard times. Archaeologist Mark Sutton points to historical documentation of raiding by Numic peoples against others and suggests that the new arrivals forced the indigenes from critical resource patches. Conflict would be only natural in the face of more and more people moving into such a harsh land. The larger populations quickly used places up, and this spurred continued movement to new places. But even raiding causes people to mix, and while some indigenes fled or died violent deaths, others surely married into the new societies and left offspring who assumed the new culture. In this way, the cultures of both immigrants and indigenes changed as a new culture was built.[30]

The linguist Sydney Lamb provided such a beautiful story in the Numic Spread, and it gave meaning to the change archaeologists had long seen in the dirt. But reality is rarely so neat, and the Numic Spread is indeed a messy concoction.

First, the underlying reasons for it are continental in scale. The Southwest and California set the stage for an otherwise improbable encounter of displacement, replacement, and mixing of foragers with foragers. The Numic Spread is not a simple extension of Southwestern farmers or dispossessed Californians, because both regions were fonts of cultural and linguistic diversity. Their similar demographic pressures, however, created a different kind of forager on their margins—one adept at moving into a vast landscape and intensifying place.

Second, the Numic Spread is not an event but a process that unfolded over centuries. It began as early as 3,000 years ago. The spread of Uto-Aztecan farmers into Utah suggests that immigration also would have flowed west into the Mojave Desert and southern Great Basin after 2,000 years ago. The demographic pressures on the Great Basin were probably greatest during the run up of population during the Medieval Warm Period, when resource stress occurred in the

FIGURE 6.5

This figure illustrates Bettinger and Baumhoff's concept of immigrant "processors" versus the indigenous "travelers" of the Great Basin. As Uto-Aztecan speakers encountered the demographic obstacles of densely populated foraging/maritime societies in coastal California and populous Fremont farmers in the eastern Great Basin, they were funnelled north. The processor culture indicates foragers with an appropriative, exploitive notion of place, because they were flung forth by the demographic pressures of farming. They contrast to the indigenous travelers, whose culture was rooted in the lower population densities of the Archaic. The travelers were no match for the processing foragers borne of the intensified economies of the Southwest and coastal California. Once Fremont farming became impossible during the Little Ice Age, the Numic, processor foragers spread into the eastern Great Basin and northern Colorado Plateau.

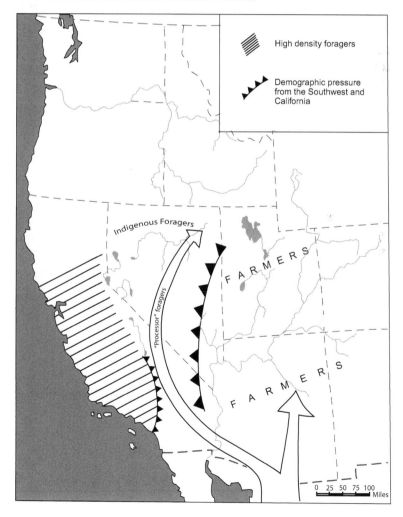

southern and western Great Basin. The upheaval brought by the collapse of farming and warfare in California in the 12th to 14th centuries continued to shape the Numic peoples of the Basin-Plateau
until only a few hundred years ago. The Numic languages are thus a
culmination.

Since the Numic Spread was a process, there is no artifact type
by which we will identify the moment of the "spread" into this or that
particular place. Whether it is pottery or arrowheads, each of these
arrives in places for its own reasons, and the artifact types layer
across cultures in different ways. The late arrival of pottery to the
western Great Basin after A.D. 1400 probably does not mark the first
arrival of Numic speakers as much as it marks the consequences of
an economic and social process regarding seed use that had been in
motion for centuries. The basketry may be the best indicator of who
people were, but in reality the sample of prehistoric basketry from
the last few millennia is so small that only gross change spanning
many human generations can be glimpsed using this artifact. A lot
can happen in only a century, let alone 10 or 20 human generations.
Basketry is a strong measure, but a coarse one.

Third, the process is not one dimensional, as is implied by the
Biblical metaphor of a Numic "homeland" located somewhere near
Death Valley, California. Original fonts from which whole peoples
spring fully formed and go forth unchanged for all time may exist in
the Bible, but they don't in history. Rather, the fan-shaped pattern of
Numic language distribution shows where people ended up, just as
Alfred Kroeber said in the 1920s. Wick Miller's "dialect continuum"
shows gradations in speech among the Numic languages that run in
more directions than the fan pattern suggests. If we know the Numic
Spread only in terms of its ending, then we miss the story.

Finally, the Numic Spread is not a simple case of population replacement. The small amount of DNA study done so far shows that
the Late Archaic people of the Carson-Stillwater marshes and the
Lovelock culture are genetically distinct from living Northern Paiute
people.[31] I suspect the same for the Fremont case, but like the Fremont,
there are elements of continuity between the newcomers and the
indigenous peoples. The assumption of population replacement
glosses over the role of the indigenous foragers, who were surely part
of the heritage of the living Numic peoples. The Numic cultures of the
Late Prehistoric were neither immigrant nor indigenous, even though
the new culture was rooted in both.[32]

The Late Prehistoric in the Great Basin looks neither South-western nor Californian—nor Great Basin Archaic. The basketry of the Numic peoples exemplifies this message. Basketry expert James Adovasio points to the "uniqueness" of prehistoric and historic period Numic basketry. It does not resemble the myriad basketry traditions of ancient California. He notes the "utter dissimilarity of Fremont and Numic basketry" and observes that "there is no discernable relationship" between Numic and Southwestern basketry traditions. Nor is Numic basketry, prehistoric or historic, similar to Late Archaic basketry of the region, especially that from western Nevada, often known as Lovelock Wickerware. Indeed, Adovasio's assertions of Numic distinctiveness are so strong that it is almost as if the Numic have no historical roots at all. It is out of this impossibility that we realize that the Numic Spread is not a debate over whose ancestors are who, but an example of culture created anew.[33]

MANY INTO THE NEW: THE LATE PREHISTORIC ON THE WASATCH FRONT

When Julian Steward reported his 1930 and 1931 excavations at the Promontory Caves and others around Great Salt Lake he was per-plexed by "certain peculiar and somewhat negative facts," and he remarked: "There is no certainty that the modern Shoshonean tribes of the region ever left important remains in these caves." He was equally mystified by the finding that "there is very little suggestion of Basketmaker or Pueblo cultures in any cave." Steward expected to find the Southwestern Puebloan cultures already known to Utah (but yet to be widely known as Fremont), and he expected to find the artifacts common to the indigenous Shoshonean peoples, whom he had been interviewing. What Steward found was a collection of basketry, moccasins, ceramics, rock art, and arrowheads that had elements of both Puebloan and Shoshone, yet collectively looked like neither. A few traits seem to come from elsewhere, and Steward speculated there might even be some influence from Native American cultures of Canada who had been moving onto the Plains. Steward labeled these finds the Promontory culture and correctly placed it after the Fremont but before the historically known Shoshone of northwestern Utah.[34]

The archaeology of the Wasatch Front and the Promontory cul-ture exemplifies the notion that the Late Prehistoric Millennium was

SIDEBAR: THE RELATIONSHIP OF MODERN TRIBES TO THE ANCIENTS

There is no question that living Native American peoples are descended from ancient Americans. They are not one of the Ten Lost Tribes of Israel, and they did not descend from Viking, Irish, Phoenician, or Libyan voyagers. They are not Chinese, Mongolian, or Siberian. Living Native Americans label their heritage according to the tribal categories of the present, akin to Americans who claim English, African, Italian, Chinese, Hispanic, or Arab ancestry. Yet none of these labels tells us about tapestry of relationships forged in the past on scales of time that transcend the lives of individuals. One of the greatest contributions of archaeology is to expand the scale of time by which we know ourselves and humanity, with the hope of uniting the many forces that often pull peoples apart.

The Great Basin and the northern Colorado Plateau are occupied during history by speakers of the Numic languages. If language is the connection to the past, then Numic speakers, as members of the Uto-Aztecan language family, have been filtering into the Basin-Plateau for perhaps 2,000 years. "They" did not always live here. Linguists suggest that the Hokan and especially the Penutian language families may be represented among Archaic foragers of the western and central Great Basin, and the archaeology largely agrees. Uto-Aztecan speakers encountered the indigenous people, and together they created the modern cultures such as the Washo (Hokan), the Northern Paiute (Numic), and the Klamath-Modoc (Penutian) and others—cultures with distinct languages, but cultures that grew out of these new connections. They were not survivals from some primeval time. Thus, we must accept that the historic Hokan and Penutian tribes of California, Oregon, and Washington have claims to millennia of antiquity in the western and northern Great Basin, even while we accept the fact of the Numic Spread.[a]

It is tempting to see genetics as the holy grail of ancestry, because it is tangible, but it tells us about only one aspect of the past. Advances in extracting mitochondrial DNA from biopsies of ancient bone show that the Fremont have the greatest affinity to modern Puebloan groups, especially those of Jemez and Zuni in New Mexico. This is a tantalizing fit with the archaeological evidence of a substantial role for Southwestern immigration in the founding of the Fremont. It is significant that the Fremont connection to the Southwest is not so much with Uto-Aztecan tribes but with Kiowa-Tanoan (Jemez) and Penutian (Zuni) speakers, symbolizing the Archaic roots not only of the Fremont but the Southwest, too.

Yet, the Fremont are distinctive even among those groups, suggesting there is more to their founding heritage than population replacement. Unfortunately, we do not have comparisons of DNA between Fremont

FIGURE 6.6

The Ancients and the Modern: Biological, linguistic, and archaeological comparisons of ancient and modern tribes.

Eastern Great Basin & Colorado Plateau
- Fremont DNA samples all from Great Salt Lake area.
- Fremont DNA similar to northern Rio Grande Valley: Kiowa-Tanoan (Jemez) and Penutian (Zuni) language families.
- Fremont DNA similar, but less so to Uto-Aztecan groups of the Southwest such as Hopi.
- Fremont DNA strikingly different from the Archaic and the Numic peoples of the western Great Basin.
- Fremont relationship to Numic peoples of the eastern Great Basin not known because DNA comparisons have yet to be made.
- Fremont cranial characteristics indicate variation across Fremont region.
- Fremont cranial characteristics are different from Numic and the Anasazi, except in the Uinta Basin.
- Possible differences in Fremont crania over time, suggesting repeated immigration and some isolation among subpopulations.
- Fremont language(s) unknown, but could be ancient Kiowa-Tanoan, Penutian, or less likely Uto-Aztecan.
- Continuity between Fremont and Late Prehistoric evident in Promontory culture of Wasatch Front.
- Continuity in chipped stone industries from Late Archaic through Late Prehistoric in southeastern Idaho.
- Discontinuity in many aspects of Fremont material culture and Numic peoples.

Western Great Basin
- DNA of Archaic peoples of western Nevada most closely related to Penutian groups of California and Oregon.
- DNA shows Archaic peoples are distantly related to Uto-Aztecan peoples and mixing was less than 2,000 years ago.
- Western Great Basin Archaic and Numic peoples are distinct from the Fremont.
- Genetic similarities and differences of western Basin and eastern Basin-Plateau Archaic peoples not yet known.
- Archaic period languages in western Nevada and southeastern Oregon most likely Penutian.
- Uto-Aztecan languages spread to Southwest over 3,000 years ago and on to California and Great Basin beginning 2,000 years ago.
- Archaeological evidence shows change in material culture such as basketry and arrowheads within the last 1,000 years, but biological, demographic, economic, and social trends suggest changes began up to 2,000 years ago.
- Significant change continues within the last 1,000 years.

and eastern Basin-Plateau Archaic populations. And, finally, all the Fremont DNA samples are from the Great Salt Lake wetlands—but this is only one part of a vast Fremont region.[b]

Statistical comparisons of complex skull measurements of Fremont are slowly being done to complement DNA analysis. These studies suggest considerable variation among the Fremont, which is consistent with the archaeology showing Fremont variants with local gene pools of interaction and marriage, even though this diversity was bound together by Fremont culture. There are significant differences in the cranial measurements between the Fremont and the Anasazi, except for the Uinta Basin. But recall that the Uinta Basin of northeastern Utah was the region to receive the earliest stimulus of Eastern Basketmaker II/Anasazi immigration out of the upper Rio Grande Valley and Four Corners area. Later immigration to the southern and western portions of Utah, and the Wasatch Front, likely brought Uto-Aztecan/Anasazi genes to the Fremont.[c]

Cranial measurements and DNA analysis show significant differences between the Fremont and both the Archaic and Numic populations of the western Great Basin. Frederika Kaestle and David Glenn Smith compared 727 DNA samples from ancient and modern California, Nevada, Utah, Arizona, and New Mexico with 39 prehistoric individuals from western Nevada ranging in age from 350–9200 B.P. The ancient western Nevadans are most closely related to the Californians, especially the Penutian tribes, and hold more distant relations with the Uto-Aztecans. DNA and studies of blood proteins suggest that mixing of Archaic western Nevadans and immigrating Uto-Aztecans may have produced the genetic patterns carried in living Native Americans of the western Great Basin. Many of the samples are dated, and the encounter between the ancient and the Numic populations of western Nevada occurred within the 2,000-year window of the Numic spreading process, but is strongly apparent after 1,500 years ago.[d]

Archaeological measures of cultural change show massive shifts in artifacts and lifeways in the Basin-Plateau during the last 2,000 years, and especially within the Late Prehistoric Millennium. Regardless of whether we use basketry, sandals, pottery, arrowheads, subsistence, settlement organization, social organization, or trade, it was change that shaped the relationships between the ancients and the moderns. These relationships are about differences, but they are also about connections. Folktales talk of difference, such as the Ute and Southern Paiute stories identifying the Fremont as a different Indian people who left the region as new groups came in from the west. The archaeology of the western Great Basin shows significant transition, but the evidence for a replacement of the old with the new is not so strong as to break the connection between the ancients and the modern tribes. In the eastern Great Basin, the Promontory culture and the archaeology of the Wasatch Front and southern Idaho attest to significant continuity, even with the demise of farming and Fremont emigration. Depopulation from European diseases strained the connection between past and present but does not deny the common heritage of all Native Americans.[e]

Every line of evidence is a different snapshot of heritage, ancestry, and identity. These are slippery notions, and our examination of peoples and place shows that ancient America did not comprise immutable entities but real people living in a complex, interacting, and cosmopolitan social landscape over many millennia. Once we move away from the myth that Indians lived in timeless, unchanging, and neatly compartmentalized cultures and beyond the fallacy that cultures must stay the same, move away, or die rather than continuously transform themselves, we will better appreciate heritage.

But even with an enlightened perspective there will be no final answer to the relationship between the ancients and the modern tribes, because identity is constructed in the present and needs no reasonable connection to the past to be real in a cultural sense. The claims of Native Americans need not be expected to align with scientific evidence. Perhaps the higher calling would be to avoid making the dead into a commodity to be dickered over in the courts and in government committees. No one owns the deceased; the heritage of America is for everyone.

a time when many heritages were entwined—not a simple historical sequence from one culture to another. It was unlike any preceding epoch, because it came in the wake of a fully occupied America with the largest populations and the most cosmopolitan societies the continent had ever seen. This milieu created new cultures.

Steward and other early 20th-century anthropologists saw some continuity between Fremont and Promontory, especially in the continued use of one-rod and bundle basketry, the distinctive basketry that marks the Archaic roots of the Fremont, and extending back at least 6,000 years. Promontory basketry did not look Anasazi, but then we now know that Fremont basketry is fundamentally different from Anasazi basketry. Nor did Promontory basketry look like the ethnographically known baskets used by the Shoshone in the last few centuries.

Artistic traditions such as rock art are more difficult to judge, because so much of it defies accurate dating. The rock art in northwestern Utah that appears to be post-Fremont is of a different tradition. It looks more like the Numic rock art best known in southeastern California. For instance, the anthropomorphs and trapezoidal figurines that held so much meaning to the Fremont were no longer expressed. Similarly, the unfired clay figurines found in Fremont sites were no longer made. The work of David Whitley shows that rock art is about much more than art—it reflects the social context of its creation. His work shows that Numic rock art is rooted in California, where for the past thousand years much of it was created in the context of rituals.

This is well documented in the history and ethnography of California and the western Great Basin and appears to extend into the past for about a millennium. This context of execution reveals the cultural roots of Numic rock art. Fremont farming society was fundamentally different, with its larger villages, more structured social and political hierarchies, and episodes of inequality arising from agricultural surplus. As Fremont society faded, the rock art changed to reflect the more individualistic and fluid contexts characteristic of Numic life, society, and place.[35]

Stone arrow tips also indicate change as the Cottonwood Triangular and Desert Side-notched points came in from the west. Their consistency in style across vast landscapes reflects a spread by far-ranging foragers on the move. In one sense, the Desert Side-notched point traces the expansion of the Uto-Aztecan language groups. In another sense, however, it indicates the degree of contact among different languages and even language families over an enormous swath of the Desert West from Mexico to Canada during the last thousand years.

The Desert Side-notched points from the Promontory caves were made to exact specifications with high side notches and a tight basal notch, giving them the distinction of being the "Sierran subtype." The Cottonwood Triangular was not given the same attention to detail, but it, too, is found across the Desert West. Both these new points mark a shift away from the regional styles found during Fremont times—distinct types corresponding to such places as the Uinta Basin, the Sevier Valley, and the Parowan Valley. Like the rock art, the social context of arrow styles comes into play. The more structured Fremont social hierarchies and the territoriality were mirrored in the regional styles of arrow points. The old Fremont social networks and hence point styles gave way to the far-flung Desert Side-notched and Cottonwood Triangular styles that signaled new times.

The changes in arrow points identify change in cultural circumstances—not necessarily the arrival of a new people. The Wahmuza site in southern Idaho spans the last 2,000 years, and the distinctive Wahmuza Lanceolate point used by the historic Shoshone on thrusting spears is found throughout the sequence and even earlier. Archaeologist Richard Holmer used this case to suggest thousands of years of heritage for the Numic peoples in southeastern Idaho. However, he makes the important point that regardless of whether the "actual spread of ancestral Shoshone" occurred this early, the stone tool tradition represented at Wahmuza is related to those of the historic period Shoshone. Holmer moves us beyond

bounded perceptions of this people or that people by casting the connection between the ancient and the modern in terms of heritage
rather than peoples.[36] The spread of Numic foragers brought encounters and conflict with indigenous peoples but at the same time
created social arrangements that yielded new cultures rooted in the
need to accommodate diversity.

As for the Fremont, many surely emigrated toward the south,
and perhaps in other directions, too, but it was unlikely a wholesale
exodus. Fremont heritage was to some extent anchored in Archaic
place extending back thousands of years. Fremont peoples lived diverse lifeways, and it is unlikely they would all see the upheaval of
the 13th and 14th centuries in the same way. The connections of the
Fremont to Southwestern cultures would make that region a natural
magnet, but the differences among peoples were significant and
the distances great, and emigration would have been a risk taken
only by those with exceptional cohesion and fortuitous leadership.
The Promontory culture is the connection between the people who
remained even as new people washed across the Basin-Plateau.

Even more telling than the arrows were changes in footwear.
One of the advantages of archaeology done in the old days before
the dry caves were looted was the recovery of numerous perishable
artifacts. Over 250 moccasins were found in the Promontory caves
and show that the distinctive Fremont deer hock moccasin made of
one piece of hide gave way in Promontory times to a two-piece gus-
seted moccasin not seen before in the region. Direct dating of the
Promontory moccasins, using AMS radiocarbon dating that requires
less than a gram of leather, shows that the new fashion trend was
taking hold by the A.D. 1200s.[37] By that time, many Fremont were
leaving, but the spasms of village construction in the late A.D. 1200s
and 1300s in central and western Utah show that the region was not
yet finished with Fremont farming. The new was literally afoot, and
the social signaling so apparent in shoes symbolizes the need to af-
firm identity when the daily lives of people from different heritages
become entwined.

Carla Sinopolli compared 172 arrows from known Numic-speaking
bands in the southeastern Great Basin collected during the J. W.
Powell expeditions in the 19th century. She found that decorations on
the arrow shafts mark band distinctions and that those distinctions
varied the most among regularly interacting groups, and the least
among groups who have little contact. Ethnic signaling thus arises
from interaction more than from isolation. Interestingly, she found that

the style of stone arrow tips did not vary according to band lines and thus carried no ethnic relevance in that case.[38]

Another indicator of a changing cultural milieu is trade. As Fremont population centers diminished and their network of social hierarchies frayed, there was far less movement of exotics, such as turquoise from Nevada and the Southwest and marine shell from California. It is not that the later peoples did not move. Indeed, they moved more as a course of daily life. But the Fremont dispersed communities linked by large villages were gone, and the trade that provided exotics to mirror the inequalities among people and place now played a different role. Like the changes in rock art, changes in the distribution of exotic items signaled change in the context of their creation and meaning. Even the sources of practical goods like obsidian changed. The obsidian sources in the Sevier Desert long used during Fremont times shifted to others located north of Malad, Idaho, and on Brown's Bench, south of Twin Falls. The social net was not only looser, but greater mobility stretched the net over the landscape in a different way once Fremont farming began to collapse.[39]

Perhaps the most apparent change was in ceramics, if for no other reason than its ubiquity enables archaeologists to compare large samples among many sites. Ceramics are indeed common, but like arrowheads they harbor a mix of information that must be teased apart. Pots are made with certain intentions for their use. One intended for cooking must resist frequent heating and cooling. A pot intended for long, reliable use may be made with better materials and greater care than one intended for only a short use. Ironically, a pot that was to be used only briefly but left at a place to be returned to and used again and again may be made to the highest standards. Pots also reflect things beyond the practical. A bowl made for social display, a gift, or trade may be manufactured and decorated with the utmost care. Pots also reflect the heritage of a potter in the manner of manufacture and the effected styles. But unlike with basketry, people can change the ways they make pots much more readily, and this makes ceramic industries sensitive indicators of change. The assemblages of broken Late Prehistoric pottery from northern Utah indicate changing circumstances of vessel function, intended use, mobility, social place, ethnicity, history, and heritage during the A.D. 1200s and 1300s.[40]

Once again, these changes were a process, not a chain of discreet events.[41] The relationship between Fremont and Promontory is not purely sequential but overlaps for a century or more. It is not so much a matter of pedigree and purity as it is about connection and diversity, and the creation of the new through the interaction of people and place. The story of continuity in the face of massive change persisted for the next several centuries on the Wasatch Front, and some of the excavated sites provide a window into that life.

LIFE AFTER THE FREMONT

The final abandonments of Fremont villages can easily imply an empty place, but the archaeology tells us otherwise. Population sizes along the Wasatch Front surely shrank, but they remained high even in the absence of farming. Amateur archaeologists, such as Mark Stuart, spent decades recording sites along the eastern flank of Great Salt Lake. Along the endlessly entwined channels that once snaked through this vast marshland (see Prologue), it is difficult to see any decline in residence between Fremont and Promontory times. A single U.S. Geological Survey map from this area yields hundreds of ancient sites so thick there are no boundaries among them. Individual sites have given up a thousand arrowheads in areas the size of an average back yard. House remains are everywhere, and refuse middens line the natural levees along the streams. The sheer numbers of sites in this archaeological landscape favor Fremont use, but the productive wetlands sustained large numbers of foraging people during Promontory times as well.[42]

Archaeologist Mel Aikens excavated a site on Injun Creek west of Ogden in the 1960s. It was a Promontory period residential camp or small village occupied by pottery-using foragers between the late A.D. 1300s and 1500s. There was no farming, but wild resources were harvested and stored in subsurface pits. Injun Creek filled just one niche in a Promontory culture reminiscent of the old Archaic period wetland pattern with one significant exception.[43] Unlike the Archaic, the Promontory came on the heels of the largest native population increase in the ancient history of North America. The Promontory and other Late Prehistoric cultures of the Basin-Plateau were thus borne of this continental upheaval that fostered processes such as the Numic Spread. Coming in the wake of the Fremont, the Promontory culture was a cultural cauldron similar to the valleys of eastern California during the Numic Spread. Farming dissolved, but the Promontory was no nostalgic return to the Archaic of millennia past.

Promontory-Late Prehistoric sites are abundant; most are known only from the remains on the surface, and countless examples have been destroyed by urbanization. Excavations in recent years show that Promontory occupation along the Wasatch Front was especially heavy in the 15th century.

The Orbit Inn near Brigham City, Utah, was a seasonal camp used repeatedly around A.D. 1450. Located on Black Slough, a slow moving spring-fed channel embedded in freshwater wetlands miles from Great Salt Lake, the Orbit Inn was occupied in the late spring and again in the late summer. People gathered there in the spring for the spawning run of Utah Sucker. The sizable catch of fish was roasted in pits and large open areas with hearths, and post holes suggest that fish may have been dried on racks over slow fires. The two houses found were domed huts covered with rushes or mats, or maybe they were just windbreaks. The refuse of living piled up behind them and abutted the walls of one structure. This was no weekend camp but at least a month-long stay. After a summer at one or more of their other residences, people used the Orbit Inn again during the late summer to hunt waterfowl during the summer molt. The birds do not fly well during the molt, and, as with the fish runs in the spring, waiting until the right time ensured a much larger take of ducks and geese than could be gained by hunters working alone. Muskrats, seeds, and starchy roots were also taken during both seasons of use. Food was stored in subsurface pits about a meter wide and half a meter deep. This type of caching tends to be short term and difficult to hide from neighbors and kin, and was thus a strong tether to place. In the winter, people likely gathered into villages and retrieved the stored foods from the many cache locations, although a clear example of a winter village has yet to be excavated. People were more mobile than in Fremont times, but the tether to place was made strong by repeated use of the same places as the Promontory foragers "farmed"—the rich ecosystems of the Wasatch Front.[44]

Trips were made to obtain things not available in the wetlands. Beads were made at the Orbit Inn out of a turquoise-like mineral called variscite that came from a source 40 miles to the northwest. The obsidian used for tools came from sources only about 60 miles to the north.

Joel Janetski excavated sites along the Wasatch Front, including Heron Springs, Sandy Beach, and Goshen Island in Utah Valley. He shows that the pattern described for Injun Creek and the Orbit Inn repeats itself over and over again during the 15th century. Heron Springs had subsurface storage pits and was used off and on between April and September during the first decades of the A.D. 1400s. Sandy

FIGURE 6.7

The Orbit Inn was used in the 15th century for about a month at a time in the late spring to harvest spawning Utah suckers and in early fall to hunt geese and ducks. The circular arrangements of stakes in the upper right and below identify circular structures. Trash was deposited to the right. The holes are the remnants of storage and roasting pits. The area in front of the individuals was an activity area with five hearths and ramadas. (Photo by Steven Simms)

Beach was a residential site dating to the same period. Located on the North Shore of Utah Lake, the excavation at Sandy Beach revealed nine hearths and three pits in one small area of what was an enormous site that had yielded artifacts to amateur archaeologists for decades. Lake edge and marsh resources were taken, just as at the Orbit Inn and Heron Springs.

Goshen Island was similar in location, artifacts, and activities to the others, but it symbolizes the dynamic nature of place. Goshen Island was used during the Archaic, ignored by the Fremont, and used again during the Late Prehistoric. The location was ideal for a campsite; yet the Fremont did not use this place. Perhaps more telling is that the foragers using the camp during Promontory times did very different things at Goshen Island than the foragers who used it in the Late Archaic. The Fremont to Promontory transition was more than a return to a one-size-fits-all notion of hunting and gathering.[45]

Given the elements of continuity that Promontory represents, even farming probably did not disappear entirely, casting into doubt the pernicious notion that Native Americans "lost" farming until the Spanish reintroduced it centuries later. As more and more of the Late Prehistoric archaeology becomes known, instances of farming will most likely be found in the microenvironments along the Wasatch Front, where fruit stands abound today. Farming was no longer the lynchpin of the economy in Promontory times, but the wetlands kept everyone tethered enough that a few farmed products could fill a niche in this intensive forager system that was neither Fremont nor Archaic.

WIDOWED CONTINENT:
DISEASE, DEPOPULATION, AND HISTORY

The last few centuries on the Wasatch Front are strangely silent in comparison to virtually all the other periods. To be sure, people were present, as testified by the Fox site on the Jordan River near Lehi that was used for fishing in the mid-1600s, the Fire Guard camp near Ogden dating to mid-1700s, and others. The pottery changed again and became even more indicative of a mobile lifeway than even the Promontory vessels that had differed somewhat from the Fremont. But the level of activity in these last centuries is sparse compared to the heyday of the Promontory.

The 17th century seems to be a time of population adjustment across the region. Dates from Ute sites in western Colorado suggest an interruption of occupation, and compilation of radiocarbon dates for the Colorado Plateau and eastern Great Basin show a pronounced dip in the mid to late A.D. 1600s. Great Salt Lake flooded in the early 17th century, and when the lake receded, people did not return in any substantial numbers as they had always done before. The Promontory period was over by the 17th century. Less than two centuries later, the first direct encounter between Native Americans in the eastern Great Basin and Europeans occurred when the Dominguez-Escalante expedition arrived in 1776. But the end of the Promontory nearly two centuries earlier may very well be when the first significant encounter occurred.[46]

There is an unfolding awareness of the enormous impact of European disease on Native American populations after the Columbian land fall—but as much as two centuries before widespread Euroamerican settlement. Contrary to conventional wisdom that holds the American continent pristine, it was, as the demographer

FIGURE 6.8

Utah radiocarbon dates in comparison to climate during the Late Prehistoric period. The rapid drop in Fremont sites is evident with the first major cold snap of the A.D.1300s, but the Promontory culture retains a strong presence until the 1500s. Additional radiocarbon dates focusing on the later centuries suggests a sharp decline in the A.D. 1600s followed by growth.

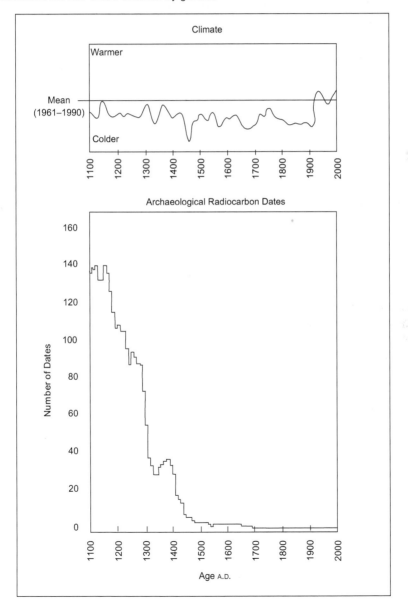

Henry Dobyns put it, a "widowed land by the time of widespread Euroamerican settlement." Did the Promontory culture decline in the 16th century, and the population anomalies of the 17th century result from European disease? Did native travelers from the Pacific coast, or perhaps the Southwest inadvertently bring disease two centuries before any white man would see the Great Basin? Several pieces of this puzzle fit, but we don't know for sure.[47]

The single greatest consequence of European and American interactions in the first centuries was the introduction of diseases including smallpox, measles, influenza, and scarlet fever. These arose in the Old World, where millennia of farming brought humans into close contact with domesticated animals, and early urbanization created the perfect storm for disease. Large populations of humans evolved with these diseases of density in the ancient cities and towns of the Middle East, China, India, and Europe. The diseases became endemic in the Old World and hence part of life, but in the New World after more than ten millennia of isolation, the same diseases brought catastrophe to a hemisphere of susceptible Americans.

Once introduced, as in the case of Cortez's army in Mexico in the early A.D. 1500s, epidemics of smallpox leapt ahead of the Spaniards in virulent waves across a densely populated native land. By the time Pizarro arrived in Andean South America in A.D. 1531, Inkan populations were already greatly diminished. Native trade routes to northern Mexico's Baja California, Sonora, and Arizona carried disease there in the early A.D. 1500s, the same active trade routes that enabled Spanish explorers such as Nuno de Guzman in A.D. 1530 to comment that the local Indians had already adopted poultry as fine as any seen in Spain. The native networks were extensive and routine, and by the time of regular exploration of the California coast and the Southwest in the 1500s and on, epidemics were finding their way into native populations. Historical records of epidemics show that mortality rates of 70% or higher were common.[48]

If the effects of European disease preceded most of the face-to-face encounters between whites and Indians, then questions about those times become an archaeological matter. Historical records, oral history, and such are not sufficient. Over the past 20 years, archaeologists have amassed a substantial body of evidence that shows America was not the "virgin land many historians and politicians have called it" but was in the process of becoming wilderness—an image that persists to this day as one of America's most indulgent myths. Ironically, America was transformed into a wilderness by the Columbian encounter well before most Europeans ever saw the continent.[49]

The discontinuity in the archaeology of the Basin-Plateau in the 17th century may be a local expression of the "population anomalies" documented elsewhere on the continent where large native populations were disrupted by disease. The anomalies are apparent in the numbers of settlements and their size, in the size of houses, in the scale of refuse production, the patterns in trade routes, and in statistical measures of radiocarbon dates. Each of these measures evaluates some aspect of population change. Large-scale declines in native populations that correlate with the expected timing of European pestilence include the Mississippi and Missouri river valleys, the Southwest, coastal California, and the Columbia Plateau. In each case, the vectors of disease were the early Spanish explorations followed by a spread among native networks. The population declines began early in the A.D. 1500s and continued, bringing massive population declines to areas with high concentrations of Native Americans.[50]

The diseases did not affect all places and all native populations equally or at the same times, and the Basin-Plateau seems so remote and wild that scholars have generally not investigated whether disease made its way here. But looking back at our excursion through the ancient Basin-Plateau, we have found that even this land was more fully used, with larger populations and villages, and more social complexity, than allowed for by our romantic longings for wildness. If there is one place in our region where it is clear native populations were large, it was the Wasatch Front during the Late Prehistoric Millennium. The ample water, the productive wetlands, and a climate moderated by Great Salt Lake and Utah Lake made the area a strip of human density in a wilderness of foragers. If diseases such as smallpox were vectored to the Wasatch Front by a sick traveler, the results could be as devastating as any of the many well-documented epidemics recorded during the historic period in America, whereby three fourths of a population might be wiped out.[51]

Difficult to imagine, there was a greater tragedy to such encounters than the mortality from the diseases. The cultural fabric was shredded as old people were often the first to die, sweeping away the libraries of knowledge held in the memories of the elders. Equally disastrous were the deaths of the young, terminating the promise of a new generation. Casualties were so high and came so swiftly that there was no one to care for the sick. The economic system faltered, because critical jobs remained undone. Those groups that survived could prey on those who became weak, fostering violence and tearing at the culture of the attackers as well as the victims. It often took several epidemic cycles for the diseases to become even tolerably endemic, and with each cycle of catastrophe, culture reinvented itself.

Whether this explains the decline in the strength of the archaeology on the Wasatch Front after A.D. 1500 or the disruptions on the Colorado Plateau and in the eastern Great Basin in the A.D. 1600s is not known, but the situation and the timing are right. A rebound of population in the A.D. 1700s apparent in the radiocarbon data would be consistent with other cases of disease introduction where epidemics were followed by a resumption of population growth, often from people moving into regions left open by the depopulation.

The end of the Promontory was abrupt, and although calamity may have befallen the people, the Wasatch Front was not depopulated completely. The horse may have been making its way into Utah as early as the mid A.D. 1600s, when the Comanche and the Ute from the north were raiding New Mexico for horses. The Mexican and native slave trade may have caused captives to be taken in Utah. Metal tools such as knives were signs of more change ahead. After the Pueblo Revolt in New Mexico in A.D. 1680, the northward flow of horses increased, and by the A.D. 1700s horses were a part of life for many people on the northern Colorado Plateau and beyond. Ethnohistoric evidence suggests that the Wasatch Front was a place used by everyone but not used as a home by anyone. Horse-mounted Commanche from the Plains, Bannock from Idaho, Shoshone, and Ute all passed along the Front, but they did not stay. The peoples who lived here were few and scattered.

In September 1776, the party led by Francisco Atanasio Dominguez and Silvestre Velez de Escalante descended Spanish Fork Canyon and entered Utah Valley to become the first known European foreigners to cross the Colorado Plateau and gaze into the Great Basin.[52] This was only two centuries after the Great Salt Lake transgression that brought closure to the archaeological signature. Of course, two centuries is a mere blink of an eye compared with the vast stretch of time since the first Americans arrived over 13,000 years ago. It is in those millennia where the real story lies and where the answers will be found.

Epilogue

America was cosmopolitan—a fully occupied, socially integrated, multicultural tapestry. The repetitive deserts and mountains of the Great Basin, and the mesas, canyons, and jutting peaks of the Colorado Plateau, remain the last wilderness in the lower 48 of the United States. Many of us may find a wilderness sense of place in the Basin-Plateau, but in the ancient past it was a human wilderness.

The many pasts of Basin-Plateau peoples are grounded in conceptions of place too diverse to be captured by the popular stereotype of a monolithic Native American culture and worldview. America was a human landscape whether it was the Paleoindian explorers and colonists, the multicultural Archaic settlers, the tethered and appropriative foragers of the Late Archaic, the Fremont farmers, or the mingling peoples of the Late Prehistoric Millennium. The stories of ancient people and place told here are anchored by the key ingredients of time and space.

Time. America's history is over 430 human generations long, and although appeals to recent history, folklore, lived experience, politics, religion, or sheer imagination bring respect to America's indigenous peoples, none of these is equipped to do justice to the sweep of time encompassed by America's deep past. That past is bigger than we think.

Space. Larger scales of geography also bring greater clarity and respect for America's past. Native Americans are connected to the other peoples of the world, not because Asians, Europeans, or any other groups explored and founded America but because the depth of time transcends the divisions rooted in our unfortunately divided present.

A third theme in our story here is epistemological—how we know about the past. Archaeology and the other sciences of the past are the only windows we have to know a past as it might have been at the time, rather than fully succumbing to the constructions we make in the present.

An empirically known past may be less than satisfying, because it is fragmentary and unsure. It is based on most probable interpretations rather than the certitude that accompanies so many ideologies of the present. The fragmentary and probabilistic nature of scientific knowledge is often stillborn, a past absent of the human touch. Archaeological information consists of things, and relationships among things, and archaeological reporting often leaves it at that for the sake of scientific responsibility. But all the archaeologists I know realize that it is the humanity that breathes life into those things and that the empirical record, known through the limitations of science, enables us to step into time machines. I believe archaeologists know more about the social and ideological past of ancient peoples than we allow ourselves to write about. I have tried to do that here, while maintaining empirical responsibility, but admittedly with only a sampling of the evidence.

Our excursion through ancient America traced changing sense of place over the more than 13,000 years humans lived in this hemisphere. The first Americans are called Paleoindians and they were Native Americans, not immigrants. Their colonization of places untouched by the hand of humanity brought an end to the American wilderness. The pathways from other parts of the world were part of one expansive land, and the settlement of what we now call the Americas was not an event but a process. The process took millennia— a span of time that transcends terms such as "historical events" and concepts that emphasize divisions, such as the term "the people." Place during the Paleoindian period was expansive and geared to newness. It was not appropriative, nor tethered, except to the mobile habitats of those who encountered a landscape with no humans. The ultimate wilderness ended then, and the worldview of these people was very different from that of *everyone* who followed.

Colonists soon grew into populations of settlers who filled in the spaces and began to part out the land. Instead of place being defined as newness, it became more anchored to tangible places. The strongest tethers were to the wetlands of the Great Basin valleys and along the ribbons of oasis tracing the canyons and floodplains of the Colorado Plateau. This was the Archaic period. Over the next seven millennia, place multiplied into divergent heritages creating the basis for a cosmopolitan America comprised of foraging societies. In the Basin-Plateau there are two main cultural heritages apparent in the archaeology: the high desert foragers and the more settled and populous foragers tethered in small villages to valley wetlands.

Place for the high desert foragers was geographically expansive, and the land was envisioned in terms of homelands, rather than a particular home. The land was socially full and created a network that cycled people among kin and across place. This pliable social net was complemented by a built environment specialized to fit many places. People were mobile, but their movements were not aimless or wandering. Food storage was episodic and particularly aimed at preparing for the winter, when people anchored to a few villages. But for the most part, the tethers to stored supplies were limited as people cycled across the land. They lived in some places for months and in others for weeks or days. Place was not appropriative, and territoriality was defined by use. In general, resources and property were seen as public. Over the life history of an individual, one might weave numerous territories into their lived experience. The broad network of kin and social obligation among the high desert foragers was synonymous with a sense of place that swathed the land, floating over it instead of dividing it up as later peoples would do.

The foragers of the valley wetlands were different. People's notions of territory became more developed as they were anchored to place. Ownership was fostered by greater reliance on food storage and a pattern of bringing the resources to the people rather than moving the people to the resources. The reduced mobility led to population growth, and by the Late Archaic some places were fully allocated both socially and economically. Place became more intensive, and the social system reflected this with a greater investment in corporate groups who identified members versus nonmembers. Access to resources and social connections is more carefully regulated in corporate groups, and greater weight is placed on the notion of private rather than public goods.

By the Late Archaic, fundamental economic, demographic, and social changes in the Southwest and in California began to send ripples of change across the Basin-Plateau.

The first agriculture made its way to southern Utah, brought by immigrant farmers from the south. For those indigenous peoples of the Four Corners region of the Southwest, who already embraced an intensive notion of place, the adoption of farming transformed their cultures quickly. Other foragers would be hold-outs. They would be driven out, subdued, and absorbed by the twin forces of immigration and the drastic changes brought by a farming economy.

Agricultural productivity drove population growth, and the Fremont culture was born. Over the next ten centuries, place in the eastern Great Basin and Colorado Plateau would fill with farmers working every available niche. Across much of southern Utah, population sizes were probably larger than they are today, when entire landscapes are considered and not just the isolated towns of modern Utah. Fremont place was extractive, and farming required a great deal of labor to attain the higher levels of production required to maintain large populations. Farming in such a tenuous place ensured that some would have larger surpluses, and others would have little. The inequality created an unsettled dynamic between connection and cooperation on the one hand and competition and conflict on the other. The system grew, but it was fragile, and global climate change brought stress that even the tightly woven Fremont social fabric could not withstand. After more than 700 years, farming was largely abandoned.

At the same time that agriculture was transforming the Southwest, forager populations grew in California. There, economic intensification was directed at processing enormous quantities of acorns, managing landscapes with fire to increase plant and animal numbers, and investing in boat and ocean hunting technology to range farther and farther from the coast. As in the Southwest, populations grew dramatically and required a great deal of labor and an appropriative sense of place to sustain it.

The Southwest and California flung excess population outward into the relatively empty high deserts of southern California and the Great Basin. The immigrants brought their appropriative, extractive cultural notions with them and imposed them on the indigenous natives of the high deserts. Both immigrants and indigenes were foragers, and the clash of the two created the peoples and cultures occupying the Basin-Plateau in the past millennium. The historically known peoples of the region—the Northern Paiute, the Shoshone, and the Ute-Southern Paiute—are at once rooted in the deep past and born of the recent past. They are not one continuous thread of antiquity, but neither are they new arrivals. The upheaval of the Late Prehistoric Millennium wove a new culture out of ancient threads of heritage.

After A.D. 1500, the edge of "history" could be felt as European exploration of North America brought a dozen diseases for which Native Americans had no natural resistance. The effects of European disease on peoples of the Basin-Plateau were surely variable, ranging from minimal to significant. But even for groups who never experienced the diseases, the depopulation that occurred elsewhere created cultural vacuums shaping everyone's lives. The repeated epidemics, and especially their social and economic consequences, created a Native America strangely disconnected from its deep past.

By the time the Basin-Plateau filled with Euroamerican settlers in the 19th and 20th centuries, images of the Native American past were drawn primarily through notions of a romanticized frontier, racial hatred, mystical reverence, and through the unbridled exploitation of Native American peoples and cultures. This is how many Americans continue to know ancient America. I argue that we really don't know them until we know their rich past as told by the actual remains from those ancient times—the archaeology.

Our time to know America's past is, in fact, short. The archaeology of America is disappearing. It is under assault by our growing population and by our ignorance. Even the Great Basin is being swallowed up by the urban sprawl of places like the Wasatch Front, Las Vegas, and Reno. Growth in the mountain and desert west, whether it be Denver, Phoenix, Albuquerque, Boise, and even St. George, Utah, all shape the landscapes of the hinterlands and endanger the only concrete lifeline we have to America's deep past—the archaeology.

Every time someone picks up the flakes of stone left from ancient tool making, or collects the arrowheads and the pottery, or lays his hands upon the rock art, he is destroying the past. Every time a housing subdivision is constructed, a water line laid, a new ATV trail is carved, or an oil well drilling pad is bulldozed, there is the potential to destroy the past.

Laws have been on the books since 1906 making collecting and digging illegal, and legislation in recent decades has greatly increased penalties and enforcement. But none of this matters as much as a public that knows and cares about the fate of our collective heritage.

Cultural resources, whether they be a spectacular Fremont village, or awe-inspiring rock art, or caves harboring fantastic stories rooted in deep time are all fragile. Then there are the hundreds of thousands, perhaps millions of tiny places across the Basin-Plateau that yield clues to the past. These are the caches and the camps, the rock art, the places of seed processing, and fishing, large-game butchering, and so much more. The casual visitor may dismiss these as minor, but collectively they constitute the bulk of our archaeological connection to the past.

All cultural resources, whether they are stunning or mundane, have one thing in common: they are nonrenewable. More fragile than endangered species, the evidence from the past cannot reproduce itself. When we destroy it, it is gone forever, and with it goes the past's only tangible record. From that day on, the only way we will know the past is through the biases of the present—the culture wars, the religious and political agendas, and through it all, the play of power. Our final disconnect from America's rich Native American past will exist only as seductive cultural images made in the present. While this is not in itself bad, it is undeniably incomplete.

Until the day comes when we destroy the tangible evidence of the past, the ancient peoples will live with us in the present through the archaeology. Knowledge of them based on evidence from *their times* instead of ours is a crucial hedge against the temptation to fashion antiquity only in terms of power, dogma, or whim.

Notes

Preface

1. I follow Julian Steward (1938) in his use of "Basin-Plateau." He included the southern edges of the Columbia Plateau to refer to southern Idaho and the Snake River Plain, but he explicitly includes the Colorado Plateau. Most importantly, he recognized the strong cultural links between the peoples "of the two plateaus and the Great Basin" (1938: Preface). There is a rich literature on the Great Basin, but it is less known than the photogenic red rock country of the Colorado Plateau. See Trimble (1999) for excellent photography, or the classic geographic treatise of Cline (1963), or McPhee's (1981) geological journal, or Grayson's (1993) ecological masterpiece.

2. Binford (1983) is a reader-friendly discussion about how archeologists "decode" the past. His phrase "the past is with us in the present" refers to the fact that archaeologists do not make "discoveries" so much as they make inferences. Binford argues that although archaeology might appear to be a social science because it is about people, the data that archaeologists must employ demand a natural science approach. Barbara Tuchman's (1978) *A Distant Mirror: The Calamitous 14th Century*, is a sweeping historical narrative set in France in the Middle Ages. It shows that our romanticized notions of the past often do not conform to what

really happened. By confronting myths with an often uncomfortable reality, we can confront the contradictions of our own times. An old idea in anthropology is that the study of the "Other" (other cultures) is really a way to learn about ourselves; Clyde Kluckhohn's (1949) *Mirror for Man: The Relation of Anthropology to Modern Life* is an example of this idea.

3. Welty (1979:128).

Chapter 1

1. Lewis Binford (1983) employs this useful phrase to focus archaeologists on harnessing the power of analogy—so fundamental to the sciences—while managing its pitfalls.

2. On the entry of the horse to the region see Callaway, Janetski, and Stewart (1986:354–355). Also see general treatises on the introduction of the horse in Roe (1955) and Ewers (1955). The Dominguez-Escalante expedition is described in Bolton (1972:179–187).

3. Callaway, Janetski, and Stewart (1986:354–355).

4. More than a dozen European diseases were introduced. Only in recent decades have scholars realized the implications of the early transmission of these diseases from native to native, often taking place well before face-to-face contact with Europeans. See, for instance, Dobyns (1983), Ramenovsky (1987), Thornton (1987).

5. For brief examples of this idea see the Foreword by Joseph Jorgenson to the book *Ute Tales* by Anne Smith (1992) and the Foreword by Catherine Fowler to the book *Shoshone Tales* by Anne Smith (1993).

6. At some risk of omission, the following are readily available ethnographic classics that attempted comprehensive description. Other important studies target specific topics (Fowler 1989; I. Kelly 1932, 1964; Lowie 1909; Murphy and Murphy 1960; Smith 1974; Steward 1938; Stewart 1939).

7. Prehistoric basketry does not occur in large sample sizes as do projectile points and ceramics. Differences in basketry are useful for identifying language associations, social connections, and group identity, because the intricacies of basketmaking demand a long apprenticeship that leads to identifiable traditions passed from teachers to students. Basketry styles and designs may also have provided social signals of ethnicity in antiquity. See Adovasio (1986a, 1986b).

8. This typology was explicitly employed in Simms (1996), but the contrast between a desert and a "lacustrine" pattern has a long history in the Great Basin region. See Janetski and Madsen (1990) for an overview.

9. See Kelly (1995:Chapter 4, "Foraging and Mobility") for an excellent overview on forager mobility around the world.

10. Ethnographic studies frequently hint at the need for fuel. In the desert-mountain settlement pattern, winter camp location traded off snow depth at higher altitudes with the need to be near forested areas with fuel. For wetland-lakeside settlement, driftwood may have been important, as well as greasewood flats and hydrologically stable areas capable of supporting larger trees. See I. Kelly (1964:150, 169, 177) for references to fuel among Southern Paiute in southwestern Utah and Fowler (1989:92) for reference to fuel among the Pyramid Lake Northern Paiute in western Nevada.

11. More and more studies actually measure the economic costs and benefits of various activities. These studies show that native foragers had intimate knowledge of their environment and took practical matters into account. Transportation costs were likely as important to shaping their behavior as much as the costs of moving oil and soda pop are important in the modern world. See Jones and Madsen (1989), Barlow, Henriksen, and Metcalfe (1993), Barlow and Metcalfe (1996).

12. See the 1938 ethnographic classic *Basin-Plateau Aboriginal Sociopolitical Groups* by Julian Steward for references to winter camp placement in several Great Basin cases.

13. Many Great Basin ethnographic studies describe camp locations, group settings and size, subsistence activities, and so on. Catherine Fowler reviews this kind of information in relationship to "food named groups" in Fowler (1982a), and with an eye to how the ethnography informs archaeology in Fowler (1982b).

14. See Janetski and Madsen (1990). The major wetlands are the Great Salt Lake and the Utah Lake wetlands of the eastern Great Basin, and the Carson-Stillwater marshes east of Reno, Nevada. Many others exist, including Malheur Lake, southeastern Oregon; Pyramid Lake, western Nevada; the Ruby marshes, northeastern Nevada; the Owens River, eastern California; and others. For the best description of the wetlands-lake lifestyle along the Wasatch Front, see Janetski (1990). For first-person demonstrations with excellent photographs of wetlands lifestyles, including building a tule mat house, a cattail boat, duck decoys, and more, see Wheat (1967).

15. See Fowler (1986) for an exhaustive overview. Thomas on animal procurement (1983:41–57) and on plants (1983:57–71) provides an outstanding synthesis of the ethnographic data on hunting and gathering with the added consideration of the archaeological implications.

16. The theoretical perspective taken throughout this book, but perhaps most explicitly apparent with subsistence, is human evolutionary ecology. Those interested in reading about this productive line of research might consult Kelly (1995:Chapter 3, "Foraging and Subsistence") and

Zeanah and Simms (1999) for an evaluation of the success of this perspective in Great Basin archaeology. See Bird and O'Connell (2006) for
a report of the significant insights of behavioral/evolutionary ecology to
archaeology in general.

17. The best classic ethnography to see for this particular point is Steward
(1938). For others, see note 6.

18. Virginia Kerns's (2003:181) book is a fascinating biography of Julian
Steward and an exploration of how autobiographical memory and life
history shape our perceptions.

19. See Janetski (1990:36) and references therein. Another excellent source
for descriptions of fishing is Willard Park's ethnography of the Pyramid
Lake Paiute in Nevada (Fowler 1989).

20. Couture, Ricks, and Housley (1986). The importance of seeds is frequently mentioned, but roots should not be underestimated, even in the
drier portions of the Basin-Plateau region.

21. See Steward (1938:34–35) for a description of an antelope drive and
Raymond (1982) for descriptions of the Box Elder county, Utah, antelope traps. The Bureau of Land Management, Elko, Nevada District,
holds records of dozens of these installations in northeastern Nevada.

22. We will see this more explicitly in later chapters, but just about any
archaeological excavation report lists the counts of animal bones found.
Most show that rabbits were the staple meat.

23. Lakeside Cave was an intensive grasshopper processing location for
three centuries, and grasshoppers were consumed at the cave for nearly
4,000 years. See Madsen and Kirkman (1988) and Madsen (1989a) for
a popular article in *Natural History* magazine.

24. Like grasshoppers, brine fly larvae are an episodic bounty that attracted
people from many places, briefly creating a large social gathering. Unlike
root crops, these kinds of resources were irregularly available and more
difficult to predict. For descriptions of brine fly larvae harvesting at
Mono Lake in eastern California see Thomas (1983:55), including the
quotes from John Ross Browne and Mark Twain.

25. See Kelly (1995:161–181) for a discussion of the patterns in sharing
and some of the reasons for it.

26. Steward (1938:33–44) is an excellent general source on hunting, but
so are some of the other classic ethnographies cited in note 6. Thomas
(1983:41–57) is the best synthesis in an ecological vein that looks toward the archaeological past.

27. See Madsen (1986) for a synthesis.

28. Steward (1938:178).

29. For a sense of how such decisions are analyzed, and the role of information in decisions about subsistence and mobility, see R. Kelly
(1995:97–98, 150–151).

30. See Fowler (1982b:121–125) and Fowler (1999) for discussions and references.
31. Kelly (1995:7–10, 333–344).
32. Steward (1969:187).
33. This section draws on a variety of ethnographies for the region, which typically include a category for "social organization." The most comprehensive source for the introductory reader are the chapters under Ethnology in the *Handbook of North American Indians*, Volume 11: Great Basin, edited by Warren L. d'Azevedo (1986).
34. Differences in male and female mobility with a high value placed on male mobility are found in foragers in various places around the world; see Kelly (1995:149–153). An accessible discussion can also be found in the chapter "Hunters in a Lifespace" in Binford (1983).
35. For an overview of Great Basin kinship see Shapiro (1986). For a personable description of how kinship and marriage worked in one area of the Great Basin see Fowler (1992:151–156).
36. Thomas (1983:37, 1986:279).
37. Fowler (1992:217). There is, of course, no magic to the number 4, but this degree of memory extension fits well with estimates of memory culture in other contexts, such as the conclusion of many folklorists that folklore may represent narrative history (in contrast to other meanings of folklore) for several generations or perhaps a few centuries.
38. Various anthropologists struggled to reconcile different findings regarding the presence and nature of bands and tribes around the region. See Shapiro (1986:621) for a broad sense of this. Better known is the debate between Julian Steward and Omer Stewart about bands and tribes during the Indian Claims Commission legal cases of the 1940s (Steward 1955 and Stewart 1966). The current popularity of revisionist interpretations of history has provoked critiques such as Ronaasen, Clemmer, and Rudden (1999) and Lewis (2002:18–22), but see Fowler (1999:57) for a less politicized and self-indulgent retrospective.
39. From among many examples in the ethnographies, see Fowler (1989: 5–6) on "Territory and Neighbors" of the Pyramid Lake Paiute studied by Willard Park in the 1930s, or the story of overlapping ranges of Northern Paiute and Western Shoshone near Austin in central Nevada (Fowler 1992:165), or in Isabel Kelly's ethnography (1964), any of the sections titled "Neighbors," "Territory and Neighbors," "Identification and Neighbors" on the four bands of Southern Paiute.
40. Kelly (1995:13, 181–189), and Fowler (1982b).
41. Fowler (1982a:117).
42. Janetski (1990) and Steward (1938).
43. Fowler (1982a).
44. See Kelly (1995:"Sharing, Exchange and Land Tenure") for a review.

45. Janetski (1991:49–51) and Bolton (1972:179–187).
46. Anthropology is finally recognizing the role of conflict in all cultures. See, for instance, Lawrence Keeley's (1996) *War Before Civilization* or Steven LeBlanc and Katherine Register's (2003) *Constant Battles: The Myth of the Peaceful, Noble Savage.*
47. Some broad patterns in Great Basin religious concepts are described by Hultkrantz (1986). Patterns in the thematic content and characters found in storytelling are described by Liljeblad (1986) and in Jorgensen (1992). For a comparative study of shamanism among several cultures see Willard Park's (1938) *Shamanism in Western North America.*
48. Fowler (1992:170) and Hultkrantz (1986).
49. Hultkrantz (1986:631).
50. Again refer to references in note 47.
51. Jorgensen (1992:xxi).
52. Peter Nabokov is a leading folklorist and champion of this idea, and his book (2002) is a well-researched discussion of the power and place of folklore in light of the fact that there are different ways to "know" the past.
53. For a hyperbolic example of the belief that Native American stories literally describe history, coupled with an unabashed willingness to exploit the past for modern purposes, see Vine Deloria's *Red Earth, White Lies* (1995).
54. Liljeblad (1986:651).
55. Nabokov (2002:70).
56. Pendergast and Meighan (1959), Franklin and Bunte (1990:27).
57. Whitley (2000) is a highly readable entré to a line of rock art research by scholars spanning several decades and continents.
58. Wolf (1982:18).
59. Fremont (1988: 218).
60. For a sweeping vision of the Desert West emphasizing the interactions among people, especially farmers and foragers, see Upham (1994:121–125) and (1990:111); and for a number of papers on this topic see Spielmann (1991).

Sidebar: Forager Cusine

a. Miller (1972:44–45).

Chapter 2

1. The writer Eudora Welty observed: "And as place has functioned between the writer and his material, so it functions between the writer and reader. Location is the ground conductor of all the currents of emotion and belief and moral conviction that charge out from the story in its

course. These charges need the warm hard earth underfoot, light and life of air, the stir and play of mood, the softening bath of atmosphere that give the likeness-to-life that life needs" (Welty 1979:128).

2. McPhee (1981:45).
3. Madsen (2001:387).
4. Russell (1965:114, 122).
5. These issues are scientifically thorny and controversial, because there are many special interests. Kay and Simmons (2002) is a strongly framed consideration of a debate that should eventually overcome the political and ideological bias that has hampered discussion.
6. Rogers (1982) features repeat photography of scenes in northwestern Utah showing the similarities and differences between the late 19th century and the present. Cottam (1947) is a visionary essay on vegetation changes during the historic period.
7. Terry Tempest Williams's (1992) *Refuge: An Unnatural History of Family and Place* is a Great Salt Lake example of this concept.
8. Nelson (1954:15).
9. Cline (1963:10).
10. Perhaps one of the best places to envision this phenomenon, despite the subdivisions, is the stretch between Bountiful and Farmington. The threshold separating the low ground east of Interstate 15 is just west of the highway and railroad tracks. Only a few decades ago, this area was watered by springs and creek overflow to produce bulrush and cattail-lined ponds and sloughs interspersed with salt grass meadows. Other stretches of inset marshland are found between Farr West and Mount Pleasant, north of Ogden. The area north of Brigham City is yet another and remains rural, even though the water is gone because of diversion and well-drilling. Captain Howard Stansbury's map of 1850 depicts substantial lakes, ponds, and streams east of the Brigham City airport, where only saltbush and greasewood flats are found today (Stansbury 1988).
11. The abundance of waterfowl along the Wasatch Front inspired observations from the Dominguez-Escalante expedition (Warner 1976:60), trappers (Russell 1965:122), explorers (Fremont 1988:149; Stansbury 1988:100), and naturalists (Pritchett, Frost, and Tanner 1981; Gwynn 2002).
12. Janetski (1991:27).
13. Janetski (1986, 1990a, 1990b, 1991). The quote by Parley Pratt (1849) is found in Janetski (1991:29).
14. See Gwynn (2002b:ix) and Alder (2002).
15. Fagan (2000) is directed at the lay reader and describes the Little Ice Age and its historical significance.
16. Compare the charts of temperature and moisture as documented by the tree ring record of climate for the "Intermountain Basins" in Fritts and Shao (1992:Figures 14.3 and 14.4, pp. 279–280). Drought occurs not

only when temperatures are high, and periods of cold do not mean that it will be wet. The two measures can coincide, but frequently they do not. This dynamic relationship holds significant implications for shaping the habitats encountered by people.

17. Fritts and Shao (1992:279–280).

18. Davis (1982:68) notes some resurgence in glaciers in the Sierra Nevada Range. Also see Currey (1969).

19. See Currey and James (1982:41), Currey (1990), and Murchison (1989) for evidence of Great Salt Lake levels. See Fritts and Shao (1992) for coordination of tree ring records among regions across the western United States.

20. Lamb (1982) is an excellent summary of this period of warming that had major effects on the expansion of European agriculture, the spread of vast grazing lands in central Asia across which the Mongols followed, and Arctic warming that opened new lands for the Vikings (and the Inuit).

21. Bright (1966) reports pollen cores into Swan Lake in the uplands north of Preston, Idaho. Wigand and Rhode (2002) describe vegetation change based largely on wood rat middens. Harper and Alder (1970) provide evidence of grassland expansion.

22. Madsen et al. (2001) report on the vegetation, fish, and small mammals from Homestead Cave and synthesize paleoenvironmental evidence from the Bonneville Basin.

23. Currey (1990), Murchison (1989).

24. Currey and James 1982:40–41.

25. Simms, Loveland, and Stuart (1991:9, 29–30, 60–61) describe low lake elevations and a site with a pithouse at 4,205–4,206 feet and likely dating between A.D. 900 and 1200. More recent field discoveries include campsites with structures at elevations of only 4,198–4,200 feet. For a preliminary report on some of these see Lambert and Simms (2003).

26. See Coltrain (2002:476–479) for discussion of the tree ring records in relationship to agriculture near Great Salt Lake. Dean et al. (1985) document climate for the Southwest and include charts showing annual variations in temperature and moisture and, importantly, the spatial uniformity and variation in the expression of climate. Some climate changes are felt uniformly across a region, while other climate changes are expressed strongly in some places and weakly in others. The implications for humans are significant, because a drought that impoverishes all the people in a region will lead to a different behavioral response than a drought that affects only some places, leaving some people without food and others with food.

27. Thompson (1990) describes vegetation histories based on wood rat middens, and Thompson (1992) describes vegetation change at the Ruby marshes. Mehringer (1985) describes pollen cores from

southeastern Oregon, and Bright (1966) describes pollen cores from southeastern Idaho.

28. Madsen et al. (2001:266); Livingston (2000).

29. Schmitt and Madsen (2005).

30. Currey (1990).

31. McKenzie and Eberlie (1987).

32. Rhode (2000); Wigand and Rhode (2002).

33. See Currey and James (1982:40) and Davis (1982:67) on glaciation; Wigand and Rhode (2002) on vegetation. Benson (2004) reports on Owens Lake levels, and Koehler, Anderson, and Spaulding (2005) is a recent treatise on Mojave Desert vegetation history. Also see Benson et al. (1990) for an excellent overview of Great Basin lake history.

34. Isostatic rebound refers to the uplift of a land mass when a weight is removed from it. When Lake Bonneville drained, the loss of the tremendous weight of the water caused the earth to rebound from a few feet up to 200 feet around the lake basin. Crittenden (1963) describes this, although new information is being added. Peter Ainsworth hypothesizes that isostatic rebound is responsible for isolating Utah Valley from the Salt Lake Valley about 5,000 years ago, causing Utah Lake to form for the first time. The evidence for this is inconclusive and unpublished, but the possibility that such a familiar landmark was not even here reminds us of how our perception of place must change to envision the past.

35. Brimhall and Merritt (1981); Janetski (1990:241–242).

36. A variety of evidence indicates there were large human populations at this time, and we will review this in subsequent chapters. General arguments about the large size of Neoglacial period populations can be found in Bettinger (1999) and Madsen (2001:400).

37. The Altithermal was first described by Ernst Antevs and is a landmark in the history of paleoclimatology. See Grayson (1993:208–216) for an excellent discussion of Antevs's ideas and subsequent studies.

38. Ross (1975) is a Masters thesis that reports submerged sand dunes. Currey (1980) describes desiccation polygons (mud cracks) seen in aerial photos. Neither sand dunes nor mud cracks can form under water.

39. See Thompson (1992) on the Ruby marshes, Mehringer (1985) and Bright (1966) on sagebrush-grass pollen, LaMarche (1974) and Thompson (1990) on treelines, Madsen (1986) on pinyon trees, and Cottam, Tucker, and Drobnick (1959) on oaks and the Altithermal. Sutton et al. (2007) summarize a great deal of archaeology in the Mojave Desert in recent years.

40. See Rhode and Madsen (1998) on Danger Cave, Madsen (2001:263) on the Onaqui Mountains. Lanner (1981) provides a lay discussion of the relationship between the trees and the birds. It remains possible that

some pinyon existed in the Basin-Plateau in the early Holocene and resurged from isolated refugia only during the mid-Holocene.

41. The owl midden at Homestead Cave in the Great Salt Lake Desert and the human debris at Camelsback Cave on Dugway Proving Ground both show this. See Madsen et al. (2001:263–264).

42. See Murchison (1989) and Murchison and Mulvey (2000) on Great Salt Lake, and McKenzie and Eberlie (1987) on isotopes.

43. There is an interesting history of debate here ably described by Donald Grayson (1993:244–255). Some speculate it was so arid that Native peoples essentially abandoned the region. Foraging societies, however, are documented in the harshest deserts on earth, so abandonment is unlikely, even in the Mojave Desert. Population densities decline with aridity, and surely the style of use changes, but the term "abandonment" is unfortunate, because it fails to consider measures of occupational intensity in the context of settlement patterns.

44. See Sutton et al. (2007) for a summary of Mojave Desert prehistory and Basgall (2000) for the relationship between the tempo of environmental trends and the structure of human land-use practices in the Mojave.

45. See Thompson (1992) on the Ruby marshes and Murchison (1989) on Great Salt Lake. Great Salt Lake probably reached 4,230 feet at this time. For a synthesis see Madsen (2001:397–398).

46. The Old River Bed can be seen today about seven miles west of Simpson Springs on the old Pony Express road. This is where Lake Gunnision, the Sevier Desert arm of Bonneville, drained north into the Great Salt Lake arm. The land for tens of miles north of this road crossing was a vast wetland that could exceed 200 square miles in extent. See Oviatt (1987), Oviatt (1997), Madsen et al. (2001:260), and Schmitt and Madsen (2005:22–27).

47. Thompson (1990) synthesizes data from wood rat middens in east-central Nevada and western Utah. Rhode and Madsen (1998) describe the vegetation from Danger Cave.

48. Madsen et al. (2001:260–261).

49. Madsen and Currey (1979).

50. The changes in the occurrence of small mammals are striking. These often-overlooked animals are often sensitive indicators of vegetation and climate. Grayson (1993:170–184 and 202–206) describes their history from Late Pleistocene to Holocene times and shows how much they tell about the past. For the Late Pleistocene-Early Holocene composition of small mammal communities in the Wasatch Front area, see Madsen et al. (2001), who report the findings from Homestead Cave.

51. Grayson (1993:207).

52. Grayson (1993:91–92) and Madsen et al. (2001:255–256). Also see Broughton, Madsen, and Quade (2000), who describe the massive die-off of many species of fish when the lake receded at about 11,200

radiocarbon years ago. There is widespread evidence of a significant drying trend in North America at about this time, sometimes called the "Clovis Drought" (see Haynes 1991). Evidence was presented at the 2007 meetings of the American Geophysical Union (Kennett et al. 2007) of a comet impact on eastern Canada about 13,000 years ago that caused the Younger Dryas and consequent changes in human ecology (also see Dalton 2007 for a readily available summary).

53. There are many lines of evidence for change associated with the rise of Great Salt Lake to the Gilbert shoreline. See Currey (1990), Madsen et al. (2001), and, for the fish, Broughton, Madsen, and Quade (2000).

54. I recall Donald Currey distinguishing Lake Bonneville and Great Salt Lake this way in his Mountains and Deserts class at the University of Utah in 1983.

55. Madsen (1999:78).

56. An excellent description of Lake Bonneville and the flood can be found in Grayson (1993:86–92). Donald Currey (1980, 1990) has written extensively on Lake Bonneville. For an excellent visual introduction to Lake Bonneville and Great Salt Lake see the map by Currey, Atwood, and Mabey (1984) published by the Utah Geological Survey.

57. Much remains to be learned about Lake Bonneville and the ancient Great Salt Lake. Jack Oviatt (e.g., 1987, 1997) has advanced knowledge about the lake a great deal, especially its early days and the relationship between the Great Salt Lake arm and the Sevier Desert arm (known as Lake Gunnison). There is evidence that around 13,000 years ago (about 11,500 radiocarbon years ago) the lake shrank to nearly its present size and may have come close to drying up. See Oviatt, Currey, and Sack (1992). The fish bones from Homestead Cave (Broughton, Madsen, and Quade 2000) show there was a relatively fresh water lake around this time, so if the lake went as low as historic Great Salt Lake, it may have done so only briefly. Again, Haynes's (1991) "Clovis Drought" may be at work here, but the details of how this affected Great Basin habitats remain murky.

Sidebar: Dates of the Past and How to Read Them

a. There are many excellent descriptions of archaeological dating, and a search on the Internet will locate sites describing the basics of dendrochronology and radiocarbon dating as good as any textbook. Of course, the Internet surfer will also find sites that only masquerade as science.

b. For details about the problem of calibrating Late Pleistocene and early Holocene radiocarbon dates see Fiedel (1999a). Minze Stuiver and Paula Reimer have long produced radiocarbon calibration curves that are widely used in archaeology and other sciences utilizing radiocarbon dating. Their software is known as CALIB and is available on the Internet at www.calib.org. Other calibration software is readily available on the Internet by simply searching for "radiocarbon calibration."

Chapter 3

1. This is a calibrated estimate for a radiocarbon age of 11,200. See chart in Chapter 2, Sidebar: "Dates of the Past and How to Read Them;" also see Fiedel (1999a).
2. The Monte Verde site in Chile is a superb example of stratigraphic excavation directed by Thomas Dillehay. The two-volume site report is Dillehay (1989, 1997). A debate of the merits of the site and dates can be found in Fiedel (1999b), Dillehay (1999), Collins (1999), and West (1999). Substantiation of the dating can be found in Meltzer et al. (1997) and Adovasio and Pedler (1997). Monte Verde was clearly occupied by 14,500 B.P. with evidence of a diverse technology including wood and fiber industries, and even the remains of a house. There is a possibility the site was occupied over 30,000 B.P., and although this date seems to be in association with stone artifacts, corroborative evidence is lacking, and most archaeologists, including Dillehay, reserve conclusion about the validity of the earlier occupation.
3. Meadowcroft Rockshelter, near Pittsburgh, Pennsylvania, was excavated between 1973 and 1978 under the direction of James Adovasio and is another example of a stratigraphically excavated early site with evidence that humans were present over 14,500 B.P. See Adovasio, Donahue, and Stuckenrath (1990), Adovasio et al. (1991), and for controversy see Haynes (1980, 1992), Adovasio et al. (1980), Tankersley and Munson (1993), Tankersley, Munson, and Smith (1987). Some archaeologists present evidence against accepting pre-Clovis dates at Meadowcroft, and although they have not falsified the case, some summarily dismiss it in the court of collegial opinion. Occupation at Meadowcroft at 14,500 B.P. is consistent with mounting evidence elsewhere on the continent and is the argument made by a skilled excavator trained in the same excavation techniques as the excavator of Monte Verde.

    The excavation evidence at Meadowcroft, as well as the continental archaeological context retains the possibility of occupation at the site before 14,500 B.P.
4. A host of new sites across the hemisphere indicate the arrival of humans to the Americas before 14,000 B.P. Many of these excavations are in progress or yet to be reported, but a popular article can be found in Bonnichsen and Schneider (2002) in *American Archaeology* magazine. However, the probability of great antiquity (30,000 +) is lowered by recent Y chromosome genetic evidence of a more recent separation from

Asian populations, and the continuing fact that sites in eastern Siberia are mostly less than 30,000 years old. The odds against extreme claims of antiquity for the Americas are also raised by an ecological conundrum. If people were here over 30,000 B.P., then for tens of thousands of years their numbers had to remain so low that we cannot detect them. We do not see such a situation even for early hominids in Africa over a million years ago, or for Europe only 50,000 years ago, or anywhere humans colonize open ecological niches. In the unlikely event that extremely early occupation is eventually demonstrated for the Americas, another interesting set of research questions is raised—in this case, the ecological circumstances that impeded colonization by the most behaviorally plastic mammal of all.

5. For the colonization of the Americas with relevance to the Great Basin see the careful presentation by Grayson (1993), the readable hemispheric synthesis by the excavator of Monte Verde in Chile (Dillehay 2000), and the flamboyant read directed at North America by Adovasio and Page (2003).

6. For decades, anthropologists thought that forager fertility varied inversely with mobility. This seems to be a less clear relationship, leaving open the age-old question of why human populations around the world grew almost imperceptibly for many millennia during the Paleolithic. A review of forager demography by Pennington (2001) shows how difficult it is even for foraging populations to obtain the incredibly slow population growth rates that apparently characterized humans for long periods in prehistory. She suggests a pattern of population boom and bust, rather than slow, steady growth. Traditional views hold that human populations grew slowly because foragers were mobile until agriculture caused fertility to spike, followed by another spike after the industrial revolution. Harpending and others (1998) use genetic data to infer that human populations were very small until about 50,000–100,000 years ago, when there was a sharp increase, followed by another long span of glacially paced growth until the appearance of agriculture. Their results also suggest a cycle of boom and bust, rather than steady "upward" progress. In the Americas, small groups of highly mobile colonists with low fertility rates might linger on the edges of archaeological visibility for a few millennia, reaching a point where the continent becomes faintly but detectably inhabited about 15,000 years ago. Surovell (2000) shows that strong population growth rates are possible, even expected, by Clovis times, because of their settlement pattern of intermittent moves among relatively settled residential bases. By Clovis times, the "light" of population growth is turned on across the continent.

7. Kelly and Todd (1988) remains a useful syntheses even as we learn more about particular Paleoindian variations around the continent. The big-game stereotype has taken a beating over the years, and everyone pretty

much acknowledges that Paleoindian people ate more than mammoth meat. The pendulum is swinging again—and with increasingly sophisticated knowledge of ecology; the issue is not just about what people ate but what drove the economic decision making. Thus, big game hunting sets off the Paleoindian period from all the later periods in prehistory. For example, see Waguespack and Surovell (2003).

8. George Frison (1989) describes the efficacy of fluted points for penetrating the hide of African elephants previously harvested by government hunters.

9. See the discussion and references in Beck and Jones (1997:199–200).

10. Grayson (1993:238–239) describes the Campbells' finds; Sutton et al. (2007) summarizes recent work in the Mojave Desert; and Basgall (2000) discusses the archaeology in terms of human land utilization.

11. A recent review of Late Paleoindian point types with pictures and dates can be found in Pitblado (2003).

12. Archaeologists have long speculated about crescents. The first systematic study was by Tadlock (1966). A photograph of a variety of crescents from the Sunshine Locality is in Hutchinson (1988). For a review see Beck and Jones (1997:206–208) and Amick (1999:162–164). Lucille Housely described her work with Marilyn Couture to me in the early 1980s, including the story of finding crescents in the root patches. To my knowledge, this tidbit has never seen the light of day, because their work focused on matters of foraging (Couture, Ricks, and Housley 1986).

13. Copeland and Fike (1988) map the location of many fluted points around Utah; see Beck and Jones (1997). During the early 1980s, when the Air Force wanted to install the MX missile in western Utah, I had the opportunity to scout private collections in Delta, Milford, and Minersville. I have seen hundreds of fluted points in private collections, including Clovis, Folsom, and many other types made of a variety of stone. Some were "classic" forms, but I was struck by the number of resharpened points. The collectors called these "Baby Clovis."

14. See Fowler and Fowler (1990) for a history of these ideas, as well as Grayson (1993:242–243) and Bedwell (1973).

15. For aficionados of Danger Cave, Smith (1942) is worth digging up, because it is a strikingly accurate cultural history of the region for such an early publication. The report by Jennings (1957) is, of course, a classic.

16. When Danger Cave was excavated, few reported on the animal bones unless they were fashioned into tools. Thus, Jennings (1957) does not identify many animal bones. Also, the screen size used in those days was 1/2-inch mesh, when screens were used at all. Today, 1/8-inch mesh is the minimum for cave excavation, and typically large samples of unscreened fill are returned to the lab for a complete inventory. Donald

Grayson (1988) examined the collections from the original Danger Cave excavation and reported on the small mammals. This shows why it is important that materials from excavations be permanently curated in museums and suggests that a great deal of original research can be found in museums, not just in the field.

17. Madsen and Rhode (1990). The oldest radiocarbon ages for the lowest levels of Danger Cave center on 10,100 radiocarbon years B.P., which calibrates to about 11,700 B.P.

18. Goebel et al. (2004). This is a preliminary report of a continuing excavation, but three radiocarbon dates on charcoal found in a hearth in the lowest level hovered between 10,000–10,100 radiocarbon years ago. T. Goebel, personal communication, provided additional updates.

19. Bryan (1979). Also see discussion in Beck and Jones (1997:192–193). The oldest reliable date for the first human presence at Smith Creek Cave is 11,140 B.P. radiocarbon years, and human presence is strongly supported by 10,700 B.P. radiocarbon years ago. Smith Creek Cave has long been controversial and a bit personalized, because Bryan and Gruhn were early advocates of pre-Clovis occupation in the Americas. I worked on this project as a draftsman of the profile drawings and maps, and to examine coprolites, and hence had some first-hand familiarity with the stratigraphy and artifact proveniences. I believe that skepticism is warranted, but that it is a mistake to confuse that with categorical dismissal of this case.

20. Beck and Jones (1997:193–194) and references. Jones and Beck (1999: 95, note 3) report some additional dates from the same site. Stemmed points were found in direct association with dates between 9820 and 9910 B.P. radiocarbon years but may be as old as 10,060 B.P. radiocarbon years. The layer containing the fluted point yields dates on natural organics and charcoal in the sediments between 10,250 and 11,020 B.P. radiocarbon years. The date on collagen from the camel bone is 11,330 B.P. radiocarbon years.

21. Madsen (2000) provides the best discussion of the human affiliation. Also see Gillette and Madsen (1993). A bone from the mammoth dated to 11,220 B.P. radiocarbon years.

22. The late Jonathan Davis was a superb field geomorphologist, and this was one of his many aphorisms.

23. Oviatt, Madsen, and Schmitt (2003).

24. Davis, Sack, and Shearin (1996) report the Hell' n Moriah site. Simms and Lindsay (1989) report 42Md300. The MX Missile Project lead to a month of reconnaissance in Utah's west deserts in 1981 (see note 12) to scout sites, interview local collectors, and examine their collections. Much of this was informal and difficult to report in a technical manner. For some sense of the project, see Simms and Lindsay (1984).

25. The Fenn Cache is presented in a beautifully photographed and illustrated volume by Frison and Bradley (1999). I think it is important to
reserve the possibility that individuals walked the landscape to collect
materials from far-flung places. Too often, archaeologists cling to pro-
vincial notions of "Indian trade" by assuming that all movement of
exotics is hand to hand simply because it seems like a long walk to us
modern folk.

26. Schroedl (1991:8–9). See Davis (1989) on the Lime Ridge site, and
Davis (1985) on the Montgomery site.

27. Plew (2000:29–30).

28. The strength of the archaeological knowledge in western Wyoming
is to a great extent a spin-off of energy development. Oil and gas and
the pipelines, reservoirs, and roads that go with them demand that the
effects on cultural resources be taken into account. Much of this literature is in technical reports, but the level of work has also spurred
broader publication. See Smith, Reust, and Richard (2003) for a recent
overview on Late Paleoindian sites and references to the technical
reports. The more difficult to procure Thompson and Pastor (1995) is
an overview of the archaeology of western Wyoming. Kelly et al. (2006)
recently re excavated at the Pine Spring site where 1964 excavations
concluded that horse and camel were part of an early occupation. The
recent excavations show the association of these animals with humans
is equivocal.

29. Donald Grayson (1993) and (2006) describes the Pleistocene megafauna
and also the many other smaller mammals that became extinct at the
close of the Pleistocene. Wade Miller provides a table of localities yielding megafauna along the Wasatch Front (2002).

30. There is persistent debate on the nature of Pleistocene habitats ranging
from Guthries' "mammoth steppe" based on faunal data to Grayson's
suspicion of great habitat diversity for the Pleistocene. Grayson (1993)
describes the debate with reference to the Great Basin. Extinction
overcame 35 genera of animals during the late Pleistocene. Also see
the references in footnote C for the Sidebar "Did Humans Kill Off the
Pleistocene Megafauna?"

31. The Spirit Cave mummy was found in 1940, and the skeleton, along with
an array of well-preserved artifacts, are reported by Tuohy and Dansie
(1997), as well as many Internet sources. Eiselt (1997) and Napton
(1997) report on the coprolites. Green et al. (1998) describe the Buhl
burial. Radiocarbon dating of two bones from the burial, dated with
the permission of the Shoshone-Bannock Tribes of Fort Hall, Idaho,
returned a date of 10,675 B.P. radiocarbon years. Stable isotopes of
carbon and nitrogen estimate the cumulative contributions of different
classes of plant and animal foods to the diet over a person's life. A DNA
biopsy was not taken and, unfortunately, this skeleton was reburied
without even a small biopsy retained to benefit humanity yet to come.

32. The photo caption on the conference flyer in fact mislabeled the source of the obsidian as "White Horse Canyon area of the Mineral Range in southern Utah." David Madsen recognized that this is the well-known Wild Horse Canyon obsidian source, and the Mineral Mountains are near Milford, in western Utah. The caretaking of this Clovis point by the Denver Museum of Natural History over the decades is another example of why it is important that artifacts be properly documented and curated by legitimate museums and not private collectors. No one knows if the material or the point itself was taken to New Mexico by one or a few people on long treks, or if it was down the line trade over perhaps many years. Both are possible.

33. Jones et al. (2003); also see Beck et al. (2002).

34. Grayson (1993:242) makes the latter argument.

35. Janetski and Nelson (1999) sourced points from 42Md300.

36. Oviatt, Madsen, and Schmitt (2003:206–207); Arkush and Pitblado (2000).

37. Bonnie Pitblado (2003) investigated the use of the southern Rocky Mountains in Colorado to determine if there were full-time mountain residents or if the mountains were used logistically by people mostly living in lower terrain. She found both, suggesting that Paleoindian settlement adjusted to diverse habitats and terrain. Her sample of projectile points included the eastern Great Basin and Colorado Plateau, but it remains unclear just how the mountains in this region were used.

38. For an overview and excellent list of references, see Kelly (1995: Chapter 3). For an overview of return rates for classes of Basin-Plateau resource types, see Simms (1985).

39. Anthropologists traditionally describe the mobility of foragers in terms of an "annual round," creating a picture of a relentless seasonal cycle that never moves in location. This conveys a false image that foragers are born, live, and die in the same place. Archaeologists exacerbate this problem by describing human behavior at the scale of individual sites. Lewis Binford (1983), in an essay titled "Hunters in a Landscape," argues that archaeologists need to recalibrate their perspective of hunters and gatherers from their small excavation units at a single site to an area of more than 300,000 square kilometers. In fact, forager mobility can encompass huge ranges over the life of a person and among generations of foragers as areas are used and abandoned. What Binford was talking about is increasingly recognized as "landscape archaeology," although we have some way to go to achieve a more realistic telling of the story.

40. Evolutionary/behavioral ecology enables models to be crafted of past adaptive systems through a combination of analogy and an understanding of evolutionary process. Nicole Waguespack (2005) applies this knowledge to the perfect case—Paleoindian society—a time so distant that modern images of Indians will not suffice. This kind of research is exemplified by Bob Elston and Dave Zeanah's (2002) use of behavioral

ecology to model ancient Paleoindian behavior for which no modern analogy exists. They compare their model to the archaeological record in Railroad Valley, eastern Nevada, and show that Paleoindian diets were narrower, men maximized encounters with large game, and residence was anchored by the reliable food procurement of women in lowland settings.

41. See Simms (1983a), who shows how the recycling of grinding stones shapes what archaeologists "see." The study includes ethnographic references to people scouring camping areas for serviceable implements before making the effort to fashion a new ground stone tool. This stimulated the hypothesis that ground stone "migrates" to later sites, and that is what the frequency of dated occurrences of grinding stones showed. As I look at the paper in retrospect, it also implies that it probably takes some time for an inventory of ground stone tools to be built up when people first arrive in a place. When these effects combine with the few incentives among the first Paleoindian colonists to make a large investment in prepared grinding stones for mass grain processing and storage, we can see why these implements are relatively infrequent at Paleoindian sites.

42. While difficult to test, Ariane Pinson's innovative study proposing settlement on ecotones is important because it directs attention to risk management as part of the decision-making process. There were probably so few people in the region during Paleoindian times that it is unlikely they were food-limited; managing risk was probably more important. See Pinson (1998, 1999, 2004).

43. Todd Surovell (2000) reconciles the paradox of high mobility, rapid colonization, and fertility rates. The Paleoindian settlement pattern was mobile but anchored by base camps of substantial size. The stereotype of isolated families of hunters moving every day is inaccurate. The most common Paleoindian settlement pattern (surely there was variability) is consistent with high fertility rates, thus resolving the paradox of how foragers that are mobile in some respects can spread rapidly across a landscape. It also implies that pre-Clovis people did things differently than Clovis and later Paleoindians did and that pre-Clovis fertility rates were relatively low.

44. See Grayson (1991) on animal extinctions.

Sidebar: Who Were the First Explorers and Colonists?

a. Meltzer (1993) is a well-illustrated, readable account of the peopling of the Americas. See Dillehay (2000:Chapter 8) for an overview of the dental, linguistic, and genetic data that includes evidence and from South America as well as North America. A collection of more specialized papers is available in Bonnichsen (2000).

b. Chatters (2000:306). As for timing, some of the claims of very early colonization (> 20,000 years) made on the basis of genetic/molecular clocks have been tempered in recent years. Larger sample sizes of ancient and modern DNA show that the rates of genetic evolution and diversification were faster than thought, bringing estimates based on genetic evidence more in line with that from archaeological evidence (see, for example, Kemp et al. 2007).

c. Jantz and Owsley (2001); also see Steele and Powell (1995) for a general statement on the evidence from biological anthropology. The Ainu of Japan are the last remnants of the indigenous people of Japan and have often provoked the observation that they have "Caucasian" traits. This same observation is often made with respect to Paleoindian crania (not as a racial referent but purely as association of physical features). The Ainu are thus a glimpse of Pleistocene Asia, as are the few Paleoindian skeletons known for the Americas. For a discussion of Kennewick man and comparisons to other Paleoindian crania see Jantz and Owsley (2001). The quote is from Chatters (2000).

d. A considerable amount of mitochrondrial DNA study has been done on modern and some ancient samples; an overview is Crawford (1998). For a recent review with many references to the primary technical literature see Jones (2003). Other recent works in this fast-paced area of research can also be followed using the Internet, with appropriate skepticism of some sites.

e. Less voluminous, the Y chromosome DNA research applicable to Native American origins can be found in Hammer (1995) and Karafet et al. (1997). The Altai region of western China is significant, because skeletons from this area provide evidence for Caucasoid-Asian interactions. Recently, genetic haplogroup X has been found there in similar frequencies to its occurrence in Europe (3.5%–4% in both regions). Haplogroup X was thought to be rare in Asia, leading some to erroneously conclude there was European migration to the Paleoindian America. It is far more likely that the paleosource of haplogroup X is central Asia for ancient migrations west to Europe and east to America (Derenko et al. 2001).

Sidebar: Did Humans Kill Off the Pleistocene Megafauna?

a. Martin has written extensively on this subject since 1958. Persistence but also change in his emphasis and position are evident in Martin (1967, 1984, 1990, 2002). I mention the hunting of horses because archaeologists have long suspected that horses were hunted, and evidence from Canada now supports this suspicion. Horse-blood proteins were found on a Clovis point from the Wally's Beach site in southern Alberta. The site yields bones of Pleistocene horse in association with artifacts, as well as the remains of other now-extinct animals (Kooyman et al. 2001).

b. Donald Grayson has long worked to stem the popularity of the overkill model, in part because it is applied so uncritically to ethical and political issues despite the fact that no one knows for sure how, let alone why, the extinctions occurred. The span of his thinking on this topic can be gleaned from Grayson (1977, 1984, 1991) and Grayson and Meltzer (2003). The classic case of well-documented human-caused extinction is that of the moas, the large birds of New Zealand. In that case, many archaeological sites yield the remains of moas, who were reduced from superabundance to extinction as humans first colonized the island. A similar situation existed across the rest of Polynesia and in Australia.

c. For overviews of the climate-habitat explanations see Grayson (1991), but also significant papers by Graham and Lundelius (1984), Guthrie (1984, 1990), Graham (1986). Daniel Fisher's work is multifaceted, showing how mammoth meat was stored in frozen ponds, and in some cases mammoths seemed to die from hunting pressure rather than food stress. Much of Fisher's work is ongoing and thus remains unpublished or as conference presentations. The paper on mammoth migration is Fisher and Beld (2003). McDonald (1984) takes the position that habitat for mammoth may have improved after 18,000 B.P., thus raising a conundrum. The suggestion about microbes is McPhee (1997). As for a comet (Kennett et al. 2007; Dalton 2007), this intriguing, even compelling finding surely helps explain the rapid habitat change associated with the Younger Dryas. Human predation would only spur on the problems experienced by the megafauna.

d. Charles Kay brings the perspective of a wildlife ecologist to this issue. His empirically prodigious study of vegetation and elk in Yellowstone shows that Native American predation was a central force in shaping the ecosystem. Kay has since expanded his thinking to other issues; a sampling of his work is Kay (1994, 1995, 2002) and an edited volume, Kay and Simmons (2002).

e. Haynes (1991:266).

f. Grayson and Meltzer (2003:591).

Chapter 4

1. The concept of the Archaic was important to mid-20th century archaeologists trying to explore an unknown American past. The Archaic arose from a desire to compare different parts of the continent to determine if there were large-scale patterns. The term described a stage of culture (a culturally loaded term that imposed Western bias on ancient peoples) that existed prior to the more visible Native American farming cultures

of the last 2,000 years. The best essay on the Desert Culture, and the relationship between the Great Basin and the concept of a continental Archaic, is Jesse Jennings's (1973) "The Short Useful Life of a Simple Hypothesis" (with homage to Hemingway). The bibliography alone is an excursion through the history of the concepts.

2. There are instances of high-density population, social hierarchies, and the other trappings of agricultural "civilization" that are based on foraging economies. The Late Prehistoric salmon fishing societies of the Northwest coast of North America are a classic example. But the foragers of the mountains and the deserts of the Basin-Plateau region would never approximate the extractive economies and population sizes of the agriculturalists that followed the Archaic period.

3. The differences between radiocarbon time and calibrated time become much less during the last 6,000 years (see Chapter 2, Sidebar: "Dates of the Past and How to Read Them"). The dates from this chapter on tend to reflect radiocarbon dates as much as they reflect the calibrated dates.

4. Jennings (1957:7).

5. I break somewhat from tradition here by finding the roots of change in the Middle Archaic rather than the Late Archaic. I agree with scholars such as Bettinger (1999) that the archaeological record of intensification is apparent only after 4,000 years ago. But the explanations of change are always rooted in the times that came before. The Middle Archaic has long been seen as a time when nothing was happening, but the dispersal of foragers in response to repeated warm and very dry times extended the human presence across the region more fully than before. In this sense, the filling of the landscape was accomplished during the Middle Archaic, setting the stage for its full exploitation in the Late Archaic.

6. Again, a debt to Robert Kelly for the term "The Foraging Spectrum." We all too often homogenize "hunters and gatherers" into one cultural form. And, the concept of a "full" landscape also takes many forms. Landscapes can be full when people accustomed to being alone encounter neighbors. This happened by the Paleoarchaic. Or, it might be full when people use all of the places, not only for visits but for regular residence. This happened by the Middle Archaic. The same landscape is full when the presence of neighbors constrains the freedom to do anything one wants. This happened by the Late Archaic. Landscapes fill to "carrying capacity" when resources are used at or beyond sustainability. This also happened in some places during the Late Archaic. The landscape continues to be full when people must invest more labor and energy to sustain larger human populations. The Fremont farmers of later prehistory certainly fit this bill. My point is that we need not reserve only the modern, Westernized world as the first time landscapes were full. To do so wrongly suggests that Native Americans did not fully occupy and own this land. They did.

7. Schmitt and Madsen (2005).
8. James Adovasio has written extensively on the manufacture and styles of basketry in the western United States. For information on basket technology see Adovasio (1977), and for an overview of Great Basin basketry in relation to other parts of the continent, see Adovasio (1974).
9. The costs of exploiting the dozens of edible seed plants that are so abundant in the region lie in the processing. Ethnographic studies such as the pioneering work of James O'Connell with the Alyawara in Australia (O'Connell and Hawkes 1981) show that seeds are rejected, no matter how abundant they are, until cheaper resources decline in availability. Simms (1987) provides experiments for Great Basin seeds that show they are the most expensive class of resource and that processing is the preponderant expense. Widespread seed use also demands a technology to process them, and their adoption by foragers is an excellent example of intensification long before the Industrial Age. Jason Bright, Lori Hunsaker, Alan Rogers, and Andrew Ugan show how the cost of an investment in technology to process food was significant to forager decision making (Bright, Ugan, and Hunsaker 2002; Ugan, Bright, and Rogers 2003).
10. We will see later that the invention of agriculture is often explained the same way—in terms of progress. Such "explanations" are really just descriptions of our own cultural perceptions and actually tend to obscure explanation. This sort of flawed logic is pervasive in the modern world of politics and culture.
11. Danger Cave (Jennings 1957), Hogup Cave (Aikens 1970), Bonneville Estates Rockshelter (Goebel et al. 2004), Camelsback Cave (Schmitt and Madsen 2005), birds from Danger Cave (Parmalee 1988), large mammals from Danger Cave (Grayson 1988).
12. The Dust Devil site (Stokes et al. 2003) was excavated as part of the Kern River Natural Gas Pipeline Project. This is one of the largest such projects in the region, and it will take years for researchers to digest the wealth of information. The combined reports of the Kern River project take up over 2 feet of my office shelf space (Reed, Seddon, and Stettler 2003).
13. Dates for the appearance of seed-processing technology appear in many site reports, but the significance of the differential appearance over time for marking fundamental decisions by people is found in O'Connell, Jones, and Simms (1982:232). References for Joe's Valley Alcove: (Barlow and Metcalfe 1993); Sudden Shelter (Jennings, Schroedl, and Holmer 1980); Gatecliff Shelter and Monitor Valley (Thomas 1973, 1983). The latest regional appearance of ground stone seems to be in the southern Great Basin (Lyneis 1982), although this is probably habitat-specific, since early grinding stones seem to be common in the Mojave Desert, especially along former streams and in now-parched wetlands (Sutton et al. 2007).

14. This was evaluated with a search of the computerized site records at the Utah Division of State History by the site records manager, Kristen Jensen. I chose 4,600 feet as the cutoff between wetlands and valley environments and upland terrain. This elevation easily captures the Salt Lake and Utah valley lowlands but also includes the slightly higher valleys in the west deserts, where many stemmed points are found.

15. For a summary see Plew (2000). Primary sources are Delisio (1970), Miller (1972), and Arkush (1999).

16. See the results of an herbalist's examination of the Patterson Bundle, found in eastern Utah (Harrison 2003).

17. My own ethnoarchaeological work in Jordan among the Bedul Bedouin showed that food hiding in remote granaries similar to Fremont and Anasazi storage contexts was almost always in competition within the extended family, not among bands or tribes (Simms and Russell 1996).

18. Aikens (1970:173).

19. Donald Grayson provides a nice summary of archaeologist's changing views on humans and the Altithermal (1993:244–248). Simms (1977) and Madsen (1982a) observe that although the shift to a stronger human presence in the uplands was known, it had yet to be explained.

20. Simms (1987) provides data on the return rates of a variety of Great Basin plant and animal foods. These rates refer to the costs of collecting (or hunting) and processing after a resource is encountered. The ranking of return rates is a prediction of the order in which resources are included or excluded from the diet to the extent people considered effort in their decisions. The abundance of the resource in the environment, however, is what determines how much of it will be collected. An item, such as a mass kill of grasshoppers at Lakeside Cave, might be taken upon encounter, because it is cheap to do so. But this may happen only occasionally. However, grass seeds may be everywhere but ignored, or taken only occasionally in small quantities, because they are expensive to collect and process. One of the most important findings of this type of study is that the decision to include a food in a forager's diet is based not on its abundance but on the abundance of more cheaply acquired alternatives. This basic tenet holds in modern ethnographic situations such as the Ache of eastern Paraguay (Hawkes, Hill, and O'Connell 1982; Kaplan and Hill 1992), the Alyawara of central Australia (O'Connell and Hawkes 1981), and others. The ethnographic cases also show that even though foragers consider reasons for taking or ignoring resources other than mere cost, they indeed have a basic concern with getting "bang for their buck." We would expect this of people who know exactly what they are doing and who are intimately familiar with their environment.

21. Sutton et al. (2007).

22. O'Connell (1975) describes Surprise Valley. See Larson (1997), Smith (2003), and Thompson and Pastor (1995) on southwestern Wyoming.

23. Dalley (1976).

24. Kristen Jensen made a search of the computer-based site database at the Utah Division of State History for the characteristics of sites in the Grouse Creek and Goose Creek Mountains at elevations between 5,000 and 7,500 feet. Of 173 sites, only 32 had projectile points indicating age. The area has seen surprisingly little study since the early 1970s.

25. Janetski (1985).

26. Madsen (1976), Simms (1999).

27. The term "finger matching" is from Bob Elston and refers to his sage advice that simply making correlations between climate and human behavior that look good does not really explain anything.

28. Danger Cave, Parmalee (1988); Hogup Cave, Aikens (1970); Black Rock Cave, Madsen (1983).

29. Mock (1971); also see Janetski (1990b).

30. Hunter (1991:52) describes the Utah Lake burial. Since the sinker was not found in direct association with the dated basketry, we cannot say for sure it is Middle Archaic. Net weights in the western Great Basin, however, show up very early, and we should expect the same on the Wasatch Front. Tuohy (1990) illustrates many net and line sinkers from western Nevada. Also see Fowler (1989:29–41) for ethnographic descriptions of native fishing at Pyramid Lake told to Willard Park in the 1930s.

31. Schmitt and Madsen (2005).

32. Sutton et al. (2007) is a review of the significant amounts of Cultural Resource Management archaeology in the Mojave Desert, much of it on military reserves protected from collecting and vandalism by the general public.

33. Madsen and Kirkman (1988) describe Lakeside Cave. Sutton (1988) summarizes insect eating across the aboriginal Great Basin. I visited Lakeside Cave in 1983 with fellow graduate students Kim Hill and Hillard Kaplan. They did fieldwork with Ache' foragers in Paraguay, and had eaten everything imaginable. Sampling the many grasshoppers dancing around the site seemed like the natural thing to do, so we roasted them briefly over a flame, pulled off their heads and legs, and ate quite a few.

34. Adovasio (1986a and 1986b).

35. For years archaeologists have been pointing out that it is risky to "assume" gendered patterns of work. Caution is good, but we depend on analogy as an investigative tool. It is important to move beyond cautionary statements instilled by concerns of political correctness, because with careful modeling and hypothesis testing, the artifacts might tell us about what might be the distinct lives of men and women playing out on the scale of landscapes over centuries.

36. An excellent survey of mobility among foragers is Kelly (1983). He explores the relationship of core and biface reduction to mobility in the Great Basin in Kelly (1988, 2001). In our studies of ceramics used by foragers we found that settlement redundancy produces similar decisions about pottery making as fully settled village life (Bright, Simms, and Ugan 2005).

37. This possibility was raised years ago by David Madsen. Richard Hughes is studying the obsidian source patterns from Hogup and Danger caves. Peter Ainsworth may have found a new obsidian source near Danger Cave.

38. The study by Fry and Adovasio (1970) was an example of interpretive excess, but I and other archaeologists have long suspected some differences among the populations, or at least the foraging ranges represented at Danger and Hogup caves. Recent geochemical sourcing of obsidian from the sites only strengthens the suspicion.

39. Robert Elston (1982:194) calls the period between 4000 and 2000 B.P. the "Mid-Archaic: Let the Good Times Roll." The date used to identify transition between the Middle and the Late Archaic varies a bit and depending on the region. Elston's Late Archaic begins at 2000 B.P. and continues to the historic period. In the eastern Great Basin, the transition is often stretched to 3,000–4,000 years ago. Here I use 3000 B.P. and note that these divisions are tools to organize ongoing processes of cultural change. Kelly (1997) is an important overview of Late Archaic archaeology in the Great Basin and employs the theoretical vantage of behavioral ecology.

40. Raven and Elston (1988, 1989), Raven (1990), Zeanah et al. (1995), and Kelly (2001). For a summary of the theoretical implications of study in the Carson-Stillwater region, see Zeanah and Simms (1999).

41. Larsen and Kelly (1995), Larsen and Hutchinson (1999), and Hemphill (1999) document a range of evidence about health. Simms and Raymond (1999) describe the consultation process with Native American tribes that permitted scientific study. See Ruff (1999) for a fascinating analysis of limb bones using CT scans to determine lifetime activity patterns.

42. The original Lovelock Cave descriptions are in Loud and Harrington (1929). Also see Ambro (1970). Heizer and Kreiger (1956) describe caches from Humboldt Cave. Thomas (1985) reports on Hidden Cave, another caching location. Kelly (2001:12–13, 296) summarizes the situation and offers an interpretation.

43. Oetting (1999) summarizes a great deal of study in the Harney Basin area and integrates it with a range of bioarchaeological analyses.

44. O'Connell (1975:44) argued that populations there did not necessarily decline despite the shift from large, communal earth lodges to lighter, wickiup style housing. He suggested people "dispersed" to exploit more habitats, but this does not mean there were few people in the region.

45. Holmer (1994), Plew (2000:79–81, 147–148).

46. Madsen and Berry (1975); see Aikens (1976) for a rebuttal.

47. Richens and Talbot (1989); Louthan (1990); Janetski, Crosland, and Wilde (1991); Lupo and Wintch (1998); Greubel (1998).

48. Split-twig figurines are long known from Grand Canyon (Schwartz, Lange, and deSaussure 1958; Schroedl 1977) and Newberry Cave in southern California (Davis and Smith 1981; Davis, Taylor, and Smith 1981). The figurines in both these cases date to 3000–4000 B.P. In recent years more have been found (Geib and Keller 1987; Jett 1991), and archaeologists are paying more attention to patterns in the context of these finds (Emslie, Mead, and Coats 1995). In a creative paper that employs basic patterns in totemism, clan composition, shamanism, and corporate descent groups across cultures worldwide, Nancy Coulam and Alan Schroedl (2004) contrast figurines from remote ritual sites with those found at domestic sites. Improved dating of sites enables them to propose two periods in which the role of split-twig figurines changed, reflecting the evolving nature of Late Archaic foraging societies on the Colorado Plateau. Their model is intriguing and refreshing, because it addresses social organization, a topic that archaeologists shy away from. It is difficult to know for sure, but their proposal is certainly consistent with cultural change among Late Archaic foragers in many areas across the Desert West.

49. A recent collection of Great Basin rock art studies exhibits the interest in the relationships between rock art and landscapes (Quinlan 2007). Chippindale and Nash (2004) is a collection that explores the "figured landscapes" of rock art around the world. Ouzman (2004) discusses the problem of understanding rock art given that it was produced in cultures with cognitive systems of communication and reality so different from us that our standard linguistic metaphors (such as "reading" or "translation") cannot capture the significance. Also see Chapter 4, note 4, Sidebar "The Built Environment." The linkage of rock art to prestige hunting is Hildebrandt and McGuire (2002) and McGuire and Hildebrandt (2005).

50. This trend was measured to some extent; see Hockett and Morgenstein (2003:Table 1, note e).

51. Elston and Budy (1990).

52. David Thomas excavated at Alta Toquima in central Nevada (1982), and Robert Bettinger excavated in the White Mountains in eastern California (1991). Grayson (1991) and Broughton and Grayson (1993) offer insights on the phenomenon of extremely high-altitude villages. Tim Canaday (1997) tirelessly explored other Great Basin mountain ranges in a largely futile search for more of them, shedding considerable light on the few places they do exist. Zeanah (2000) attempts to explain the pattern, and Zeanah and Simms (1999) summarize the theoretical implications of high-altitude study.

53. Hughes (1994); Hughes and Bennyhoff (1986).
54. Wylie (1974); Janetski (1979).
55. Madsen (1979); Arkush (1998). The Hot Springs and Airport site reports are in preparation by James Allison of Baseline Data, Inc., but see Allison, Colman, and Webb (1997) for a preliminary report.
56. McDonald (2000) reports on the Wasatch Plateau.
57. Dave Madsen and Mike Berry (1975) interpreted the stratigraphy of Hogup Cave differently than Aikens (1970) did and argued for a significant period with no occupation between the Archaic and Fremont levels. They found other sites with a hiatus. Aikens (1976) pointed to other evidence suggesting there was no regional abandonment. Over the years, it is apparent that some sites have gaps and others do not during the Archaic-Fremont transition, and Madsen has now scaled back his view to a less sweeping interpretation. Berry employs counts of radiocarbon dates to estimate population and continues to argue for scant occupation of the Colorado Plateau in the Late Archaic. Obviously, something was going on during this time that is different from the periods before and after, but the possibilities extend beyond stark visions of depopulation.
58. Stuart (1992) reports on the Burch Creek site. Geologists excavated Green Canyon Cave, near Logan, in the 1960s. Artifacts collected at that time were salvaged and studied by Gordon Keller, an anthropologist at Utah State University. Projectile points from Early through Late Archaic attest to a long occupation. There is no shortage of Late Archaic projectile points, such as Gypsum, Elko Contracting Stem, and Gatecliff Contracting stem, in private collections from northern Utah valleys. These date to between 2,500 and 1,500 years ago. Finally, the Kern River Expansion Project shows there were significant changes during the Late Archaic in the eastern Great Basin (Reed, Seddon, and Stettler 2003, Volume IV: Prehistoric Synthesis).
59. Byers and Broughton (2004).
60. Robert Bettinger (1999) considers the well-known increase in activity in the Late Archaic in light of the social causes and implications. He casts the issue as one of cultural versus environment explanations, but most of Bettinger's work shows that he treats culture as one part of the environment that organisms in evolving ecosystems must face.
61. I find the notion of recruitment among some foraging societies fascinating. I suspect this varies by circumstances but also is structured by the basic social organization in place; some were more open than others. Some tantalizing sources on this include Blurton-Jones, Hawkes, and O'Connell (1996) and Woodburn (1988).
62. The distinction between public and private goods is a useful tool for seeing similarities and differences among cultures past and present. It helps us move beyond simply judging other cultures by our own standards and through the lens of modern times. Perhaps even more

important for us here is to see beyond the stereotypes of prehistoric Native Americans as doing all one thing, thinking all one way, and living in one kind of "Indian" society. The concepts are from economic theory, but Kristen Hawkes (1993) applies the concept of public goods to forager behavior. Robert Bettinger (1999) did a great service by applying the concept to the prehistoric Great Basin, and Bettinger (1989, 1994), among others, shows the range of evidence for fundamental changes in forager social organization in the Late Archaic. Jelmer Eerkens (2004) discusses public and private goods systems in light of seed exploitation and ceramic use and provides an up-to-date summary and bibliography of these concepts as applied to Great Basin foragers.

63. McGuire and Hildebrandt (2005) extend ecological analysis to prestige and costly signaling behavior. There is debate about which places show intensified big game hunting (Broughton and Bayham 2003; Byers and Broughton 2004; Hockett 2005) and debate over the technicalities of how we differentiate between prestige hunting and change in the abundance of game caused by climate and predation (including human predation). The debate also unfortunately pits the notions of hunting efficiency against the acquisition of prestige as if they were completely different things, when they are really just facets of the same gem. I see both as employing foraging theory and both "positions" as fully informed by the research strategy of evolutionary ecology. What is cast as a debate should really be a discussion about the role of alternative currencies and the circumstances that select for the role those currencies will play in human decision making in different times and places. Sometimes scientists are, in the words of Marvin Harris (1991), "ships crashing in the night."

64. Coulam and Schroedl (2004:note 52).

65. The earliest corroborated dates for maize in Utah are from a pit associated with a burial near Elsinore, Utah (Wilde and Newman 1989). Wilde and Newman provide direct dates on the corn, but some wood charcoal was mixed with the sample, making it appear older. Coltrain (1994) obtained slightly younger dates using a biopsy of bone from the burial. The context and patterning in the appearance of early maize in Utah can be found in Madsen and Simms (1998).

66. Maize domestication was once thought to be much earlier in the Tehuacan Valley of central Mexico, but more accurate dating shows it is younger than 5000 B.P. Maize was clearly in northern Mexico and at least as far north as Tucson, Arizona, between 3,200 and 2,800 years ago. For a summary of early agriculture in the Southwest, see Cordell (1997); however, this picture continues to change rapidly with new research.

67. Simms (1985, 1987).

68. This study was Renee Barlow's doctoral dissertation at the University of Utah, and her inquiry into this complex issue continues (Barlow 2002, 2006).
69. Robert McC. Adams (1966) recognized the significance of this for the development of social complexity and urban societies in the Near East, as did Frederick Barth (1961) writing on pastoral societies in Persia. I quote Steadman Upham because I always like the way he phrased this important insight (1994:123).

Sidebar: The Built Environment

a. Two of the 11 duck decoys found in Lovelock Cave in 1924 were dated using AMS 14C technology (requiring only a few milligrams). One dated to 2080 ± 330 B.P. and the other to 2250 ± 230 B.P. (radiocarbon years). These dates are statistically equivalent. See Tuohy and Napton (1986).
b. Simms (1989) describes this case of incredible preservation of five wickiups built in the early 19th century.
c. I learned of this cache from a former student who grew up in Willard. The points were probably in a bag placed in the pit over a layer of burned corn cobs and clay. They are Rose Spring Corner-notched points, a common type about 1,000 years ago. Six hundred points might seem like a lot, but not to someone who used his bow and arrow as often as we might use our dishwashers. Unfortunately, the collection was broken up, his wife knows nothing about it, and the farmer has Alzheimer's disease. This case provides yet another reason why such irreplaceable information and collections should not be held in unknowing hands.
d. Rock art is increasingly discussed in terms of social landscapes (Arsenault 2004); studies in the Great Basin show that rock is part of the built environment for everyday activities (Cannon and Ricks 2007; Shock 2007) and for ritual and symbolic activities (Whitley 1998). Heizer and Krieger (1956) interpreted the Humboldt Cave cache as a shaman's bundle. The Patterson Bundle was found by collectors in east-central Utah. Merry Harrison (2003), a Salt Lake City herbalist, saw it in a display case at the Bureau of Land Management office in Moab, Utah, and gained permission to examine it. She found that several of the pouches contained medicinal roots in dosage-size portions and combinations.
e. Isabel Kelly's quotes from her Southern Paiute informants are a gold mine of ideas. In the early 1980s, I searched the state site data records and found a higher frequency of grinding stones at later sites (Simms 1983a). This could reflect real changes in the tools and food that people used over time. Or, it could simply reflect an inexorable movement of reusable tools toward later sites, where, at the dawn of the historic period, the objects were left for the last time.

f. The pronghorn enclosures in Matlin Basin, near Park Valley, Utah, are described by Raymond (1982), and he quotes a well worn but exciting description of a pronghorn drive by Howard Egan that was published in 1917. Brooke Arkush has studied pronghorn drives in great detail and summarizes the current state of knowledge about these, with a dose of revisionism (Arkush 1999).

Sidebar: Humans and the Pinyon Pine

a. Thomas (1973, 1983).
b. An overview of pinyon ecology is Ronald Lanner's *The Pinyon Pine* (1981). Madsen (1986) summarizes pinyon use as known at that time. The Danger Cave pinyon is described by Madsen and Rhode (1990), and a more recent review can be found in Rhode and Madsen (1998). Simms (1985) tried to explain and predict the use of pine nuts at different times and introduced transport as a limiting cost. Jones and Madsen (1989) were the first to calculate data on resource transport costs. Bettinger (1999) argues for a very late intensification of pinyon use.

Chapter 5

1. Morss (1931). The Fremont River in central Utah was named after the explorer John C. Fremont, and the ancient culture was named after the river, so the connection to the explorer is secondhand.
2. Talbot (1997) is the definitive summary of Fremont architecture.
3. Ambler (1966) and Jennings (1978).
4. Judd (1919) describes the layout of the Paragonah site based on excavations in 1916–1917. Judd (1919:1) mentions the report of the Wheeler expedition in 1872 estimating between 400 and 500 "mounds" in the area around Paragonah. The mounds were created by the accretion of homes and other structures of adobe that fell into disrepair and were superimposed by other structures. Judd described the layout of houses, granaries, and public space. Excavations at Paragonah in the 1950s found many more granaries (Meighan 1958:6–7). Similar layouts are known from Fremont "mound" sites in the Parowan Valley and across the region extending from the Nevada-Utah border at the Garrison and Baker Village sites to eastern Utah almost to the Colorado border at the Turner-Look site. Reviews of Fremont sites include Janetski et al. (1997) and Madsen and Simms (1998).
5. Hockett and Morgenstein (2003) trace the source of materials used to make ceramics using inductively coupled plasma (ICP), mass spectrometry, and scanning electron microscopy. A small, forager site near Elko, Nevada, yielded Fremont ceramic vessels made primarily from local

materials. A few vessels, however, were carried in from elsewhere, and one was tempered with quartz from lithified dunes such as those found in Navajo Sandstone in central Utah over 300 miles away.

6. The Nawthis site is reported in Jones and O'Connell (1981), Jones and Metcalfe (1981), and Metcalfe (1983). The irrigation ditch at Nawthis is reported in Metcalfe and Larrabee (1985).

7. Schaafsma (1971) remains an accessible summary of Fremont rock art and its variations, and Cole (1990) provides a concise description. Schaafsma (1980:166) observes: 'The hallmark of Fremont rock art everywhere is the broad-shouldered human figure in ceremonial regalia."

8. The extensive work in Clear Creek Canyon was led by Richard Talbot and Lane Richins, and reported in a multivolume set. The synthesis volume (Janetski et al. 1997) contains chapters on specific topics, including Fremont architecture, social organization, and trade.

9. Madsen and Simms (1998:293–295) summarize this information and provide references. Geib (1996) is a comprehensive study in the rugged country north of the Colorado River that now drains into Lake Powell. The appearance of maize cultivation along the Wasatch Front is not known. There is a pre A.D. 500 date from the Grantsville site west of Salt Lake City, but it is not certain the date is associated with farming or simply the occupation of the site. Tantalizingly early dates have long cropped up in Great Salt Lake Fremont sites prompting Marwitt (1970:145–148) to place the beginning of the Great Salt Lake Fremont at A.D. 400. Structures at the Levee site near the mouth of the Bear River may date to the A.D. 500–600 (but could be later, given the large error ranges on those dates). The Levee site continued to be occupied, and the locale became an obvious case of Fremont farming and settlement. Dating of over 50 human skeletons recovered by the Great Salt Lake Wetlands Project (Simms 1999) found five individuals dating between A.D. 250–750, most likely near the middle of this range. The archaeology of the Wasatch Front is rich but so damaged by urbanization that it remains an open question as to when farming arrived and whether it was really that much later than areas to the east and south.

10. The Steinaker Gap site is reported by Talbot and Richens (1996), and they went on to synthesize the northeastern Fremont region (Talbot and Richens 2004). Early houses in the Sevier Valley, the North Richfield sites along Interstate 70, are reported by Talbot and Richens (1993). The Confluence site (formerly the Muddy Creek site), west of the San Rafael Swell near the Basin-Plateau interface may be the clearest case of early pithouses that might predate the introduction of maize agriculture. The site was excavated by several organizations and is described by Greubel (1996, 1998). Sites with pithouse or habitation structures of

some kind, with varying degrees of stratigraphic context, well-associated dating, and such, include Sandy Ridge (Richens and Talbot 1989), the Orchard site (Louthan 1990), Carcass Corners (Lupo and Wintch 1998), Hog Canyon Dune (Schleisman and Nielson 1988), Cockelbur Wash (Tucker 1986). Janetski summarizes many of these in light of the question of Fremont-Basketmaker II relationships (1993).

11. For a discussion of the history of Fremont and Southwest contacts see Madsen and Simms (1998), but especially Janetski (1993, 2002) and Talbot and Richens (2004). For more of a Southwestern perspective on the Fremont see Matson (2002).

12. This is a much discussed topic, and there are ethnographic examples and prehistoric settings where agriculture is integrated to varying degrees in forager systems (e.g., Minnis 1985, Wills 1988, Wills and Huckell 1994). Talbot and Richens (1996:178–198) describe an ethnographic analogy for the early Fremont situation. Barlow (2002) comes closest to an explanation of the ultimate causation regarding these decisions, a level of understanding that moves beyond historical circumstance and cultural particulars.

13. Osteological evidence for Basketmaker II populations include Reed (1955), Hurst and Turner (1993), and Turner (1993).

14. I draw this distinction from the book by Gertrude Bell, *The Desert and the Sown* (1907). Bell was a British traveler, writer, and diplomat important to the creation of Iraq after World War I. Her travels among the Bedouin made her aware that local lifeways and cultures superseded notions of national Arab unity, even as the Bedouin of "the desert" held the common ground of Islam with "the sown," the farmers of the villages and towns. The desert and the sown was a theme that would run through Fremont history for over 700 years.

15. Matson (2002) is a concise overview.

16. Demographic changes associated with the maintenance of the elderly and the effects of this on younger generations are found in ethnographies around the world. Ethnographic analogy cannot be forced uncritically onto particular situations in the past but helps us to recognize processes that we sometimes do not take into account, or even see as a possibility. For a discussion of this and other evidence explaining how people become migrants see Fiedel and Anthony (2003:157–160). Their article appears in a book with a very seductive title for those interested in the origins of the Fremont: *Colonization of Unfamiliar Landscapes: The Archaeology of Adaptation* (Rockman and Steele 2003).

17. Schlegel (1992) discusses matrilineality among the Hopi. The Hopi language is in the Uto-Aztecan family and split off about 3000 B.P. See Peregrine (2001) for a recent treatise on matrilineality in the prehistoric Southwest.

18. Talbot and Richens (2004:88–114) and Janetski (1993) describe "the Fremont of the Southwest." For the larger context of prehistoric Southwestern genetic relationships using ancient DNA research see Carlyle et al. (2000), and for a specific comparison of Great Salt Lake Fremont and Anasazi from Grand Gulch, Utah, see O'Rourke, Parr, and Carlyle (1999). Anthropologists are becoming more aware that variation in the migration propensity of males and females under different circumstances is a key. See Gagnon et al. (2006) for a discussion of some possibilities. Recent DNA research is indeed consistent with a model of male-biased sex ratios among early populations of migrant farmers (Mahli et al. 2003).

19. Rasmussen Cave was excavated by local ranchers, and portions of the collections were observed by Noel Morss and the Claflin-Emerson Expedition (Morss 1931). Although much about this find will never be known, and it can hardly be conclusive, this burial symbolizes the far-flung nature of cultural connections as well as the local indigenous traditions of the Fremont (Gunnerson 1969:97–104).

20. The stark differences in basketry between the Fremont and the Southwest are summarized by Adovasio (1986a) and Adovasio, Pedler, and Illingworth (2002). Adovasio and Pedler (1994) trace the historically known Numic peoples in the prehistoric Great Basin and counter those who advocate that the Basketmaker II peoples simply migrated into a land vacated by indigenes.

21. The historian Frederick Jackson Turner's (1920, 1932) notion that the frontier and ethnic distinctions ("sectionalism") shaped the American people and history is interesting to consider for the problem of Fremont origins. Incorporating the concept of frontier can help move our understanding of the interactions of farmers and foragers beyond the merely descriptive notions of population replacement, acculturation, and diffusion that at times become rote among archaeologists (but see, for example, Headland and Reid 1989 and Moore 1985). Donald Holly (2005) refers to periods when there is overlap among different groups of hunter-gatherers and applies this to a case in Newfoundland. Changes in the "social landscape," specifically, the intrusion of new foragers in an area already occupied, actually spur the indigenous foragers toward intensification of their food procurement, processing, and storage—the very things that are part and parcel of the road to farming. The interaction itself is the driving force for change. We will find later that this is relevant to the Numic Spread.

22. Eric Wolf (1982) coins the term "people without history" to refer to those who are very real but pushed out of consideration as significant players in historical and cultural affairs. Archaeologists have done this, much to the detriment of their understandings of the past. Steadman Upham (1994:123) suggests the power of this perspective by considering what

happened to people when farmers and foragers collided in the ancient American Southwest.

23. Polarizing the discussion of indigenous development versus population replacement does little to move us toward a deeper understanding. We all can acknowledge "blending," but by itself this term is thoroughly non-explanatory. Lightfoot, Martinez, and Schiff (1998) employ the example of Russian, Native Alaskan, and Native Californian interaction at Fort Ross on the northern California coast. Their interaction was not a "mixture" of the three but produced a new culture out of the interaction. In the same way, the Fremont is the product of interaction, not something that occurred in spite of it.

24. "Sprinkled with neolithic communities" was the phrase used by the archaeologist V. Gordon Childe in the 1950s to describe the Middle East of 10,000 years ago at the dawn of farming. Even in that region so widely known as the world's first case of plant and animal domestication, the "Neolithic Revolution" was much more of a sprinkling of new ways than it was a wave of advancing progress that was obvious to all. Childe realized that the context of the first farmers comprised "a great diversity in culture" with a background of "scattered groups of hunters and fishers, survivals of the pre-neolithic economy," along with "migratory horticulturalists." Steadman Upham reminded Southwesternists of Childe's foresight (1994:118) as he attempted to move beyond the telling of history in terms of progress among monolithic cultural entities.

25. Cynthia Irwin-Williams (1973) argued for connections between the Late Archaic and Durango Basketmaker II, and R. G. Matson (1991, 2002) developed the idea. Cultural resource management archaeology provides large-scale projects such as the TransColorado Natural Gas Pipeline that examine many sites. The larger sample only stimulates the suspicion that it was a mixed bag of indigenes and immigrants all struggling to carve a niche, and all using the new forms of maize (e.g., Firor 2001).

26. Matson (1991) and especially (2002) bring considerable traction to this issue by reconciling very different lines of evidence—artifacts, language, and knowledge about the production and maintenance of ethnicity. LeBlanc (2002) furthers the discussion by considering the issue in light of how conflict molds societies and history.

27. The osteological evidence suggesting east-west biological variation in Basketmaker II populations is of varying sample sizes and quality (Reed 1955; Hurst and Turner 1993; Turner 1993). LeBlanc (2002:360) refers to more recent analysis of multivariate cranial measurements by Douglas Owsley that also suggests Eastern Basketmaker and Western Basketmaker are distinct biological populations. The rock art exhibits spatial and temporal variation that seems to indicate different ethnicities (Cole 1993, 2004). Janetski (1993), and especially Howard and Janetski

(1992), describe the scalp stretchers and the basis for their attribution to Basketmaker II, not Archaic or Fremont times.

28. Richard Talbot and Lane Richens (2004) report on the Steinaker Gap site and the irrigation features, as well as the stable carbon isotope work of Joan Coltrain suggesting that maize constituted 40%–50% of the diet during this very early portion of the Fremont period.

29. James Wilde and Deborah Newman (1989:717) recognized that something in the local Late Archaic was already afoot even as the first hints of the Southwest appeared in the form of early maize in the Sevier Valley. Their previous experience was in the northwestern Great Basin, and they were familiar with the fact that huge changes took place among Late Archaic foragers with or without the direct presence of farming or Southwestern peoples.

30. The idea that the Fremont was founded by migrants from the Southwest dates to Julian Steward (1941) and was championed by James Gunnerson (1969:170). Marie Wormington's (1955) "Uncompagre Complex" was a Late Archaic, Durango Basketmaker II-like culture that had Fremont migrants coming from the Four Corners region. Michael Berry took these ideas in a new direction through a reanalysis of stratigraphic associations and the compilation of radiocarbon and tree ring dates from the Southwest that suggested gaps in the record of occupation (Berry 1982). A role for migration in the origins of the Fremont was a logical inference, and Berry and Berry (1986) proposed that Late Archaic foragers abandoned the region because of declining moisture. The Berrys made an important contribution by maintaining a role for migration when pretty much the rest of us ignored this fundamental human behavior. Berry continues to compile chronometric data and finds a lull in dates in eastern Utah between 500 to 700 B.C. Yet, when I examine his radiocarbon charts, I notice other, similar punctuations throughout the Archaic. In other regions of the West, these often mark changes in the way people organized themselves on the land, but not abandonment. I think foragers were concentrating settlement and abandoning some environments, much as happened in the western Great Basin in the Middle to Late Archaic. I doubt they left the region.

31. Arrow points were found at Dirty Shame Rockshelter in southeastern Oregon in Cultural Level II, and this level began to accumulate at 2700 B.P. (Aikens, Cole, and Stuckenrath 1977). This is quite early, and given the association within a layer subject to long deposition, the introduction of the bow and arrow there is probably later. A general spread after 2000 B.P. from the Columbia Plateau and heading southeast into the Great Basin and onto the Snake River Plain (Plew 2000) seems to occur with a clear presence of Rose Spring corner-notched/Rosegate points by 1500 B.P. (Holmer 1986). The precise dating of the

spread of the bow and arrow remains murky, because of the problem of association between the points and the organic materials used for radiocarbon dating.

32. Blitz (1988) remains a basic guide to the adoption of the bow and arrow and shows it is more than a simple tale of progress caused by "better" technology. The relationship between the bow and arrow to conflict and to the problem of public and private goods remains underdeveloped by researchers. James Creek Shelter is Elston and Budy (1990).

33. Phil Geib (1996:64–66) and Geib and Bungart (1989) improve our understanding of the appearance of bow technology in Utah more than anyone in recent decades. The bow and arrow was in the Glen Canyon area in the first few centuries A.D., clearly earlier than its regional presence by A.D. 500–600. But bow and arrow appearance is patchy—some places have it and other places "less than a two-day walk away" do not have it until several centuries later (Geib 1996:65). Many Western "White Dog" Basketmaker II people south of the Colorado River continued to use the atlatl.

34. The evidence for early arrow points in southwestern Colorado at the Tamarron site and site 5DL896 reported by Reed (1990) is tantalizing and consistent with linkages between the indigenous peoples of the Durango Basketmaker II and Archaic traditions of the Basin-Plateau. Large-scale contract archaeology from the Trans Colorado Natural Gas Pipeline project adds to the realization that arrows are making their way into southwestern Colorado before A.D. 500 (for instance, Reed 2001: Figure 41–4 and text).

35. See Janetski (2002) for an overview and references to the large-scale movement of ceramics among the Fremont, yet limited ceramic trade between the Fremont and Anasazi. Neutron activation analysis done as part of the Kern River gas transmission pipeline project also found that substantial fractions of Fremont ceramic assemblages resulted from trade and that there were various production centers in southwestern Utah (Reed 2005). Common Fremont symbolism over large areas is indicated even in the absence of direct ceramic trade by a case of Snake Valley Red on Buff pottery found at a Great Salt Lake Fremont site. Analysis of the temper of three sherds showed that although the painted design on the vessel was a copy of a style from southwestern Utah, it was in fact made of local materials from the Wasatch Front (Simms, Bright, and Ugan 1997:789). Fremont ceramics are a combination of cultural notions defining appropriate morphology and design, some instances of ceramic manufacturing centers, and local circumstances. Our work to explain some of the variability in Fremont ceramics by reference to mobility and the intended use of pots (Simms, Bright, and Ugan 1997; Bright, Simms, and Ugan 2005) does not deny or even challenge previous studies of Fremont ceramic style and types. The different

forces that produce the characteristics of Fremont ceramics are not mutually exclusive.

36. The evidence for early maize in southern Utah is reviewed by Geib (1996:53–77). The Clyde's Cavern sample and the relationships of those samples to other Southwestern maizes are discussed by Winter (1973, 1976). Also see Jett (1991) for evidence of an early appearance of Maiz de Ocho in Utah.

37. Coltrain (1993).

38. Simms (1999:30–31) discusses the importance for interpretation of a large sample that results not from excavation bias but from a naturally caused exposure of everyone buried in a large area. Coltrain and Stafford (1999) found a broad range of diets from forager to farmer using stable carbon isotopes. Stable carbon isotopes reflect accumulated diets over many years; perhaps not an entire life, but a significant percentage of it given the shorter life expectancies of the time. The dietary variability is unlikely to be exclusive to the Great Salt Lake area—the Wasatch Front was an excellent microclimate in which to grow maize, and there were as many large villages between Brigham City and Provo as any place in Fremont land.

39. Mike Berry (1974) hit on this essential pattern when he proposed that people went west from the large villages in the Parowan Valley to the rich pinyon pine groves near the Nevada border during years of crop shortfall. The upshot of his model is that the foragers in the hinterlands were the same people as the farmers, at least to some extent. Simms (1986) used the excavation of light, wickiup-type housing at the Topaz Slough site, a small Fremont campsite yielding ceramics and maize, to propose several different adaptive strategies for the Fremont from foraging to farming. The essence of the ecological concept of adaptive diversity (see Upham 1984) is that it incorporates the fact that culture is plastic, not just resistant, especially over the life spans of individuals. We find transition among lifeways, "cultures" if you will, all the time in the historic world. Ironically, archaeologists have been so obsessed with typological cubbyholes that we even treated adaptive diversity that way—as one more type. Fortunately, we seem to be outgrowing this habit.

40. Christopher Ruff (1999) did the fascinating analysis of activity patterns using CT scans. The sexual dimorphism he reports for the Great Salt Lake skeletons is similar to what he found among the Stillwater Marsh wetland village foragers in western Nevada. Ryan Parr and Shawn Carlyle worked under the direction of Dennis O'Rourke (O'Rourke, Parr, and Carlyle 1999) and added the Great Salt Lake ancient DNA to the growing inventory from the western U.S. These analyses suggest that the Great Salt Lake sample that showed so much variation in diet looked like a single population. This is as close as we have come to a

test of whether adaptive diversity better explains Fremont pattern and variation or if all the variation can be classified into distinct cultures and variants.

41. I once heard that A.V. Kidder, one of the founders of Southwestern archaeology, said "the Anasazi always abandoned" to emphasize that this was not aberrant behavior but typical. But the tendency to associate abandonment with failure is strong. Archaeologists are steadily losing this bias and increasingly realize that "abandonment" is not a failure but a highly workable lifeway. Nelson and Hegmon (2001) summarize and further develop this thinking. We might also be losing the bias that episodes of abandonment must mean that each new occupation brought a new culture or a new people. More often than not it was probably the same people, or at least their children and grandchildren. We tend to hold ancient cultures as timeless and unchanging, yet plasticity over the life history of individuals was often great. A study of pinyon pine in the Uinta Basin by Gray, Jackson, and Betancourt (2004:953, Figure 3) illustrates swings of precipitation so frequent and sharp, the graphs of climate shifts look like cat scratches on a tree. Abandonment as a way of life would be the only solution to living with such variability.

42. The Evan's burial is described by Jera Pecotte in Dodd (1982:117–120). It was excavated in 1973, and I remember this burial from my field school. Joel Janetski (2002:363) estimates that about 15% of excavated Fremont burials contain grave "offerings."

43. The Clear Creek Canyon report has a chapter on Fremont "Social and Community Organization" and a discussion of community aggregation (Janetski et al. 1997:284–286 and Chapter 15). Also see Coltrain and Leavitt (2002:454–455). An early consideration of Fremont complexity is found in Jones and Metcalfe (1981).

44. Judd (1919:1 and 1926) and an excellent summary in Janetski et al. (1997:272–277).

45. Judd (1919); Steward (1936).

46. Talbot uses the term "dispersed community" in Janetski et al. (1997: 267–269). For the first brave steps to a return to discussing "complex-ity" in the Fremont we owe Pat Barker (1994) for a paper on sequential hierarchies presented at the Great Basin Anthropological Conference. Jim Wilde presented a paper at the same conference that dubbed Baker Village a "planned community." Bryan Hockett (1998) made a sig-nificant contribution using faunal analysis to document social ranking at Baker Village. Barker and Hockett (and Talbot to some extent, see Janetski et al. 1997:220–221) attributed some of the inattention to Fremont social organization to the "types of models" used, especially models from evolutionary ecology. Unfortunately, this omits some im-portant facts in the history of Fremont archaeology. During the 1960s and 1970s, the Fremont were interpreted as distinct from the cultures

of the Southwest; the food remains indicated that they did more hunting and gathering. In those days, village size was estimated using the most conservative reading of the stratigraphy to provide a minimum count, ignoring the fact that many more houses could have been occupied at one time. Oddly, this meant that the negative evidence drove the perception that there were no big villages and, of course, no complexity. In fact, the interest of Fremont researchers in complexity occurred at the same time there is a resurgence of interest in complexity in the Southwest in the early 1990s. That had nothing to do with evolutionary ecology. Since evolutionary ecology is not inherently about subsistence, calories, or efficiency but about animal social systems, its potential to contribute to our understanding of Fremont complexity is great; it is the perspective employed throughout this book.

47. A pioneer in recognizing the different paths to social complexity is Gary Feinman (1995), although Steadman Upham's much earlier (1982) work on the Western Pueblo certainly stimulated a lot of discussion about complexity in the Southwest. A recent article by Michelle Hegmon (2005) and published in a North American archaeology textbook is an excellent primer.

48. Hegmon (2005:228–229).

49. Hegmon (2005:226–227).

50. Matrilineal kinship and matrilocal postmarital residence may not have come to the Southwest until the development of Puebloan villages between A.D. 700–900, and it was probably never as strongly developed among the Fremont as it was at early historic Pueblos such as Zuni and the Hopi mesas, and perhaps Chaco Canyon. Most kinship systems are mixes of behaviors, and I am speaking of evolutionary trends toward matrilineality, not categorical culture types. Classic ethnographic studies such as Aberle (1961), Schneider (1961), and Ember, Ember, and Pasternak (1974) show that matrilineal societies arise from female work groups in horti-cultural economies where migrants displace indigenes, where conflict is possible, and where men must move across the landscape. The spread of farming into the Southwest initiated pressures for matrilineality even during Basketmaker II times, and the historic period pueblos see its full development. Matrilineal kinship was probably strongest where Fremont populations were the largest and most dependent on farming, but where variable access to resources demanded the movement of goods among villages. A recent paper by Peter Peregrine (2001) breathes life into the subject.

51. Janetski (2002:358).

52. Schaafsma (1971:136–149) summarizes relationships among styles and heritage. Cole (2004) is an excellent evaluation of the Barrier Canyon style that began in the Late Archaic and shows change with the influence of Basketmaker II, as well as the Fremont and the

Anasazi who followed. Matheny (2004) contains up-to-date papers and references on Fremont rock art.

53. Brigham Young University excavated sites near the town of Escalante (Baer and Sauer 2003; Harris 2005; Jordan and Talbot 2002), and they conducted surveys in Capitol Reef National Park (Janetski et al. 2005). Shannon Novak, an osteologist trained in Doug Owsley's statistical approach to cranial measurement, mentions the distinctive variation in Fremont crania around the region. These intriguing observations remain unpublished but certainly fit with other lines of evidence suggesting that the Fremont included different genetic populations and varying degrees of gene flow among populations bound together by the material and symbolic connections. Like many archaeological cultures, the Fremont probably included local ethnic and linguistic variations.

54. Hockett (1998) argues that the central structure at Baker Village was a chief's house where feasting occurred. The bones, however, occur in a series of depositional events in this central area, each sealed by silts eroding from the adobe walls of the houses, suggesting they may not have been deposited inside the same home. The large number of such bones deposited in a village farming site is nevertheless clear and of significant interest. Whether it was a chief's residence and deposited by communal feasting remain debatable.

55. Wilde and Soper (1999); Hockett (1998).

56. Madsen and Schmitt (2005); Schmitt and Madsen (2005); Bright, Simms, and Ugan (2005).

57. The archaeology of Nine Mile Canyon remains spotty—many of the sites were harmed before they could be carefully studied. Jerry Spangler (2000a) offers an intriguing synthesis. The recent exposure of well-preserved archaeological sites in nearby Range Creek should greatly stimulate more research and offers a second chance at preservation.

58. It is fashionable to question whether granaries on cliffs that a modern urban American would find difficult to access were really defensive or remote. Explanations based on vague notions of Fremont (or New Age) religion seem to be popular. In fact, there are examples of food hiding and remote storage elsewhere in the world. The Bedul Bedouin used their structures like a shell game, moving supplies among several storage units over weeks and months. They even placed bear-trap-like spring traps at the entrances. The traps would not necessarily stop a thief, but if he was injured by one, he would be publicly identifiable. Thus, such storage is not only about the defense of food, or about making it difficult to steal, but also about power and authority—the social management of food saving and its eventual distribution (Simms and Russell 1996).

59. Experienced Fremont archaeologists have long commented quietly on this sort of thing. Novak and Kollmann (2000) report butchering of humans from Backhoe Village, Nawthis Village, and Snake Rock Village,

three Fremont sites occupied mostly in the A.D. 1000s and all in central Utah. Another case that might involve violence and modification of human bone is the Sky Aerie site in extreme northwest Colorado (Baker 1999). This is a technical report in the cultural resource management literature. It was apparently not well received but does appear to be a case of violence, dismemberment, and ritual cooking that, although ambiguous, cannot be summarily dismissed. Violence in Fremont times deserves to be investigated.

Sidebar: The Big Village at Willard

a. Maguire (1879).
b. Steward (1933). The quote is from O. A. Kennedy (1930).
c. Steward (1936).
d. J. T. Edwards, personal communication with Mark Stuart. The figurine is illustrated in Steward (1933:28).

Sidebar: Farming, Language, and Immigrants

a. Fritz (1994) summarizes this, and Long et al. (1989) report on the AMS redating of the Tehuacan maize that revised the ages downward (also see Benz and Long 2000). There is evidence that the first flirtations with maize in Mexico were very early, but it does not seem to take off until about 5,000 years ago. Early Southwestern dates for maize and villages in the Late Archaic are reviewed by Huckell (1996). Finds of early farming in southern Arizona continue to be made (e.g., Mabry 1998) and are reported in contract archaeology monographs and as presentations at professional meetings. It is increasingly apparent that farming and even village life arrived in the Southwest before 3000 B.P., long before there is any evidence of Basketmaker II farming by indigenes or immigrants on the Colorado Plateau.
b. Jane Hill (2001, 2002a, 2002b) reevaluated Uto-Aztecan and Kiowa-Tanoan linguistic data in light of the new dating of maize and current archaeological knowledge about the Southwest to produce a significant new synthesis. Research showing the relationship between the spread of farming and the distribution of languages in other cases around the world shows that the Southwestern case is not unique (e.g., Bellwood and Renfrew 2002; Diamond and Bellwood 2003).
c. For research on the prehistoric rates of change in the maize plant see Benz and Long (2000).
d. Matson's model of Archaic roots for the Eastern Basketmaker (1991) gained some momentum from the recent linguistic research when Hill (2002a:471) observed: "The linguistic evidence presented here suggests that the Eastern Basketmaker II people were ancestral Kiowa-Tanoan."

Hill reports comparisons of key words between the Uto-Aztecan and Tanoan linguistic families to suggest various relationships between ancient and modern tribes.

Chapter 6

1. Steward (1937:83) estimated the Promontory culture to be "sometime after about 1000 A.D." and later estimated that it had been "800 years" since the deposits in Promontory Cave Number 1 were laid down (1940: 460). The quotes from Harrington and Hayden are Harrington, Hayden, and Schellbach, III (1930: 125) and Hayden (1930:87). David Madsen (1994) reminded us that it was archaeologists not linguists who first recognized the abrupt change at the end of the farming period and attributed it to migration and popu-lation replacement.
2. There is so much more to climate than wet and dry. The "tempo" of climatic change, the frequency at which climate swings from one event to another, may be more important. Further, climate does not cause culture change per se. How large was the population? How intensive was the economic system? Was it ratcheted up to the point where risk was high, or were there buffers against risk? What was the social system like—hierarchical with haves and have nots, or more equable? Nor does climate change affect all places equally. Tree ring charts for the Four Corners area of the Southwest (Dean et al. 1985:541, Figure 1d) depict spatial variability in climate in addition to climate over time. Some droughts were expressed across the entire Four Corners region, thus affecting everyone. Other droughts were expressed in a patchwork fashion that increased the frequency of haves and have nots. Each set of circumstances produces different expressions of social reaction, whether these are cooperation or conflict, and they vary in their likelihood of bringing fundamental change to the cultures.
3. Fagan (2000) on the Little Ice Age; Gray, Jackson, and Betancourt (2004:958) show the severity of droughts in the Uinta Basin, northeastern Utah.
4. Coltrain and Leavitt (2002) discuss changing climate relevant to the Fremont demise.
5. Great Salt Lake carbon isotope data are reported in Coltrain and Stafford (1999) and Coltrain and Leavitt (2002). Clear Creek Canyon radio-carbon trends are found in Janetski et al. (1997:287). The Evans Mound is reported in Dodd (1982:18), and Nawthis Village descriptions and radio-carbon dates are found in Jones and Metcalfe (1981), Jones and O'Connell (1981), Metcalfe (1984), and Metcalfe and Heath (1990).
6. Madsen and Simms (1998:307–308). Based on work at Ticaboo, near Lake Powell, Madsen used the terms "Freazi" or "Anamont" to prod

archaeologist's preoccupation with labels based on objects, and the tendency for labels repeated often enough to become peoples (Madsen 1982b, 1989b:42).

7. Fagan (2000:65–67).

8. Lindsay (1986) describes the patchwork nature of "Fremont fragmentation."

9. Emil Haury (1958) proposed migration of 50 to 60 families at a time by the Kayenta Anasazi in the 13th and 14th centuries, and his work was confirmed by later excavations showing that fairly large, organized migrations were not exceptional. Since then, Southwestern archaeologists have recognized that both large-scale and small-scale, household-sized migrations occur (e.g., Duff and Wilshusen 2000). Stephen Lekson's popular treatise *The Chaco Meridian* (1999) lends some force to the expansiveness of place by ancient Southwestern farmers that could entail the organized movement of entire communities over large distances. This is most likely under conditions of social hierarchy and control. Lekson et al. (2002) report on the Pinnacle Ruin in southwestern New Mexico as a bona fide example of large-scale migration from Mesa Verde, Colorado. The Southwest is not a distant analogy for the Fremont. Small-scale migration from Fremont hamlets is the most palatable to most Fremont archaeologists, but there is an increasing awareness that Fremont villages were common. Large-scale Fremont migration should also be considered a likely mechanism for the depopulation of the Fremont region. It needs to be studied.

10. The late sites in northwestern Colorado are described in Creaseman and Scott (1987), and Spangler (2000b) focuses on the chronology of the region. For the subject of changes in material culture marking at the end of the Fremont see Janetski (1994). As for Fremont emigration, possible movement to the north into Wyoming and the more likely emigration to the Southwest are summarized in Madsen and Simms (1998:316–317). Surely, the Fremont exercised various options during their demise.

11. Rhode (1994); Hockett and Morgenstein (2003).

12. See Adovasio (1974, 1986b) on basketry. Connolly (1999) is an excellent discussion of cultures in the northwestern Great Basin, because he considers their prehistory in light of relationships with peoples to the south and north.

13. The western Great Basin, especially the Owens Valley and other areas of eastern California, have been subject to a great deal of systematic archaeological investigation and more excavation than most places in the Basin. The work of archaeologists such as Mark Basgall, Robert Bettinger, Mike Delacorte, Bill Hildebrandt, Kelly McGuire, and others documents a late arrival of ceramics and a late increase in the reliance on small seeds, both in the context of major changes in the western

Great Basin preceding these changes and continuing with them. The analysis of these changes has often been explained in historical terms—the arrival of the Numic peoples. But Great Basin archaeology has long played a significant role in the development of anthropological theory about foraging societies, and this led to explanations for the history itself. Models from evolutionary ecology from beginnings based on simple time and energy foraging models, concepts such as adaptive peaks, adaptive diversity, and others, led to consideration of more complex variables such as transport costs, risk, and, more recently, costly signaling and prestige. Jelmer Eerkens (2004) continues the investigation by linking pots and seeds and the relationships these have to patterns of sharing and ownership known among living foragers. Archaeologist's discussions about evolutionary ecology have sometimes been ships passing in the night, but the steady building of models to systematically explain more and more variability has been productive and exciting.

14. Sutton and Rhode (1994) summarize linguists' investigation of Great Basin languages. After decades of archaeologists pronouncing the word Numic with the "u" as in fruit and/or with the "u" as in "abut" or "nut," David Thomas finally affirmed with the linguist Sidney Lamb that the latter is the correct pronunciation (Thomas 1994:57). The quote is from Kroeber (1925:577), and it is aptly contextualized by Sutton and Rhode (1994:7).

15. Lamb (1958) deserves to be carefully read in the original and reread after one has examined some of the subsequent analysis and comments by linguists and archaeologists.

16. The papers in Madsen and Rhode (1994) provide a sense of the continuing discussion.

17. The discussion among linguists is important to an evaluation of the archaeology. Linguist James Goss (1968) agreed with Lamb and then changed positions completely (Goss 1977) by interpreting the linguistic data from a different vantage and concluding that the Numic languages have been in the Great Basin for many thousands of years. Shaul (1986) took us somewhere new by appealing to analogy from Australia to understand the rates of language change among foraging societies instead of an uncritical reliance on analogy from European languages. Lamb's discussion with David Thomas is in Thomas (1994). Wick Miller's work and his observations about the nature of a "dialect continuum" add greatly to the discussion (Miller, Tanner, and Foley 1971; Miller 1986) and should be required reading for all archaeologists. Simms (1983b) suggested that we might be expending a lot of energy explaining something that did not happen. This was a spasm of excessive caution, but I still wonder if we have created an "it" out of something bigger, more interesting, and more dynamic than a mere historical event (Simms 1994).

18. This basic trajectory in California's past was understood decades ago and first summarized by Chartkoff and Chartkoff (1986). Jones and Klar (2007) summarize improved chronologies and changes in how the California's culture history has been viewed and explained. Other chapters in the same volume provide considerable detail.

19. Broughton (1994a, 1994b).

20. Basgall (1987), Bouey (1987).

21. Hildebrandt and McGuire (2002) began their quest to extend the application of evolutionary ecology into the currencies of food sharing, social prestige, and power with the case of resource intensification in California.

22. Bill Hildebrandt and Terry Jones (1992) investigated the effects of human predation on sea mammal populations and the consequences for changes in everything from hunting patterns to technology, settlement location, and social organization. Resistance to the notion that foragers have any significant impact on the animals and plants they live among is ingrained in anthropologists, but as more research has been done, such as Jones et al. (2004), it is apparent that much can be learned by studying humans as part of ecosystems, not apart from them. On the subject of plank canoes (tomols), Arnold (1995) shows how they played a central role in the development of social complexity in the last 1,500 years, whereas Fagan (2004) shows that the technology had been around for many millennia but played a different role in the earlier societies.

23. Lambert and Walker (1991) summarize the evidence from physical anthropology for increased social complexity, including bone collagen isotopes, to evaluate (1) the source of subsistence, dental wear, and caries to in connection with diet and health, (2) osteoarthritis in an assessment of lifetime workloads, and (3) osteological measures of health and the quality and consistency of human diets. Lambert (1997) summarizes the research revealing changing patterns of violence in coastal southern California.

24. Complexity among California foragers, and the reasons for it, constitutes a long academic discussion. See Arnold (1992), papers in Erlandson and Jones (2002), Glassow et al. (2007), Jones and Klar (2007), Kennett (2005), and Raab and Larsen (1997). For evidence that complexity in California has early roots and is variable in its expression over time and space see Byrd and Raab (2007).

25. Holly (2005:Chapter 5, note 21).

26. See Chapter 5, Sidebar: "Farming, Language, and Immigrants" and references therein. Great Basin archaeology has yet to digest the fundamental revision holding that Uto-Aztecan languages spread north from Mexico with farming rather than the traditional view that Uto-Aztecans spread south from somewhere in the Southwest. The new model corroborates

a wealth of evidence from archaeology, linguistics, and the study of migrations and farming in other world cases. The traditional model always made me wonder how one of the harshest deserts and lowest population densities of foragers in the world could give birth to cultures ranging from the Anasazi to the Toltecs and the Aztecs. Perhaps my skepticism is influenced by the Biblical undertones of wandering new peoples arising from desert sands. The recent thinking about the Uto-Aztecan spread helps resolve a number of issues about the Numic spread and, importantly, places it in continental context.

27. The expansion of Uto-Aztecan languages into southern California has long been known and referred to as the "Shoshonean Wedge" for its spatial pattern (Bright and Bright 1976; Kroeber 1953). Recent analysis of mitochondrial DNA is consistent with the older view based on language (Johnson and Lorenz 2006).

28. Mitochondrial DNA indicates that, unlike the mixing between Uto-Aztecan and Hokan speakers in some places, there was little mixing between the immigrants and the indigenous Chumash and other groups farther north in the populous San Joaquin Valley (Johnson and Lorenz 2006).

29. Bettinger and Baumhoff (1982) introduced the notion that immigrating Numic speaking foragers had an advantage over the indigenous foragers and that this was a case of competitive exclusion. The Numic were at an adaptive peak, and it was one of those moments in evolution when the traditions of one culture, for better or worse, simply outdo the competition under the circumstances of that historical moment; "sometimes you're the windshield—sometimes you're the bug." The Numic were in such a position because they were pioneer foragers emanating from farming centers. In addition, the run up of indigenous forager populations during the last few thousand years in the western Great Basin led to a situation already very competitive with prestige hunting, large villages, and food hoarding. It could have been a place where Numic-speaking "processors may have simply walked into a cultural landscape on the verge of collapse" (McGuire and Hildebrandt 2005:708).

30. Eerkens (2004); Sutton (1986); Sutton et al. (2007).

31. Kaestle and Smith (2001). I suspect that ancient DNA on skeletal remains from the eastern Great Basin will show distinction between Late Prehistoric/Numic and the Fremont. I also suspect that "Numic" DNA from the eastern Basin will not be identical to that in the west.

32. Lightfoot, Martinez, and Schiff (1998) employs the case of Ft. Ross, California, to explore the archaeological implications of a mixed ethnic community comprising Native Alaskan men, Native Californian women, and the mostly male Russian colony at Ft. Ross. The practices of daily life created identities and social ways that had elements of diverse cultures. Together, these did not create a melting pot but a completely

novel culture. The distinction is significant for archaeologists, because we rely so much on metaphors of cultural purity versus mixture that we obscure our recognition of the new.

33. Adovasio and Pedler (1994:121–122).

34. Steward (1937:121). Some of the materials from the many caves on Promontory Point and others around Great Salt Lake are curated at the Utah Museum of Natural History in Salt Lake City. However, other items are unfortunately in private collections in northern Utah and southern Idaho. The best synthesis of the Promontory culture is Janetski (1994).

35. Whitley (2000) provides an excellent overview of his often misunderstood position. Essentially his is a thorough and responsible use of two types of analogy: the direct historical approach and analogy from principle. He uses these to hypothesize that the shamanic social and ritual context of some California rock art from certain regions was operant in the past for about 1,000 years. He finds support for this hypothesis. Most of all, he shifts attention from the art itself to the social context of its production and reproduction, making rock art informative of the nature of societies fundamentally different from our own.

36. The report of excavations at the Wahmuza site are Holmer and Ringe (1986), and a prehistory of the area is found in Holmer (1990). An overview of the relevance of the work for the Numic Spread is Holmer (1994).

37. Janetski and Smith (2007:331–332) reports AMS C-14 dating on three Promontory moccasins from the collections at the Utah Museum of Natural History, Salt Lake City. The calibrated ages of the moccasins are A.D. 1165–1291, A.D. 1194–1376, and A.D. 1222–1383. Obviously, these dates overlap significant Fremont occupations in the region through the late 13th century.

38. Sinopolli (1991).

39. Janetski (1994:172–173). The Kern River gas pipeline project produced a large data set on obsidian procurement that shows changes in mobility over time (Seddon 2005).

40. For discussions of Late Prehistoric ceramics relevant to questions of type and culture history see Janetski (1994) and Janetski and Smith (2007). For studies of ceramic variability on a landscape level aimed at elucidating aspects of human mobility see Simms, Bright, and Ugan (1997) and Bright, Simms, and Ugan (2005).

41. The recognition that the end of the Fremont was a process that was time and space transgressive was recognized long ago (Lindsay 1986).

42. Mark Stuart is an avocational archaeologist from Ogden, Utah, who has recorded the local archaeology for decades. Most of these data remain in site forms, but some references for the Promontory-Late Prehistoric archaeology near Great Salt Lake include Enger and Blair (1947);

Hassel (1960, 1961); Russell (1989); Russell et al. (1989); Simms (1990); Stuart (1990); Simms, Loveland, and Stuart (1991); Baker et al. (1992); Cornell, Stuart, and Simms (1992); Loveland, Furlong, and Gregg (1992); Fawcett and Simms (1993); Simms (1999). Simms and Stuart (2002) provide an overview.

43. Aikens (1966).

44. Simms and Heath (1990). The Orbit Inn is on Brigham City property and was excavated and analyzed with volunteer labor including donated professional analyses. A descriptive report of the full details has yet to be produced. Janetski (1990b) and Janetski and Smith (2007) report the many years of effort excavating Promontory-Late Prehistoric sites in Utah Valley, which constitute the bulk of the data on the period.

45. Janetski (2002); Janetski and Smith (2007).

46. Stuart (1993) and Janetski and Smith (2007) report on the Wasatch Front. Reed (2001) describes the data from western Colorado. Lindsay (2005) reports the radiocarbon compilations of Mike and Claudia Berry for the region that shows a sharp dip in the 17th century before rising again.

47. Dobyns (1966) was the salvo that forced rethinking of the effects of epidemics on Native American population sizes. The quote is from Dobyns's (1983:8) book *Their Number Become Thinned*, a polemic that accomplished three important things: It (1) showed that depopulation from disease was earlier and greater than thought, because it was not just a matter of spreading from whites to Indians but a spread among Indians in a fully occupied continent; (2) showed that the inability and reluctance to explore this are rooted in the myth that America was a wilderness with few Indians living in a benign state of nature; and (3) stimulated analysis of the proposition that aboriginal population sizes were far higher than anyone thought. In retrospect, Dobyns's estimates of pre-Columbian population sizes of North America north of civilized Mesoamerica of 18 million people are surely too high. It is more common to see estimates of 5–7 million, a likely range. Even the conservative estimates of a few contemporary scholars of only 2 million are double the figure of 1 million Indians north of central Mexico that anthropologists have recited since the early 20th century. Simms (1990), Beck and Jones (1992), and Simms and Stuart (2002) suggest the possibility that European disease depopulated peoples of the Great Basin before face-to-face Indian-European contact. Better chronology suggests a population anomaly in the 17th century in the eastern Great Basin, followed by a rebound about a century later (Lindsay 2005). The samples are still not large enough to rule out sampling bias, but population declines and rebounds were frequent demographic characteristics of the encounters between Native Americans and European diseases.

48. This is now a rich literature. For example, see Reff (1991), Roberts (1989), Thornton (1987), and Verano and Ubelaker (1992). These and other scholars vary in their estimates of how large the North American populations were. The implications of native depopulation before most Euro-Americans ever saw large parts of the country are significant for comprehending the myth of American wilderness and how we understand ancient peoples and ecosystems. See Butzer (1992), Denevan (1992), Kay and Simmons (2002), Krech (1999), as well as counterarguments represented by scholars such as Vale (1998).

49. The quote is from Dobyns (1983:8).

50. A true test of the hypothesis of early depopulation in most of North America can be achieved only using archaeological data because no matter how early the eyewitness accounts, the question revolves around material evidence of regional depopulation prior to Euro-American presence. Oral history can provide enticing retrospectives, but it is not explicit and not able to evaluate regional patterns. The major archaeological tests are Ramenovsky (1987) and Campbell (1990). The significance of California and the Southwest as disease sources for the Great Basin and Colorado Plateau are shown especially by Preston (1996, 2001); also see Reff (1991), Kealhofer (1996), and Erlandson et al. (2001). For an excellent general treatment of the issue on a hemispheric scale see Mann (2005).

51. Reff (1991) and Preston (2001) document epidemics in the Southwest and California, respectively.

52. An article in the Utah Archaeology newsletter by John Dewey (1966) describes the transient use of the Wasatch Front by groups en route between the Snake River Plain, the Wyoming plains and high country, and the high mountain valleys behind the Wasatch Front. The sense of this is a very sparse population on the Front itself. Of course, by the 19th century acculturation had come to some natives and not to others. But when Escalante arrived in Utah Valley, the Front seemed to house villages in some places, while others, such as the Salt Lake Valley, and perhaps places to the north, were largely depopulated. Whether this depopulation resulted from disease or some other demographic circumstance remains unknown; it is worthy of investigation.

Sidebar: The Relationship of Modern Tribes to the Ancients

a. Great time depth for Hokan and Penutian languages on the western fringe of the Great Basin has long been recognized (Kroeber 1955). Archaeologists such as Heizer and Krieger (1956) noted similarities in material culture between northern California and western Nevada, and Hattori (1982) explicitly linked the Lovelock culture to Penutian speakers, whereas Pettigrew (1980) suggested the same for the prehistoric

Chewaucan culture of southeastern Oregon. Even Northern Paiute folktales tell of others living in the region in ancient times (Hopkins 1883, Kelly 1932). Aikens and Witherspoon (1986) extended this to an argument for long-term Numic presence in the Great Basin, and Aikens continued to promote consideration of this alternative (Aikens 1994). Connolly (1999:3–21) implies complex relationships for southwestern Oregon without direct reference to linguistic families and shows that multiple patrimonies for peoples of the northern and western Great Basin are in order. There is also a genetic basis for Penutian and Hokan residence in the prehistoric western Great Basin (Kaestle and Smith (2001). Since the Numic spread spanned millennia, elements of several models previously seen as competing probably yield some truth.

b. Comparisons of the Great Salt Lake wetlands Fremont mtDNA with Anasazi are O'Rourke, Parr, and Carlyle (1999) and Carlyle et al. (2000). As more samples accumulate, broader comparisons are possible, such as Mahli et al. (2003).

c. Doug Owsley and Shannon Novak spent several days at Utah State University in 1997 measuring skulls from the Great Salt Lake wetlands. Owsley and associates were steadily making their way through collections across the Basin-Plateau. Owsley has long been known for comparing populations based on statistical correlations among numerous cranial measurements. My sense of this largely unpublished work is that, although Fremont is a unified cultural entity, there was diversity in the sources of immigration and degrees of continuity with Archaic indigenes. These combined with sufficient isolation to produce local populations evident in cranial attributes. The Fremont are distinct from the Anasazi when compared en masse. However, on closer examination, the Fremont of eastern Utah have the strongest Southwestern connection, but Owsley's data also show that Anasazi skulls vary across their region. Owsley and Jantz prepared an unpublished draft report of some of their findings for the U.S. Bureau of Reclamation. Years ago in an obscure publication on a cultural resource management survey on the White River south of Vernal, Utah, Michael and Claudia Berry (1976) suggested that immigration from the Southwest had a role in founding the Fremont. Others, such as Marie Wormington, had speculated on this, and the Berrys pursued a good idea that had languished for lack of attention.

d. Kaestle, Lorenz, and Smith (1999) and Kaestle and Smith (2001) compare the western Great Basin ancient and Numic populations to other parts of the west. Many of their samples from the Stillwater marsh are radiocarbon dated. When I plotted the presence of haplogroups D and B, those common among Penutian speakers, the frequencies decreased after 2000 B.P. but did so strongly after 1500 B.P., as predicted by the Numic spread: D before 2000 B.P., N = 8; D after 2000 B.P., N = 5 and D before 1500 B.P., N = 11; D after 1500 B.P., N = 2 and B before 2000 B.P.,

N = 2; B after 2000 B.P., N = 8 (does not fit my hypothesis) and B before 1500 B.P., N = 7; B after 1500 B.P., N = 3. Kaestle and Smith thus find support for the "Numic Expansion Hypothesis." I see an expanded time window for this process that correlates with the massive social and economic upheaval of the Middle to Late Archaic as it is defined in the western Great Basin. Note that DNA study has not been done on modern eastern Great Basin and Colorado Plateau peoples. Thus, it is premature to assume that the genetics of western Basin tribes such as Northern Paiute are representative of the Northwestern Band of the Shoshone of northern Utah and southern Idaho, or the Ute of the Uinta Basin. The scenarios developed here would suggest more, rather than less variability arising from the different evolutionary processes leading to the peoples and cultures of the historic period.

e. The edited volume *Across the West: Human Population Movement and the Expansion of the Numa* (Madsen and Rhode 1994) contains papers that thoroughly document the massive evidence for change and stability as seen in material culture. Less often cited are the Southern Paiute and Ute folktales distinguishing the Numic tribes from the Fremont (Pendergast and Meighan 1959; Smith 1974:16).

References

Aberle, D. 1961. Matrilineal Descent in Cross-Cultural Perspective. In *Matrilineal Kinship,* edited by D. Schneider and K. Gough, pp. 655–729. University of California Press, Berkeley and Los Angeles.

Adams, R. McC. 1966. *The Evolution of Urban Society.* Aldine, Chicago.

Adovasio, J. M. 1974. Prehistoric North American Basketry. In *Collected Papers on Aboriginal Basketry,* edited by D. R. Tuohy and D. L. Rendall, pp. 98–148. Nevada State Museum Anthropological Papers, No. 16. Carson City.

———. 1977. *Basketry Technology: A Guide to Identification and Analysis.* Aldine Publishing Co., Chicago.

———. 1986a. Artifacts and Ethnicity: Basketry as an Indicator of Territoriality and Population Movements in the Prehistoric Great Basin. In *Anthropology of the Desert West, Essays in Honor of Jesse D. Jenning,* edited by C. J. Condie and D. D. Fowler, pp. 43–88. Anthropological Papers No. 82, University of Utah Press, Salt Lake City.

———. 1986b. Prehistoric Basketry. In *Handbook of North American Indians,* Vol. 11: Great Basin, edited by W. L. d'Azevedo, pp. 194–205. Smithsonian Institution Press, Washington D.C.

Adovasio, J. M., J. Donahue, and R. Stuckenrath. 1990. The Meadowcroft Rockshelter Radiocarbon Chronology 1975–1990. *American Antiquity* 55:348–354.

329

Adovasio, J. M., J. D. Gunn, J. Donahue, R. Stuckenrath, J. E. Guilday, and K. Volman. 1980. Yes Virginia, It Really Is That Old: A Reply to Haynes and Mead. *American Antiquity* 45:588–595.

———. 1991. Never Say Never Again: Some Thoughts on Could Haves and Might Have Beens. *American Antiquity* 57:327–331.

Adovasio, J. M., and J. Page. 2003. *The First Americans: In Pursuit of Archaeology's Greatest Mystery.* Modern Library, Random House, New York.

Adovasio, J., and D. Pedler. 1994. A Tisket, a Tasket: Looking at the Numic Speakers through the "Lens" of a Basket. In *Across the West: Human Population Movement and the Expansion of the Numa,* edited by D. B. Madsen and D. Rhode, pp. 114–123. University of Utah Press, Salt Lake City.

———. 1997. Monte Verde and the Antiquity of Humankind in the Americas. *Antiquity* 71:573–580.

Adovasio, J., D. R. Pedler, and J. S. Illingworth. 2002. Fremont Basketry. *Utah Archaeology* 15:5–26.

Aikens, C. M. 1966. *Fremont-Promontory-Plains Relationships, Including a Report of Investigations at the Injun Creek and Bear River No. 1 Sites, Northern Utah.* Anthropological Papers No. 82. University of Utah Press, Salt Lake City.

———. 1967. *Excavations at Snake Rock Village and the Bear River No. 2 Site.* Anthropological Papers No. 87. University of Utah Press, Salt Lake City.

———. 1970. *Hogup Cave.* Anthropological Papers No. 93. University of Utah Press, Salt Lake City.

———. 1976. Cultural Hiatus in the Eastern Great Basin? *American Antiquity* 41:543–550.

———. 1994. Adaptive Strategies and Environmental Change in the Great Basin and Its Peripheries as Determinants in the Migrations of Numic-Speaking Peoples. In *Across the West: Human Population Movement and the Expansion of the Numa,* edited by D. B. Madsen and D. Rhode, pp. 35–43. University of Utah Press, Salt Lake City.

Aikens, C. M., D. L. Cole, and Robert Stuckenrath. 1977. *Excavations at Dirty Shame Rockshelter, Southeastern Oregon.* Miscellaneous Papers No. 4. Idaho State Museum of Natural History, Pocatello.

Aikens, C. M., and Y. T. Witherspoon. 1986. Great Basin Numic Prehistory: Linguistics, Archeology, and Environment. In *Anthropology of the Desert West, Essays in Honor of Jesse D. Jenning,* edited by C. J. Condie and D. D. Fowler, pp. 8–20. University of Utah Anthropological Papers No. 110. Salt Lake City.

Alder, W. 2002. The National Weather Service, Weather Across Utah in the 1980s, and Its Effect on Great Salt Lake. In *Great Salt Lake: An Overview of Change,* edited by J. W. Gwynn, pp. 295–301. Utah

Department of Natural Resources Special Publication, Utah Geological Survey, Salt Lake City.

Allison, J. R., A. Colman, and A. Webb. 1997. *Archaeology at the Salt Lake Airport: 1996–1997 Test Excavations and Data Recovery Plan.* Baseline Data, Inc. Orem, Utah.

Ambler, J. R. 1966. *Caldwell Village and Fremont Prehistory.* Ph.D. dissertation, Department of Anthropology, University of Colorado, Boulder.

Ambro, R. D. 1970. A Basket-Maker's Work Kit from Lovelock Cave, Nevada. *Contributions of the University of California Archaeological Research Facility* 7:73–79.

Amick, D. S. 1999. Using Lithic Artifacts to Explain Past Behavior. In *Models for the Millennium: Great Basin Anthropology Today,* edited by C. Beck, pp. 161–170. University of Utah Press, Salt Lake City.

Arkush, B. S. 1998. *Archaeological Investigations at Mosquito Willie Rockshelter and Lower Lead Mine Hills Cave, Great Salt Lake Desert, Utah.* Coyote Press Archives of Great Basin Prehistory, Coyote Press, Salinas, California.

———. 1999a. Recent Small-Scale Excavations at Weston Canyon Rockshelter in Southeastern Idaho. *Tebiwa* 27:1–64.

———. 1999b. Numic Pronghorn Exploitation: A Reassessment of Stewardian-Derived Models of Big-Game Hunting in the Great Basin. In *Julian Steward and the Great Basin: The Making of an Anthropologist,* edited by R. O. Clemmer, L. D. Myers, and M. E. Rudden, pp. 35–52. University of Utah Press, Salt Lake City.

Arkush, B. S., and B. L. Pitblado. 2000. Paleoarchaic Surface Assemblages in the Great Salt Lake Desert, Northwestern Utah. *Journal of California and Great Basin Anthropology* 22:12–42.

Arnold, J. 1992. Complex Hunter-Gatherer-Fishers of Prehistoric California: Chiefs, Specialists, and Maritime Adaptations of the Channel Islands. *American Antiquity* 57:60–84.

———. 1995. Transportation Innovation and Social Complexity among Maritime Hunter-Gatherers. *American Anthropologist* 97:733–747.

Arsenault, D. 2004. Rock-Art, Landscape, Sacred Places: Attitudes in Contemporary Archaeological Theory. In *Pictures in Place: The Figured Landscapes of Rock-Art,* edited by C. Chippindale and G. Nash, pp. 69–84. Cambridge University Press.

Baer, S., and J. Sauer. 2003. *The BYU Escalante Drainage Project: Little Desert, Main Canyon and Escalante Desert Areas 2002.* Museum of Peoples and Cultures Technical Series 02-08. Brigham Young University, Provo, Utah.

Baker, S. A., S. E. Billat, L. D. Richens, and R. K. Talbot. 1992. *An Archaeological Survey of Bureau of Reclamation Lands around Willard Bay Reservoir, Northern Utah.* Brigham Young University Museum of Peoples and Cultures Technical Series No. 92-2. Provo, Utah.

Baker, S. G. 1999. *Fremont Archaeology on the Douglas Creek Arch, Rio Blanco County, Colorado: The Sky Aerie Promontory Charnel Site (5RB104)*. Centuries Research, Montrose, Colorado.

Barker, J. P. 1994. *Sequential Hierarchy and Political Evolution along the Western Fremont Frontier*. Paper presented at the 24 Biennial Great Basin Anthropological Conference, Elko, Nevada.

Barlow, K. R. 2002. Predicting Maize Agriculture among the Fremont: An Economic Comparison of Farming and Foraging in the American Southwest. *American Antiquity* 67:65–88.

———. 2006. A Formal Model for Predicting Agriculture among the Fremont. In *Behavioral Ecology and the Transition to Agriculture*, edited by D. J. Kennett and B. Winterhalder, pp. 87–102. University of California Press, Berkeley and Los Angeles.

Barlow, K. R., P. R. Henriksen, and D. Metcalfe. 1993. Estimating Load Size in the Great Basin: Date from Conical Burden Baskets. *Utah Archaeology* 6:27–36.

Barlow, K. R., and D. Metcalfe. 1993. *1990 Excavations at Joes Valley Alcove*. University of Utah Archaeological Center Reports of Investigations 93–1. Salt Lake City.

Barlow, K. R., and D. Metcalfe. 1996. Plant Utility Indices: Two Great Basin Examples. *Journal of Archaeological Science* 23:351–371.

Barth, F. 1961. *Nomads of South Persia: The Basseri Tribe of the Khamseh Confederacy*. Oslo University Press, Norway.

Basgall, M. E. 1987. Resource Intensification among Hunter-Gatherers: Acorn Economies in Prehistoric California. *Research in Economic Anthropology* 9:21–52.

———. 2000. The Structure of Archaeological Landscapes in the North-Central Mojave Desert. In *Archaeological Passages: A Volume in Honor of Claude Nelson Warren*, edited by J. S. Schneider, R. M. Yohe II, and J. K. Gardner, pp. 123–138. Western Center for Archaeology and Paleontology Publications in Archaeology 1.

Beck, C., and G. T. Jones. 1992. New Directions? Great Basin Archaeology in the 1990s. *Journal of California and Great Basin Anthropology* 14:22–36.

———. 1997. The Terminal Pleistocene/Early Holocene Archaeology of the Great Basin. *Journal of World Prehistory* 11:161–236.

Beck, C., A. K. Taylor, G. T. Jones, C. M. Fadem, C. R. Cook, S. A. Millward. 2002. Rocks are Heavy: Transport Costs and Paleoarchaic Quarry Behavior in the Great Basin. *Journal of Anthropological Archaeology* 21:481–507.

Bedwell, S. F. 1973. *Fort Rock Basin: Prehistory and Environment*. University of Oregon Books, Eugene.

Bell, G. 1907. *The Desert and the Sown*. W. Heinemann, London.

Bellwood, P., and C. Renfrew (eds.). 2002. *Examining the Farming/ Language Dispersal Hypothesis.* McDonald Institute Monographs, Oxbow Books, Oxford.

Benson, L. V. 2004. Western Lakes. In *The Quaternary Period of the United States,* edited by A. Gillespie, S. Porter, and N. Atwater, pp. 185–204. Elsevier, Amsterdam.

Benson, L. V., D. R. Curry, R. I. Dorn, K. R. Lajoie, C. G. Oviatt, S. W. Robinson, G. I. Smith, and S. Stine. 1990. Chronology of Expansion and Contraction of Four Great Basin Lake Systems during the Last 35,000 Years. *Palaeogeography, Palaeoclimatology, Palaeoecology* 78:241–286.

Benz, B. F., and A. Long. 2000. Prehistoric Maize Evolution in the Tehuacan Valley. *Current Anthropology* 41:459–465.

Berry, M. S. 1974. *The Evans Mound: Cultural Adaptation in Southwestern Utah.* Master's Thesis, Department of Anthropology, University of Utah, Salt Lake City.

———. 1982. *Time, Space and Transition in Southwestern Prehistory.* University of Utah Press, Salt Lake City.

Berry, M. S., and C. F. Berry. 1976. *An Archeological Reconnaissance of the White River Area, Northeastern Utah.* Antiquities Section Selected Papers, Vol. 2: No. 4. Utah State Historical Society, Salt Lake City.

———. 1986. Chronological and Conceptual Models of the Southwestern Archaic. In *Anthropology of the Desert West, Essays in Honor of Jesse D. Jennings,* edited by C. J. Condie and D. D. Fowler, pp. 253–327. University of Utah Anthropological Papers No. 110. Salt Lake City.

Bettinger, R. L. 1989. *The Archaeology of Pinyon House, Two Eagles, and Crater Middens: Three Residential Sites in Owens Valley, Eastern California.* Anthropological Papers of the American Museum of Natural History Vol. 67: American Museum of Natural History, New York.

———. 1991. Aboriginal Occupation at High-Altitude: Alpine Villages in the White Mountains of Eastern California. *American Anthropologist* 93:656–679.

———. 1994. How, When and Why the Numic Spread. In *Across the West: Human Population Movement and the Expansion of the Numa,* edited by D. B. Madsen and D. Rhode, pp. 44–55. University of Utah Press, Salt Lake City.

———. 1999. *What Happened in the Medithermal.* In *Models for the Millennium: Great Basin Anthropology Today,* edited by C. Beck, pp. 62–74. University of Utah Press, Salt Lake City.

Bettinger, R. L., and M. A. Baumhoff. 1982. The Numic Spread: Great Basin Cultures in Competition. *American Antiquity* 47:485–503.

Binford, L. R. 1983. *In Pursuit of the Past: Decoding the Archaeological Record.* Thames and Hudson, New York. New edition in 2002, University of California Press, Berkeley and Los Angeles.

Bird, D. W., and J. F. O'Connell. 2006. Behavioral Ecology and Archaeology. *Journal of Archaeological Research* 14:143–188.

Blitz, J. 1988. The Adoption of the Bow in Prehistoric North America. *North American Archaeologist* 9:123–145.

Blurton-Jones, N., K. Hawkes, and J. O'Connell. 1996. The Global Process and Local Ecology: How Should We Explain Differences between the Hadza and the !Kung? In *Cultural Diversity among 20th Century Foragers: An African Perspective,* edited by S. Kent, pp. 159–187. Cambridge University Press, New York.

Bolton, H. E. 1972. *Pageant in the Wilderness: The Story of the Escalante Expedition to the Interior Basin, 1776.* Utah State Historical Society, Salt Lake City.

Bonnichsen, R. (ed.). 2000. *Who Were the First Americans? Proceedings of the 58th Annual Biology Colloquium, Oregon State University.* Center for the Study of the First Americans, Oregon State University, Corvallis.

Bonnichsen, R., and A. L. Schneider. 2002. The Case for Pre-Clovis People. *American Archaeology* 5(4):35–39.

Bouey, P. D. 1987. The Intensification of Hunter-Gatherer Economies in the Southern North Coast Ranges of California. *Research in Economic Anthropology* 9:53–101.

Bright, J., S. R. Simms, and A. Ugan. 2005. Ceramics from Camels Back Cave and Mobility in Farmer-Forager Systems in the Eastern Great Basin. In *Camels Back Cave,* by D. N. Schmitt and D. B. Madsen, pp. 177–192. Anthropological Papers No. 125. University of Utah Press, Salt Lake City.

Bright, J., A. Ugan, and L. Hunsaker. 2002. The Effect of Handling Time on Subsistence Technology. *World Archaeology* 34:164–181.

Bright, R. C. 1966. Pollen and Seed Stratigraphy of Swan Lake, Southeastern Idaho: Its Relation to Regional Vegetational History and to Lake Bonneville. *Tebiwa* 9:1–47.

Bright, W., and M. Bright. 1976. Archaeology and Linguistics in Prehistoric Southern California. In *Variation and Change in Language: Essays by William Bright,* edited by A. S. Dil, pp. 189–205. Stanford University Press, Palo Alto.

Brimhall, W. H., and L. B. Merritt. 1981. Geology of Utah Lake: Implication for Resource Management. In *Utah Lake Monograph,* pp. 24–42. Great Basin Naturalist Memoirs No. 5. Provo, Utah.

Broughton, J. M. 1994a. Late Holocene Resource Intensification in the Sacramento Valley, California: The Vertebrate Evidence. *Journal of Archaeological Science* 21:501–514.

———. 1994b. Declines in Mammalian Foraging Efficiency during the Late Holocene, San Francisco Bay, California. *Journal of Anthropological Archaeology* 13:371–401.

Broughton, J. M., and F. E. Bayham. 2003. Showing Off, Foraging Models, and the Ascendance of Large-Game Hunting in the California Middle Archaic. *American Antiquity* 68:783–789.

Broughton, J. M., and D. K. Grayson. 1993. Diet Breadth, Adaptive Change, and the White Mountain Faunas. *Journal of Archaeological Science* 20:331–336.

Broughton, J. M., D. B. Madsen, and J. Quade. 2000. Fish Remains from Homestead Cave and Lake Levels of the Past 13,000 Years in the Bonneville Basin. *Quaternary Research* 53:392–401.

Bryan, A. L. 1979. Smith Creek Cave. In *The Archaeology of Smith Creek Canyon, Eastern Nevada*, edited by D. R. Tuohy and D. L. Rendall, pp. 162–253. Nevada State Museum Anthropological Papers, No. 17. Carson City.

Butzer, K. W. 1992. The Americas Before and After 1492: Current Geographical Research. *Annals of the Association of American Geographers*, 82(3).

Byers, D. A., and J. M. Broughton. 2004. Holocene Environmental Change, Artiodactyl Abundances and Human Hunting Strategies in the Great Basin. *American Antiquity* 69:235–256.

Byrd, B. F., and L. M. Raab. 2007. Prehistory of the Southern Bight: Models for a New Millennium. In *California Prehistory: Colonization, Culture, and Complexity*, edited by T. L. Jones and K. A. Klar, pp. 215–227. AltaMira Press, Walnut Creek.

Callaway, D. G., J. C. Janetski, and O. C. Stewart. 1986. Ute. In *Handbook of North American Indians*, Vol. 11: *Great Basin*, edited by W. L. d'Azevedo, pp. 336–367. Smithsonian Institution Press, Washington D.C.

Campbell, S. K. 1990. *PostColumbian Culture History in the Northern Columbia Plateau* A.D. *1500–1900*. Garland, New York.

Canaday, T. W. 1997. *Prehistoric Alpine Hunting Patterns in the Great Basin*. Ph.D. dissertation, Department of Anthropology, University of Washington, Seattle.

Cannon, W. J., and M. F. Ricks. 2007. Contexts in the Analysis of Rock Art: Settlement and Rock Art in the Warner Valley Area, Oregon. In *Great Basin Rock Art: Archaeological Perspectives,* edited by A. R. Quinlan, pp. 107–125. University of Nevada Press, Reno.

Carlyle, S. W., R. L. Parr, G. Hayes, and D. H. O'Rourke. 2000. Context of Maternal Lineages in the Greater Southwest. *American Journal of Physical Anthropology* 113:85–101.

Chatters, J. C. 2000. The Recovery and First Analysis of an Early Holocene Human Skeleton from Kennewick, Washington. *American Antiquity* 65:291–316.

Chippindale, C., and G. Nash. 2004. *Pictures in Place: The Figured Landscapes of Rock-Art*. Cambridge University Press.

Cline, G. G. 1963. *Exploring the Great Basin*. University of Oklahoma Press, Norman.

Cole, S. 1990. *Legacy on Stone: Rock Art of the Colorado Plateau and Four Corners Region*. Johnson Books, Boulder, Colorado.

———. 1993. Basketmaker Rock Art at the Green Mask Site, Southeastern Utah. In *Anasazi Basketmaker: Papers from the 1990 Wetherill-Grand Gulch Symposium*, edited by V. M. Atkins, pp. 193–222. Bureau of Land Management, Utah, Cultural Resource Series No. 24. Salt Lake City.

———. 2004. Origins, Continuities, and Meaning of Barrier Canyon Style Rock Art. In *New Dimensions in Rock Art Studies*, edited by R. T. Matheny, pp. 7–78. Brigham Young University Museum of Peoples and Cultures, Occasional Papers No. 9. University of Utah Press, Salt Lake City.

Collins, M. B. 1999. Monte Verde Revisited: Reply to Fiedel, Part II, *Scientific American Discovering Archaeology* 1:14–15.

Coltrain, J. B. 1993. Fremont Corn Agriculture: A Pilot Stable Carbon Isotope Study. *Utah Archaeology* 6:49–55.

———. 1994. *Fremont Foragers and Farmers: A Stable Carbon Isotope Study*. Paper presented at the 24th Great Basin Anthropological Conference, Elko, Nevada.

Coltrain, J. B., and S. W. Leavitt. 2002. Climate and Diet in Fremont Prehistory: Economic Variability and Abandonment of Maize Agriculture in the Great Salt Lake Basin. *American Antiquity* 67:453–485.

Coltrain, J. B., and T. W. Stafford, Jr. 1999. Stable Carbon Isotopes and Great Salt Lake Wetlands Diet: Toward an Understanding of the Great Basin Formative. In *Prehistoric Lifeways in the Great Basin Wetlands: Bioarchaeological Reconstruction and Interpretation*, edited by B. E. Hemphill and C. S. Larsen, pp. 55–83. University of Utah Press, Salt Lake City.

Connolly, T. J. 1999. *Newberry Crater: A Ten-Thousand Year Record of Human Occupation and Environmental Change in the Basin-Plateau Borderlands*. University of Utah Anthropological Papers No. 121. Salt Lake City.

Copeland, J. M., and R. Fike. 1988. Fluted Projectile Points in Utah. *Utah Archaeology* 1:5–28.

Cordell, L. 1997. *Archaeology of the Southwest,* 2nd Edition. Academic Press, San Diego.

Cornell, A., M. E. Stuart, and S. R. Simms. 1992. An Obsidian Cache from the Great Salt Lake Wetlands, Weber County, Utah. *Utah Archaeology* 5:154–159.

Cottam, W. P. 1947. *Is Utah Sahara Bound?* Bulletin of the University of Utah 37:1–40.

Cottam, W. P., J. M. Tucker, and R. Drobnick. 1959. Some Clues to Great Basin Postpluvial Climates Provided by Oak Distributions. *Ecology* 40:361–377.

Coulam, N. J., and A. R. Schroedl. 2004. Late Archaic Totemism in the Greater American Southwest. *American Antiquity* 69:41–62.

Couture, M. D., M. L. Ricks, and L. Housley. 1986. Foraging Behavior of a Contemporary Northern Great Basin Population. *Journal of California and Great Basin Anthropology* 8:150–160.

Crawford, M. H. 1998. *The Origins of Native Americans: Evidence from Anthropological Genetics.* Cambridge University Press, New York.

Creaseman, S. D., and L. J. Scott. 1987. Texas Creek Overlook: Evidence for Late Fremont (Post A.D. 1200) Occupation in Northwest Colorado. *Southwestern Lore* 53:1–16.

Crittenden, M. D., Jr. 1963. *New Data on Isostatic Deformation of Lake Bonneville.* U.S. Geological Survey Professional Paper 454-E. Washington D.C.

Currey, D. R. 1980. Coastal Geomorphology of Great Salt Lake and Vicinity. In Great Salt Lake: A Scientific, Historical and Economic Overview, edited by J. W. Gwynn, pp. 69–82. Utah Geological and Mineral Survey Bulletin No. 116. Salt Lake City.

———. 1990. Paleolakes in the Evolution of Semi-Desert Basins, with Special Emphasis on Lake Bonneville and the Great Basin. *Palaeogeography, Palaeoclimatology, Palaeoecology* 76:189–214.

Currey, D. R., G. Atwood, and D. R. Mabey. 1984. *Major Levels of Great Salt Lake and Lake Bonneville.* Utah Geological and Mineral Survey Map 73. Salt Lake City.

Currey, D. R., and S. R. James. 1982. Paleoenvironments of the Northeastern Great Basin and Northeastern Great Basin Rim Region: A Review of Geological and Biological Evidence. In *Man and Environment in the Great Basin,* edited by D. B. Madsen and J. F. O'Connell, pp. 27–52. Society for American Archaeology Papers 2. Washington D.C.

Curry, R. R. 1969. Holocene Climatic and Glacial History of the Central Sierra Nevada, California. In *United States Contributions to Quaternary Research,* edited by S. A. Schumm and W. C. Bradley, pp. 1–47. Geological Society of America Special Paper No. 123.

Dalley, G. F. 1976. *Swallow Shelter and Associated Sites.* Anthropological Papers No. 96. University of Utah Press, Salt Lake City.

Dalton, R. 2007. Blast in the Past? *Nature* 447:256–257.

Davis, C. A., and G. A. Smith. 1981. *Newberry Cave.* San Bernardino County Museum Association, Redlands, California.

Davis, C. A., R. E. Taylor, and G. A. Smith. 1981. New Radiocarbon Determinations from Newberry Cave. *Journal of California and Great Basin Anthropology* 3:144–147.

Davis, J. O. 1982. Bits and Pieces: The Last 35,000 Years in the Lahontan Area. In *Man and Environment in the Great Basin,* edited by D. B. Madsen and J. F. O'Connell, pp. 53–75. Society for American Archaeology Papers 2. Washington D.C.

Davis, W. E. 1985. The Montgomery Folsom Site. *Current Research in the Pleistocene* 2:11–12.

———. 1989. The Lime Ridge Clovis Site. *Utah Archaeology* 2:66–76.

Davis, W. E., D. Sack, and N. Shearin. 1996. The Hell' n Moriah Clovis Site. *Utah Archaeology* 9:55–70.

d'Azevedo, W. L. (ed.). 1986. *Handbook of North American Indians*, Vol. 11: Great Basin. Smithsonian Institution Press, Washington D.C.

Dean, J. S., R. C. Euler, G. J. Gumerman, F. Plog, R. H. Hevly, and T. N. V. Karlstrom. 1985. Human Behavior, Demography, and Paleoenvironment on the Colorado Plateaus. *American Antiquity* 50:537–554.

Delisio, M. P. 1970. *The Natural and Cultural Stratigraphy of the Weston Canyon Rockshelter, Southeastern Idaho.* Unpublished Master's thesis, Department of Anthropology, Idaho State University, Pocatello.

Deloria, V., Jr. 1995. *Red Earth, White Lies.* Scribners, New York.

Denevan, W. M. (ed.). 1992. *The Native Population of the Americas in 1492,* 2nd ed. (1st edition 1976). University of Wisconsin Press, Madison.

Derenko, M. V., T. Grzybowski, B. A. Malyarchuk, J. Czarny, D. Miścicka-Śliwka, and I. A. Zakharov. 2001. The Presence of Mitochondrial Haplogroup X in Altaians from South Siberia. *American Journal of Human Genetics* 69:237–241.

Dewey, J. R. 1966. Evidence of Acculturation among the Indian of Northern Utah and Southeast Idaho: A Historical Approach. *Utah Archaeology* 12:3–10. Utah Division of State History, Salt Lake City.

Diamond, J., and P. Bellwood. 2003. Farmers and Their Languages: The First Expansions. *Science* 300:597–603.

Dillehay, T. D. 1989. *Monte Verde, A Late Pleistocene Settlement in Chile,* Vol. 1: *Palaeoenvironment and Site Context.* Smithsonian Institution Press, Washington D.C.

———. 1997. *Monte Verde: A Late Pleistocene Settlement in Chile,* Vol. 2: *The Archaeological Context and Interpretation.* Smithsonian Institution Press, Washington D.C.

———. 1999. Monte Verde Revisited: Reply to Fiedel, Part I: *Scientific American Discovering Archaeology* 1:12–14.

———. 2000. *The Settlement of the Americas: A New Prehistory.* Basic Books, New York.

Dobyns, H. F. 1966. Estimating Aboriginal American Population: An Appraisal of Techniques with a New Hemispheric Estimate. *Current Anthropology* 7:395–416.

———. 1983. *Their Number Become Thinned: Native American Population Dynamics in Eastern North America.* University of Tennessee Press, Knoxville.

Dodd, W. A., Jr. 1982. *Final Year Excavations at the Evans Mound Site.* Anthropological Papers No. 106. University of Utah Press, Salt Lake City.

Duff, A. I., and R. H. Wilshusen. 2000. Prehistoric Population Dynamics in the Northern San Juan Region, A.D. 950–1300. *Kiva* 66:167–190.

Eerkens, J. W. 2004. Privatization, Small-Seed Intensification, and the Origins of Pottery in the Western Great Basin. *American Antiquity* 69:653–670.

Eiselt, B. S. 1997. Fish Remains from the Spirit Cave Paleofecal Material: 9,400-Year-Old Evidence for Great Basin Utilization of Small Fishes. In *Papers on Holocene Burial Localities Presented at the Twenty-Fifth Great Basin Anthropological Conference, October 10–12, 1996*, edited by D. Tuohy and A. Dansie. *Nevada Historical Society Quarterly* 40(1): 117–139.

Elston, R. G. 1982. Good Times, Hard Times: Prehistoric Culture Change in the Western Great Basin. In *Man and Environment in the Great Basin*, edited by D. B. Madsen and J. F. O'Connell, pp. 186–206. Society for American Archaeology Papers No. 2. Washington D.C.

Elston, R. G., and E. E. Budy (eds.). 1990. *The Archaeology of James Creek Shelter*. University of Utah Anthropological Papers No. 115. Salt Lake City.

Elston, R. G., and D. W. Zeanah. 2002. Thinking Outside the Box: A New Perspective on Diet Breadth and Sexual Division of Labor in the Pre-archaic Diet. *World Archaeology* 34:103–130.

Ember, M., C. Ember, and B. Pasternak. 1974. On the Development of Unilineal Descent. *Journal of Anthropological Research* 3:87–111.

Emslie, S D., J. I. Mead, and L. Coats. 1995. Split-Twig Figurines in Grand Canyon, Arizona: New Discoveries and Interpretations. *Kiva* 61: 145–173.

Enger, W. D., and W. Blair. 1947. Crania from the Warren Mounds and Their Possible Significance to Northern Periphery Archaeology. *American Antiquity* 13:142–146.

Erlandson, J. M., and T. L. Jones (eds.). 2002. *Catalysts to Complexity: Late Holocene Societies of the California Coast*. Perspectives in California Archaeology 6. Cotsen Institute, University of California, Berkeley and Los Angeles.

Erlandson, J. M., T. C. Rick, D. J. Kennett, and P. L. Walker. 2001. Dates, Demography, and Disease: Cultural Contacts and Possible Evidence for Old World Epidemics among the Protohistoric Island Chumash. *Pacific Coast Archaeological Society Quarterly* 37:11–26.

Ewers, J. 1955. *The Horse in Blackfoot Indian Culture*. Bureau of American Ethnology, Bulletin 159. Washington D.C.

Fagan, B. 2000. *The Little Ice Age: How Climate Made History 1300–1850*. Basic Books, New York.

———. 2004. The House of the Sea: An Essay on the Antiquity of Planked Canoes in Southern California. *American Antiquity* 69:7–16.

Fawcett, W. B., and S. R. Simms (eds.). 1993. *Archaeological Test Excavations in the Great Salt Lake Wetlands and Associated Analyses, Weber and*

Box Elder Counties, Utah. Utah State University Contributions to Anthropology No. 14. Logan.

Feinman, G. M. 1995. The Emergence of Inequality: A Focus on Strategies and Processes. In *Foundations of Inequality,* edited by T. D. Price and G. M. Feinman, pp. 255–279. Plenum, New York.

Fiedel, S. J. 1999a. Older Than We Thought: Implications of Corrected Dates for Paleoindians. *American Antiquity* 64:95–115.

———. 1999b. Monte Verde Revisited: Artifact Provenience at Monte Verde: Confusion and Contradictions, *Scientific American Discovering Archaeology* 1:1–12.

Fiedel, S. J., and D. W. Anthony. 2003. Deerslayers, Pathfinders, and Icemen: Origins of the European Neolithic as Seen from the Frontier. In *Colonization of Unfamiliar Landscapes: The Archaeology of Adaptation,* edited by M. Rockman and J. Steele, pp. 144–168. Routledge, New York.

Fisher, D., and S. G. Beld. 2003. *Growth and Life History Records from Mammoth Tusks.* Paper presented at the 3rd International Mammoth Conference, Dawson City, Yukon Territory, Canada.

Firor, J. 2001. The Myron Taylor Site (5LP696). In *The TransColorado Natural Gas Pipeline Archaeological Data Recovery Project, Western Colorado and Northwestern New Mexico.* Compiled by Alan D. Reed, pp. 29, 50–51. Alpine Archaeological Consultants, Montrose, Colorado.

Fowler, C. S. 1982a. Food-Named Groups among Northern Paiute in North America's Great Basin: An Ecological Interpretation. In *Resource Managers: North American and Australian Hunter-gatherers,* edited by N. Williams and E. Hunn, pp. 113–129. American Association for the Advancement of Science Selected Symposium 67, Boulder, Colorado.

———. 1982b. Settlement Patterns and Subsistence Systems in the Great Basin: The Ethnographic Record. In *Man and Environment in the Great Basin,* edited by J. F. O'Connell and D. B. Madsen, pp. 121–138. Society for American Archaeology Papers No. 2. Washington D.C.

———. 1986. Subsistence. In *Handbook of North American Indians,* Vol. 11: Great Basin, edited by W. L. d'Azevedo, pp. 64–97. Smithsonian Institution Press, Washington D.C.

———. 1989. *Willard Z. Park's Ethnographic Notes on the Northern Paiute of Western Nevada, 1933–1940.* Anthropological Papers No. 114. University of Utah Press, Salt Lake City.

———. 1992. *In the Shadow of Fox Peak: An Ethnography of the Cattail-Eater Northern Paiute People of Stillwater Marsh.* Cultural Resource Series 5. U.S. Department of Interior, Fish and Wildlife Service, Region 1.

———. 1999. Current Issues in Ethnography, Ethnology, and Linguistics. In *Models for the Millennium: Great Basin Anthropology Today,* edited by C. Beck, pp. 55–61. University of Utah Press, Salt Lake City.

Fowler, C. S., and D. D. Fowler. 1990. A History of Wetlands Anthropology in the Great Basin. In *Wetlands Adaptations in the Great Basin*, edited by J. C. Janetski and D. B. Madsen, pp. 5–16. Museum of Peoples and Cultures Occasional Papers No. 1. Brigham Young University, Provo, Utah.

Franklin, R. J., and P. A. Bunte. 1990. *The Paiute.* Chelsea House Publishers, New York.

Fremont, J. C. 1988. *The Exploring Expedition to the Rocky Mountains.* Originally published 1845. Smithsonian Institution Press, Washington D.C.

Frison, G. C. 1989. Experimental Use of Clovis Weaponry and Tools on African Elephants. *American Antiquity* 54:766–783.

Frison, G., and B. Bradley. 1999. *The Fenn Cache: Clovis Weapons and Tools.* One Horse Land and Cattle Company, Santa Fe, New Mexico and distributed by the University of Utah Press, Salt Lake City.

Fritts, H. C., and X. M. Shao. 1992. Mapping Climate Using Tree-Rings from Western North America. In *Climate Since A.D. 1500*, edited by R. S. Bradley and P. D. Jones, pp. 269–295. Routledge, New York.

Fritz, G. J. 1994. Are the First American Farmers Getting Younger? *Current Anthropology* 305–309.

Fry, G. F., and J. M. Adovasio. 1970. Population Differentiation in Hogup and Danger Caves, Two Archaic Sites in the Eastern Great Basin. In *Five Papers on the Archaeology of the Desert West*, edited by D. R. Tuohy, D. L. Rendall, and P. A. Crowell, pp. 207–215. Nevada State Museum Anthropological Papers No. 15. Carson City.

Fry, Gary F. and Gardiner F. Dalley. 1979. *The Levee Site and the Knoll Site.* Anthropological Papers No. 100. University of Utah Press, Salt Lake City.

Gagnon, A., B. Toupance, M. Tremblay, J. Beise, and E. Heyer. 2006. Transmission of Migration Propensity Increases Genetic Divergence between Populations. *American Journal of Physical Anthropology* 129:630–636.

Geib, P. R. 1996. *Glen Canyon Revisited.* University of Utah Anthropological Papers No. 119. Salt Lake City.

Geib, P. R., and P. W. Bungart. 1989. Implications of Early Bow Use in Glen Canyon. *Utah Archaeology* 2:32–47.

Gillette, D. D., and D. B. Madsen. 1993. The Columbian Mammoth, *Mammuthus columbi*, from the Wasatch Mountains of Central Utah. *Journal of Paleontology* 66:669–680.

Glassow, M. A., L. H. Gamble, J. E. Perry, and G. S. Russell. 2007. Prehistory of the Northern California Bight and the Adjacent Transverse Ranges. In *California Prehistory: Colonization, Culture, and Complexity*, edited by T. L. Jones and K. A. Klar, pp. 191–213. AltaMira Press, Walnut Creek.

Goebel, T., K. Graf, B. Hockett, and D. Rhode. 2004. Late Pleistocene Humans at Bonneville Estates Rockshelter, Eastern Nevada. *Current Research in the Pleistocene* 20:20–23.

Goss, J. A. 1968. Culture-Historical Inference from Utazetecan Linguistic Evidence. In *Utazetecan Prehistory*, edited by E. H. Swanson, Jr., pp. 1–42. Occasional Papers of the Idaho State University Museum No. 22. Pocatello.

———. 1977. Linguistic Tools for the Great Basin Prehistorian. In *Models and Great Basin Prehistory: A Symposium,* edited by D. D. Fowler, pp. 48–70. Desert Research Institute Publications in the Social Sciences No. 12.

Graham, R. W. 1986. Plant-Animal Interactions and Pleistocene Extinctions. In *Dynamics of Extinctions*, edited by D. K. Elliot, pp. 131–154. John Wiley and Sons, Chicago.

Graham, R. W., and E. L. Lundelius. 1984. Coevolutionary Disequilibrium and Pleistocene Extinctions. In *Quaternary Extinctions: A Prehistoric Revolution,* edited by P. S. Martin and R. G. Klein, pp. 223–249. University of Arizona Press, Tucson.

Gray, S. T., S. T. Jackson, and J. L. Betancourt. 2004. Tree-Ring Based Reconstructions of Interannual to Decadal Scale Precipitation Variability for Northeastern Utah Since 1226 A.D. *Journal of the American Water Resources Association.* August 2004.

Grayson, D. K. 1977. Pleistocene Avifaunas and the Overkill Hypothesis. *Science* 195:691–693.

———. 1984. Explaining Pleistocene Extinctions: Thoughts on the Structure of a Debate. In *Quaternary Extinctions: A Prehistoric Revolution,* edited by P. S. Martin and R. G. Klein, pp. 807–823. University of Arizona Press, Tucson.

———. 1988. *Danger Cave, Last Supper Cave, and Hanging Rock Shelter: The Faunas.* Anthropological Papers of the American Museum of Natural History Vol. 66: Pt. 1. American Museum of Natural History, New York.

———. 1991a. Late Pleistocene Mammalian Extinctions in North America: Taxonomy, Chronology, and Explanations. *Journal of World Prehistory* 5:193–232.

———. 1991b. Alpine Faunas from the White Mountains, California: Adaptive Change in the Late Prehistoric Great Basin? *Journal of Archaeological Science* 18:483–506.

———. 1993. *The Desert's Past: A Natural Prehistory of the Great Basin.* Smithsonian Institution Press, Washington D.C.

———. 2006. The Late Quaternary Biogeographic Histories of some Great Basin Mammals (western USA). *Quaternary Science Reviews* 25:2964–2991.

Grayson, D. K., and D. J. Meltzer. 2003. A Requiem for North American Overkill. *Journal of Archaeological Science* 30:585–593.

Green, T. J., B. Cochran, T. W. Fenton, J. C. Woods, G. L. Titmus, L. Tieszen, M. A. Davis, S. J. Miller. 1998. The Buhl Burial: A Paleoindian Woman from Southern Idaho. *American Antiquity* 63:437–456.

Greubel, R. A. 1996. *Archaeological Investigations of 11 Sites Along Interstate 70: Castle Valley to Rattlesnake Bench.* Alpine Archaeological Consultants, Montrose, Colorado.

———. 1998. The Confluence Site: An Early Fremont Pithouse Village in Central Utah. *Utah Archaeology* 11:1–32.

Gunnerson, J. H. 1969. *The Fremont Culture: A Study in Culture Dynamics on the Northern Anasazi Frontier.* Papers of the Peabody Museum of Archaeology and Ethnology, Harvard University, Vol. 59: No. 2.

Guthrie, R. D. 1984. Mosaics, Allelochemics and Nutrients: An Ecological Theory of Pleistocene Megafaunal Extinctions. In *Quaternary Extinctions: A Prehistoric Revolution,* edited by P. S. Martin and R. G. Klein, pp. 259–298. University of Arizona Press, Tucson.

———. 1990. Late Pleistocene Faunal Revolution: A New Perspective on the Extinction Debate. In *Megafauna and Man: Discovery of America's Heartland,* edited by L. D. Agenbroad, J. I. Mead, L. W. Nelson, pp. 42–53. The Mammoth Site of Hot Springs, South Dakota Scientific Papers 1.

Gwynn, J. W. 2002a. History of the Bear River Migratory Bird Refuge, Box Elder County, Utah. In *Great Salt Lake: An Overview of Change,* edited by J. W. Gwynn, pp. 375–386. Utah Department of Natural Resources Special Publication, Utah Geological Survey, Salt Lake City.

———. 2002b. Introduction. In *Great Salt Lake: An Overview of Change,* edited by J. W. Gwynn, pp. ix–x. Utah Department of Natural Resources Special Publication, Utah Geological Survey, Salt Lake City.

Hammer M. F. 1995. A Recent Common Ancestry for Human Y Chromosomes. *Nature* 378: 376–378.

Harpending, H. C., M. A. Batzer, M. Gurven, L. B. Jorde, A. R. Rogers, and S.T. Sherry. 1998. Genetic Traces of Ancient Demography. *Proceedings of the National Academy of Sciences USA* 95:1961–1967.

Harrington, M. R., I. Hayden, and L. Schellbach, III (eds.). 1930. *Archaeological Explorations in Southern Nevada: Report of the First Sessions Expedition, 1929.* Southwest Museum Papers No. 4. Los Angeles.

Harris, D. C. 2005. *The BYU Escalante Drainage Project: Black Hills, Escalante Flats, and Escalante Canyon 2003.* Museum of Peoples and Cultures Technical Series 03-12. Brigham Young University, Provo, Utah.

Harris, M. 1991. Anthropology: Ships That Crash in the Night. In *Perspectives on Social Science: The Colorado Lectures,* edited by R. Jessor, pp. 70–114. Westview Press, Boulder, Colorado.

Harrison, M. L. 2003. The Patterson Bundle: An Herbalist's Discovery. *Utah Archaeology* 16:53–62.

Hassel, F. K. 1960. Archaeological Notes on the Northeastern Margin of the Great Salt Lake. *Utah Archaeology* 6:10–15.

Hassel, F. K. 1961. An Open Site Near Plain City, Utah. *Utah Archaeology* 7:5–13.

Hattori, E. M. 1982. *The Archaeology of Falcon Hill, Winnemucca Lake, Washoe County, Nevada.* Nevada State Museum Anthropological Papers 18. Carson City.

Haury, E. W. 1958. Evidence at Point of Pines for a Prehistoric Migration from Northern Arizona. In *Migrations in New World Culture History,* edited by R. H. Thompson, pp. 1–8. University of Arizona Bulletin 29, Social Science Bulletin 27.

Hawkes, K. 1993. Why Hunter-Gatherers Work: An Ancient Version of the Problem of Public Goods. *Current Anthropology* 34:341–361.

Hawkes, K., K. Hill, and J. F. O'Connell. 1982. Why Hunters Gather: Optimal Foraging and the Ache' of Eastern Paraguay. *American Ethnologist* 9:379–398.

Hayden, I. 1930. Mesa House. In Archeological Explorations in Southern Nevada: *Report of the First Sessions Expedition, 1929.* Southwest Museum Papers No. 4(2):26–92. Los Angeles.

Haynes, C. V. 1980. Paleoindian Charcoal from Meadowcroft Rockshelter: Is Contamination a Problem? *American Antiquity* 45:582–587.

————. 1991. Geoarchaeological and Paleohydrological Evidence for a Clovis-Age Drought in North America and Its Bearing on Extinction. *Quaternary Research* 35:438–450.

————. 1992. More on Meadowcroft Rockshelter Radiocarbon Chronology. *The Review of Archaeology* 12:8–14.

Haynes, G. 1991. *Mammoths, Mastodonts, and Elephants: Biology, Behavior, and the Fossil Record.* Cambridge University Press, New York.

Headland, T. N., and L. A. Reid. 1989. Hunter-Gatherers and Their Neighbors from Prehistory to the Present. *Current Anthropology* 30:43–66.

Hegmon, M. 2005. Beyond the Mold: Questions of Inequality in Southwest Villages. In *North American Archaeology,* edited by T. R. Pauketat and D. D. Loren, pp. 212–234. Blackwell Publishing, Malden, Massachusetts.

Heizer, R. F., and A. D. Krieger. 1956. The Archaeology of Humboldt Cave, Churchill County, Nevada. *University of California Publications in American Archaeology and Ethnology* 47(1):1–190.

Hemphill, B. E. 1999. Wear and Tear: Osteoarthritis as an Indicator of Mobility among Great Basin Hunter-Gatherers. In *Prehistoric Lifeways in the Great Basin Wetlands: Bioarchaeological Reconstruction and Interpretation,* edited by B. E. Hemphill and C. S. Larsen, pp. 241–289. University of Utah Press, Salt Lake City.

Hemphill, B. E., and C. S. Larsen. 1999. *Prehistoric Lifeways in the Great Basin Wetlands: Bioarchaeological Reconstruction and Interpretation.* University of Utah Press, Salt Lake City.

Hildebrandt, W. R., and T. L. Jones. 1992. Evolution of Marine Mammal Hunting: A View from the California and Oregon Coasts. *Journal of Anthropological Archaeology* 11:360–401.

Hildebrandt, W. R., and K. R. McGuire. 2002. Ascendance of Hunting during the California Middle Archaic: An Evolutionary Perspective. *American Antiquity* 67:231–256.

Hill, J. H. 2001. Proto-Uto-Aztecan: A Community of Cultivators in Central Mexico? *American Anthropologist* 103(4):913–934.

———. 2002a. Toward a Linguistic Prehistory of the Southwest: "Azteco-Tanoan" and the Arrival of Maize Cultivation. *Journal of Anthropological Research* 58:457–475.

———. 2002b. Proto-Uto-Aztecan Cultivation and the Northern Devolution. In *Examining the Farming/Language Dispersal Hypothesis*, edited by P. Bellwood and C. Renfrew, pp. 331–340. McDonald Institute for Archaeological Research, University of Cambridge, United Kingdom.

Hockett, B. 1998. Sociopolitical Meaning of Faunal Remains from Baker Village. *American Antiquity* 63:289–302.

———. 2005. Middle and Late Holocene Hunting in the Great Basin: A Critical Review of the Debate and Future Prospects. *American Antiquity* 70:713–731.

Hockett, B., and M. Morgenstein. 2003. Ceramic Production, Fremont Foragers, and the Late Archaic Prehistory of the North-Central Great Basin. *Utah Archaeology* 16:1–36.

Holly, D. H., Jr. 2005. The Place of "Others" in Hunter-Gatherer Intensification. *American Anthropologist* 107:209–220.

Holmer, R. N. 1986. Common Projectile Points of the Intermontane West. In *Anthropology of the Desert West, Essays in Honor of Jesse D. Jennings*, edited by C. J. Condie and D. D. Fowler, pp. 98–115. Anthropological Papers No. 110, University of Utah Press, Salt Lake City.

———. 1990. Prehistory of the Northern Shoshone. In *Fort Hall and the Shoshone-Bannock*, edited by E. S. Lohse and R. N. Holmer, pp. 41–59. Idaho State University Press, Pocatello.

———. 1994. In Search of Ancestral Northern Shoshone. In *Across the West: Human Population Movement and the Expansion of the Numa*, edited by D. B. Madsen and D. Rhode, pp. 179–187. University of Utah Press, Salt Lake City.

Holmer, R. N., and B. L. Ringe. 1986. Excavations at Wahmuza. In *Shoshone-Bannock Culture History*, edited by R. N. Holmer. Swanson-Crabtree Anthropological Research Laboratory Reports of Investigations 85–16: 39–203.

Hopkins, S. W. 1883. *Life among the Paiutes: Their Wrongs and Claims.* Putnam, New York.

Howard, J., and J. C. Janetski. 2002. Human Scalps from Eastern Utah. *Utah Archaeology* 5:125–132.

Huckell, B. B. 1996. Archaic Prehistory of the North American Southwest. *Journal of World Prehistory* 10:305–373.

Hughes, R. E. 1994. Mosaic Patterning in California-Great Basin Exchange. In *Prehistoric Exchange Systems in North America*, edited by T. G. Baugh and J. E. Ericson, pp. 363–383. Plenum Press, New York.

Hughes, R. E., and J. A. Bennyhoff. 1986. Early Trade. In *Handbook of North American Indians*, Vol. 11: Great Basin, edited by W. L. d'Azevedo, pp. 238–255. Smithsonian Institution Press, Washington D.C.

Hultkrantz, A. 1986. Mythology and Religious Concepts. In *Handbook of North American Indians*, Vol. 11: Great Basin, edited by W. L. d'Azevedo, pp. 630–640. Smithsonian Institution Press, Washington D.C.

Hunter, R. J. 1991. Archaeological Evidence of Prehistoric Fishing at Utah Lake. *Utah Archaeology* 4:44–54.

Hurst, W. B., and C. G. Turner, II. 1993. Rediscovering the "Great Discovery": Wetherill's First Cave 7 and Its Record of Basketmaker Violence. In *Anasazi Basketmaker: Papers from the 1990 Wetherill-Grand Gulch Symposium*, edited by V. M. Atkins, pp. 143–191. Bureau of Land Management, Utah, Cultural Resource Series No. 24. Salt Lake City.

Hutchinson, P. W. 1988. The Prehistoric Dwellers at Lake Hubbs. In *Early Human Occupation in Far Western North America: The Clovis-Archaic Interface*, edited by J. A. Willig, C. M. Aikens, and J. L. Fagan, pp. 303–318. Nevada State Museum Anthropological Papers No. 21. Carson City.

Janetski, J. C. 1979. Implications of Snare Bundles in the Great Basin and Southwest. *Journal of California and Great Basin Anthropology* 1: 306–321.

———. 1985. *Archaeological Investigations at Sparrow Hawk (42TO261): A High Altitude Prehistoric Hunting Camp in the Southern Oquirrh Mountains, Tooele County, Utah*. Brigham Young University Museum of Peoples and Cultures Technical Series No. 85–37.

———. 1986. The Great Basin Lacustrine Subsistence Pattern: Insights from Utah Valley. In *Anthropology of the Desert West, Essays in Honor of Jesse D. Jennings*, edited by C. J. Condie and D. D. Fowler, pp. 145–168, Anthropological Papers No. 110, University of Utah Press, Salt Lake City.

———. 1990a. Utah Lake: Its Role in the Prehistory of Utah Valley. *Utah Historical Quarterly* 58:5–31.

———. 1990b. Wetlands in Utah Valley Prehistory. In *Wetlands Adaptations in the Great Basin*, edited by J. C. Janetski and D. B. Madsen, pp. 233–258. Museum of Peoples and Cultures Occasional Papers No. 1. Brigham Young University, Provo, Utah.

———. 1991. *The Ute of Utah Lake*. Anthropological Papers No. 116. University of Utah Press, Salt Lake City.

———. 1993. The Archaic to Formative Transition North of the Anasazi: A Basketmaker Perspective. In *Anasazi Basketmaker: Papers from the 1990 Wetherill-Grand Gulch Symposium*, edited by V. M. Atkins, pp. 223–241. Bureau of Land Management, Utah, Cultural Resource Series No. 24. Salt Lake City.

———. 1994. Recent Transitions in Eastern Great Basin Prehistory: The Archaeological Record. In *Across the West: Human Population Movement and the Expansion of the Numa,* edited by D. B. Madsen and D. Rhode, pp. 157–178. University of Utah Press, Salt Lake City.

———. 2002. Trade in Fremont Society: Contexts and Contrasts. *Journal of Anthropological Archaeology* 21:344–370.

Janetski, J. C., R. Crosland, and J. D. Wilde. 1991. Preliminary Report on Aspen Shelter: An Upland Deer Hunting Camp on the Old Woman Plateau. *Utah Archaeology* 4:33–45.

Janetski, J. C., L. Kreutzer, R. K. Talbot, L. D. Richens, and S. A. Baker. 2005. *Life on the Edge: Archaeology in Capitol Reef National Park.* Occasional Papers No. 11. Museum of Peoples and Cultures, Brigham Young University, Provo, Utah.

Janetski, J. C., and D. B. Madsen. 1990. *Wetlands Adaptations in the Great Basin.* Museum of Peoples and Cultures Occasional Papers No. 1. Brigham Young University, Provo, Utah.

Janetski, J. C., and F. W. Nelson. 1999. Obsidian Sourcing of Paleoindian Points from the Sevier Desert, Utah. *Current Research in the Pleistocene* 16:96–97.

Janetski, J. C., and G. C. Smith. 2007. *Hunter-Gatherer Archaeology in Utah Valley.* Occasional Papers No. 12. Museum of Peoples and Cultures, Brigham Young University, Provo, Utah.

Janetski, J. C., R. K. Talbot, D. E. Newman, L. D. Richens, J. D. Wilde, S. A. Baker, and S. E. Billat. 1997. *Clear Creek Canyon Archaeological Project, Vol. 5: Results and Synthesis.* Museum of Peoples and Cultures Technical Series 95-9. Brigham Young University, Provo, Utah.

Jantz, R., and D. Owsley. 2001. Variation among Early North American Crania. *American Journal of Physical Anthropology* 114:146–155.

Jennings, J. D. 1957. *Danger Cave.* Anthropological Papers No. 27. University of Utah Press, Salt Lake City.

———. 1973. The Short Useful Life of a Simple Hypothesis. *Tebiwa* 13:1–9.

———. 1978. *Prehistory of Utah and the Eastern Great Basin.* Anthropological Papers No. 98. University of Utah Press, Salt Lake City.

Jennings, J. D., A. R. Schroedl, and R. N. Holmer. 1980. *Sudden Shelter.* Anthropological Papers No. 103. University of Utah Press, Salt Lake City.

Jett, S. C. 1991. Split-Twig Figurines, Early Maize, and a Child Burial in East-Central Utah. *Utah Archaeology* 4:24–32.

Johnson, J. R., and J. G. Lorenz. 2006. Genetics, Linguistics, and Prehistoric Migrations: An Analysis of California Indian Mitochondrial DNA Lineages. *Journal of California and Great Basin Anthropology* 26:33–64.

Jones, G. T., and C. Beck. 1999. Paleoarchaic Archaeology in the Great Basin. In *Models for the Millennium: Great Basin Anthropology Today,* edited by C. Beck, pp. 83–95. University of Utah Press, Salt Lake City.

Jones, G. T., C. Beck, E. E. Jones, and R. E. Hughes. 2003. Lithic Source Use and Paleoarchaic Foraging Territories in the Great Basin. *American Antiquity* 68:5–38.

Jones, K. T., and D. B. Madsen. 1989. Calculating the Cost of Resource Transportation: A Great Basin Example. *Current Anthropology* 30:529–534.

Jones, K. T., and D. Metcalfe. 1981. Preliminary Report: *Archeological Research at Nawthis Village, 1981.* University of Utah Archaeological Center Reports of Investigations No. 81–19. Salt Lake City.

Jones, K. T., and J. F. O'Connell. 1981. *Archeological Research at Nawthis Village, 1980.* University of Utah Archaeological Center Reports of Investigations No. 81-4. Salt Lake City.

Jones, M. 2003. Ancient DNA in Pre-Columbian Archaeology: A Review. *Journal of Archaeological Science* 30:629–635.

Jones, T. L., W. R. Hildebrandt, D. J. Kennett, and J. F. Porcasi. 2004. Prehistoric Marine Mammal Overkill in the Northeastern Pacific: A Review of New Evidence. *Journal of California and Great Basin Anthropology* 24:69–80.

Jones, T. L., and K. A. Klar. 2007. Colonization, Culture, and Complexity. In *California Prehistory: Colonization, Culture, and Complexity,* edited by T. L. Jones and K. A. Klar, pp. 299–315. AltaMira Press, Walnut Creek.

Jordan, A., and R. K. Talbot. 2002. *The BYU Escalante Drainage Project: Big Flat and Escalante Canyon 2001.* Museum of Peoples and Cultures Technical Series 01-13. Brigham Young University, Provo, Utah.

Jorgensen, J. 1992. Foreword. In *Ute Tales* by A. M. Smith, pp. xi–xxiv. University of Utah Press, Salt Lake City.

Judd, N. M. 1919. *Archaeological Investigations at Paragonah, Utah.* Smithsonian Institution Miscellaneous Collections 70:1–22.

———. 1926. *Archaeological Observations North of the Rio Colorado.* Bulletin No. 82. Bureau of American Ethnology, Smithsonian Institution, Washington D.C.

Kaestle, F. A., J. G. Lorenz, and D. G. Smith. 1999. Molecular Genetics and the Numic Expansion: A Molecular Investigation of the Prehistoric Inhabitants of Stillwater Marsh. In *Understanding Prehistoric Lifeways in the Great Basin Wetlands: Bioarchaeological Reconstruction and Interpretation,* edited by B. E. Hemphill and C. S. Larsen, pp. 167–183. University of Utah Press, Salt Lake City.

Kaestle, F. A., and D. G. Smith. 2001. Ancient Mitochondrial DNA Evidence for a Prehistoric Population Movement: The Numic Expansion. *American Journal of Physical Anthropology* 115:1–12.

Kaplan, H., and K. Hill. 1992. The Evolutionary Ecology of Food Acquisition. In *Evolutionary Ecology and Human Behavior,* edited by E. A. Smith and B. Winterhalder, pp. 167–202. Aldine de Gruyter, New York.

Karafet T. S., L. Zegura, J. Brady, L. Osipova, V. Weibe, F. Romero, J. C. Long, S. Harihara, F. Jin, B. Dashnyam, T. Gerelsaikhan, K. Omoto, and M. F. Hammer. 1997. Y Chromosome Markers and Trans-Bering Strait Dispersals. *American Journal of Physical Anthropology* 102:301–314.

Kealhofer, L. 1996. The Evidence for Demographic Collapse in California. In *Bioarchaeology of Native American Adaptation in the Spanish Borderlands*, edited by B. J. Baker and L. Kealhofer, pp. 56–92. University Press of Florida, Gainesville.

Kay, C. E. 1994. Aboriginal Overkill: The Role of Native Americans in Structuring Western Ecosystems. *Human Nature* 5:359–396.

———. 1995. Aboriginal Overkill and Native Burning: Implications for Modern Ecosystem Management. *Western Journal of Applied Forestry* 10:121–126.

———. 2002. Are Ecosystems Structured from the Top-Down or Bottom-Up? A New Look at an Old Debate. In *Wilderness and Political Economy: Aboriginal Influences and the Original State of Nature*, edited by C. E. Kay and R. T. Simmons, pp. 215–237. University of Utah Press, Salt Lake City.

Kay, C. E., and R. T. Simmons (eds.). 2002. *Wilderness and Political Economy: Aboriginal Influences and the Original State of Nature*. University of Utah Press, Salt Lake City.

Keeley, L. H. 1996. *War Before Civilization*. Oxford University Press, New York.

Kelly, I. T. 1932. *Ethnography of the Surprise Valley Paiute*. University of California Publications in American Archaeology and Ethnology 31:67–210.

———. 1964. *Southern Paiute Ethnography*. Anthropological Papers No. 69. University of Utah Press, Salt Lake City.

Kelly, R. L. 1983. Hunter-Gatherer Mobility Strategies. *Journal of Anthropological Research* 39:277–306.

———. 1988. The Three Sides of a Biface. *American Antiquity* 53:717–734.

———. 1995. *The Foraging Spectrum: Diversity in Hunter-Gatherer Lifeways*. Smithsonian Institution Press, Washington D.C.

———. 1997. Late Holocene Great Basin Prehistory. *Journal of World Prehistory* 11:1–49.

———. 2001. *Prehistory of the Carson Desert and Stillwater Mountains: Environment, Mobility, and Subsistence in a Great Basin Wetland*. Anthropological Papers No. 123. University of Utah Press, Salt Lake City.

———. 2003. Maybe We Do Know When People First Came to North America; and What Does It Mean If We Do? *Quaternary International* 109–110:133–145.

Kelly, R. L., D. A. Byers, W. Eckerle, P. Goldberg, C. V. Haynes, R. M. Larsen, J. Laughlin, J. I. Mead, and S. Wall. 2006. Multiple Approaches to Formation Processes: The Pine Spring Site, Southwest Wyoming. *Geoarchaeology* 21:615–638.

Kelly, R. L., and L. C. Todd. 1988. Coming into the Country: Early Paleo-Indian Hunting and Mobility. *American Antiquity* 53:231–244.

Kemp, B. M., R. S. Mahli, J. McDonough, D. A. Bolnick, J. A. Eshleman, O. Rickards, C. Martinez-Labarga, J. R. Johnson, J. G. Lorenz, E. J. Dixon, T. E. Fifield, T. H. Heaton, R. Worl, and D. G. Smith. 2007. Genetic Analysis of Early Holocene Skeletal Remains from Alaska and Its Implications for the Settlement of the Americas. *American Journal of Physical Anthropology* 132:605–621.

Kennedy, O. A. 1930. *Old Indian Relics of Willard Puzzle*. Salt Lake Tribune. Charles Kelly collection, scrapbook on archaeology, box 8, file 7. Utah State Historical Society, Salt Lake City.

Kennett, D. J. 2005. *The Island Chumash: Behavioral Ecology of a Maritime Society*. University of California Press, Berkeley and Los Angeles.

Kennett, D. J., J. Erlandson, T. J. Braje, and B. J. Culleton. 2007. Exploring the Human Ecology of the Younger Dryas Extraterrestrial Impact Event. Joint Assembly of the American Geophysical Union. May 22–25. Acapulco, Mexico.

Kerns, V. 2003. *Scenes from the High Desert: Julian Steward's Life and Theory*. University of Illinois Press, Urbana.

Kluckhohn, C. 1949. *Mirror for Man: The Relation of Anthropology to Modern Life*. Whittlesey House, New York.

Koehler, P A., R. Scott Anderson, and W. Geoff Spaulding. 2005. Development of Vegetation in the Central Mojave Desert of California during the Late Quaternary. *Palaeogeography, Palaeoclimatology, Palaeoecology* 215:297–311.

Kooyman, B., M. E. Newman, C. Cluney, M. Lobb, S. Tolman, P. McNeil, and L. H. Hills. 2001. Identification of Horse Exploitation by Clovis Hunters Based on Protein Analysis. *American Antiquity* 66:686–691.

Krech, S. 1999. *The Ecological Indian: Myth and History*. W. W. Norton and Co., New York.

Kroeber, A. L. 1953. *Handbook of the Indians of California*. California Book Company. Originally, Bureau of American Ethnology Bulletin 78.

———. 1955. Linguistic Time Depths Results So Far and Their Meaning. *International Journal of American Linguistics* 21:91–109.

LaMarche, V. C. 1974. Paleoclimatic Inferences from Long Tree-Ring Records. *Science* 183:1043–1048.

Lamb, H. H. 1982. *Climate, History and the Modern World*. Methuen, London.

Lamb, S. 1958. Linguistic Prehistory in the Great Basin. *International Journal of American Linguistics* 24:95–100.

Lambert, P. M. 1997. Patterns of Violence in Prehistoric Hunter-Gatherer Societies in Coastal Southern California. In *Troubled Times*, edited by D. L. Martek and D. W. Frayer, pp. 77–109. Gordon and Breach, Amsterdam.

Lambert, P. M., and S. R. Simms. 2003. *Archaeology and Analysis of Prehistoric Human Remains Near Willard Bay, Utah*. Utah State University Contributions to Anthropology No. 33. Logan.

Lambert, P. M., and P. L. Walker. 1991. Physical Anthropological Evidence for the Evolution of Social Complexity in Coastal Southern California. *Antiquity* 65:963–973.

Lanner, R. 1981. *The Pinyon Pine: A Natural and Cultural History.* University of Nevada Press, Reno.

Larsen, C. S., and D. L. Hutchinson. 1999. Osteopathology of Carson Desert Foragers: Reconstructing Prehistoric Lifeways in the Western Great Basin. In *Prehistoric Lifeways in the Great Basin Wetlands: Bioarchaeological Reconstruction and Interpretation,* edited by B. E. Hemphill and C. S. Larsen, pp. 184–202. University of Utah Press, Salt Lake City.

Larsen, C. S., and R. L. Kelly. 1995. *Bioarchaeology of the Stillwater Marsh: Prehistoric Human Adaptation in the Western Great Basin.* Anthropological Papers of the American Museum of Natural History 77.

Larson, M. L. 1997. Housepits and Mobile Hunter-Gatherers: A Consideration of the Wyoming Evidence. *Plains Anthropologist* 42:353–369.

LeBlanc, S. A. 2002. Conflict and Language Dispersal: Issues and a New World Example. In *Examining the Farming/Language Dispersal Hypothesis,* edited by P. Bellwood and C. Renfrew, pp. 357–365. McDonald Institute Monographs, Oxbow Books, Oxford.

LeBlanc, S., and K. E. Register. 2003. *Constant Battles: The Myth of the Peaceful, Noble Savage.* St. Martins Press, New York.

Lekson, S. H. 1999. *The Chaco Meridian: Centers of Political Power in the Ancient Southwest.* AltaMira Press, Walnut Creek, California.

Lekson, S. H., C. P. Nepstad-Thornberry, B. E. Yunker, T. S. Laumbach, D. P. Cain, K. W. Laumbach. 2002. Migrations in the Southwest: Pinnacle Ruin, Southwestern New Mexico. *Kiva* 68:73–97.

Lewis, H. T. 2002. An Anthropological Critique. In *Forgotten Fires: Native Americans and the Transient Wilderness* by O. C. Stewart, pp. 17–36. University of Oklahoma Press, Norman.

Lightfoot, K., A. Martinez, and A. M. Schiff. 1998. Daily Practice and Material Culture in Pluralistic Social Settings: An Archaeological Study of Culture Change and Persistence from Fort Ross, California. *American Antiquity* 63:199–222.

Liljeblad, S. 1986. Oral Tradition: Content and Style of Verbal Arts. In *Handbook of North American Indians,* Vol. 11: Great Basin, edited by W. L. d'Azevedo, pp. 660–672. Smithsonian Institution Press, Washington D.C.

Lindsay, C. 2005. Late Prehistoric/Protohistoric Demography. In *Kern River 2003 Expansion Project,* Vol. 4: Chapter 20, edited by A. D. Reed, M. T. Seddon, and H. K. Stettler, pp. 381–392. Alpine Archaeological Consultants, Montrose, Colorado and SWCA Environmental Consultants, Salt Lake City.

Lindsay, L. W. 1986. Fremont Fragmentation. In *Anthropology of the Desert West: Essays in Honor of Jesse D. Jennings,* edited by C. J. Condie and D.

D. Fowler, pp. 229–251. Anthropological Papers No. 110. University of Utah Press, Salt Lake City.

Livingston, S. D. 2000. The Homestead Cave Avifauna. In *Late Quaternary Paleoecology in the Bonneville Basin,* by D. B. Madsen, pp. 91–102. Utah Geological Survey Bulletin 130. Salt Lake City.

Long, A., B. Benz, J. Donahue, A. Jull, and L. Toolin. 1989. First Direct AMS Dates on Early Maize from Tehuacan, Mexico. *Radiocarbon* 31:1035–1040.

Loud, L. L., and M. R. Harrington. 1929. *Lovelock Cave.* University of California Publications in American Archaeology and Ethnology 25. Berkeley and Los Angeles.

Louthan, B. D. 1990. Orchard Pithouse. *Canyon Legacy* 7:24–27.

Loveland, C. J., D. Furlong, and J. B. Gregg. 1992. Deformity and Left Hip Fusion in a Prehistoric Great Basin Skeleton. *Utah Archaeology* 5:107–115.

Loveland, C. J., and J. B. Gregg. 1994. Probable Metastatic Carcinoma in a Prehistoric Great Basin Skeleton. *Utah Archaeology* 7:81–87.

Lowie, R. 1909. *The Northern Shoshone.* Anthropological Papers of the American Museum of Natural History, Vol. 2:165–306. New York.

Lupo, K. D., and K. L. Wintch. 1998. Carcass Corners (42WN1975): A Late Archaic Site in Wayne County, Utah. *Utah Archaeology* 11:33–42.

Lyneis, M. M. 1982. Prehistory in the Southern Great Basin. In *Man and Environment in the Great Basin,* edited by D. B. Madsen and J. F. O'Connell, pp. 172–185. Society for American Archaeology Papers No. 2. Washington D.C.

MacPhee, R., and P. Marx. 1997. The 40,000-year Plague: Humans, Hyperdisease, and First-Contact Extinctions. In *Natural Change and Human Impact in Madagascar,* edited by S. M. Goodman and B. D. Patterson, pp. 169–217, Smithsonian Institution Press, Washington D.C.

Madsen, D. B. 1976. *Bulldozer Dune(42SL46).* Antiquities Section Selected Papers, Vol. 2: No. 6. Utah State Historical Society, Salt Lake City.

———. 1979. *Preliminary Analysis of Prehistoric Occupation Patterns, Subsistence Adaptations, and Chronology in the Fish Springs Area, Utah.* Prepared for the U.S. Fish and Wildlife Service and the Bureau of Land Management by the Antiquities Section, Utah Division of State History, Salt Lake City.

———. 1982a. Get It Where the Gettin's Good: A Variable Model of Great Basin Subsistence and Settlement Based on Data from the Eastern Great Basin. In *Man and Environment in the Great Basin,* edited by D. B. Madsen and J. F. O'Connell, pp. 207–226. Society for American Archaeology Papers No. 2. Washington D.C.

———. 1982b. Salvage Excavations at Ticaboo Town ruin (42Ga2295). In *Archaeological Investigations at Fish Springs, Clay Basin, Northern San Rafael Swell, Southern Henry Mountains,* edited by D. B. Madsen and R. L. Fike. Utah Bureau of Land Management Cultural Resources Series 12. Salt Lake City.

———. 1983. *Black Rock Cave Revisited*. Bureau of Land Management, Utah, Cultural Resource Series No. 14. Salt Lake City.

———. 1986. Great Basin Nuts. In *Anthropology of the Desert West: Essays in Honor of Jesse D. Jennings*, edited by C. J. Condie and D. D. Fowler, pp. 21–41. Anthropological Papers No. 110. University of Utah Press, Salt Lake City.

———. 1989a. A Grasshopper in Every Pot. *Natural History*. July.

———. 1989b. *Exploring the Fremont*. Utah Museum of Natural History. University of Utah Press, Salt Lake City.

———. 1994. Mesa Verde and Sleeping Ute Mountain: The Geographical and Chronological Dimensions of the Numic Expansion. In *Across the West: Human Population Movement and the Expansion of the Numa*, edited by D. B. Madsen and D. Rhode, pp. 24–31. University of Utah Press, Salt Lake City.

———. 1999. The Nature of Great Basin Environmental Change during the Pleistocene/Holocene Transition and Its Possible Impact on Human Populations. In *Models for the Millennium: Great Basin Anthropology Today*, edited by C. Beck, pp. 75–82. University of Utah Press, Salt Lake City.

———. 2000. A High-Elevation Allerod-Younger Dryas Megafauna from the West-Central Rocky Mountains. In *Intermountain Archaeology*, edited by D. B. Madsen and M. D. Metcalf, pp. 100–115. Anthropological Papers No. 122. University of Utah Press, Salt Lake City.

———. 2001. Great Basin Peoples and Late Quaternary Aquatic History. In *Great Basin Aquatic System History*. Smithsonian Contributions to Earth Sciences No. 33, edited by R. Hershler, D. B. Madsen, and D. R. Currey, pp. 387–405. Smithsonian Institution Press, Washington D.C.

Madsen, D. B., and M. S. Berry. 1975. A Reassessment of Northeastern Great Basin Prehistory. *American Antiquity* 40:391–405.

Madsen, D. B., and J. E. Kirkman. 1988. Hunting Hoppers. *American Antiquity* 53:593–604.

Madsen, D. B., and D. Rhode. 1990. Early Holocene Pinyon (*Pinus monophylla*) in the Northeastern Great Basin. *Quaternary Research* 33: 94–101.

Madsen, D. B., and D. Rhode (eds.). 1994. *Across the West: Human Population Movement and the Expansion of the Numa*. University of Utah Press, Salt Lake City.

Madsen, D. B., D. Rhode, D. K. Grayson, J. M. Broughton, S. D. Livingston, J. Hunt, J. Quade, D. N. Schmitt, and M. W. Shaver III. 2001. Late Quaternary Environmental Change in the Bonneville Basin, Western USA. *Palaeogeography, Palaeoclimatology, Palaeoecology* 167:243–271.

Madsen, D. B., and D. N. Schmitt. 2005. *Buzz-Cut Dune and Fremont Foraging at the Margin of Horticulture.* Anthropological Papers No. 124. University of Utah Press, Salt Lake City.

Madsen, D. B., and S. R. Simms. 1998. The Fremont Complex: A Behavioral Perspective. *Journal of World Prehistory* 12:255–336.

Mahli, R. S., H. M. Mortensen, J. A. Eshleman, B. M. Kemp, J. G. Lorenz, F. A. Kaestle, J. R. Johson, C. Gorodezky, and D. G. Smith. 2003. Native American mtDNA Prehistory in the American Southwest. *American Journal of Physical Anthropology* 120:108–124.

Mann, C. C. 2005. *1491: New Revelations of the Americas Before Columbus.* Alfred A. Knopf, New York.

Martin, P. S. 1958. Pleistocene Ecology and Biogeography of North America. In *Zoogeography*, edited by C. L. Hubbs, pp. 375–420. American Association for the Advancement of Science Publication 51. Washington D.C.

———. 1984. Prehistoric Overkill: The Global Model. In *Quaternary Extinctions: A Prehistoric Revolution*, edited by P. S. Martin and R. G. Klein, pp. 354–403. University of Arizona Press, Tucson.

———. 1990. 40,000 Years on the Planet of Doom. *Palaeogeography, Palaeoclimatology, Palaeoecology* 82:187–201.

———. 2002. Prehistoric Extinctions: In the Shadow of Man. In *Wilderness and Political Economy: Aboriginal Influences and the Original State of Nature*, edited by C. E. Kay and R. T. Simmons, pp. 1–27. University of Utah Press, Salt Lake City.

Marwitt, J. P. 1970. *Median Village and Fremont Culture Regional Variation.* Anthropological Papers No. 95. University of Utah Press, Salt Lake City.

Matheny, R. T. (ed.). 2004. *New Dimensions in Rock Art Studies.* Brigham Young University Museum of Peoples and Cultures, Occasional Papers No. 9. University of Utah Press, Salt Lake City.

Matson, R. G. 1991. *The Origins of Southwest Agriculture.* University of Arizona Press, Tucson.

———. 2002. The Spread of Maize Agriculture in the U.S. Southwest. In *Examining the Farming/Language Dispersal Hypothesis*, edited by P. Bellwood and C. Renfrew, pp. 341–356. McDonald Institute Monographs, Oxbow Books, Oxford.

McDonald, J. N. 1984. The Reordered North American Selection Regime and Late Quaternary Megafaunal Extinctions. In *Quaternary Extinctions: A Prehistoric Revolution*, edited by P. S. Martin and R. G. Klein, pp. 404–439. University of Arizona Press, Tucson.

McDonald, S. 2000. Archaic Use of the Wasatch Plateau Uplands: A Preliminary View. In *Intermountain Archaeology*, edited by D. B. Madsen and M. D. Metcalf, pp. 124–131. Anthropological Papers No. 122. University of Utah Press, Salt Lake City.

McGuire, K. R., and W. R. Hildebrandt. 2005. Re-Thinking Great Basin Foragers: Prestige Hunting and Costly Signaling during the Middle Archaic Period. *American Antiquity* 70:695–712.

McKenzie, J. A., and G. P. Eberlie. 1987. Indications for Abrupt Holocene Climatic Change: Late Holocene Oxygen Isotope Stratigraphy of the Great Salt Lake, Utah. In *Abrupt Climatic Change*, edited by W. H. Berger and L. D. Labeyrie, pp. 127–136. Reidel, Dordrecht, The Netherlands.

McPhee, J. A. 1981. *Basin and Range.* Farrar, Straus, and Giroux, New York.

Mehringer, P. 1985. Late Quaternary Pollen Records from the Interior Pacific Northwest and Northern Great Basin of the United States. In *Pollen Records of Late-Quaternary North American Sediments*, edited by V. M. Bryant, Jr. and R. G. Holloway, pp. 167–190. American Association of Stratigraphic Palynologists, Dallas.

Meighan, C. W. 1958. Archaeology of Paragonah. Ms. on file, Department of Anthropology, University of California, Los Angeles.

Meltzer, D. 1993. *Search for the First Americans.* Smithsonian Institution Press, Washington D.C.

Meltzer, D., D. Grayson, G. Ardila, A. Barker, D. Dincauze, C. Vance Haynes, Jr., F. Mena, L. Nunez, and D. Stanford. 1997. On the Pleistocene Antiquity of Monte Verde, Southern Chile. *American Antiquity* 62: 659–663.

Metcalfe, D. 1983. 1982 Excavations at Nawthis Village. *The UPAC News* 1:4–5. Utah Division of State History, Salt Lake City.

———. 1984. *Gooseberry Archaeological Project: 1983.* University of Utah Archeological Center Reports of Investigations No. 83-1. Salt Lake City.

Metcalfe, D., and K. Heath. 1990. Microrefuse and Site Structure: The Hearths and Floors of the Heartbreak Hotel. *American Antiquity* 55:781–796.

Metcalfe, D., and L. Larrabee. 1985. Fremont Irrigation: Evidence from Gooseberry Valley. *Journal of California and Great Basin Anthropology* 7:244–253.

Miller, S. J. 1972. *Weston Canyon Rockshelter: Big-Game Hunting in Southeastern Idaho.* Unpublished Master's thesis. Department of Anthropology, Idaho State University, Pocatello.

Miller, W. R. 1972. *Newe Natekwinappeh: Shoshoni Stories and Dictionary.* Anthropological Papers No. 94. University of Utah Press, Salt Lake City.

———. 1986. Numic Languages. In *Handbook of North American Indians*, Vol. 11: Great Basin, edited by W. L. d'Azevedo, pp. 98–107. Smithsonian Institution Press, Washington D.C.

Miller, W. R., J. L. Tanner, and L. P. Foley. 1971. A Lexicostatistical Study of Shoshoni Dialects. *Anthropological Linguistics* 13:142–164.

Minnis, P. E. 1985. Domesticating Plants and People in the Greater American Southwest. In *Prehistoric Food Production in North America,* edited by R. I. Ford, pp. 309–340. Museum of Anthropology Papers No. 75. University of Michigan, Ann Arbor.

Mock, J. M. 1971. Archaeology of Spotten Cave, Utah County, Central Utah. Unpublished Masters Thesis, Department of Anthropology, Brigham Young University, Provo, Utah.

Moore, J. A. 1985. Forager/Farmer Interactions: Information, Social Organization, and the Frontier. In *The Archaeology of Frontiers and Boundaries,* edited by S. W. Green and S. M. Perlman, pp. 93–112. Academic Press, Orlando.

Morss, N. 1931. *The Ancient Culture of the Fremont River in Utah.* Papers of the Peabody Museum of American Archaeology and Ethnology 12(2). Cambridge, Massachusetts.

Murchison, S. B. 1989. *Fluctuation History of Great Salt Lake, Utah, during the Last 13,000 Years.* Limnotectonics Laboratory Technical Report 89–2. Department of Geography, University of Utah, Salt Lake City.

Murchison, S., and W. E. Mulvey. 2000. Late Pleistocene and Holocene Shoreline Stratigraphy on Antelope Island. In *Geology of Antelope Island,* edited by J. K. King and Grant C. Willis, pp. 77–83. Utah Geological Survey Miscellaneous Publication 00-1.

Murphy, R. F., and Y. Murphy. 1960. *Shoshone-Bannock Subsistence and Society.* University of California Anthropological Records, Vol.16: pp. 293–338. Berkeley.

Nabokov, P. 2002. *A Forest of Time: American Indian Ways of History.* Cambridge University Press, United Kingdom.

Napton, L. K. 1997. The Spirit Cave Mummy: Coprolite Investigations. In *Papers on Holocene Burial Localities Presented at the Twenty-Fifth Great Basin Anthropological Conference, October 10–12, 1996,* edited by D. Tuohy and A. Dansie. *Nevada Historical Society Quarterly* 40(1): 97–104.

Nelson, M. C., and M. Hegmon. 2001. Abandonment Is Not as It Seems: An Approach to the Relationship Between Site and Regional Abandonment. *American Antiquity* 66:213–235.

Nelson, N. F. 1954. *Factors in the Development and Restoration of Waterfowl Habitat at Ogden Bay Refuge, Weber County, Utah.* Utah State Department of Fish and Game Publication No. 6. Salt Lake City.

Novak, S. A., and D. D. Kollmann. 2000. Perimortem Processing of Human Remains among the Great Basin Fremont. *International Journal of Osteoarchaeology* 10:65–75.

O'Connell, J. F. 1975. *The Prehistory of Surprise Valley.* Ballena Press, Ramona, California.

O'Connell, J. F., and K. Hawkes. 1981. Alyawara Plant Use and Optimal Foraging Theory. In *Hunter-Gatherer Foraging Strategies: Ethnographic and Archaeological Analyses,* edited by B. Winterhalder and E. Smith, pp. 99–125. University of Chicago Press.

O'Connell, J. F., K. T. Jones, and S. R. Simms. 1982. Some Thoughts on Prehistoric Archaeology in the Great Basin. In *Man and Environment in the Great Basin,* edited by D. B. Madsen and J. F. O'Connell, pp. 227–240. Society for American Archaeology Papers No. 2. Washington D.C.

Oetting, A. C. 1999. An Examination of Wetland Adaptive Strategies in Harney Basin: Comparing Ethnographic Paradigms and the Archaeological Record. In *Prehistoric Lifeways in the Great Basin Wetlands: Bioarchaeological Reconstruction and Interpretation,* edited by B. E. Hemphill and C. S. Larsen, pp. 203–218. University of Utah Press, Salt Lake City.

O'Rourke, D. H., R. L. Parr, and S. Carlyle. 1999. Molecular Genetic Variation in Prehistoric Inhabitants of the Eastern Great Basin. In *Prehistoric Lifeways in the Great Basin Wetlands: Bioarchaeological Reconstruction and Interpretation,* edited by B. E. Hemphill and C. S. Larsen, pp. 84–102. University of Utah Press, Salt Lake City.

Ouzman, S. 2004. Toward a Mindscape of Landscape: Rock-Art as Expression of World-Understanding. In *The Archaeology of Rock Art,* edited by C. Chippindale and P. S. C. Tacon, pp. 30–41. Cambridge University Press.

Oviatt, C. G. 1987. Lake Bonneville Stratigraphy at the Old River Bed. *American Journal of Science* 287:383–398.

———. 1997. Lake Bonneville Fluctuations and Global Climate Change. *Geology* 25:155–158.

Oviatt, C. G., D. R. Currey, and D. Sack. 1992. Radiocarbon Chronology of Lake Bonneville, Eastern Great Basin, USA. *Palaeogeography, Palaeoclimatology, Palaeoecology* 99:225–241.

Oviatt, C. G., D. B. Madsen, and D. N. Schmitt. 2003. Late Pleistocene and Early Holocene Rivers and Wetlands in the Bonneville Basin of Western North America. *Quaternary Research* 60:200–210.

Park, W. Z. 1938. *Shamanism in Western North America: A Study in Cultural Relationships.* Cooper Square Publishers, New York.

Parmalee, P. W. 1988. Avian Remains from Danger Cave. In *Danger Cave, Last Supper Cave, and Hanging Rock Shelter: The Faunas,* by D. K. Grayson, pp. 37–43. Anthropological Papers of the American Museum of Natural History Vol. 66: Pt. 1. American Museum of Natural History, New York.

Pendergast, D. M. 1961. *Excavations at the Bear River Site, Box Elder County, Utah.* Utah Archaeology 7, No. 2.

Pendergast, D. M., and C. W. Meighan. 1959. Folk Traditions as Historical Fact: A Paiute Example. *Journal of American Folklore* 73:132.

Pennington, R. 2001. Hunter-Gatherer Demography. In *Hunter-Gatherers: An Interdisciplinary Perspective,* edited by C. Panter-Brick, R. H. Layton, and P. Rowley-Conwy, pp. 170–204. Cambridge University Press, New York.

Peregrine, P. N. 2001. Matrilocality, Corporate Strategy, and the Organization of Production in the Chacoan World. *American Antiquity* 66:36–46.

Pettigrew, R. M. 1980. *The Ancient Chewaucanians: More on the Prehistoric Lake Dwellers of Lake Abert, Southwestern Oregon*. Association of Oregon Archaeologists, Occasional Papers 1:49–67.

Pinson, A. O. 1998. Subsistence and Settlement Patterns during the Pleistocene-Holocene Transition in the Northern Great Basin: The View from Dietz Basin. *Current Research in the Pleistocene* 15:60–62.

———. 1999. *Foraging in Uncertain Times: The Effects of Risk on Subsistence Behavior during the Pleistocene-Holocene Transition in the Oregon Great Basin*. Ph.D. dissertation, University of New Mexico, Albuquerque. University Microfilms, Ann Arbor, Michigan.

———. 2004. Of Lakeshores and Dry Basin Floors: The Early Holocene Record of Environmental Change and Human Adaptation at the Tucker Site in Regional Perspective. In *Early and Middle Holocene Archaeology of the Fort Rock Region in the Northern Great Basin*, edited by D. Jenkins, T. Connolly, and C. M. Aikens. University of Oregon Anthropological Papers 62, Eugene.

Pitblado, B. L. 2003. *Late Paleoindian Occupation of the Southern Rocky Mountains: Early Holocene Projectile Points and Land Use in the High Country*. University Press of Colorado, Boulder.

Plew, M. G. 2000. *The Archaeology of the Snake River Plain*. Department of Anthropology, Boise State University. Boise, Idaho.

Pratt, P. Y. 1849. Correspondence from America. Letter dated July 8. *The Millennial Star* 11:342–343.

Preston, W. L. 1996. Serpent in Eden: Dispersal of Foreign Disease into Pre-Mission California. *Journal of California and Great Basin Anthropology* 18:2–37.

———. 2001. Portents of Plague from California's Protohistoric Period. *Ethnohistory* 49:69–121.

Pritchett, C. L., H. H. Frost, and W. W. Tanner. 1981. Terrestrial Vertebrates in the Environs of Utah Lake. In *Utah Lake Monograph*, pp. 125–169. Great Basin Naturalist Memoirs No. 5. Provo.

Quinlan, A. 2007. *Great Basin Rock Art: Archaeological Perspectives*. University of Nevada Press, Reno.

Raab, L. M., and D. O. Larsen. 1997. Medieval Climatic Anomaly and Punctuated Cultural Evolution in Coastal Southern California. *American Antiquity* 62:319–336.

Ramenovsky, A. F. 1987. *Vectors of Death: The Archaeology of European Contact*. University of New Mexico Press, Albuquerque.

Raven, C. 1990. *Prehistoric Human Geography in the Carson Desert*, pt. 2, *Archaeological Field Tests of Model Predictions*. U.S. Fish and Wildlife Service Cultural Resource Series No. 4. Portland, Oregon.

Raven, C., and R. G. Elston (eds.). 1988. *Preliminary Investigations in Stillwater Marsh: Human Prehistory and Geoarchaeology*. U.S. Fish and Wildlife Service Cultural Resource Series No. 1. Portland, Oregon.

———. 1989. *Prehistoric Human Geography in the Carson Desert*, pt. 1, *A Predictive Model of Land-Use in the Stillwater Wildlife Management Area*. U.S. Fish and Wildlife Service Cultural Resource Series No. 3. Portland, Oregon.

Raymond, A. 1982. Two Historic Game Drive Enclosures in the Eastern Great Basin. *Journal of California and Great Basin Anthropology* 4:23–33.

Reed, A. 1990. Evidence of Arrow Points from Basketmaker II Sites in Southwestern Colorado. *Utah Archaeology* 3:139–141.

———. 2001. *The TransColorado Natural Gas Pipeline Archaeological Data Recovery Project, Western Colorado and Northwestern New Mexico*. Alpine Archaeological Consultants, Inc., Montrose, Colorado.

———. 2005. Instrumental Neutron Activation Analysis. In *Kern River 2003 Expansion Project*, Vol. 4: Chapter 15, edited by A. D. Reed, M. T. Seddon, and H. K. Stettler, pp. 295–306. Alpine Archaeological Consultants, Montrose, Colorado and SWCA Environmental Consultants, Salt Lake City.

Reed, A. D., M. T. Seddon, and H. K. Stettler. 2003. *Kern River 2003 Expansion Project*. Alpine Archaeological Consultants, Montrose, Colorado and SWCA Environmental Consultants, Salt Lake City.

Reed, E. 1955. Human Skeletal Remains from the Turner-Look Site. In *A Reappraisal of the Fremont Culture* by H. M. Wormington, pp. 38–43. Proceedings of the Denver Museum of Natural History No. 1.

Reff, D. T. 1991. *Disease, Depopulation, and Culture Change in Northwestern New Spain A.D. 1518–1764*. University of Utah Press, Salt Lake City.

Rhode, D. 1994. Direct Dating of Brown Ware Ceramics Using Thermoluminescence and Its Relation to the Numic Spread. In *Across the West: Human Population Movement and the Expansion of the Numa*, edited by D. B. Madsen and D. Rhode, pp. 124–132. University of Utah Press, Salt Lake City.

———. 2000. Holocene Vegetation History in the Bonneville Basin. In *Late Quaternary Paleoecology in the Bonneville Basin*, by D. B. Madsen, pp. 149–163. Utah Geological Survey Bulletin 130. Salt Lake City.

Rhode, D., and D. B. Madsen. 1998. Pine Nut Use in the Early Holocene and Beyond: The Danger Cave Archaeological Record. *Journal of Archaeological Science* 25:1199–1210.

Richens, L. D., and R. K. Talbot. 1989. Sandy Ridge: An Aceramic Habitation Site in Southeastern Utah. *Utah Archaeology* 2:77–88.

Rockman, M., and J. Steele (eds.). 2003. *Colonization of Unfamiliar Landscapes: The Archaeology of Adaptation.* Routledge, New York.

Roe, F. G. 1955. *The Indian and the Horse.* University of Oklahoma Press, Norman.

Rogers, G. F. 1982. *Then and Now: A Photographic History of Vegetation Change in the Central Great Basin Desert.* University of Utah Press, Salt Lake City.

Ronaasen, S., R. O. Clemmer, and M. E. Rudden. 1999. Rethinking Cultural Ecology, Multilinear Evolution, and Expert Witnesses: Julian Steward and the Indian Claims Commission Proceedings. In *Julian Steward and the Great Basin: The Making of an Anthropologist,* edited by R. O. Clemmer, L. D. Myers, and M. E. Rudden, pp. 170–202. University of Utah Press, Salt Lake City.

Ruff, C. B. 1999. Skeletal Structure and Behavioral Patterns of Prehistoric Great Basin Populations. In *Prehistoric Lifeways in the Great Basin Wetlands: Bioarchaeological Reconstruction and Interpretation,* edited by B. E. Hemphill and C. S. Larsen, pp. 290–320. University of Utah Press, Salt Lake City.

Russell, D. J. 1989. Bone Whistles of Northern Utah. *Utah Archaeology* 2:48–55.

Russell, K. W., M. E. Stuart, J. A. Brannan, and H. M. Weymouth. 1989. *Archaeological Reconnaissance in the Ogden/Weber River Marshes.* Weber State College Reports of Investigation No. 89-1. Ogden, Utah.

Russell, O. 1965. *Journal of a Trapper (1834–1843),* edited by A. L. Haines. Originally published 1955. University of Nebraska Press, Lincoln.

Schaafsma, P. 1971. *The Rock Art of Utah.* University of Utah Press, Salt Lake City.

———. 1980. *Indian Rock Art of the Southwest.* University of New Mexico Press, Albuquerque.

Schlegel, A. 1992. African Political Models in the American Southwest: Hopi as an Internal Frontier Society. *American Anthropologist* 94:376–397.

Schmitt, D. N., and D. B. Madsen. 2005. *The Archaeology of Camels Back Cave.* Anthropological Papers No. 125. University of Utah Press, Salt Lake City.

Schneider, D. 1961. Introduction: The Distinctive Features of Matrilineal Descent. In *Matrilineal Kinship,* edited by D. Schneider and K. Gough, pp. 1–31. University of California Press, Berkeley and Los Angeles.

Schroedl, A. R. 1977. The Grand Canyon Figurine Complex. *American Antiquity* 42:254–265.

———. 1991. Paleo-Indian Occupation in the Eastern Great Basin and Northern Colorado Plateau. *Utah Archaeology* 4:1–16.

Schwartz, D. W., A. L. Lange, and R. deSaussure. 1958. Split-Twig Figurines in the Grand Canyon. *American Antiquity* 23:264–274.

Seddon, M. T. 2005. A Revised Model of Obsidian Procurement and Use in the Eastern Great Basin. In *Kern River 2003 Expansion Project,* Vol. 4: Chapter 35, edited by A. D. Reed, M. T. Seddon, and H. K. Stettler, pp. 687–708. Alpine Archaeological Consultants, Montrose, Colorado and SWCA Environmental Consultants, Salt Lake City.

Shapiro, J. 1986. Kinship. In *Handbook of North American Indians,* Vol. 11: Great Basin, edited by W. L. d'Azevedo, pp. 620–629. Smithsonian Institution Press, Washington D.C.

Shaul, D. L. 1986. Linguistic Adaptation and the Great Basin. *American Antiquity* 51:415–416.

Shock, M. P. 2007. A Regional Settlement System Approach to Petroglyphs: Application to the Owyhee Uplands, Southeastern Oregon. In *Great Basin Rock Art: Archaeological Perspectives,* edited by A. R. Quinlan, pp. 69–91. University of Nevada Press, Reno.

Simms, S. R. 1977. A Mid Archaic Subsistence and Settlement Shift in the Northeastern Great Basin. In Models and Great Basin Prehistory: A Symposium, edited by D. D. Fowler. *Desert Research Institute Publications in the Social Sciences* 12.

———. 1983a. The Effects of Grinding Stone Reuse on the Archaeological Record of the Eastern Great Basin. *Journal of California and Great Basin Anthropology* 5:98–102.

———. 1983b. Comments on Bettinger and Baumhoff's Explanation of the "Numic Spread" in the Great Basin. *American Antiquity* 48:825–834.

———. 1985. Acquisition Cost and Nutritional Data on Great Basin Resources. *Journal of California and Great Basin Anthropology* 7:117–125.

———. 1986. New Evidence for Fremont Adaptive Diversity. *Journal of California and Great Basin Anthropology* 8:204–216.

———. 1987. *Behavioral Ecology and Hunter-Gatherer Foraging: An Example from the Great Basin.* BAR International Series 381. British Archaeological Reports, Oxford, England.

———. 1989. The Structure of the Bustos Wickiup Site, Eastern Nevada. *Journal of California and Great Basin Anthropology* 11:2–34.

———. 1990. Fremont Transitions. *Utah Archaeology* 3:1–18.

———. 1994. Unpacking the Numic Spread. In *Across the West: Human Population Movement and the Expansion of the Numa,* edited by D. B. Madsen and D. Rhode, pp. 76–83. University of Utah Press, Salt Lake City.

———. 1996. North American Prehistory and Early History of the North American West. In *The Oxford Companion to Archaeology,* edited by B. M. Fagan, pp. 523–525. Oxford University Press, New York.

———. 1999. Farmers, Foragers, and Adaptive Diversity: The Great Salt Lake Wetlands Project. In *Prehistoric Lifeways in the Great Basin Wetlands: Bioarchaeological Reconstruction and Interpretation,* edited by

B. E. Hemphill and C. S. Larsen, pp. 21–54. University of Utah Press, Salt Lake City.

Simms, S. R., and K. M. Heath. 1990. Site Structure of the Orbit Inn: An Application of Ethnoarchaeology. *American Antiquity* 55:797–812.

Simms, S. R., and L. W. Lindsay. 1984. The MX Intuitive Surveys, 1980–1981. In *Prehistoric and Historic Settlement in the Southeastern Great Basin*, edited by R. N. Holmer and J. F. O'Connell. University of Utah Archaeological Center Reports of Investigations 82–28.

———. 1989. 42Md300: An Early Holocene Site in the Sevier Desert. *Utah Archaeology* 2:56–66.

Simms, S. R., J. R. Bright, and A. Ugan. 1997. Plain-Ware Ceramics and Residential Mobility: A Case Study from the Great Basin. *Journal of Archaeological Science* 24:779–792.

Simms, S. R., C. J. Loveland, and M. E. Stuart. 1991. *Prehistoric Human Skeletal Remains and the Prehistory of the Great Salt Lake Wetlands*. Utah State University Contributions to Anthropology No. 6. Logan.

Simms, S. R., and A. W. Raymond. 1999. No One Owns the Deceased! The Treatment of Human Remains from Three Great Basin Cases. In *Prehistoric Lifeways in the Great Basin Wetlands: Bioarchaeological Reconstruction and Interpretation*, edited by B. E. Hemphill and C. S. Larsen, pp. 8–20. University of Utah Press, Salt Lake City.

Simms, S. R., and K. W. Russell. 1996. *Ethnoarchaeology of the Bedul Bedouin of Petra, Jordan: Implications for the Food Producing Transition, Site Structure, and Pastoralist Archaeology*. Utah State University Contributions to Anthropology, Logan, Utah.

Simms, S. R., D. N. Schmitt, and K. Jensen. 1999. Playa View Dune: A Mid-Holocene Campsite in the Great Salt Lake Desert. *Utah Archaeology* 12:31–50.

Simms, S. R., and M. E. Stuart. 2002. Ancient American Indian Life in the Great Salt Lake Wetlands: Archaeological and Biological Evidence. In: *Great Salt Lake: An Overview of Change*, edited by J. W. Gwynn, pp. 71–83. Utah Department of Natural Resources Special Publication, Utah Geological Survey. Salt Lake City.

Sinopolli, C. M. 1991. Style in Arrows: A Study of an Ethnographic Collection from the Western United States. In *Foragers in Context: Long-Term Regional and Historical Perspectives in Hunter-Gatherer Studies*, edited by P. T. Miracle, L. E. Fisher, and J. Brown, pp. 63–87. Michigan Discussions in Anthropology, Vol. 10. Ann Arbor.

Smith, A. M. 1974. *Ethnography of the Northern Utes*. Museum of New Mexico Papers Anthropology No. 17. Museum of New Mexico Press, Santa Fe.

———. 1992. *Ute Tales*. University of Utah Press, Salt Lake City.

———. 1993. *Shoshoni Tales*. University of Utah Press, Salt Lake City.

Smith, C. S. 2003. Hunter-Gatherer Mobility, Storage, and Houses in a Marginal Environment: An Example from the Mid-Holocene Of Wyoming. *Journal of Anthropological Archaeology* 22:162–189.

Smith, C. S., T. P. Reust, and R. D. Richard. 2003. Site 48UT375: Late Paleoindian Period Subsistence and Land Use Patterns in the Green River Basin, Wyoming. *Plains Anthropologist* 48:133–149.

Smith, E. 1942. Early Man in the Great Salt Lake Area. *Mineralogical Society of Utah* 3(2):27–32.

Spangler, J. D. 2000a. One-Pot Pithouses and Fremont Paradoxes: Formative Stage Adaptations in the Tavaputs Plateau Region of Northeastern Utah. In *Intermountain Archaeology*, edited by D. B. Madsen and M. D. Metcalf, pp. 25–38. Anthropological Papers No. 122. University of Utah Press, Salt Lake City.

————. 2000b. Radiocarbon Dates, Acquired Wisdom and the Search for Temporal Order in the Uinta Basin. In *Intermountain Archaeology*, edited by D. B. Madsen and M. D. Metcalf, pp. 48–99. Anthropological Papers No. 122. University of Utah Press, Salt Lake City.

Spielmann, K. 1991. *Farmers, Hunters, and Colonists: Interactions between the Southwest and the Southern Plains.* University of Arizona Press, Tucson.

Stansbury, H. 1988. *Exploration of the Valley of the Great Salt Lake.* Originally published 1852. Smithsonian Institution Press, Washington D.C.

Steele, D. G., and J. F. Powell. 1995. Peopling of the Americas: Paleobiological Evidence. *Human Biology* 64:303–336.

Steward, J. H. 1933. *Early Inhabitants of Western Utah. Part 1: Mounds and House Types.* University of Utah Bulletin 23, No. 7:1–34.

————. 1936. *Pueblo Material Culture in Western Utah.* Bulletin No. 287. Anthropological Series Vol. 1: No. 3. University of New Mexico, Albuquerque.

————. 1937. *Ancient Caves of the Great Salt Lake Region.* Bureau of American Ethnology Bulletin 116. Washington D.C.

————. 1938. *Basin-Plateau Aboriginal Sociopolitical Groups.* U.S. Bureau of American Ethnology Bulletin 120. Washington D.C.

————. 1940. Native Cultures of the Intermontane (Great Basin) Area. In *Essays in Historical Anthropology of North America, Published in Honor of John R. Swanton*, pp. 445–502. Smithsonian Miscellaneous Collections No. 100. Washington D.C.

————. 1941. *Archeological Reconnaissance of Southern Utah.* Bureau of American Ethnology Bulletin 128, pp. 227–356. Washington D.C.

————. 1955. *Theory of Culture Change: The Methodology of Multilinear Evolution.* University of Illinois Press, Urbana.

————. 1969. Observations on Bands. In *Contributions to Anthropology: Band Societies*, edited by D. Damas, pp. 187–190. National Museum of Canada Bulletin 228. Ottawa.

Stewart, O. 1939. *The Northern Paiute Bands*. University of California Anthropological Records, Vol. 2: No. 3. Berkeley.

———. 1966. Tribal Distributions and Boundaries in the Great Basin. In *Current Status of Anthropological Research in the Great Basin: 1964*, edited by W. L. d'Azevedo, W. A. Davis, D. D. Fowler, and W. Suttles, pp. 167–238. Desert Research Institute Social Sciences and Humanities Publication No. 1, Reno.

Stokes, W. L., A. Hutchinson, S. Hutmacher, J. Hasbargen, C. Lindsay, M. T. Seddon, D. Mullins, K. Taite, and T. Sharp. 2003. Site 42JB394—The Dust Devil Site. In *Kern River 2003 Expansion Project*, Vol. III: Chapter 8, edited by A. D. Reed, M. T. Seddon, and H. K. Stettler, pp. 821–977. Alpine Archaeological Consultants, Montrose, Colorado and SWCA Environmental Consultants, Salt Lake City.

Stuart, M. E. 1990. *Human Osteology and Archaeological Survey of the Weber River Wetlands, Weber County, Utah*. Promontory/Tubaduka Reports of Investigations No. 90-1. Ms. On file Utah Division of State History, Salt Lake City.

———. 1992. Salvage Excavations at the Burch Creek Site, 42WB76, Weber County, Utah. *Utah Archaeology* 5:115–124.

———. 1993. Salvage Excavations at the Fire Guard Hearth 42WB54 Weber County, Utah. *Utah Archaeology* 6:71–78.

Surovell, T. A. 2000. Early Paleoindian Women, Children, Mobility, and Fertility. *American Antiquity* 65:493–508.

Sutton, M. Q. 1986. Warfare and Expansion: An Ethnohistoric Pespective on the Numic Spread. *Journal of California and Great Basin Anthropology* 8:65–82.

———. 1988. *Insects as Food: Aboriginal Entomophagy in the Great Basin*. Ballena Press Anthropological Papers No. 33. Menlo Park, California.

Sutton, M. Q., M. E. Basgall, J. K. Gardner, and M. W. Allen. 2007. Advances in Understanding Mojave Desert Prehistory. In *California Prehistory: Colonization, Culture, and Complexity*, edited by T. L. Jones and K. A. Klar, pp. 229–245. AltaMira Press, Walnut Creek.

Sutton, M. Q., and D. Rhode. 1994. Background to the Numic Problem. In *Across the West: Human Population Movement and the Expansion of the Numa*, edited by D. B. Madsen and D. Rhode, pp. 6–15. University of Utah Press, Salt Lake City.

Tadlock, D. R. 1966. Certain Crescentic Stone Objects as a Time Marker in the Western United States. *American Antiquity* 31:662–675.

Talbot, R. K. 1997. Fremont Architecture. In *Clear Creek Canyon Archaeological Project*, Vol. 5: *Results and Synthesis*. Museum of Peoples and Cultures Technical Series 95-9. Brigham Young University, Provo, Utah.

Talbot, R. K., and L. D. Richens. 1993. *Archaeological Investigations at Richfield and Vicinity*. Museum of Peoples and Cultures Technical Series No. 93-15. Brigham Young University, Provo, Utah.

Talbot, R. K., and L. D. Richens. 1996. *Steinaker Gap: An Early Fremont Farmstead*. Museum of Peoples and Cultures Occasional Papers No. 2. Brigham Young University, Provo, Utah.

———. 2004. *Fremont Farming and Mobility on the Far Northern Colorado Plateau*. Museum of Peoples and Cultures Occasional Papers No. 10. Brigham Young University, Provo, Utah.

Talbot, R. K., L. D. Richens, J. D. Wilde, J. C. Janetski, and D. E. Newman. 1999. *Excavations at Icicle Bench, Radford Roost, and Lott's Farm, Clear Creek Canyon, Central Utah*. Museum of Peoples and Cultures Occasional Papers No. 4. Brigham Young University, Provo, Utah.

Tankersley, K. B., and C. A. Munson. 1993. Comments on the Meadowcroft Rockshelter Radiocarbon Chronology and the Recognition of Coal Contaminants. *American Antiquity* 57:321–326.

Tankersley, K. B., C. A. Munson, and D. Smith. 1987. Recognition of Bituminous Coal Contaminants in Radiocarbon Samples. *American Antiquity* 52:318–330.

Thomas, D. H. 1973. An Empirical Test for Steward's Model of Great Basin Settlement Patterns. *American Antiquity* 38:155–176.

———. 1982. *The 1981 Alta Toquima Village Project: A Preliminary Report*. Desert Research Institute Social Sciences and Humanities Publication No. 27. Reno, Nevada.

———. 1983a. *The Archaeology of Monitor Valley 1: Epistemology*. Anthropological Papers of the American Museum of Natural History Vol. 58: Pt. 1. American Museum of Natural History, New York.

———. 1983b. *The Archaeology of Monitor Valley 2: Gatecliff Shelter*. Anthropological Papers of the American Museum of Natural History Vol. 59: Pt. 1. American Museum of Natural History, New York.

———. 1985. *The Archaeology of Hidden Cave, Nevada*. Anthropological Papers of the American Museum of Natural History Vol. 61: Pt. 1. American Museum of Natural History, New York.

———. 1994. Chronology and the Numic Expansion. In *Across the West: Human Population Movement and the Expansion of the Numa*, edited by D. B. Madsen and D. Rhode, pp. 56–61. University of Utah Press, Salt Lake City.

Thomas, D. H., L. S. A. Pendleton, and S. C. Cappannari. 1986. Western Shoshone. In *Handbook of North American Indians*, Vol. 11: Great Basin, edited by W. L. d'Azevedo, pp. 262–283. Smithsonian Institution Press, Washington D.C.

Thompson, K. W., and J. V. Pastor. 1995. *People of the Sage: 10,000 Years of Occupation in Southwestern Wyoming*. Archaeological Services, Western Wyoming Community College, CRM Report 57. Rock Springs.

Thompson, R. S. 1990. Late Quaternary Vegetation and Climate in the Great Basin. In *Packrat Middens: The Last 40,000 Years of Biotic Change*, edited by J. L. Betancourt, T. R. Van Devender, and P. S. Martin, pp. 200 239. University of Arizona Press, Tucson.

Thompson, R. S. 1992. Late Quaternary Environments in Ruby Valley, Nevada. *Quaternary Research* 37:1–15.

Thornton, R. B. 1987. *American Indian Holocaust and Survival: A Population History since 1492.* University of Oklahoma Press, Norman.

Trimble, S. 1999. *The Sagebrush Ocean: A Natural History of the Great Basin.* University of Nevada Press, Reno.

Tuchman, B. W. 1978. *A Distant Mirror: The Calamitous 14th Century.* Alfred Knopf, New York.

Tuohy, D. R. 1990. Pyramid Lake Fishing: The Archaeological Record. In *Wetlands Adaptations in the Great Basin,* edited by J. C. Janetski and D. B. Madsen, pp. 121–158. Museum of Peoples and Cultures Occasional Papers No. 1. Brigham Young University, Provo, Utah.

Tuohy, D. R., and L. K. Napton. 1986. Duck Decoys from Lovelock Cave, Nevada, Dated By ^{14}C Accelerator Mass Spectroscopy. *American Antiquity* 51:813–816.

Turner, C. G., II. 1993. Southwest Indian Teeth. *National Geographic Research and Exploration* 9:32–53.

Turner, F. J. 1920. *The Frontier in American History.* Henry Holt & Co., New York.

———. 1932. *The Significance of Sections in American History.* Henry Holt & Co., New York.

Ugan, A., J. Bright, and A. Rogers. 2003. Is Technology Worth the Trouble? *Journal of Archaeological Science* 30:1315–1329.

Upham, S. 1982. *Politics and Power: An Economic and Political History of the Western Pueblo.* Academic Press, New York.

———. 1984. Adaptive Diversity and Southwestern Abandonments. *Journal of Anthropological Research* 40:235–256.

———. 1990. Analog or Digital: Toward a Generic Framework for Explaining the Development of Emergent Political Systems. In *The Evolution of Political Systems: Sociopolitics in Small-Scale Sedentary Societies,* edited by S. Upham, pp. 87–115. Cambridge University Press.

———. 1994. Nomads of the Desert West: A Shifting Continuum in Prehistory. *Journal of World Prehistory* 8:113–167.

Vale, T. 1998. The Myth of the Humanized Landscape: An Example from Yosemite National Park. *Natural Areas Journal* 18:231–236.

Verano, J. W., and D. H. Ubelaker (eds.). 1992. *Disease and Demography in the Americas.* Smithsonian Institution Press, Washington D.C.

Waguespack, N. M. 2005. The Organization of Male and Female Labor in Foraging Societies: Implications for Early Paleoindian Archaeology. *American Anthropologist* 107:666–676.

Waguespack, N. M., and T. A. Surovell. 2003. Clovis Hunting Strategies, Or How to Make Out on Plentiful Resources. *American Antiquity* 68:333–352.

Warner, T. J. (ed.). 1976. *The Dominguez-Escalante Journal*. Translated by Fray Angelico Chavez. Brigham Young University Press, Provo, Utah.

Welty, E. 1979. Place in Fiction. In *The Eye of the Story: Selected Essays and Reviews*, pp. 116–133. Vintage Books, Random House, New York.

West, F. 1999. Monte Verde Revisited: The Inscrutable Monte Verde. *Scientific American Discovering Archaeology*, November/December 1999, pp. 15–16.

Wheat, M. M. 1967. *Survival Arts of the Primitive Paiute*. University of Nevada Press, Reno.

Whitley, D. M. 1998. Finding Rain in the Desert: Landscape, Gender, and Far Western North American Rock Art. In *The Archaeology of Rock Art*, edited by C. Chippindale and P. S. C. Tacon, pp. 11–29. Cambridge University Press.

———. 2000. *The Art of the Shaman: Rock Art of California*. University of Utah Press, Salt Lake City.

Wigand, P., and D. Rhode. 2002. Great Basin Vegetation and Late Quaternary Aquatic History. In *Great Basin Aquatic System History*. Smithsonian Contributions to Earth Sciences No. 33, edited by R. Hershler, D. B. Madsen, and D. R. Currey, pp. 309–368. Smithsonian Institution Press, Washington D.C.

Wilde, J. D., and D. E. Newman. 1989. Late Archaic Corn in the Eastern Great Basin. *American Anthropologist* 91:712–720.

Wilde, J. D., and R. A. Soper. 1999. *Baker Village: Report of Excavations, 1990–1994*. Museum of Peoples and Cultures Technical Series No. 99–12. Brigham Young University, Provo, Utah.

Williams, T. T. 1992. *Refuge: An Unnatural History of Family and Place*. Vintage Books, New York.

Wills, W. H. 1988. *Early Prehistoric Agriculture in the American Southwest*. School of American Research Press, Santa Fe.

Wills, W. H., and B. B. Huckell. 1994. Economic Implications of Changing Land-Use Patterns in the Late Archaic. In *Themes in Southwest Prehistory*, edited by G. J. Gumerman, pp. 33–52. School of American Research Press, Santa Fe.

Winter, J. 1973. The Distribution and Development of Fremont Maize Agriculture: Some Preliminary Interpretations. *American Antiquity* 38:439–452.

———. 1976. The Processes of Farming Diffusion in the Southwest and Great Basin. *American Antiquity* 41:421–429.

Wolf, E. R. 1982. Europe and the People without History. University of California Press, Berkeley and Los Angeles.

Wormington, H. M. 1955. *A Reappraisal of the Fremont Culture*. Denver Museum of Natural History, Proceedings, No. 1.

Wylie, H. G. 1974. Promontory Pegs as Elements of Great Basin Subsistence Technology. *Tebiwa* 16:46–67.

Zeanah, D. W. 2000. Transport Costs, Central Place Foraging, and Hunter-Gatherer Alpine Land Use Strategies. In *Intermountain Archaeology,* edited by D. B. Madsen and M. D. Metcalf, pp. 1–14. Anthropological Papers No. 122. University of Utah Press, Salt Lake City.

———. 2004. Sexual Division of Labor and Central Place Foraging: A Model for the Carson Desert of Western Nevada. *Journal of Anthropological Archaeology* 23:1–32.

Zeanah, D. W., J. A. Carter, D. P. Dugas, R. G. Elston, and J. E. Hammett. 1995. *An Optimal Foraging Model of Hunter-Gatherer Land Use in the Carson Desert.* Prepared for U.S. Fish and Wildlife Service and U.S. Department of the Navy by Intermountain Research, Silver City, Nevada.

Zeanah, D. W., and S. R. Simms. 1999. Modeling the Gastric: Great Basin Subsistence Studies Since 1982 and the Evolution of General Theory in Archaeology. In *Models for the Millennium: The Current Status of Great Basin Anthropological Research,* edited by C. Beck, pp. 118–140. University of Utah Press, Salt Lake City.

Index

abalone, 236
abandonment, 233; Fremont, 189,
    216, 234, 263; Late Archaic,
    176, 177; Mesa Verde, 234
absolute time, 75
adornment, 198, 217, 221
Adovasio, James, 161, 166, 255,
    288n2, 301n38, 309n20
affinity, 108, *164, 186*
Agate Basin, *121*
Agate Basin/Haskett II projectile
    point, 115
agriculture, 43, 49, 55–56,
    230, *250*; arrival to North
    America, 141; Californian,
    244; European, 85, 90, 107;
    Fremont, 58, 194, 197,
    206–207; Late Archaic, 173,
    181, 183, 274; maize 63, 73,
    307; modern, 29; Uinta Basin
    232
Ainu, 108, 295nc
Airport site, UT, 176–177
Allen Village site, UT, 239
alliances, 22, 47–48, 216, 223,
    227
Altithermal, 86, 94, 96, 176
Alvey site, UT, 195
Anasazi, 201, 218, 221–228,
    233–234, 257, 258–259;
    abandonment, 216, 314n31;
    basketry, 203, *204*, 224;
    ceramics, 195, 201–202,
    211–212; farmers, 212–214,
    230, 231, 236

andesite, 113
Angostura projectile point, 115
annual round, 54, 153
aquifers, 91
architecture, 187, 194, 224
Arkush, Brooke, 131
arrows, 27, 29–30, *40*, 54, 63,
    178–179; cane, 23; Fremont,
    190–192, 209–211, 226;
    Californian, 247–248; Late
    Archaic, 143, 167; shafts,
    152–153, 261; styles, 260
arrowheads, 11, 18, 31, 254–255,
    257–258, 262–263; Fremont,
    190–191
art. *See* rock art
artistic expression, 124
aspen, 67
atlatl, 30, *40*, 113, 114, 179, 198;
    Fremont, 209, 211. *See also*
    spear, spear thrower
Aspen Shelter site, UT, *145*, 171, *186*
awl, 31, 188, 192
Aztec Empire, 191; Aztec site 228

Backhoe Village site, UT, *186*, 214
bags, 152
Baker Village site, UT, *186*, 193,
    224–226, 233
balsam, 45
bands, 28–55, 165, *172*, 178, 181;
    lines, 21–22, 52, 135, 161,
    261–262; Numic-speaking,
    261–262
Bannock people, *30, 240*, 270

369

About the Author

Steven R. Simms is Professor of Anthropology at Utah State University, where he has taught since 1988. Raised in California, he has done archaeology since 1972 and has directed over 50 archaeological research projects in most western states and in the southeast. He studied the ethnoarchaeology of the Bedul Bedouin in Jordan between 1986 and 1997. Simms has authored over 50 published articles and 80 research reports. He served as President of the Great Basin Anthropological Association and editor of the journal *Utah Archaeology*. His interests are archaeological method and theory, human behavioral ecology, ethnoarchaeology, the paleoecology of the American Desert West, and the history and theory of anthropology. He believes that archaeologists should be proficient at theory because there is no such thing as field archaeology done in the absence of the paradigms that suffuse our interpretations about the past. On the practical side, however, Dr. Simms now focuses on training students to enter cultural resource management, the primary employment sector for archaeologists.